And One Was a Priest

And One Was a Priest

THE LIFE AND TIMES OF DUNCAN M. GRAY JR.

ARAMINTA STONE JOHNSTON

University Press of Mississippi
Jackson

www.upress.state.ms.us

Designed by Peter D. Halverson

The University Press of Mississippi is a member of the
Association of American University Presses.

All photographs provided by Duncan M. Gray Jr., unless otherwise noted.

Copyright © 2011 by University Press of Mississippi
All rights reserved
Manufactured in the United States of America

First printing 2011
∞
Library of Congress Cataloging-in-Publication Data

Johnston, Araminta Stone.
  And one was a priest : the life and times of Duncan M. Gray, Jr. /
Araminta Stone Johnston.
      p. cm.
  Includes bibliographical references (p.   ) and index.
  ISBN 978-1-60473-828-5 (cloth : alk. paper) —
  ISBN 978-1-60473-829-2 (ebook) 1. Gray, Duncan Montgomery.
2. Episcopal Church—Bishops—Biography. 3. Southern States—Race
relations—History. 4. Race relations—Religious aspects—Episcopal
Church—History. I. Title.
  BX5995.G73J64 2011
  283.092—dc22
  [B]   2010020374

British Library Cataloging-in-Publication Data available

In loving memory of the rest of my family

PHIL STONE (1893–1967)

EMILY WHITEHURST STONE (1909–1992)

PHILIP ALSTON STONE (1940–1966)

Writers all.

CONTENTS

I sing a song of the saints of God . . .
Patient and brave and true,
Who toiled and fought and lived and died
For the Lord they loved and knew
And one was a doctor, and one was a queen;
And one was a shepherdess on the green:
They were all of them saints of God
—and I mean, God helping, to be one too.

They loved their Lord so dear; so dear,
And his love made them strong;
And they followed the right for Jesus' sake,
The whole of their good lives long.
And one was a soldier, and one was a priest,
And one was slain by a fierce wild beast;
And there's not any reason—no, not the least—
Why I shouldn't be one too.

They lived not only in ages past,
There are hundreds of thousand still,
The world is bright with the joyous saints
Who love to do Jesus' will
You can meet them in schools, or in lanes, or at sea,
In church, or in trains, or in shops, or at tea,
For the saints of God are just folk like me,
And I mean to be one too.[1]

IN THE WORLD of the twenty-first century the words of this children's hymn tend to strike us as quaintly naïve and perhaps impossibly hopeful, but fifty years ago these were impressive words to me. In the apparently safe, secure world of 1950s Mississippi in which I, a privileged and somewhat overly sensitive white child, grew up, these words from the 1940 edition of *The Hymnal of the Protestant Episcopal Church in the United States of America* were familiar ones. We sang them so frequently at the Sunday morning children's service at St. Peter's Episcopal Church in Oxford, Mississippi, that even these many years later I still have them all but committed to memory.

But those words from the "Hymns for Children" section of the Episcopal hymnal are only one set of words that represent for me a kind of partial frame for the story I have to tell. The second set of lyrics is very different:

> *Oxford Town, Oxford Town*
> *Ev'rybody's got their heads bowed down*
> *The sun don't shine above the ground*
> *Ain't a-goin' down to Oxford Town.*[2]

These words are, of course, the lyrics to a song written and sung by folk-singer Bob Dylan in the early 1960s after two people had been killed and many more injured in the small, peaceful, segregated campus community of Oxford. The violence occurred during a riot fomented in reaction to the efforts of a black Mississippian by the name of James Meredith to enroll as the first African American student at the University of Mississippi.

I first heard the Dylan song, I believe, when I left Mississippi to enroll as a freshman at Duke University in the fall of 1966. My enrollment at Duke came four years after Meredith finally registered as a student at Ole Miss—with the help of the NAACP Legal Defense Fund, the Fifth District Court of Appeals and the Supreme Court, the U.S. Justice Department, a federalized contingent of the Mississippi National Guard, twenty-four federal marshals, and two battalions of U.S. Army troops. Needless to say, my enrollment at Duke was an uneventful as Meredith's at Ole Miss had been full of incident.

Even though I was only thirteen years old on September 30, 1962, when the outbreak of mob violence over Meredith's admission took place, I was well aware of the event that occurred on the campus that night and of the reactions of university faculty and Oxford residents to them. In a town of a few thousand and a university community of a few thousand more, one couldn't help but be. In addition, I had seen with my own eyes the beginning of the disturbance.

My mother, who taught in the university's English Department, had come for me and a friend after our church youth group meeting at St. Peter's that Sunday evening and had driven us around the campus just as crowds of students began to gather outside the university's administration building.

She wanted us to see for ourselves "history in the making" and help us to understand better what it was like to be present at such a time. When we saw the groups of students early that evening, their mood most resembled the high spirits of a pep rally to us. Spirits were high, and mischief seemed bound to occur, but as things appeared early in the evening, the events of the night didn't seem likely to be much more serious than that. Something historic was almost certainly about to occur—the registration of the first African American as a student at the University of Mississippi, familiarly known as "Ole Miss" after the title slaves had given to their owners' wives and mothers—and these students weren't about to miss the excitement. Undoubtedly, most of them were not happy about the prospect of Meredith as a fellow student, given the values and beliefs they had imbibed growing up in Mississippi. Nevertheless, few, if any, at that point contemplated a night of violence, death, injury, and destruction.

On Monday morning, however, my mother awakened me to watch as U.S. Army troops marched down the street in front of our house on their way to the campus. In the days that followed I learned something of the reaction of the nation to those events that night of September 30 on the Ole Miss campus. Even so, it came as something of a shock four year later during freshman orientation at Duke when my fellow students asked where I was from, and I responded, I almost invariably heard in reply, "Oxford Town, Oxford Town." What seventeen-year-old away from home for the first time wants to be from a place about which people say, "The sun don't shine above the ground"?

And besides, I knew that however much Dylan's song might capture a real piece of the truth about Oxford in 1962, I knew also that that truth was a far more complicated one than the popular lyrics and the popular perceptions. But who was going to listen to some seventeen-year-old freshman apologist for Mississippi in 1966?

The truth *was* complicated, and "Oxford Town" *does* describe a piece of the truth. Another piece, however, is captured by the unfashionably earnest, sincere, and hopeful words of "I sing a song of the saints of God." In Oxford, Mississippi, in 1962, it was possible to meet these saints the children's hymn spoke of. And one of them *was* a priest. In what follows it is his story that I want to tell.

So although I begin with a piece of *my* story, I tell it because if it were not my story, I would not be writing about Duncan Montgomery Gray Jr., rector of St. Peter's Episcopal Church in Oxford, Mississippi, in 1962.

* * *

How does one tell the story of a good person? Gray is a good person, and telling the story of a truly good person presents problems.

We are all familiar with the sentiment, "Why would anybody want to go to heaven? It must be an awfully boring place!" We ourselves may even have felt a certain sympathy with the assumption behind the sentiment: any place where everyone is *good* all the time couldn't possibly be any fun; indeed, it must be pretty damned dull. But even if we've never felt sympathy with this proposition about heaven, surely many of us, although perhaps secretly, tend to agree that a really good person, while doubtless very edifying and perhaps uplifting to be around, would, like heaven, get to be an awful bore rather quickly.

But Gray is not a bore. Indeed, people who have known him over the years describe him as a sparkling social companion—in other words, "fun." And yet, they agree, he is a truly good man.

Another difficulty arises, however, and it is a peculiarly Christian one. The Jewish philosopher Hannah Arendt has probably done as good a job of explaining it as anyone:

> The one activity taught by Jesus in word and deed is the activity of goodness, and goodness obviously harbors a tendency to hide from being seen or heard. . . . For it is manifest that the moment a good work becomes known and public, it loses its specific character of goodness, of being done for nothing but goodness' sake. When goodness appears openly, it is no longer goodness, though it may still be useful as organized charity or as an act of solidarity. Therefore: "Take heed that ye do not give your alms before men, to be seen of them." Goodness can exist only when it is not perceived, not even by its author; whoever sees himself performing a good work is no longer good, but at best a useful member of society or dutiful member of a church. Therefore: "Let not thy left hand know what thy right hand doeth.[3]

Although Gray is not a philosopher, but rather a man of action, he instinctively knows the truth of Arendt's reflections.

Gray's younger son, Lloyd, is a newspaper editor and thus experienced in learning and telling people's stories. When I first told him about my plans for this project, his response was, "I don't envy you. Dad doesn't like to talk about himself." Gray's reluctance to talk about himself, which his son had observed, is neither shyness nor reserve but, in my judgment, the result of Gray's implicit understanding that "when goodness appears openly, it is no longer goodness." Likewise, when I told Gray's wife that after several years of observing her husband and talking with those who knew him well, I had come to the conclusion that he is indeed that very rare being, a truly good man, she responded, "Yes. And you know what's so wonderful is that he doesn't even know it." To quote Arendt again, "Goodness can exist only when it is not perceived, not even by its author; whoever sees himself performing a good work is no longer good."

While, however, Arendt is certainly right that true goodness exists only when its author is unaware of his or her goodness and "doesn't let the left hand know what the right hand is doing," she is wrong to say that goodness can exist *only* when it is not perceived. Those who aspire to true goodness must tell each other the stories of the truly good; we *must* have the examples of the truly good before us for the formation of our own characters into goodness. It is for this reason that in the Christian tradition we have the Gospels, the stories of Jesus manifesting his goodness. If those of us aspiring to goodness did not need these "open appearances" of goodness in story form, it would be sufficient for Christians to have simply the proclamations of the apostles and the creeds of the church: "Jesus Christ is God in human form who has come to save us from evil and death." The same is true for the church's tradition of hagiography—the stories of the lives of saints. Roman Catholics have long understood their importance.

But do I "sing a song" of a saint here? Surely, we often think, real saints are those people who lived in "ages past" and performed miracles, acts that defy natural law. Or we may be more cynical and believe that saints are people who, as American humorist Ambrose Bierce defined them, are "dead sinners, revised and edited." Or if there are saints today, we tend to think, they're people like Mother Teresa, who give up all semblance of a normal life for one of poverty, chastity, and obedience, tending to the world's outcasts. Certainly not "folk just like me."

I have had much cause to think about these propositions and others like them since I began work on this biography of Duncan Gray.

If I "sing a song of the saints of God," I have a difficult task before me, do I not? Even the great English Puritan poet John Milton, in his epic poem *Paradise Lost*, is widely agreed to have failed in his effort to make Christ the hero of this poem and, by default, in effect to have portrayed Satan in the role! For the reasons I have already mentioned, true goodness is difficult to portray effectively.

But I do have a number of advantages that Milton lacked. Although Gray has absorbed and in his life manifests much of the teachings and example of Jesus, he is still in many ways "just folk" like you and me.

For instance, he describes himself as "a big sports fan" and for years has gotten a special pleasure out of taking his sons and grandsons to St. Louis to see the Cardinals play. Football and basketball are among his passions too, and he has put in his time coaching his children's teams as they were growing up. He doesn't hunt, but enjoyed fishing for many years, especially with his children.

When he is pressed as to whether or not he has a "besetting sin," he replies, "Some people would say gluttony, I guess."

But if they do, they are wrong. Gray is a man who clearly appreciates food and eats it with gusto and a certain appreciative concentration. Even in his eighties, however, he is a trim, fit man who would still play tennis if his bad knee didn't give him so much trouble.

He's the fast driver in the family and has been known to be stopped for speeding. And yet even here his unthinking truthfulness can get him into trouble. His family enjoys telling the story of the late night that a Mississippi highway patrolman stopped Gray speeding down the Natchez Trace, an old Indian trail that is now a very limited access, two-lane highway that runs through forests and fields. The speed limit along the Trace is fifty miles an hour, lower than on most highways, especially those like the Trace on which traffic is sparse even during the day. After Gray stopped, the patrolman ordered him out of the car. Gray climbed out, pointing at his clerical collar as he did so. The patrolman approached, saying, "I'm sorry, Father, but you were going over the speed limit." Gray responded, "Officer, I can't have been. I had my cruise control set at sixty-five!"

This quality of unthinking truthfulness, like that of uncalculating trustfulness, seems to be a habit of Gray's.

Several years ago a crew of workmen was doing some repairs on the Grays' house in Jackson. The workmen had about one more day's work in order to finish their job, and the Grays were leaving town the next day on a trip. If the Grays were to go ahead and pay them, would they return the next day to finish the job? Oh, yes! Surely!

Sure. When the Grays came back home a week later, there was, of course, no sign of either workmen or of a finished job. And yet, more recently Gray contracted with a man who promised to keep the Gray's lawn cut for the summer. In fact, he was paid in advance to do so. Yes, now there's a new lawn man who's paid weekly for the work he does.

And so again, despite Gray's real enjoyment of variety of worldly goods—good food, scotch, parties, sports, marriage, children and grandchildren and great-grandchildren—some of these tales sound like ones about a saint, a man who takes people at their word again and again, and again and again is snookered. A trusting, but hopelessly unworldly man who couldn't possibly be *effective* in the real world.

And yet this is a man who is fascinated by secular politics and who also successfully negotiated the politics of the church for over forty years, nineteen of them as bishop of Mississippi during the turbulent period when Episcopalians dealt with the highly controversial issues of prayer book revision and the ordination of women to the priesthood.

And this is a man with whom a number of the Episcopal clergy and laity of Mississippi repeatedly disagreed. But this is a man of whom many Mississippi clergy and laity say, "We loved our bishop."

* * *

> *I sing a song of the saints of God. . . .*
> *They lived not only in ages past.*
> *There are hundred of thousands still!*
> *You can meet them in school, or in lanes, or at sea,*
> *In church, or in trains, or in shops, or at tea!*[4]

Again, the children's hymn with which I began this preface seems completely foreign to the sophistication, suspicion, and cynicism of America in the late twentieth and early twenty-first centuries. It seems completely foreign to Mississippi in the 1950s and '60s, where very public and almost matter-of-fact expressions of the horribly ugly and frequently death-dealing racism, hatred, and evil the culture had harbored within it for nearly 150 years were the order of the day. Apparently foreign, too, to the politics of the church, often described as politics in one of its nastiest forms.

And yet, "I sing a song of the saints of God. . . . They lived not only in ages past. . . . You can meet them in school, or in lanes, or at sea, in church, or in trains, or in shops, or at tea. . . . And one was a priest."

My story, then, is of a truly good man who has lived a life of goodness as a Christian and who, despite the usual response of a sinful world and some real suffering on his part, has not only succeeded in the world's terms, but also remained a truly good man.

ACKNOWLEDGMENTS

A WORK OF MANY YEARS means many, many people to thank for all their support, physical, emotional, and spiritual.

First, thanks to Duncan and Ruthie Gray, who could not have been more wonderful to work with. In addition to offering me the hospitality of their home and table, they were always open to my inquiries. Bishop Gray spent many hours in conversation with me, and Mrs. Gray put in her share too. Bishop Gray made his files completely available to me; in fact, early in this project the two of them took a European trip of several weeks duration, leaving me with twelve open drawers of files, both professional and personal, to peruse at my leisure.

Next, I must thank my husband, Steve, who supported me through fifteen long summers of research and writing, including during my sometimes long absences from home. When I was about five years into this project and our children had grown and gone off on their own, he began to press me about moving to a smaller house. "I can't do that until I finish this project," I exclaimed. "How long do you think that will take?" he asked. "Oh, probably about five more years," I answered. He was exceedingly patient as the additional five turned into ten.

To all the Mississippians who have opened their homes to me and given their time to me, I owe a huge debt of thanks.

In Oxford, Sue Smith, former neighbor, retired Ole Miss librarian, and member of St. Peter's Episcopal Church, made her attached apartment available to me summer after summer and let me come and go at my pleasure, while also feeding me night after night. She also introduced me around the university library, further ensuring that my work would find a welcome there.

My old Oxford friends Debbie Slade, Jo Dale Slade Mistilis, and Angelo Mistilis (whose restauranteur father had a deal with Duncan Gray that provided food for any hungry souls who showed up at the church down the street) could always be counted on for good food, good conversation, and, from Angelo (almost always) good jokes.

In Oxford, too, I so much appreciated the help of conversations with the late Frank Peddle and the late Chooky Falkner.

In Meridian, I thank Nancy LaPrade Hamilton and Anne Tobias Hamilton for welcoming me to the town and David and Loretta Hamilton for their generosity in letting me have the use of their home during my stay there. Also in Meridian, I must thank St. Paul's members Tile Howell and Gil and Deanie Carmichael for their time, their willingness to talk, and their memories of days forty years earlier. Bill Johnson, retired from the Meridian Chamber of Commerce and a voice for reason and justice in the town in the difficult years, gave me lunch in a wonderful Chinese restaurant and much good information about the founding of the Committee of Conscience and the temper of Meridian in the mid-1960s. Thanks also to St. Paul's Rector Greg Proctor, who provided me with a welcome, a space for interviewing, and a helpful history of St. Paul's.

Thanks, too, to Duncan and Ruthie's children, two of whom still live in Mississippi (the other two in Tennessee). Duncan III, Anne, Lloyd, and Catherine helped me see the events that they and their parents lived through from a different perspective, that of growing children. And thanks to Isabel Gray Kelly for her thoughts and memories of her brother and her father.

In Tupelo, Mississippi, the Reverend Cecil Jones Jr. gave me wonderful perspectives on Bishops Duncan M. Gray Sr. and Duncan M. Gray Jr., not to mention another good lunch.

My appreciation goes also to the staff of the Diocese of Mississippi, who welcomed me into their offices, answered my questions, and helped me find materials and the copier. Thanks also to Bishop Chip Marble and later Bishop Duncan M. Gray III for their time and for making the diocesan offices available.

Thanks to my cousin, Pat Guest, and her husband, Jim Guest, for the hospitality they offered me many times about halfway on the drive from Charlotte, North Carolina, to Mississippi.

Thanks also to the numerous others who were willing to take the time to talk to me about the Grays and the Episcopal Church in Mississippi.

Thanks to my colleagues at Queens University of Charlotte who provided me with financial support for this project and to Charles Reed and Bob Whalen of the History Department, who read all or parts of this in manuscript form. And thanks to Emily Seelbinder, who lent me that history of Cleveland, Mississippi.

And thanks to my daughter, Abigail J. Cudabac, proof reader and editor extraordinaire. I took some of her suggestions, just as she takes some of mine.

Finally, thanks to Stanley Hauerwas, Gilbert T. Rowe Professor of Theological Ethics at Duke University, who retaught me what I learned from my parents but had almost forgotten: that ethics is about stories.

And One Was a Priest

Chapter 1

"STOP THIS VIOLENCE!"

University of Mississippi, September 1962

L ATE IN THE EVENING of September 30, 1962, the Rev. Duncan M. Gray Jr. mounted the base of the Confederate monument on the campus of the University of Mississippi.

A slight, balding man in glasses, he shouted to be heard above the din. "General! General! Speak to these students! *You* can persuade them! Tell them to stop this violence and rioting! Tell them to go back to their dormitories!"

The "General" whom Gray addressed was the same Major General Edwin Walker who, at President Dwight D. Eisenhower's orders, had led U.S. Army troops into Little Rock, Arkansas, to ensure the desegregation of Little Rock's Central High School seven years earlier. More recently, he had been disciplined for insubordination. In response, he had resigned from the army in public protest over what he had described as the Kennedy administration's "collaboration and collusion with the international Communist conspiracy." Still more recently—indeed, only four days before his appearance on the university campus—he had given a radio speech in which he apologized for being "on the wrong side" in Little Rock and had called on supporters to rally to the campus to help resist the admission of the first African American student—James H. Meredith—to the University of Mississippi.[1]

Now Walker ignored Gray. Instead, he continued his harangue of the crowd as tear gas fumes swirled around them all.

"I want to congratulate you on what you are doing here this evening!" he cried. "You have every right to protest. Stand fast, stand firm! There are thousands who support you. You will win in the end! The federal government is encroaching on your rights as American citizens. It is your duty to resist!"[2]

Gray persisted, however. "General, please try to quiet these students! Ask them to stop their rioting and go back to their dormitories."

Walker paused for a moment. Then he spoke again to those gathered around him who eagerly awaited his words. "There's a man here. . . . I am an Episcopalian, but there's a man here tonight, a man wearing the cloth, a man who makes me ashamed I've ever called myself an Episcopalian." He pointed at Gray.

Quickly taking advantage of the crowd's attention, Gray spoke to the group composed partially of student but largely of outsiders, many of whom had come to the university in response to Walker's radio plea.

Although Gray knew the attitude this group was likely to have toward his words, he pleaded with them. "Stop this violence! You'll only get hurt and you'll hurt the University and the community!"

But the crowd, inflamed by Walker's rhetoric and eager for a target, howled in reply. "Get the bastard!" "Kill him!" "Kill the s.o.b!"[3] Swiftly they pulled Gray down from the monument and pushed him to the ground.

As some members of the mob began to rough him up, other members of the crowd almost as quickly surrounded him. Two students and a deputy sheriff, an avowed segregationist but, unlike some others in the crowd, a man reluctant to stand passively by in the face of potential murder, began to move Gray from the center of the throng to its edges.[4]

The deputy shouted, "You've got to get out of here, preacher, or they're go'n get you!" He and the students escorted Gray several yards away from the crush to the steps of the nearby YMCA building and relative safety.

Just at that moment, two other members of the crowd, also students, approached Gray as Walker continued to hold forth to his listeners. These two, however, came with apparently good intentions, if not perhaps the most careful judgment. "Reverend Gray! Come on back. We think that crowd will listen to you!"[5]

Yet as Gray and the student turned to head back in Walker's direction, Gray realized the cause was lost; the mob, bent on violence, moved in the direction of the already embattled federal marshals President John F. Kennedy had ordered in to protect Meredith and the university campus.

* * *

By the time twenty-nine-year-old James H. Meredith, an Air Force veteran and Mississippi native, enrolled at Ole Miss on the morning of October 1, he had been pursuing his quest to gain admission to the university for twenty months. One of ten children, he was the son of a man unusual among Mississippi blacks because he owned the land he farmed in the hill country of central Mississippi. It was almost certainly Moses A. Meredith's economic self-sufficiency that made it possible for him to raise his children to maintain a fierce personal pride and dignity in the face of the racism that surrounded them.

It may also have been James's father's example that supplied the son with the determination and single-mindedness required to break the color barrier at Ole Miss. According to author Taylor Branch, Meredith's father was determined that in the case of his son, no white Mississippian would be able to follow the standard practice of calling a black person always by first name alone, no matter what the age or position of the individual. Mr. Meredith's solution was to name his son "J. H."; technically speaking, he had no first name until he was forced to adopt one when he entered the Air Force and became James Howard Meredith.[6]

Meredith had deliberately chosen the day after John F. Kennedy's inauguration as president to begin his effort to gain admission to the state's most highly regarded educational institution. Although he had seen it as his "personal responsibility" to do his part to change Mississippi's segregated system since he was eighteen, he chose this particular action and date because he believed it was the way he could best contribute to the democratic system that Kennedy had celebrated in his inaugural address.[7]

He knew that his goal would not be easily achieved, so before he sent the university his first letter requesting admission, he wrote Thurgood Marshall at the NAACP's Legal Defense Fund (LDF) to notify Marshall of his plans and to ask for legal aid, something the Fund eventually supplied. When Marshall received Meredith's first letter he took it in to his colleague Constance Baker Motley, threw it on her desk, and said, "This man has got to be crazy!" Motley says Marshall's comment meant "that it would be my case if I wanted it." So Motley became Meredith's LDF attorney.[8]

Meredith's letter was received in the university admissions office on January 25, 1961, and got prompt attention. The university registrar wrote him the following day, enclosing the requested material and encouraging him to continue the admissions process. What neither the registrar, nor anyone else at Ole Miss, knew, however, was that Meredith was African American; he had not mentioned that piece of information in his first letter.

Meredith filled the lacuna with a polite letter dated January 31 (and sent registered mail, return receipt requested) in which he wrote the registrar,

I am pleased with your letter that accompanied the application forms you recently sent me. I sincerely hope that your attitude toward me

as a potential member of your student body reflects the attitude of
the school and that it will not change upon learning that I am not a
white applicant.

I am an American-Mississippi-Negro citizen. . . .

I am requesting that immediate action be taken on my application
and that I be notified of its status, as registration begins on February
6, 1961, and I am hoping to enroll at this time.[9]

As Meredith surely anticipated, the "immediate action" he had requested
and hoped for was not forthcoming. But even he may not have anticipated
that reaching his goal would involve not only the efforts of his Legal Defense
Fund lawyer; it would also mean nearly two years of delaying, diversionary
tactics on the part of government officials in all three branches of state
government (tactics which occasionally reached the level of farce), a legal
battle waged in federal courts from the district level to the Supreme Court
and in state courts ranging from the lowly justice of the peace court to the
Hinds County Chancery Court in Jackson, the state's capital. In addition,
during this time neither Mississippi Governor Ross Barnett nor Lieutenant Governor Paul Johnson nor the state legislature missed an opportunity
to involve themselves in what became, from early 1961 to late 1962 (and in
its aftereffects well beyond that), a highly compelling and divisive series of
political events in Mississippi.

On one level the battle was once again between the old Southern cry
of "states' rights" and Washington's insistence that ours is a *federal* system
with states and other governments finally subject to the requirements of
the federal government. On another level, of course, the battle was over the
South's—and in this case Mississippi's—perpetuation of blatant, legalized
racism.

The results of this concatenation of persons, assertions, actions, and
institutions were manifold, but on the night of September 30–October 1,
1962, in the effort to restore order and some measure of civility to the campus and the small adjoining town of Oxford, they included the interven-
tion of federal marshals, the introduction of a federalized National Guard
unit composed of white area residents, and the interposition of U.S. Army
troops (eventually numbering 23,000—several times more than the population of Oxford and the university combined) to quell a riot that took the
lives of two persons and injured many others on the campus of the University of Mississippi.

In the days and months preceding this ugly outbreak of racist violence,
however, courage and concern for justice also appeared in a number of

places in the town and the university. Some of the courage and concern was rooted in good secular liberal principles and some in Christian conviction. Of the latter variety, such courage and concern for justice appeared nowhere so fully as in the person of Duncan M. Gray Jr.

By the time Gray, at the age of thirty-one, became rector of St. Peter's Episcopal Church in Oxford in August 1957, he already had something of a record in the Episcopal Diocese of Mississippi for civil rights activity. Yet he did not immediately get directly involved in James Meredith's effort to become a student at the university, familiarly known as "Ole Miss." (As I noted earlier, this familiar term for the university is derived from an African American slave practice of referring to the older mistress of a household as "ole miss"; the younger mistress, daughter or daughter-in-law of ole miss, was known as "young miss." Once one knows the origin of the nickname, the question of its appropriateness obviously arises, but since it continues to be a familiar one widely used even today by Mississippians both black and white, including black students at the university, I will also use the term from time to time in what follows.) In his lack of involvement, Gray was like the vast majority of Mississippians; the only exceptions to this rule in 1961 were a few university administrators, some elected officials, and a handful of lawyers and judges. Indeed, after Meredith's first letter to the university inquiring about application, it took a full year for his request to reach a point where there seemed to be any immediate possibility of his entering Ole Miss as a student. Part of the delay was the result of the normal lumbering pace of the judicial process. But much of it was the result of concerted and often coordinated efforts by university administrators and trustees, elected state officials, and two federal judges to prolong the battle as long as possible in the apparent hope that postponement would win the day or that, in other words, justice delayed would indeed result in justice denied.

The issue of equal justice arose almost immediately after Meredith, in his second letter to the university, advised officials of his race. In reply to this January 31 letter, the university registrar telegraphed Meredith on February 4: "It has been found necessary to discontinue consideration of all applications for admission or registration received after January 25, 1961 [the date of Meredith's initial letter of inquiry]. Your application was received subsequent to such date and thus we must advise you not to appear for registration."[10] In his 1965 account, *Integration at Ole Miss*, Russell H. Barrett, at the time a professor of political science at the University of Mississippi, concluded, "It is clear that the sending of telegrams marked the real beginning of the policy of changing the rules as abruptly as necessary to keep Negroes out of Ole Miss."[11]

"Changing the rules as abruptly as necessary" did represent something of a new policy for dealing with efforts to integrate Mississippi colleges and universities. In the previous decade several other African Americans had applied for admission to institutions of higher learning in Mississippi, and their fates did not encourage others to follow their steps. The realities of life for an African American citizen of Mississippi who in any way challenged the Jim Crow system were frightening.

The last black applicant to the University of Mississippi prior to Meredith had been dealt with in a summary fashion by state officials. When Clennon King, an instructor at black Alcorn A&M College (now Alcorn State University) in the southwestern part of the state, applied for admission to Ole Miss in 1958, his admission was officially denied on the grounds that he was applying for a program in history beyond the MA level, and the university had no such program. But to be certain that there were no slip-ups in keeping King out of the university, Mississippi Governor James P. Coleman (generally regarded among state politicians as a moderate on race), a representative of the state Highway Patrol, and a number of plainclothesmen were on hand when King arrived on campus in hopes of registering. These state officials quickly removed King to the state's mental hospital for a psychiatric exam. Doctors there, apparently not under the influence of the state officials, declared King sane and released him. Governor Coleman commented at the time that any black person who wanted to attend a white college in Mississippi must be at least a little crazy, a comment which, as we have seen, was Thurgood Marshall's offhand reaction to Meredith's letter.[12]

In 1959, Clyde Kennard had applied for admission to the University of Southern Mississippi in Hattiesburg. Kennard had served as a U.S. paratrooper in Korea and Germany and was discharged in 1952. After his discharge, he had been a student at the University of Chicago for three years. He returned to his native Mississippi after his stepfather's death in order to help his mother run the family chicken farm and, he hoped, to complete his college education. When he appeared on the University of Southern Mississippi campus in the fall of 1959 in an attempt to register, he was told that there were "irregularities" in his application, he was questioned about his "moral character," and then denied admission. Almost immediately after leaving the campus, Kennard was arrested for speeding and reckless driving. The speeding charges were eventually dismissed, but not until the case reached the Mississippi Supreme Court two years later.

By then, however, Kennard's troubles were far more serious: he was serving seven years in Parchman, the state's infamous penal farm, after being found guilty of stealing three bags of chicken feed, each worth $3.57. The sentence for such a crime would ordinarily be on the order of ninety days in the county jail, but local and state officials clearly did not consider Kennard an ordinary person. Those familiar with the case are convinced that Kennard was framed on the theft charge; the primary witness against him was an African American boy who worked on a nearby white-owned farm. The boy, according to the case made against Kennard, was the one responsible for "transporting" the three bags of feed from the farm where he worked to Kennard's farm. No charges were filed against the boy nor did he lose his job.[13]

It was not until the 1960s, then, that the national political climate was such, especially on the federal level, that Mississippi officials, in their efforts to prevent the desegregation of the state's colleges and universities, were forced to resort to such mundane tactics as delay, friendly judges, and changing the rules.

After Meredith began his fight for admission, rule changing continued apace. On February 7, 1961, in a special meeting that coincided with the date of registration for the spring semester at Ole Miss, the board of trustees voted to adopt two new rules for admission. One provided that state institutions would accept only transfer students whose previous institution and program, whether accredited or not, were "acceptable to receiving institution and the Board of Trustees." The second stated that a student would not be allowed to transfer from one institution to another when that student was in the middle of a quarter, semester, or trimester at his or her current institution "except that the student be an exceptional student and where the best interest of the student can be shown and the receiving institution and the Board of Trustees consents to the acceptance."[14]

Aside from the timing "coincidence" of the board's meeting, both new rules were clearly aimed at Meredith, who was then a student at Jackson State University, an accredited institution on the quarter system. Ole Miss operated on a semester system. Thus, in order to comply with this new admissions policy, Meredith would have been forced to remain out of school for a quarter, thereby endangering his veteran's educational benefits. So, except in the extremely unlikely event that the university and the trustees were willing to declare Jackson State an "acceptable institution" and to decide that attending Ole Miss was in Meredith's "best interest," rejecting Meredith as a student became even more surely a foregone conclusion.

Other ad hoc rule changes followed, but by then Meredith and Motley, his LDF lawyer, thought they had sufficient evidence to act. In early April, Meredith wrote the university's dean of arts and sciences that he had reached the conclusion that "the university registrar had failed to act on my application solely because of my race and color."[15] Two months later he and Motley filed suit in federal district court.

The issue over which Meredith's attorneys chose to file suit was an admission requirement that the state board of trustees had put into place nearly a decade earlier in response to the Supreme Court's *Brown* decision. In September 1954, the board unanimously adopted a requirement that all Mississippi residents who applied to the state's public colleges and universities provide five letters from alumni in their county of residence that would certify to the applicant's good character. Since all the alumni of Ole Miss were white, for Meredith the requirement meant that he would have to find five white individuals who were residents of his home county and also alumni of the University of Mississippi to recommend him for admission as a student. The chance of him finding a snowball lying on the grounds of the Mississippi state capital in August was greater.

It was on this issue, then, that Meredith's attorneys chose to present a constitutionally based challenge to Mississippi's admissions policies and practices. They argued, reasonably enough, that the alumni letter requirement placed a special burden on African Americans which white Mississippians did not bear. But the federal court in which Meredith's attorneys were forced to file the suit was one presided over by one of the "friendly judges" that the state could rely upon, Judge Sidney C. Mize.

Judge Mize quickly showed where his sympathies lay. Above all, as the federal Court of Appeals later noted, he used his judicial powers to do all he could to delay the progress of the suit in his court. As a result, Meredith missed several opportunities to register at the university.[16]

Seven months after the suit's filing, Mize denied Meredith's request for a preliminary injunction against the defendants which, if it had been granted, would have required them to suspend for the time being the alumni letter requirement. The trial of Meredith's request for a permanent injunction against the board's and the university's requirement of alumni recommendations began a month later in Mize's court. Meredith's attorneys argued that the alumni letter requirement failed to provide equal protection under the laws as required by the Fourteenth Amendment to the U.S. Constitution.

On February 3, Mize denied Meredith's request for injunctive relief. In a remarkable opinion, the judge stated that "the University is not a segregated institution" and that while it may have been so before 1954, the Supreme Court's *Brown* decision ended that.[17] In the Alice-in-Wonderland world that many white Mississippians inhabited at the time, such statements as Mize's could be accepted at their face value.

Meredith's lawyers immediately filed notice of appeal and asked the appeals court to issue a preliminary injunction against the state and the university which would order Meredith's immediate admission as a student.

* * *

Although Duncan Gray had not been directly involved up to this point in Meredith's struggle to gain admission to the university, he had been doing what he could to help the community prepare for Meredith's arrival since February, shortly after Judge Mize heard and denied Meredith's request for admission and the case went to the appeals court. He and other white clergy in Oxford approached their African American colleagues and began meeting with them on a monthly basis, "mainly," Gray said, "for the purpose of discussion and fellowship." Although the group did not pursue what he called "significant plans or programs," he added that these relationships were "helpful to us in the fall of '62 as one means of communication between the white and Negro community in Oxford itself."[18] In fact, the very existence of such a group was radical for the time.

Although fellowship and communication between black and white clergy in Oxford would undoubtedly be helpful, Gray knew there was much more to be done. As a minister of the Christian gospel, he genuinely believed not only that we should love our neighbors as ourselves, but that, like the Good Samaritan, we should also speak and act on that belief.

On February 11, the Sunday following Meredith's appeal of Mize's ruling, Gray preached his first sermon to his Oxford congregation on the subject of the coming desegregation of the university. In the little antebellum brick church with its stained glass windows, Gray stood in the high wooden pulpit to the right of his congregation, where his maternal grandfather as rector and his father as bishop had stood before him. He spoke to his congregation about how, as Christians, they should respond to the coming events, even if they were personally opposed to the university's desegregation, as, indeed, he knew that many of them were. He preached the sermon when he did, he said, because he and others expected that the appeals court would issue the preliminary injunction that Meredith had requested, allowing Meredith to participate in the fast-approaching registration for the 1962 spring semester.[19]

Unlike many preachers, Gray left his hearers in no doubt as to the specifics of how, on a highly controversial issue, he believed they should apply Jesus' teaching to their everyday speech and action. February 11 had been designated "Race Relations Sunday" throughout the nation. In addition, the day's lectionary prescribed a New Testament reading from the fifth chapter of Matthew's gospel, that portion known as the Sermon on the Mount, in which Jesus sets out for his followers how they should live and what their ethic should be. Gray took as the text for his sermon Matthew 5:13: "Ye are the salt of the earth: but if the salt has lost its savor, wherewith shall it be salted? It is thenceforth good for nothing, but to be cast out, and to be trodden under foot by men."

The congregation had heard the passage read just before Gray stepped into the pulpit. He began his sermon by reminding his hearers of the importance and value of salt in the ancient world, and he added, "When our Lord told his disciples they were 'the salt of the earth,' He was attaching great value to their lives and their role in human history.

"Without salt," he said, "in those days food would spoil. In the same way," he went on, "human society can easily become corrupt. Greed, lust, self-centeredness, and indifference lead to decay. These are forces which are always at work in the world, and if God's will is to be done, there must be those dedicated persons who serve as the salt of society, those persons who will resist and overcome the corrupting forces of decay.

"To be a Christian, then, is to be put on the spot. . . .

"We are more or less sensitive to our responsibility for our personal behavior—no matter how well or poorly we may carry it out. But," he continued, developing his point, "we are much *less* sensitive to our responsibility for the customs and practices of the society in which we live. Even if we are concerned about a just and proper ordering of the world, we so often salve our consciences by telling ourselves there is so little that we as individuals can do. . . . We fancy ourselves like the dispossessed sharecropper" in John Steinbeck's *The Grapes of Wrath* who, when he set out to revenge himself on the person who foreclosed on his land, discovered only a vast corporate bureaucracy in which no one person was responsible for his misfortune.

While Gray acknowledged the reality in modern society of situations like the sharecropper's, he went on to say, "But there are times when pressing social problems, no matter how complex their background, boil down to a single specific situation in which our duties and responsibilities as Christians are clear and unequivocal. Such a situation now faces us—or soon will—in the admission of the first Negro to the University of Mississippi. . . .

"And since this is Race Relations Sunday in most American churches, it is appropriate—and, indeed, imperative—that we ask ourselves—students, faculty, and townspeople alike—just where *our* responsibility as Christians lies.

"We may not like the prospect," he said, speaking to a congregation in which he knew there were many who, indeed, had no fondness at all for the idea of giving African Americans a place in society equal to that of Americans of European extraction. "But . . . we can no longer be concerned with our like and dislikes, but only with what is just and right for us to do in the situation as it now faces us."

Gray went on to tell his listeners that as Christians they had three duties.

The first was to prevent violence in every way possible, which included, he said, not only *not participating* in violent acts, but also doing all they could "by word and deed" to prevent their eruption. He reinforced his point by adding, "No matter what our feelings, no matter what the pressures, there can be *no possible* justification or excuse from a Christian standpoint for violence in this situation. We must not delude ourselves about this. If we call ourselves Christians, let us act accordingly."

Their second responsibility, he said, was to uphold the law. "As Christian citizens of a democratic society, we cannot permit any man or any group of men to become a law unto themselves. When a Negro enters the University, the law admitting him will be quite clear, and our duty under it will be just as clear."

Finally, Gray told them, "As Christians, we will have the *continuing* duty to see that this new student is accepted and treated *as a person*; that he is not exposed to badgering, torment, or ridicule; that he is given the opportunity to stand on his own merits as a student among students, person among persons, regardless of the color of his skin. Ultimately, this is where the real test of our Christianity will come. This is where we will know if the salt has kept, or lost, its savor."[20]

But the eventuality that Gray had anticipated when he preached the sermon—that the appeals court would issue a preliminary injunction that would make possible Meredith's registration for the spring semester—did not occur. On the day after Gray had addressed his congregation about their Christian duty, a three-judge panel of the federal appeals court denied Meredith's request on a two-to-one vote. In a dissenting opinion Judge Elbert Tuttle argued that the court should have granted Meredith's request not only because in the long run he was almost certain to win his case on its merits, but also because delaying Meredith's admission further would allow time for tensions to build and "massive resistance" to be organized.[21] His words were prophetic.

Changing the rules continued as one of the state's strategies, but Mississippi had not entirely given up on its harassment strategy either. As the spring term wound down, anticipation built that the federal appeals court would rule in Meredith's favor in time for him to register for the summer term on June 8. On June 7, however, state officials announced that Meredith would be arrested for violating state voting laws. The officials justified their announcement by referring to testimony given in Mize's court that Meredith had registered and voted in Hinds County while claiming residence in another county. Motley quickly flew to New Orleans, where she obtained an order from Appeals Court Judge John Minor Wisdom enjoining the state from such action against Meredith.[22]

On June 25, Meredith's twenty-ninth birthday, he received a favorable ruling from the Fifth Circuit Court of Appeals striking down Mize's decision. Wisdom, who gradually became well known and later even respected throughout the South for his favorable rulings in civil rights cases, wrote a scathing opinion in which he made no secret of his view of both the state's and the university's machinations preventing Meredith's enrollment or of Judge Mize's conduct of the trial, as well as his decision.

Of the state and the university, Wisdom wrote, "A full review of the record leads the Court inescapably to the conclusion that from the moment these defendants discovered Meredith was a Negro they engaged in a carefully calculated campaign of delay, harassment, and masterly inactivity." Wisdom added that the state and university, rather than rejecting Meredith for admission on "valid, non-discriminatory grounds," had instead engaged in "a well-defined pattern of delays and frustrations, part of a Fabian policy of worrying the enemy into defeat while time worked for the defenders."[23]

In addition to pointing out Mize's multiple erroneous legal rulings, Wisdom's opinion raked the district judge for his conclusion that there was no "custom or policy" of segregation in Mississippi institutions of higher learning. Of this Wisdom wrote, "This about-face in policy, news of which may startle some people in Mississippi, could have been accomplished only by telepathic communication among the University's administrators [and] the Board of Trustees of State Institutions of Higher Learning." In response to Mize's claim that Mississippi had no policy of segregation in its educational institutions, Wisdom went on to cite several Mississippi statutes prescribing segregation and quoted from a state publication that described five of Mississippi's public higher educational institutions as "White" and the other three as "Negro."[24]

Meredith, his attorneys, and indeed all those who supported the desegregation of Mississippi institutions could not have asked for a more favorable or stronger ruling from the appeals court. Wisdom's opinion made
clear that the court's decision applied to *all* African Americans and to *all* of
Mississippi's public colleges and universities. Wisdom also made clear the
appeals court was directing Mize to issue an injunction that would prevent
the state and university from engaging in further delaying tactics and direct
it to admit Meredith as a student at Ole Miss.[25]

The state, however, was far from the end of its rope. Among other weapons in its arsenal, it still had friendly judges on its side. Thus began a bizarre duel among members of the Fifth Circuit Court of Appeals, which
had just issued the ruling ordering the state and the university to admit
Meredith as a student. Although the intramural struggle among members
of the court was eventually resolved in Meredith's favor, its playing out was
nearly enough to convince Meredith to abandon his fight, and only Motley's persuasion prevented this.[26]

The court's rules provided that Mize would not officially receive its order until twenty-one business days after it was handed down, that is, not
until July 18. At 9:30 a.m. on July 18, however, an attorney for the state
of Mississippi appeared in the clerk of court's office with another order
signed by Fifth Circuit Judge Ben Cameron, a colleague of Wisdom's and a
native Mississippian, that granted a stay of Judge Wisdom's order until the
Supreme Court could rule in the case. Cameron granted his stay without
giving Meredith's lawyers opportunity to argue against it. About Cameron's
action, political scientist Barrett comments that the judge "acted with a
degree of speed usually reserved for saving convicted murderers from the
gas chamber," and added, "In the odd world in which they lived and which
they helped create, the Mississippi defendants and their attorneys felt their
position was precisely" analogous to that of the convicted murderer about
to be executed.[27]

Meredith's attorneys returned to the three-judge panel that had given
them their victory less than a month before and asked them to vacate Cameron's stay. The judges did so on July 27 and ordered Mize to issue an order
for Meredith's admission immediately.

Again, Wisdom could not have been clearer about the panel's desires and
intentions. He not only made plain his opinion of Cameron's action (". . . it
is unthinkable that a judge who was not a member of this panel should be
allowed to frustrate the mandate of the court"), but on the panel's behalf
he also issued an injunction prohibiting the state and the university from
further frustrating Meredith's enrollment. The injunction was to remain in

effect until Mize had issued and enforced the order demanded by the appeals court and until "there has been full and actual compliance in good faith" on the part of the state and the university.[28]

But neither the state and the university nor Judge Cameron had given up. The day after the three-judge panel's injunction, Cameron issued his second stay. This time the panel responded the same day with an even more specific injunction ordering Meredith's immediate admission. The summer school term was too far gone for Meredith to enroll immediately, but he announced his plans to enroll on September 21 for the fall semester. Judge Cameron, however, was still not willing to concede the judicial scuffle, and on July 31 he issued a third stay, overruled by the court on August 4. This time Cameron took two days to issue a fourth stay.

Since Cameron had by then made quite clear that his defiance of the court's ruling would continue indefinitely, Meredith's attorney announced that she would petition the Supreme Court to throw out the stays. On August 31, the U.S. Justice Department became involved in the suit for the first time by filing a friend of the court brief in support of her petition.

And so anticipating that Meredith's registration at Ole Miss would take place very soon, in time for him to be a student during the fall semester, on September 9, Gray again spoke to his congregation about what Christian profession required of them in a situation that they might not like. He knew from past experience that his message would be received with very mixed responses by his congregation.

The Episcopal Church is a lectionary church, meaning that certain prayers and scriptural readings are appointed for each day. On this Sunday the "collect," or short prayer, designated for the day as part of the service was one that Gray had come to appreciate more and more in the years he had pursed his ministry both within the church and outside it.

In the prayer book in use in the Episcopal Church at that time, the collect read, "Almighty and everlasting God, who art always more ready to hear than we are to pray, and art wont to give us more than we desire or deserve; Pour down upon us the abundance of thy mercy; forgiving us those things whereof our conscience is afraid, and giving us those good things which we are not worthy to ask, but through the merits and mediation of Jesus Christ, thy Son, our Lord. Amen."[29]

Gray understood and agreed wholeheartedly with the straightforward theology behind the prayer: God's love and mercy are so limitless that they are not only always well beyond what we deserve, but also even beyond what we can desire, because they are beyond what we, as humans, can even imagine. As he had practiced his ministry and had repeatedly found himself in situations that he believed required him to speak and act out of Christian conviction in ways that his neighbors and his parishioners might well oppose, he had also come to see another, slightly different message in the prayer's theology: God often sends us challenges that we really have little or no desire to meet, but he sends them out of the same love and mercy that he sends those other goods that we *do* desire, that are *still* more than we deserve. Gray could hardly say the prayer without a little smile at what he took to be its slightly ambiguous message.

On September 9, he took this collect as the text for his sermon and proceeded to explain how the prayer book's Elizabethan language (scarcely modified since its origins in sixteenth-century England) and also how much older biblical claims and commands applied directly to his listeners' lives in Oxford, Mississippi, on September 9, 1962.

The sermon began with exegesis of the collect's statement on prayer, that God is always more willing to hear than we are to pray, and Gray talked about the difficulty Christians have in practicing the life of prayer they are called to.

Then he quickly moved on to the second part of the collect, its statement of God's infinite giving, and pointed out the double meaning implicit in it language.

He told his congregation, "The real hitch must come with that last word 'desire.' Even though we can see how God gives us more than we deserve, can we really say that he is 'wont,' or inclined, to give us more that we *desire*? Surely not, we say, for our desires are, quite literally, insatiable. Can we ever get enough acceptance and recognition to satisfy us? Can we ever get enough of success? Can we ever really get more of the things of this world than we want?"

Then he moved on to the specific situation faced by the members of his congregation, from the freshman women going through sorority rush who saw the rest of their career at Ole Miss as dependent on whether they got a bid from the "right" sorority or not, to the far graver situation faced by the entire community and the university.

Of the latter he told his listeners,

No one would ask to be born in these trying and troublous times. We would have preferred a quieter age of peace and security. But God has given us *more* than we desire. He has given us the opportunity to serve Him and His purpose in this world at a time when such service can be more significant and more meaningful than ever before. All of us shy away from the heavy responsibility which probably will soon

be placed upon us for the peaceful admission and acceptance of the
first Negro student at the University. We didn't *choose* this responsibility. Most of us would have preferred to have come along later
after everything was settled and all problems resolved. But *God has
chosen us.* He has given us *more* than we desire: the opportunity to
make a significant contribution to the history of our University, our
community, and our state by seeing to it that this student is accepted
peacefully and quietly and in an atmosphere of Christian charity and
goodwill.[30]

As words on a page, these may seem relatively innocuous, especially
nearly fifty years after the fact. But we must imagine ourselves in the situation that Gray and his congregation found themselves—a highly charged
atmosphere in which many respected citizens of the community, including
members of Gray's congregation, were of the opinion that Meredith's attempted entrance as a student had nothing to do with the will of God but,
if anything, was more likely the work of the devil. If then, we, like Gray and
other members of his congregation, took seriously the sermon's admonitions and acted on them, we would know that we would almost surely face
ridicule and rejection by some members of our church and our community.
We also would be justified in fearing that such a stand on our parts could
well harm us economically, just as it had other Mississippians, both black
and white. Finally, we might even be putting at risk our own and our family's health and safety. In the preceding decade in Mississippi, there had
been others, including whites such as those in Gray's congregation, who
had sometimes given up much, including occasionally even their lives, for
speaking and acting in favor of equal justice for African Americans.
     Such contemporary realities had discouraged many otherwise well-
meaning white Mississippians, citizens who understood the necessity or
even the justice of equal opportunities for African Americans and who
would neither resort to nor encourage violence, from speaking out and
taking public stands. But these same realities had not prevented Duncan
Gray from saying and doing what he believed he was called to say and do
as a Christian and a minister of the Gospel.
     As Gray had anticipated, the end of the legal battle over Meredith's
enrollment at the University was near. The day following Gray's sermon,
less than two weeks before fall registration at the university was scheduled
to begin, U.S. Supreme Court Justice Hugo Black ordered that all Judge
Cameron's stays be vacated and that the federal appeals court's judgment
be made effective "immediately." He also enjoined the Mississippi board

of trustees and university officials from interfering with the enforcement of the appeals court's decision until and unless the Supreme Court ruled on their appeal, although he warned that the Court was unlikely to agree to hear the appeal since it "essentially only involves factual issues." Black added that he had consulted all the other Supreme Court justices about his order, and all agreed "that under the circumstances I should exercise that power as I have done here."[31]

The state of Mississippi, then, had apparently reached the end of the line when it came to reliance upon changing the rules, friendly judges, and delay. On Wednesday, September 13, Judge Mize issued the required permanent injunction against the state and the university that would make possible Meredith's admission and enrollment.[32]

All was far from quiet, however, both on the university campus and throughout the state; indeed, as it turned out, things were far from quiet throughout much of the Deep South.

On the Ole Miss campus, tensions continued to build, even as university administrators began to make some efforts to prepare for Meredith's arrival. A number of students were already on campus to prepare for such activities as student orientation and fraternity and sorority rush. Administrators had met with student leaders even before Justice Black's order was handed down, and the groups discussed avoiding violence, dealing with outsiders attracted to the campus by Meredith's enrollment, and ensuring that the university remain open. The decision was made to conduct an "educational campaign," mainly through the campus newspaper, the *Mississippian*, and student leaders agreed to do all they could to help maintain law and order.[33]

Early in the morning of September 11, however, a small group of students and others erected a large cross near Fraternity Row. Campus police arrived on the scene before the cross could be lighted and successfully persuaded the students not to set it afire. When the dean of students arrived, students told him that they had simply wanted to protest Meredith's admission. He persuaded them to remove the cross, and the university took no disciplinary action against them.

The following afternoon, university officials, including the chancellor, the university's top administrator, met with fraternity presidents, and that night administrators met with fifty men's dormitory managers to enlist their cooperation in the effort to avoid violence and ensure that the university remained open.

But later that same night a cross *was* set afire, again near Fraternity Row. This time those responsible were apparently not students. Fraternity members who went outside to investigate said they saw a camera flash and four or five men running away. The next day a photo of the burning cross appeared on the front page of the *Jackson Daily News*, a newspaper then notorious throughout the state for its slanted coverage of racial matters, its racist editorial stance, and, indeed, for its rabble rousing on all matters related to race. The headline above the photo read, "Meredith Cross Blazes at Oxford." The story accompanying the picture claimed that over one hundred students and members of the campus police force watched the cross burn, and that police and university officials finally dispersed the crowd with "threats of expulsion." *Daily News* editors knew full well that reporting such disciplinary threats, whether true or not, could be counted on to outrage parents of Ole Miss students throughout the state. The newspaper's fabrication is a good example of *Daily News* coverage of racially charged events at the time.

Foremost among the political fomenters of the crisis was Mississippi governor Ross Barnett, although other elected officials also did not miss their opportunities to stir the pot. On September 13, the day that Judge Mize finally had been forced to issue his injunction against the university and the state, Governor Barnett delivered an evening television address. The next morning the *Jackson Daily News* headlined its story "Ross Risks Jail to Halt Race Mixing."

Although it had been clear to Mississippi voters since Barnett's 1959 campaign for governor that he was a race-baiting demagogue (an approach that a majority of the voters obviously favored at that time), Barnett reached what may have been a new low given the crisis that was building. On September 13, Barnett declared that "no school will be integrated while I am your governor." He then went on to "especially call upon all public officials both elected and appointed to join hands with the people and resist by every legal and constitutional means and [in a departure from his text] by *every* means the tyrannical edicts which have been and will be directed against the patriotic citizens of our state."[34]

Other elected officials did not miss their opportunity to jump on the governor's bandwagon, quickly praising the governor's statement. From Washington, both of Mississippi's senators telegraphed Barnett. Their message read, "We congratulate you on your effort and determination to preserve the sovereign rights and privileges of our state and pledge you and the people of Mississippi our full and unqualified support." As Barrett says, "The reaction to the governor's message was a wave of approval which drowned out the few voices of dissent, plus silence from some who feared what lay at the end of Barnett's road."[35]

Voices of dissent there certainly were, and Duncan Gray's was one of the foremost among them. His reaction to Barnett's speech and the positive response it received from all but a handful of Mississippi politicians was, however, one of "discouragement, depression, and great sadness." Gray was very much concerned that Barnett should "take this stand at this time, because with the climate what it was—already bordering on hysteria—and the firm conviction in the minds of so many people that somehow Meredith would never be admitted, no matter how many court orders came along, and with the governor giving encouragement to this and more or less promising that he would not be, we felt that the speech more or less set the stage for a kind of back-to-the-wall resistance—a last ditch resistance— that was bound to create problems. Certainly the possibility of violence was very much in our minds at that time."[36]

Gray's "discouragement, depression, and great sadness" did not, however, prevent him from acting. He met with a group of eight other white Oxford ministers representing four other denominations (Methodist, Catholic, Baptist, and Presbyterian). Although these other ministers had not spoken as frequently and publicly on the issue as Gray had, now they all agreed to a statement that they read in their churches on the Sunday following the governor's speech.

In their statement, the ministers urged their congregations to "solemnly and prayerfully . . . act in a manner consistent with the Christian teaching concerning the value and dignity of man," to "exert whatever leadership and influence possible to maintain peace and order among us," to "pray unceasingly for God's guidance of the leaders in this community and in our beloved state and nation," and to "make every effort to resist the pressures placed upon us by emotionally excited groups."[37]

Like Episcopal chaplain Wofford K. Smith and Murphey C. Wilds, minister of Oxford's First Presbyterian Church, Gray went beyond the statement itself to warn his congregation once again that each "professing Christian bears a *heavy responsibility* to see that no acts of intimidation or violence take place," and he called for "the leadership necessary to assure the peaceful admission of James Meredith to the University, insofar as we have the power to do so."[38]

Despite these admonitions from clergy, as Gray says, "the tension certainly grew and deepened as the days went on, and I found it difficult to explain to people outside of Mississippi and maybe particularly people outside Oxford just what state this hysteria had reached in those early weeks in September prior to Meredith's first arrival on the Ole Miss campus."[39]

CHAPTER 2

"WHAT IS JUST AND RIGHT"

Oxford, Mississippi, 1962

INDEED, during those early September weeks, Mississippi officials, both elected and appointed, as well as anonymous troublemakers, continued to ratchet up the level of hysteria in the state and increase the potential for violence.

Other Mississippians agreed with Gray's assessment of the situation. Barrett comments, "The absence of serious *public* discussion of the problem in *Mississippi* clearly indicated how far Ross Barnett and his supporters had led the state toward public insanity."[1] Ira Harkey, editor of the newspaper in the small Gulf Coast city of Pascagoula, predicted that Barnett would resort to violence to keep Meredith out of Ole Miss. In an editorial published the day before Meredith was expected to register, Harkey described the state's condition as schizophrenic and wrote, "In a madhouse's din, Mississippi waits." He added, "God help Mississippi."[2]

On the same day the pastors' statement was read in Oxford churches, a rumor spread that a forty-two car caravan carrying Ku Klux Klan members was on it way to Oxford. That turned out to be false.

On Monday, September 17, the board of trustees of the state's colleges and universities met, and it was apparently becoming fairly clear to them that further resistance was useless and meant only the real risk of a contempt citation from the courts. But Barnett and his allies managed to take control of the meeting, and Barnett outlined his plans for further resistance.[3]

On September 18, the state legislature was called into special session by the governor; after a rousing speech from him, the legislators resolved to "commend" Barnett "for his fearless and courageous stand against political aggression . . . designed to destroy Southern institutions, traditions, and way of living" and promised "our full support in the staunch stand he had taken to uphold and defend by every lawful and honorable means available the laws and sovereign powers of our state against the unlawful, unwarranted aggression and usurpation by the federal government."[4]

Although the resolution claimed to support only "lawful" resistance, one apparently insurmountable problem at the heart of the situation was that the legislators who voted for the resolution, as well as their supporters, defined the word "lawful" in terms of "state's rights." But federal courts had already rejected their interpretation of that part of the Constitution. As long as Mississippians refused to recognize the final authority of the federal courts to interpret the Constitution, the impasse could only be resolved by unlawful means, which almost certainly meant physical force.

Very early in the hours of September 19, a fourteen-by-seventeen-foot cross made of cloth sacks was set afire in a street between two of the men's dormitories. Firemen arrived at the scene and put out the fire in about ten minutes, while student stood by cheering—whether for the fireman or the burning cross was not entirely clear.[5]

Early the same morning, the state legislature approved a bill that would automatically deny admission to any state school to any person "who has a criminal charge of moral turpitude pending against him" or "has been convicted of any criminal offense and not pardoned."[6]

The law was drawn carefully, however, and did not cover "any charge or conviction of traffic law violation, violation of the state conservation laws and state game and fish laws, or manslaughter as the result of driving while intoxicated or under the influence of intoxicants."[7] One can only assume that these exceptions in the new law came into being when some legislator or another realized that without the exclusion, he or some member of his family or that of a friend would be barred from enrolling at a Mississippi college or university under the new provisions.

But the reasons for the legislature's new law quickly became clear. On the day after the bill passed, the day new students were scheduled to enroll at Ole Miss, James Meredith was tried in absentia in a Jackson justice of the peace court on the charges that had been raised in Mize's court: that Meredith had voted in a different county from his home county. The trial, of course, was in direct defiance of the appeals court's June ruling forbidding such action. Under the circumstances though, it was not surprising that the justice of the peace who tried Meredith found him guilty as charged and sentenced him to a fine of $100 and a full year in the county jail.[8]

In this atmosphere of defiance, registration of returning students began later in the morning of September 19, the day the legislature passed its

"Meredith law." On the same day, Gray preached again, this time to the entire community over local radio, his recent sermon about how God often sends us *more* than we desire.

On Wednesday, September 20, the day that new Ole Miss students, including James Meredith, were scheduled to register, Gray again took to local radio to repeat his earlier sermon about the Christian calling to be "the salt of the earth."

The day of Meredith's trial and of new student registration was a busy one for Gray. He and Smith, the Episcopal chaplain, spent most of it on the campus, manning a table at registration for the purpose of greeting and giving out information to Episcopal students as they arrived.

He recalls, "Everybody was anticipating Meredith's arrival. Nobody knew the exact time. I can remember at one point—I suppose it was shortly after noon—we were in the vicinity of the Lyceum [the university's main administrative building at the heart of the campus] and saw a large crowd gathered at that point. . . . I remember a few organized cheers—first, to begin with, rather spontaneous cheers. . . . Later on these became a bit more organized with some students seeming to take the lead. It was not long until the cheers began to take on segregationist overtones—one I can recall: 'Two, four, six, eight. We don't want to integrate! . . .

"Finally, after a goodly number were joining in cheers and anti-integration shouts and slogans, a group of, I'd say, a half dozen students made a dash down to the flagpole in front of the Lyceum and started to haul down the American flag that was flying there. At that point a couple of student leaders stepped in between them and the flagpole, grabbed them by the arms, told them to stop what they were doing and go away. . . .

"The cheers stopped and the crowd began to disperse, students going off in small groups began to wander out into the Circle [the street in front of the Lyceum] and around the Lyceum. It struck me. . . this is my own interpretation—that they had been carried away a bit and then suddenly realized. . . maybe the seriousness of some of the implication of what they were doing, and this had a sobering effect, and it did break up for the time being."[9]

The day was a busy one for a number of Mississippians. The board of trustees had told Meredith that he should present himself at its Jackson offices at 3:00 p.m. "for registration or other disposition of his application." At its 10:00 a.m. meeting the trustees learned of the new "Meredith law" and of Meredith's conviction on the false swearing charge. And by lunchtime the trustees learned that matters had been further taken out of their hands. The state's plan was to direct Meredith to come to the university campus to register. The board, quickly conceding its loss of authority and thereby attempting to avoid the risk of a contempt citation, voted "to invest Honorable Ross R. Barnett, the Governor of the State of Mississippi, with the full power, authority, right and discretion of his Board to act upon all matters pertaining to or concerned with the registration or non- registration, admission or non-admission, and/or attendance of James H. Meredith at the University of Mississippi."[10]

Thus Meredith was told to appear that afternoon at a building on the campus's east edge known as the University Continuation Center or, more popularly, the Alumni House. Barnett arrived from Jackson at the tiny Oxford airport around 2:30 p.m. When he was asked if Meredith would be allowed to register, he responded, "Hell, no."[11]

Word began to spread on the campus that Meredith would not register at the campus gymnasium like other students, but would be arriving shortly at the Continuation Center. A large crowd began to gather there, as well as state highway patrolmen and sheriff's deputies, one of whom said that their orders were to arrest Meredith and, if necessary, shoot it out with the federal marshals accompanying him.[12]

Meredith, escorted by U.S. Justice Department officials and three federal marshals, including their chief, James P. McShane, arrived between 4:30 and 5:00 p.m. The crowd greeted them with boos, chants of "we want Ross!" and renditions of the university's favorite athletic cheer: "Hotty toddy, God A'mighty, who in the hell are we? Flim flam, bim bam! Ole Miss, by damn!"

Once Meredith and his protectors were inside, the scenario proceeded according to Barnett's plans. Meredith said to the university and state officials present, "I want to be admitted to the university." Barnett, acting as registrar, refused to grant him admission, invoking the widely discredited legal doctrine of "interposition," which claims the right of a state to "interpose" its sovereignty between the federal government and its citizens. John Doar, the Justice Department attorney, responded, "Do you realize that this puts you and other officials in contempt of a federal court order?" Barnett responded, "Are *you* telling me I'm in contempt, or does it take a judge?" Although federal power was fast closing on him, Barnett apparently still could not believe that the day of friendly judges willing to defy the federal government for what he and others believed was for "the good of Mississippi" had come to an end.

But to a degree Barnett's wager was correct; the federal government was not yet willing to exert its power further. The encounter with Barnett ended quietly with Meredith and his escorts leaving the building, getting in their car, and driving away. Since the federal government was not yet ready to confront state authorities to any greater extent, the car with Meredith in it left the campus. The crowd did not realize this, and speculation immediately spread among them that Meredith was headed for the campus gymnasium, where he would actually register. And so they made a mad rush in that direction, only later realizing they were to be cheated out of their excitement.

Although some members of the crowd were present mainly for the excitement of the occasion, others had more sinister intent. Gray had been present at the Continuation Center when Meredith arrived. He saw that while the crowd was still composed largely of students, there were others among them whom he recognized as outsiders, including "a rather militant segregationist and Citizens' Council member" from Jackson. The presence of such individuals and the mood of the crowd gave him pause. "But again, with Meredith having left the campus, . . . no real incident developed; it was just the frightening thought of what could have happened where you began to see the potential for violence there and that had us worried."[13]

Still picking their way carefully, the Kennedy administration and Attorney General Robert Kennedy's Justice Department decided not to ask the appeals court for a contempt citation against Barnett for his direct defiance of the court's orders, although as Barrett notes, by "failing to seek immediate action . . . the Department of Justice insured further delay of Meredith's enrollment." And, of course, further time for tensions to build and plans for "massive resistance" to be formulated. At the same time, there was some sense to the Kennedy administration's excuse that it considered Barnett's actions a political ploy and had chosen not to give him and his supporters the additional ammunition that jailing him would create. But the Justice Department released a statement that said: "It is our responsibility, together with the courts to see that these orders [to admit Meredith] are obeyed no matter what course is ultimately necessary."[14]

Legal and political maneuvering filled the next several days. On Sunday, September 23, however, Gray spoke once more to his congregation about the crisis at hand. From the day's prescribed readings, Gray took as his text verse 15 and part of verse 16 in the Apostle Paul's great letter to the Romans: "Rejoice with those who rejoice, weep with those who weep. Live in harmony with one another." Much of the book of Romans, as Gray noted in his sermon, is soaringly theological, but in the chapter from which Gray took his text, Paul takes the occasion to remind the Christians in Rome very specifically of the ethic that Jesus had set forth for them in such teachings as the Sermon on the Mount.

In his sermon, Gray did the same, telling his congregation that "in his theology, St. Paul concentrates upon our essential unity in Christ, the essential kinship and oneness of all mankind in the Incarnation." Gray went on to assert that for Paul "the primary goal of Christian living" is the recognition of this essential unity. It is for this reason, Gray said, that Paul exhorted his readers to "rejoice with those who rejoice" and "weep with those who weep." Such behavior is an acting out of the realization of our essential unity as children of God.

"Yet all too often," Gray continued, "the tragedy of life is that we seem to rejoice alone and weep alone. We are separated from each other, no matter how close we appear on the surface, and in our joys and in our sorrows, we have a sense of profound *loneliness*."

To the extent that this is true, Gray went on, this loneliness poses real dangers for us. Loneliness, he warned, is a kind of vacuum which may fill itself with relationships with our fellows that are far from the kind that Paul had in mind when he spoke of laughing and weeping together.

"For example," he said, "it can make us so easily susceptible to the pressures of the crowd. We don't want to go against the mood and temper of the crowd in which we find ourselves for fear of isolating further and risking whatever tenuous relationship we do have with our fellows. So often we find ourselves going against our better judgment—doing things which we would not do on our own—when placed with a group whose mood and temper seems to be different."

Speaking of the crowds of students and others that he had observed on the Ole Miss campus the preceding Thursday, Gray told his congregation, "Every student with whom I have talked—and this has been quite a few— seems to sense deeply the need for calm, orderly, and peaceful conduct on the part of all of us at this trying time. And, yet, some of our students found themselves led astray last Thursday by the pressures of a crowd. They were induced to boo and jeer and demonstrate at a time when the object of their jeers was conducting himself with dignity and poise that it would behoove us to imitate."

Quoting Ralph Waldo Emerson, "The mob is man voluntarily descending to the nature of the beast," Gray went on in good Anglican fashion to recommend the application of reason: "For no thinking person could believe that those jeers and curses *helped* the situation. They only made matters worse. But people lose their perspective and their reason when they become members of a crowd, or mob.

"Consequently," he concluded, "it behooves us all to resolve once again that as Christians we will use whatever leadership and influence we have to prevent not only violence, but also any sort of riotous demonstration where reason is so easily lost and where the University, the community, and the state are so easily hurt.

"I have real faith and confidence in this congregation and in the students whom I know. I know you want your contribution to be on the side of peace and goodwill. Just don't let a crowd carry you in the other direction."[15]

Although there was no threat of violence the next day, peace was far from at hand. Monday morning, a collection of university officials and board members had been summoned to appear at a hearing before all eight judges of the Fifth Circuit Court of Appeals to explain why they should not be held to contempt of court for their failure to register Meredith the preceding week. Their defense was that the matter had been taken out of their hands when they had made Barnett registrar, but the court had little sympathy for this argument. One judge incredulously asked the board's attorney, "Did you advise [the board] that this monkey business of coming around pretending to take over the school was legal?"[16]

University registrar Robert Ellis hastened to assure the court that "when the decision became ours . . . we would do exactly what the court told us to do," that is, register Meredith. Given such an expression of cooperation, Meredith's lawyer moved that "the appellant be registered right here and now in open court by the Registrar of the University of Mississippi." Although her motion was not accepted by the judges, all eight of them concurred that "the twelve members of the Board of Trustees have willfully and intentionally violated the Court's order." When, in response, the board's chair assured the court that board members would "enter any order and do any act that this Court may direct them to do as, if, and when the Court directs them to do it," the judges decided not find them in contempt, but contented themselves with ordering that Meredith should be registered by 4:00 p.m. the next day.[17]

Barnett, however, quickly moved to do what he could to prevent the registration from taking place. Still relying on the doctrine of interposition, which one judge at the previous day's hearing had described as "knocked out at Appomattox," he issued an executive order requiring the arrest of any federal official attempting to prevent a state official from carrying out his "official duties."

Although university trustees and administrators proceeded to attempt to fulfill their promise to the court, they were outfoxed again the next day. Registrar Ellis arrived in Jackson on Tuesday only to find that he was summoned to appear before a committee of the state legislature. Waiting in his place in the board's meeting room was none other than Governor Barnett, and outside the building a mob of over two thousand of his supporters. When Justice Department lawyer John Doar, one of Meredith's escorts, attempted to hand Barnett a restraining order from the court of appeals, Barnett refused it and read a statement that concluded with a sentence addressed to Meredith: "I do hereby finally deny you admission to the University of Mississippi." This brought cheers for Barnett and jeers for Meredith from others gathered in the room, including some state legislators. At this, Meredith and his escorts again left the building, protected from the mob by members of the Mississippi highway patrol.[18]

In addition to the legal proceedings in federal court, negotiations by phone attempting to resolve the impasse had also been underway between Barnett and Attorney General Robert Kennedy. When Kennedy learned the result of the latest attempt to register Meredith, he was furious and called Barnett, threatening to have Meredith simply show up in classes on the Ole Miss campus on Wednesday. (Barnett's protest to Kennedy was, "How can you do that without registering? . . . They're going to give him special treatment? They can't do that, General.") Setting aside the threat to have Meredith simply show up in classes, Kennedy put Barnett on notice that Meredith would arrive on the Ole Miss campus at ten the next morning to register. Barnett politely agreed.

In response to Barnett's actions earlier in the day, the appeals court ordered him to appear before them on Friday for a contempt of court hearing, and the following morning a banner headline on the front page of the *New York Times* proclaimed, "U.S. Is Prepared to Send Troops as Mississippi Governor Defies Court and Bars Negro Student."[19]

Gray had a worship service to conduct on Wednesday morning, so he missed that day's encounter between Meredith and Mississippi officials. The scene played itself out in what was coming to seem a scripted way. This time it was Lieutenant Governor Paul Johnson who stated to Doar, Meredith, and his other escorts, "We do not intend to allow Meredith to enter." After this, there ensued what Barrett describes as "an almost comic elbowing match" between the federal and state officials, but once again Meredith and his escorts left peacefully. For his actions Johnson won a contempt citation for himself from the appeals court, and from Barnett praise for having "stood tall." (When Johnson ran for governor of Mississippi in 1963, Barnett's praise became his campaign slogan: "Stand tall with Paul." Barnett's slogan had been "Roll with Ross. He's his own boss!")

Although Gray had been tending to his priestly duties Wednesday morning, later that day he joined six other Oxford ministers in a telegram to Barnett which read, "We, the following members of Oxford clergy and chaplains to the university, fearful of the anarchy upon us and our people through continued defiance of the federal court and convinced of the Christian's call both to obey the laws of the land, and to be himself a peacemaker, do hereby call upon you above all else to avoid the closing of the university, to protect its accreditation and to uphold the good name and dignity of the university."[20]

On Thursday, Barnett continued his telephone negotiations with Robert Kennedy, and early in the afternoon they seemed near to reaching an agreement for a scenario that would create the impression of Barnett being forced to give in to federal officials at gunpoint, thereby saving face for him and allowing Meredith to register. But an hour later a crowd was beginning to gather on the campus, and Barnett began to hint at the possibility of violence if Meredith were brought to register.

Gray was on campus again on Thursday and observed the crowd, which he described as "large." He recalls that "there were several of us, faculty members and two or three clergy, who tried to talk to the students and ask them to go back to their dormitories. . . . We had some measure of success—a few would go on—but then for the most part the students stayed. . . .

"It was this point also," he says, "that we saw quite a few strange faces. . . . [C]ertainly they were not students. That began to get us even more worried. Their numbers were more impressive at this point, more numerous than they had been the week before. Of course rumors were flying through the crowd. . . . Nobody seemed to know anything much for sure, but . . . as the crowd began to build up . . . [the] tension was very obvious."[21]

Although university officials and even Lieutenant Governor Johnson tried to get the crowd to disperse, all were unsuccessful, despite Johnson's warning that "someone might get killed." In fact, this was the less offensive form of the lieutenant governor's attempt to disperse the crowd; he also told them, "If you want this nigger to get in, just stay here."[22]

Johnson's appearance was followed by one from Barnett, who was received with cheers by a crowd now numbering somewhere between fifteen hundred and two thousand. Barnett acknowledged the cheers and, as Gray remembers it, "said a few words, something to the effect that he didn't know just what was happening or what to expect, . . . but the result was a pretty enthusiastic pep rally at that point—the waving of Confederate flags and so forth and so on."[23]

Gray's usual tendency is to speak carefully and charitably; other observers remember the situation in more threatening terms. One former *Mississippian* editor wrote of the scene: "After a couple of wars and a revolution, you learn how to smell death and danger. And that smell was in the air between 5 and 5:55 p.m. yesterday on the street corner. The trouble was that too few people realized it—too few people could recognize the smell."[24]

A reporter for *U.S. News and World Report* was quoted as observing, "I swear that at one minute it was bunch of happy, good natured school kids—but the next minute it was a mob."[25] In other words, exactly the situation that Gray had warned of in his sermon the previous Sunday.

By 6:00 p.m. Thursday as it became clear to the crowd that Meredith would not appear on the campus that day, its members began to disperse.

But if tensions were not already high enough, other Mississippi officials continued to fan them higher. Both of Mississippi's senators and all but one of its congressmen sent a telegram to President Kennedy that read, "A holocaust is in the making. You are the only person that can stop it."[26] Although some might suppose the message was intended to encourage the president to restrain Barnett, in fact, as all Mississippians knew, the opposite was actually the case; the message was a warning to the president that he should desist from trying to enforce the law.

That same day, General Edwin Walker delivered his radio address, calling for "ten thousand strong, from every state in the union" to come to Oxford to "rally for the cause of freedom."[27]

On the side of law and order, however, the court of appeals in New Orleans found Barnett guilty of contempt of court, gave him until 11:00 a.m. the following Tuesday to purge himself, and fined him ten thousand dollars a day until he complied.

But Barnett was still far from a compliant mood. On Saturday, September 29, Ole Miss met the University of Kentucky in a football game played in Jackson. Before the game began, Ole Miss students had displayed what was billed as "the largest Confederate flag in the world." At halftime, Ole Miss was ahead 7–0, and hysteria was reaching a new peak. When the crowd began to chant, "We want Ross! We want Ross!" Barnett could not resist. He stepped from his box onto the field and approached the microphone. When the cheering finally died, he raised a clenched fist and cried, "I love Mississippi! I love her people! I love her customs! And I love and respect her heritage!" That was all he said, but in response the crowd went wild, waving a sea of Confederate flags and joining in a new ditty that the *Jackson Daily News* had published and urged on football fans the previous day: "Never, Never, Never, Never, Never, N-o-o-o Never Never Never! We will not yield an inch of any field! Fix us another toddy, ain't yielding to nobody. Ross's standin' like Gibraltar, he shall never falter. Ask us what we say? It's 'to hell with Bobby K!' Never shall our emblem go from Colonel Reb to Old Black Joe!"[28]

It was in this atmosphere, then, that the following morning Gray preached once again to a congregation that he knew included both those who opposed Meredith's admission and those who favored it, as well as those in fundamental sympathy with and those disgusted and frightened by the political and moral insanity that had been building during the last week.

"For the past two Sundays," he began, "this congregation has heard sermons on the present crisis at the University; and I'm sure there are many here today who would rather not hear another one! Indeed, there are probably some who came here this morning primarily to get a little peace and quiet, to get away from the maddening problems which now confront us. It is very easy to understand and sympathize with an attitude such as this. The burden of this crisis hangs so heavily upon us that all of us would like to get out from under it for awhile, even if only an hour."

"But this," he went on, "I do not believe we can conscientiously do. To use our religion as a means of escape from the pressing problems that face our community, our state and our nation would be to make of our religion precisely what Karl Marx called it: an 'opiate.' God in Christ has never promised us *this* kind of peace, a peace brought at the price of ignoring what's going on in the world around us. Our Christian faith is *vitally* relevant to this crisis in our community; and if it were not, we would do well to give it up forthwith.

"The atmosphere of a church *is* one of peace and quiet, however, and this is an atmosphere that it has been hard to find in Oxford during the past two weeks. It might be well, then, for us to take advantage of this hour to give calm and prayerful thought to our present situation. Could we, then, for a few moments this morning, consider reverently and rationally just where we are, where we are headed, and what we, as Christians, are doing about it?

"I think we should ask ourselves, first of all, if we are really sufficiently aware of the *deadly serious* nature of our present predicament. This may seem like a silly question to ask in the light of the anxiety and concern which has burdened us all in the past several days. But one wonders if it is so silly when we see legislators . . . wearing [Confederate] centennial uniforms on the floor of the House. One wonders if it is so silly when we see students cheering and laughing in a situation where even the lieutenant governor said someone might get killed. I am afraid that there may be many—and not just freshman at the university—who seem to put this whole matter in the category of waving Confederate flags and singing 'Dixie' at a football game; or standing up and proclaiming to the world that we are proud to be Mississippians. We need to remind ourselves that we are now on an entirely different level from this," Gray said.

He went on to speak to his listeners of the dangers to the university's, the town's, and the state's reputations inherent in the situation before them, and also of the duty of Christians to oppose anarchy and lawlessness.

"But finally, and most important of all," he said, "I ask you as Christian people to consider the real moral issue that lies at the base of this whole crisis: Are we *morally* justified in refusing to admit to the University of Mississippi any student who meets all the necessary requirements except for the color of his skin? Remember, the question here is not 'What would I like?' or 'What do I want?' The question is simply 'What is *just* and *right*?' . . .

"I do not believe that any one of us here today could stand in the presence of Jesus of Nazareth, look Him squarely in the eye, and say, 'We will not admit a Negro to the University of Mississippi.' For it was our Lord who said, 'Inasmuch as you have done it unto the least of these my brethren, you have done it unto me.'

"Surely most of us realize by now that there can be only one resolution to this crisis: the admission of James Meredith to the University. Our leaders have tried to make us think it could be otherwise, and they have succeeded in convincing many people that this is possible. This is especially tragic, because it will make our adjustment to the new situation all the more difficult. But we, as Christians, should now accept this fact, if we have not already done so. Not only is this the only practical and reasonable solution, but it is also the only answer that is just and right. It is our business now to get to work at once to do all that we can to make the adjustment to this new situation as peaceful and as orderly as possible on our campus and in our community.

"Brethren," he concluded, "we need to *pray*; pray for our university and our community, our state and our nation. Perhaps, above all, we need to pray for *ourselves*. For these are times which not only *try* men's souls, but also *infect* and *poison* them. The seeds of anger and hatred, bitterness and prejudice, are already widely sown, and, as Christians, we need to do our utmost to uproot them and cast them out. You and I have a heavy responsibility in the days and weeks to come. Let us pray daily, even hourly, for God's guidance and direction that we may faithfully fulfill this responsibility to the end that God's will may be done."[29]

Even as Gray was speaking these words, negotiations between Barnett and President Kennedy and his brother Attorney General Robert Kennedy were continuing.

All but a handful of Mississippians, both Barnett's supporters and his opponents, would have been amazed to learn that on the same day that he had delivered his halftime oration before thousands, he had been on the phone with the Kennedys frequently, engaged in political bargaining designed both to get Meredith registered and to save the governor's face as much as possible. The latter became more and more difficult as Barnett's public defiance (which, as Gray had noted, raised both the governor's supporters' emotions and their expectations) continued, and also as Barnett continued to back out of commitments and promises he had made to Kennedy administration officials. But Barnett continued to try to persuade the Kennedys to agree to a show of federal force that would be sufficient to make his "surrender" look inevitable.

Both Kennedys, highly conscious of the potential political costs to them and the Democratic Party if they acted in ways that would inflame white Southerners' still lively memories of Civil War defeat and Reconstruction, had been remarkably patient with Barnett up to this point. Yet they were also fully aware of the seriousness of the building constitutional crisis they were facing, and now their patience was wearing thinner and thinner.

The president was scheduled to deliver an address to the nation on television Sunday night, and Robert Kennedy made use of this fact to pressure Barnett. When, once again, the governor waffled on Meredith's registration, Kennedy told him that if he did not cooperate and bargain in good faith, the president could not avoid telling the nation that he had been forced to send troops onto the Ole Miss campus because Barnett had broken the commitments he had made to the Kennedys the day before. This got the governor's attention as nothing before had, and he quickly came up with a new proposal: "Why don't you bring him in this afternoon?" Kennedy was cautious, in part because advisors had warned him about Mississippians' religious sensibilities being offended by a Sunday registration. Barnett, although a well-publicized Southern Baptist, dismissed that concern and continued to warm to his proposal. Its chief virtue, as he saw it, was that it would allow him to claim that he had been tricked by the Kennedys, who, he would say, had led him to believe that the registration would not take place until Monday or Tuesday. Kennedy, reasonably confident that he had backed Barnett into a corner from which he could not escape, finally agreed to the proposal.

Preparations began immediately for Meredith's fifth attempt at registration, and he was quickly removed from the professional football game he was watching on television at the air station in Memphis, Tennessee, and, with his escorts Doar and McShane, he boarded a small plane to fly the short distance to Oxford. At around 6:00 p.m. the three looked out the plane's windows to see the one-runway airport littered with army trucks, jeeps, buses, cars, and government planes, as well as piles of tents, riot equipment, and giant searchlights. The three men were met by Justice Department officials who had arrived earlier from Washington and who informed them that three hundred federal marshals armed with tear gas had already been posted around the Lyceum, the university's main administration building, where it was assumed that Meredith would register.[30]

Gray already knew about the marshals, as did most residents of Oxford, but, to his amusement, he had the opportunity to inform out-of-town newsmen, who had swarmed to the town, of the marshals' presence. Two reporters had asked him after the morning service for a meeting and a copy of his sermon. He agreed to meet them at the church after lunch. The two did not show up, but eight to ten other journalists were waiting for him when he returned, having heard a rumor that he would hold a news conference at 2:00 p.m. Gray denied the press conference rumor and insisted on waiting for the two reporters who had spoken to him earlier. As time passed, the journalists became increasingly restless and pressed Gray about where he thought the missing two were. "Well," he said, "I imagine they're out at the airport where the marshals are coming in." Remembering the occasion later, Gray chuckled with amusement. "Seems that none of these reporters had even listened to the radio to know what was going on, because by then the marshals were coming in at the airport. Well, at that they broke out in a hurry and left!"[31]

Gray tried to reach the airport himself, but found "the roads so clogged with traffic" that he gave it up. He returned to the church to meet with its youth group, Episcopal Young Churchmen. "They were pretty tense," he recalls. "They were all Oxford kids, of course. We could think about nothing else but what was going on, so we sat and listened to the radio for a while."[32]

At just about the time that Meredith, Doar, and McShane were arriving at the Oxford airport, Gray received a call from the mother of an Ole Miss student worried about her daughter's safety. Gray offered to go get the girl and take her to his house for the night.

Leaving the teenagers with their advisor, he left for the campus. When he arrived at the girl's dorm, she was not ready, so he strolled over to the nearby Lyceum building.

"By then the marshals were ringing the Lyceum . . . [and] truckloads of marshals were coming in about then. A pretty fair-sized crowd had gathered by then—mostly students, I think—most of them in the Circle . . .

across the road from the Lyceum. There were highway patrolmen . . . more or less keeping the crowd back. A crowd was also gathering on the north side of the Lyceum, but the crowd in front of the Lyceum—that is, on the east side—were the ones that were rather boisterous at this time and doing a lot of cheering and jeering and speaking to the marshals. I heard taunts and insults, I suppose you'd say, at the marshals. . . . I stayed a few minutes more there doing nothing much more than observing, and then I went back to the dormitory to pick up the coed that I'd come there to get. I picked her up, took her back home, left her at my house, and went back to the church to meet with Canterbury, our Episcopal student group, . . . college students.

"Naturally there were very few present that night. There was too much excitement on campus. I suppose there were about a dozen of us. We sat down, had a brief supper, argued a few points about what was going on, and then we left. . . .

"I had an appointment with a faculty member, Dr. [William H.] Willis, at his home which was just inside the east gate of the University, and I was to get out there as soon as I could after the Canterbury meeting, and we were to watch the president's speech on television together. We . . . found the television not working and then went to another faculty member's house to watch the president's speech there.

"I mention this only because I remember passing across the Eastgate bridge to the University at about ten minutes to eight in the Willis' car, and we were stopped there by the highway patrol, asked who we were and what we were doing, and when we were identified as faculty members and a local resident, they let us go on through. . . . I also noticed at that time that although cars were being stopped by the patrolmen, people on foot, mostly teenage boys and some older men, seemed to be moving freely across the bridge without being stopped.

"Dr. and Mrs. Willis and about three or four other faculty members watched the president's speech on television at the home of Dr. [James W.] Silver. . . . While we were there, the Rev. Wofford Smith [Episcopal chaplain to the university] came and joined us . . . and we watched the speech together. Just after the speech was over, we heard on the television . . . that violence had broken out on the campus. . . . We also heard a report that a faculty member had been beaten by some students, and at this point we were thinking maybe that it was the man whose house we were in, and so Mr. Smith and two faculty members . . . and I started up toward the Lyceum on the main part of the campus walking rather rapidly, maybe even running at times."

The group encountered Silver's wife driving toward the center of the campus and learned from her that her husband was fine. Silver was anxious to remove a second car from the campus because he was afraid that it would be damaged by the mob, but he lacked the car key, which Mrs. Silver had. She turned the key over to the group of men to give to her husband.

Gray continued, "We . . . found Dr. Silver, gave him the key, and Wofford Smith and I proceeded toward the Circle [which is in front of the Lyceum]. . . . [W]hen we got to the edge of the Y[MCA] building [which faces the Circle on its north side] . . . the tear gas that had been fired by this time was pretty heavy, [and it] began to get in our eyes, and we ducked into the Y building rather quickly to get out of the tear gas, but when we got inside there we found that it was not entirely clear inside, so we stayed just a very few minutes and then came back out, and, as we came out, of course, and looked out on the Circle, we could see clouds of tear gas up towards the Lyceum, hundreds of students for the most part, although there were others who seemed not to be students, running back and forth in the Circle carrying bricks and bottles and sticks and stones, one with a shovel, any weapon that seemed close at hand, many of them running toward the Lyceum, others away from it, and others just in one direction or another—general chaos and confusion.

"A car passed slowly in front of the Y at that time, moving very slowly because it was so difficult to get through the crowd of people that were milling around. We saw though that it had a law enforcement officer's insignia on it . . . and we went to the man and stopped him. Mr. Smith said, 'Well, how about getting out and let's see if we can do something to get these students back to the dormitory?' And he said there was nothing he could do and drove on the direction toward the Confederate monument and away from the Lyceum.

"So then Mr. Smith and I went out into the Circle and began to stop students individually or in small groups, those that were carrying weapons of some sort, and would ask them to drop their weapons or to give them to us, and many of them did. . . . Many of them seemed to be in a daze almost, and when we would stop them, grabbing an arm or simply standing in front of them and asking for their bricks or the bottles or whatever they had, and asking them to go back to their dormitories, many of them would give up their weapons and go off. Whether they went back to their dormitories is something else again, but I couldn't help feeling that so many of them were hysterical and carried away with emotion at this point that seeing us— particularly [since] both of us were wearing clerical collars—that it maybe tended to bring them a little back to their senses—temporarily at least.

"There were, of course, those who resisted. One, I remember, threatened me with a shovel and . . . chased me, . . . but most of them were not resisting in that manner. By this time, though, there were a number of outsiders, as I'll call them. I say they certainly were not Ole Miss students. They apparently were mostly young boys, though, teenagers, that is, or maybe in their early twenties, who were much tougher looking, and most of these would simply brush you aside and go on.

"I . . . remember . . . going back into the Y one time to sort of get a breather and finding some students in there with bricks in their hands, both of whom I stopped, took the bricks away from them, dropped them in the wastebasket in the Y, and they left with rather sheepish grins on their faces. I remember seeing some other boys run into the Y and empty the rack of empty Coke bottles, taking these out for weapons to throw at the marshals.

"Then back into the Circle again and moving over a little bit south of the Confederate statue—south and west of the statue—I remember seeing the highway patrol cars—about fifteen or twenty of them, I should say, at this point—moving off the campus . . . and across the east bridge. I stood there and watched this briefly and observed that many of the students in the crowd were standing along the side the street cheering . . . as the cars were leaving."

Around nine o'clock, after he had been on the campus about an hour and a half, Gray saw General Edwin Walker standing in the Circle between the flagpole and the Confederate monument and surrounded by about a dozen older men. "Walker," Gray recalls, "more or less stood out in his Texas hat and as tall as he was with this small group of ten or twelve men out in the Circle.

"I had heard just prior to this some small student groups saying, 'Now we have a leader, now we have a leader!' And as soon as I saw him I associated that remark with his presence, assuming that he must have been the one they were talking about.

"At any rate, I went up to him and asked him if he were General Walker. He said he was, and I asked him if he would say a word to the students to try and help us send them back to the dormitories.

"I must say that I certainly had no illusions about being able to stop the riot as such, but being able to get as many as we could of the students particularly to go back to the dormitories; I thought this would be of help.

"And I told him that I thought his word would carry considerable weight, since the students identified him with their cause and would listen respectfully to anything he had to say and would probably follow his leadership.

. . . But when I asked him to do what he could to help stop the rioting, he said that he was there just as an observer, he was not there to stop them. He said he didn't think he could do anything even if he wanted to, but he wasn't particularly interested in doing anything. He said something about 'they had every right to protest,' and as I persisted and kept asking him to do this, to try and speak to the students in some way to dissuade them from what they were doing, he finally turned on me and said, 'Who are you, anyway?'

"And I told him—I gave him my name and said that I was an Episcopal minister, a local Episcopal minister, this was my home and my community, and I was deeply concerned about what was happening to it, I was out there to do anything I could to stop the rioting or to get some of the rioters—the students—to go back.

"And he said at this point, 'You are the kind of Episcopal minister that makes me ashamed to be an Episcopalian.' And he turned around and walked off."[33]

Gray would meet Walker again later in the evening as he stood on the Confederate monument and addressed the crowd, and Walker would repeat his remark about Gray being "kind of Episcopal minister that make me ashamed to be an Episcopalian," thereby encouraging the crowd to turn on Gray, as I have described.

After that encounter, when Gray was rescued by a Mississippi deputy sheriff and a few students, he stood silently for a moment on the steps of the YMCA building and watched "what I suppose you would call a charge on the marshals. This was the largest single movement . . . or charge there had been up to this point just in terms of pure numbers, because the whole crowd . . . that been there listening [to Walker] then started to move toward the Lyceum."

At the sight of this, Gray moved into the middle of the crowd, "again trying to restrain whatever individuals or small groups I could. This time I got very little response in terms of giving up weapons. I did have a few that would stop and argue with me, but then they would move on past.

"I remember particularly being struck at this point by many of the students with tears in their eyes, and, of course, I know there was tear gas, but the tears came from emotion and rage as much as anything else. In fact, at that point they were comparing themselves to the Hungarian freedom fighters [a reference to the 1956 Hungarian anti-communist, popular uprising that was crushed with the aid of Russian troops and tanks]. They were really prepared to charge with rocks and stones and whatever they might have. They felt, certainly, that what they were doing was a fight for freedom.

"I gave ground with the crowd, trying to stop and talk to and slow down any that I could, but, as I say, with very little success, and had given ground mostly with my back to the Lyceum, and moving backward with the crowd, until finally the tear gas became very heavy as we got to the proximity of the Lyceum. It got too bad for me, and I turned around finally and came on back—this time, once more to the Y. As I stood on the steps there I saw that pretty much the whole charge was broken by this time, and most of the crowd were retreating again and moving back in the direction of the Y and the Confederate monument."[34]

Although the charge inspired by Walker had been broken, neither the night's violence nor Gray's attempts to stop it were finished.

Soon afterward he saw a small car with four U.S. marshals in it providing an escort for the truck carrying tear gas supplies to the marshals in front of the Lyceum. The crowd also saw them and let loose a barrage of bricks, bottles, and pieces of concrete from a nearby construction project. Again Gray moved among the crowd, attempting to persuade its members to drop their weapons, but this time with no success at all. The truck sustained little damage, but the windows of the marshals' car were smashed out. Despite Gray's fears for the safety and success of its occupants, the vehicles did finally manage to reach the Lyceum, and the marshals were resupplied with their only weapon against the crowd.

As the night wore on, and Gray continued his efforts to discourage the violence, he remembered, "A man . . . attracted my attention because he looked so out of place: white shirt, tie, with heavy beard, a rather large man. And I was headed back into the Circle at the time, and he was going back around the Y building. . . . [F]rom pictures I realize that this was [French photographer] Paul Guiot, who was killed that night. . . . It couldn't have been more than five or ten minutes before he was shot. The place where he was shot was back away from the real scene of action . . . and he was headed in that direction when I saw him. It was not long after that I heard an ambulance or a siren. . . . I went back in that direction, thinking someone had been hurt. But the time I got to the ambulance, they had pulled out and left."[35]

Gray finally called his wife shortly after this, around 10:00 p.m., from the Y building. After helping a female employee of the university get her car off the campus and headed toward home, he returned briefly to the Circle, but realized then that he had done all he could and that the crowd was beyond his reach, so he headed toward the Silver's house, from which he had started out more than three hours earlier.

He returned by car with the Willises to their house, where he had left his own car, and reached his home shortly before midnight.[36]

The violence continued for several more hours.

Finally at 2:00 a.m. the first regular army troops arrived on campus. A platoon of the riot-trained 503rd Military Police Battalion marched in "V" riot formation, bayoneted rifles fixed. More arrived behind them. The soldiers were the ones who managed to begin to disperse the rioters, and they did so without a single fatality. General Charles Billingslea, who commanded the troops, finally declared the campus secure at 6:15 a.m.

James Meredith registered at 8:00 a.m. that morning, but the violence and its aftermath were far from over, as Gray discovered when he arrived at his office at St. Peter's Episcopal Church in Oxford the same morning.

To that day we shall return, but first we must examine how it is that Gray, in so many ways a child of privilege, became the man who spent the evening of September 30, 1962, among the rioters on the Ole Miss campus.

CHAPTER 3

"THE FAMILY IS A PRIMARY SOURCE OF GRACE"

Lineage

"MISSISSIPPI'S NOT A STATE; IT'S A CLUB." This saying, once common among white Mississippians of an older generation, aptly describes, for better and for worse, the most "Southern" of states; and, to a remarkable degree, these words remain true even today. Mississippians, when they meet, especially outside the state, tend to greet each other with a certain *bon homie* that seems to signify an immediate sense of rapport seldom matched by natives or residents of most other states in the Union.

The bond that these expressions represent would seem to be rooted in the experience of growing up in a place that until recently was almost completely rural, and therefore sparsely and diffusely populated; a place largely poor for both black and white; a place where black and white, rich and poor often contended against the superior and sometimes overwhelming forces of nature. All these elements—relatively small population, relative-to-absolute poverty, and the joint battles against nature—combined to create neighbor-like bonds, even sometimes between dominant whites and oppressed blacks.

In addition, Mississippi was, of course, a place that in the mid-twentieth century was the locus of great moral battles and the intense emotions that accompany them. Those moral battles also made Mississippi the focus of frequently negative national and international attention, a fact that in itself tended to create an odd kind of sympathy between opposing sides, especially once the battles were past.

Today this "clubbiness" of Mississippi often transcends race and sometimes even class, especially for expatriates, but in the first half of the twentieth century the "club" was very much a white, usually upper-class, male one.

Duncan Gray Jr., therefore, had automatic membership.

What makes a man like him? A person who as a child lived a life of relative privilege, sheltered from all but the most genteel and softly institutionalized forms of the South's racism, and who yet as a man was willing to risk his membership in the "club" as well as his vocation, and even his life, to speak and act against the racism from which he, as white man, in many ways benefited.

One might facilely attribute Gray's actions to his "Christian upbringing," and, as with most clichés, there is truth to this one. But the story itself is, not surprisingly, much richer and more complex than the cliché. After all, we all know hell-raising and/or self-centered and self-indulgent "preacher's kids" as well as "Mercedes Christians." Few self-described Christians are willing to live out the radicalism of Jesus' teachings.

In addition to the significant role that Christianity has played in the lives of Gray and his ancestors, privilege also has long roots in Gray's family. The stories that the family genealogists tell read like a compendium of European and American history told according to the old model: history from the perspective of leadership and privilege.

Gray's mother, Isabel, was a member of the McCrady family, prominent in Charleston, South Carolina. The McCradys were linked by marriage in the nineteenth century with the originally Norman deBernieres family, a line that "includes princes, dukes, counts, one viscount, innumerable landed gentry, bishops, priests, professors, lawyers, physicians, generals, colonels, one Nobel Prize winner in physics, one world-famed theologian, one industrialist described as the greatest benefactor of Ireland" but also "barbers, hairdressers [and] wine merchants." Two members of the deBernieres family are said to have saved the life of French King Louis XI, and, as a result, the family was granted the right to add the golden fleur-de-lis to its coat of arms.[1]

Like other Norman families, the deBernieres split themselves along Roman Catholic and Protestant Huguenot lines in the sixteenth and seventeenth century. Just before Louis XIV repealed the Edict of Nantes in 1685 and resumed persecution of the Huguenots, Jean Antoine deBernieres, like other Huguenots, fled France for Holland. When William of Orange traveled to England in 1688 to pursue his "Glorious Revolution" and to become King William III of England, Jean Antoine deBernieres traveled with him and later fought in Spain on William's behalf, losing a hand in the process. He eventually settled in Ireland, marrying the daughter of another Huguenot who had become a great Irish linen manufacturer.[2]

The following generations of deBernieres continued the tradition of military service in their new British homeland. Jean Antoine's grandson and namesake John Anthony and his father fought with British troops at Ft. Duquesne and at Quebec during the French and Indian Wars. In the late 1770s John Anthony deBerniere (the final "s" had been dropped from the name after the family left France) married Anne Jones, a descendant of Bishop Jeremy Taylor, chaplain to England's Charles I. In 1799, deBerniere resigned his commission as a lieutenant colonel and left with his wife and children for the new United States.[3]

Rather than returning to the northern reaches of the country, John Anthony settled his family in North Carolina, where he acquired plantations in the area of Fayetteville and Deep River and also Columbia, South Carolina. Eventually he moved to Charleston, where his married daughters, Mrs. Robert Lane and Mrs. John Johnson, lived. In 1829, John Anthony's granddaughter, Louisa Rebecca Lane, daughter of Louisa deBerniere and Robert Lane, married Edward McCrady in Charleston.[4]

On Gray's father's side the ancestry was less exalted, but its roots no less deep. In a two-page memorandum, William Franklin Gray (d. 1929), a well-known Louisiana and Mississippi newspaper editor, passed on to his son Duncan M. Gray (father of Duncan Jr.) his knowledge of the family's lineage in a style typical of late nineteenth- and early twentieth-century Southern pride in family and history. William Gray wrote, "Your antecedents on both sides of the house give you a pretty fair background of which you have no reason to be ashamed. They were of the South—'native and to the manner [*sic*] born'—steeped in its traditions. They adhered to its standards and were loyal to its ideals. Their men were honest and brave, their women were gentle and tender and true."[5]

According to William Franklin Gray's memorandum, the family could trace its roots as far back as another William F. Gray, a captain in the American revolutionary army "who commanded the escort of Lafayette at the surrender of Cornwallis at Youngstown." Captain Gray had been a resident of Virginia, but soon after the war he moved to South Carolina. His son, following a pioneer-era pattern, left South Carolina for Huntsville, Alabama, where he is said to have donated the land on which the town's First Presbyterian Church stood. In fact, the family was known in Huntsville as the "Presbyterian Grays" to distinguish them from another family of the same last name.[6]

In his memorandum, William Gray says of the family, "They were landholders and slave owners, but not rich. They believed strongly in education, and gave their children every opportunity that the times afforded. I know that my father was very bookish, had studied medicine as a young man, but never engaged in its practice, and was better educated than most of his contemporaries, as numerous letters of his which I have read attest."[7]

Perhaps typically for the attitudes of the time, William Gray does not speak of his mother's family, but later twentieth-century descendents of Sara Fuqua Gray think the Fuqua family may be "a descendent or relative of Nicholas Fouquet (1615–1680)," who was minister of finance to the same Louis XIV whose repeal of the Edict of Nantes had sent the Huguenot de-Bernieres family into exile.[8]

In any case, the Fuquas traced their American ancestry back to Guilliam (or Guillaume) Fouquet, who came to Virginia in the late 1600s. Three generations later, Fouquet's great grandson Joseph Fuqua came with his wife, Mary, from South Carolina to settle in Wilkinson County, in the southwestern corner of Mississippi, shortly after the Louisiana Purchase in 1803.[9]

Joseph and Mary later moved further west to Terrebone Parish, Louisiana. When their son Nathaniel married in 1824, Joseph gave him "the Lerette Place about 3 miles above Houma [LA] and 18 negroes," a frequent parental wedding gift among land and slave owners. Nathaniel's father-in-law gave the couple "4 or 5 negroes. It looks like they were pretty well off."[10]

At the onset of the Civil War, Joseph "raised a company of volunteers and served throughout as their captain," says the family genealogist, but adds that official war records show him "as a lieutenant in Cole's Cavalry from July to November 1861."

Like other well-to-do white Southerners, the Fuquas clearly suffered financially after the war. In 1871, Nathaniel and his son Joseph signed an agreement pledging that year's cotton crop in return for seed and expenses. Joseph and his wife left the plantation later that same year, "so I guess the crop wasn't much," Joseph Elsbury says. Nathaniel died in 1875, and "his debts exceeded his assets." Sarah Fuqua, Joseph's sister, widow of David Ichabod Gray and mother of William, declared she had no interest in trying to recover any of the assets. She herself died only five years later.[11]

Her son William, if not a planter like his forbearers, went on to achieve success as a political writer and editor of a number of newspapers in Louisiana and Mississippi. Gray began his career in New Orleans working for a paper known as the *New Delta*. In a day when newspapers made little pretence of objective reporting and instead relied on their numbers to present multiple perspectives on an issue or event, the *New Delta* had been founded by a chief justice of the Louisiana Supreme Court with the intent of fighting a state lottery.[12]

Gray's journalistic career continued in a similar vein. He moved to Mississippi, where he wrote for and edited papers in Jackson, Meridian, and Cleveland, Mississippi. He became known as "one of the leading political writers" in the state, where he "espous[ed] the cause of James K. Vardaman, former [governor and] United States Senator from Mississippi, and Gov. Theo. G. Bilbo."[13]

William Gray's support of Vardaman and Bilbo is ironic in the light of grandson Duncan's later involvement in civil rights. In the early part of the twentieth century when Jim Crow laws were firmly in place and unchallenged, the issue of class and the power of special interests were nearly as important in Mississippi politics as race. Race was, of course, seldom absent as a political issue, but when it arose, it was often inextricably bound up with the issue of class. Vardaman's and Bilbo's careers were embodiments of this complex intermingling of populism and racism in early twentieth-century Mississippi politics—an intermingling in which the populism would eventually be dissolved by the acid of racism. Although each of them at times took populist positions against entrenched interests in Mississippi, each of them was, as a Vardaman biographer says of him, "a hard-shell racist."[14]

Although editor Gray outlived Vardaman, Bilbo served as one of the honorary pallbearers at the editor's funeral, as did a number of other ranking state officials. By now, the formerly "Presbyterian Grays" had become Episcopalians, and Gray's funeral service was conducted by the Right Reverend William Mercer Green, bishop of Mississippi.

Gray was survived by several children, including his son Duncan Montgomery Gray, an Episcopal clergyman who at the time of his father's death was serving as rector of Grace Church in Canton, Mississippi, near the state capital of Jackson. Some fourteen years later this same Duncan would succeed Green as bishop of Mississippi.

Well before he became bishop, however, the fortunes of the McCrady and the Gray families intersected, and Duncan met and married Isabel Denham McCrady, herself the daughter of a prominent Episcopal clergyman, in 1925. The two produced three children: Duncan Montgomery Gray Jr., Mary Ormond Gray, and Isabel McCrady Gray.

Duncan Sr. had been born in Meridian, Mississippi, in 1898 while his father edited the *Meridian Star* and the *Meridian Dispatch*. Meridian was a railroad town, and according to the Mississippi diocese's official history, Gray "enjoyed the disadvantages and advantages" of that, "including the pleasure of drinking coffee brewed on the stove of a caboose, which he later maintained was the best coffee anywhere."[15]

As he grew up, he filled a succession of jobs at the newspapers, first as a paper carrier and later in more responsible positions. He graduated from Meridian High School, where he played tackle on the school's football team. Ironically, his coach was Ben F. Cameron, the same man later appointed by President Dwight Eisenhower as a judge on the Fifth Circuit Court of Appeals in New Orleans. Fifty years later, Cameron, as we have seen, played a significant if obstructionist role in the battle to integrate the University of Mississippi.

In an interview Gray gave to a Mississippi newspaper columnist years after his consecration as bishop, he said he thought that athletic programs were "beneficial to participants and spectators alike," but rejected the idea that athletics "builds character."

"The place to build character," he told the writer, "is in the home. And the mistakes and shortcomings of parents are not likely to be corrected by a boy or girl joining this, that, or another organization or program or group activity which claims to 'build character.' The characters of boys and girls are molded before they get into sports and other group activities."

Still, Gray remained a sports fan all his life, although when the same columnist asked him whether he continued his football career in college, he replied, "I went out for football one day at Rice Institute [now Rice University] . . . but I was too light for the line in college. They stuck me on the third team and put me to work running back punts in practice." With typical dry humor, Gray concluded, "After about 10 or 15 minutes of that I knew my football career was ended. I did not report for practice the next day."[16]

Gray spent one year at Rice and then transferred to the University of the South in Sewanee, Tennessee, where he graduated in 1925 with a degree that prepared him to go into the ministry. His first churches were the ones in Cleveland and Rosedale, Mississippi, in the center of the Mississippi Delta, where he remained for three years.

It was also in 1925 that Gray married Isabel McCrady on June 17.

Less than six weeks before the wedding, in the same year that John T. Scopes was tried and convicted for teaching evolutionary theory in a Tennessee high school, Gray received a three-and-half-page, single-spaced letter from his father-in-law-to-be, the Reverend Dr. Edward McCrady, a well-regarded scholar on contemporary issues relating to science and religion, and also a parish priest.

The letter was written in response to a letter from Gray in which he apparently inquired about the acceptability for ministry of a person (un-named, but possibly recent seminarian Gray himself) who questioned the factual and historical nature of Gospel infancy narratives and the literal,

historical truth of the Christian doctrine of the Virgin Birth. In his opening paragraph McCrady assured his future son-in-law that "a warm welcome awaits you in our midst," but the rest of his missive, which McCrady
describes as "necessarily . . . brief and so, to some extent, disappointing,"
is a dense and closely argued philosophical and theological disquisition
in which the author declares that the Episcopal Church could not recommend such a person for ordination to the priesthood, and then goes on at
length to explain why this was the case. McCrady concluded with an as-
surance of his confidence—not unusual among more "liberal" students of
science and religion at the time—that eventually, as theologians gained a
better understanding of science, they will come to realize that the "truths"
of science and the "truths" of religion are not in contradiction, but instead
can be harmonized with one another. For example, the Virgin Birth can
be explained as a form of parthogenesis and thus need not be rejected by
educated people as truth.

McCrady concludes: "To quote a remark recently made in regard to the
view of a certain well-known authority in Science, not only do I not believe
that there is any incompatibility between Science and Christianity, but 'the
scientific account of nature may *actually suggest and enhance the religious
view.*'" He adds, "I only differ from the writer in saying that it *does* so suggest and enhance the religious view."[17]

Whatever theological agreements or differences may or may not have
existed between Gray and McCrady after this exchange of letters, Gray
could not have remained in any doubt that his soon-to-be-father-in-law
was a man who was accustomed to having himself and his complex philosophical and theological conclusions honored and accepted with little if any
question. What the less scholarly, more down-to-earth Gray thought about
this we can only imagine.

In any case, the marriage between Gray and McCrady's daughter took
place. A little more than a year later, on September 21, 1926, the Grays had
their first child, a boy, named Duncan Montgomery after his father. When
his son was not quite three years old, Gray became rector of St. Paul's Episcopal Church in Columbus, Mississippi, where he remained for ten years.
It was in Columbus, then, that Duncan Jr. would spend his childhood.

Columbus is located in east central Mississippi not far from its border
with Alabama, an area known as Mississippi's "Black Belt" because of the
color and fertility of its soil. Although Columbus lies on the other side of
the state from the Mississippi Delta on its western edge, it shares with the
Delta both fertile soil and the large landholdings that sprang up in such
areas of the South, with their accompanying concentrations of slavery and

the enormous, stubborn inequalities of wealth and privilege that persisted long after Emancipation, into the Jim Crow era and, indeed, throughout the twentieth century.

Until the very last decades of that century, "wealth" in much of Mississippi was something very different from what we think of as wealth today, not only in scale but also in flavor. Today wealth is almost always something urban, usually technological and bureaucratized. In twentieth-century Mississippi, although the gap between rich and poor was certainly comparable to what it is in the United States today, both rich and poor found themselves significantly further down the scale. "Rich" was poorer, and "poor" was poorer still. In the early decades of the century, technology was beginning to make some inroads, but it was still almost nonexistent by today's standards. Bureaucracy, with its policies, rules, and regulations, was despised, and personal relationships (including between blacks and whites, however unequal the relationship) and personal honor (to some degree for all whites, but especially among upper-class ones) took its place.

So twentieth-century Mississippi remained poor relative to much of the rest of the nation; it also remained very largely rural, its countryside punctuated by towns such as Columbus where the small-town culture was an outgrowth of the agriculture that surrounded it. In churches on Sunday mornings, prayers offered for rain or for fair weather were heartfelt since economies, and sometimes lives, depended on them.

Unlike many other such Mississippi towns, Columbus had not only the economic advantage of its fertile soil, but also the cultural advantage of a small women's college, founded in 1884 primarily for the purpose of educating women to be teachers. And like Natchez, just south of the Delta, Columbus had escaped the ravages of Union armies and so had preserved its antebellum homes, which by the mid-twentieth century became, again like Natchez, the focus of a "pilgrimage" in which residents dressed in antebellum costumes and conducted tours of the old homes for the growing middle class of the state.

But in the 1930s, Columbus, like the rest of the nation, was in the grips of the Great Depression, and even the town's more comfortable citizens felt its pinch, again in a different way from those in more urban parts of the nation. In the middle of this fertile soil, sufficient food need not be a problem if one had a little land available to plant, and the surrounding countryside was full of game for hunting. As long as the rest of the nation needed the area's agricultural products, work was available, even while money was scarcer as demand and prices dropped. For many rural and small-town white Southerners, however, the Depression seemed hardly more than a continuation of the "hard times" that had marked the South since the Civil War and its end two generations earlier.

Duncan Jr. himself remembers the Depression and his childhood years as a lean but not a desperate time. "I never had any new clothes—I got hand-me-downs from my cousin—but I liked them, and so I thought it was just fine.

"I don't remember ever being in want during the Depression. I always had enough to eat. It wasn't fancy food—cereal for breakfast and we had our share of peanut butter and jelly sandwiches. It hadn't been that long since George Washington Carver had invented peanut butter, and it was cheap, probably cheaper than it is now.

"But I do remember my mother making a platter of peanut butter and jelly sandwiches every night. The rectory where we lived was right next to the church, and during the Depression there would be people nearly every night, black and white, who would come by looking for something to eat, and she'd hand out those sandwiches.

"The people who came didn't look like bums or anything. They looked like the people you'd see every day. The whites were usually just men, but the blacks would often be a whole family. I was pretty young, so I didn't think of this as anything unusual, and I certainly don't have any memories of going hungry."[18]

He remembered his growing-up years in Columbus primarily as a round of family, friends, school, sports, and church—the activities of a typical middle- to upper-middle-class child. From the time he entered nursery school to the time he finished sixth grade, he attended the Demonstration School on the campus of what was then Mississippi State College for Women. Like most such schools of the time, it offered a place for student teachers to practice their teaching—Gray remembers "many student teachers, eight or ten a year, one for each subject each semester, with a supervising teacher watching over the whole process." He says that he remembers *"enjoying* learning and reading, especially history." Many years later, after he himself became bishop and traveled the state, he still ran into elderly women who told him they had done their practice teaching with his class at the Demonstration School.

Along with church attendance and related church activities, sports played a significant role in Duncan's life from the time he was a child. He sang in the children's choir at St. Paul's, but even that memory is linked to athletics. "We sang for weekday services during Lent—Monday through Friday—with a baseball game following the service every day on a vacant lot next to the rectory." Pee Wee football was also a part of his fifth- and sixth-grade years.

In young Duncan's neighborhood was a group of more than half a dozen boys who were all within a year or two of each other's age. Most of them were also members of St. Paul's, although some of these same children came from families of Greek or Lebanese immigrants. The Episcopal Church was about as close to their native Orthodox Christianity as one was likely to find in small-town Mississippi in the 1930s.

In any case, there were always enough children around for a pick-up game of football or baseball, and the vacant lot next door to the rectory provided a handy field.

Young Duncan's father was often willing to join—or even help create— some of the fun on Saturdays. Many of the other boys' fathers were retailers, and for them Saturday was the busiest day of the week—the day when people from the country came into town to do their shopping and socializing. For the rector, however, Saturday was often the slow day before Sunday, so he would sometimes take the group to the high school's football field or to the local semi-pro baseball team's field to play, where the elder Gray served as coach and referee. Or sometimes he would join the group of boys in a nearby woods off the town's golf course for a game of "cowboys and Indians," which might feature the minister waving his lasso and bringing it down around a nearby tree stump.

Other boys' fathers had advantages to offer too. One owned two of the town's three movie theaters, and his son's friends could gain admittance for only a penny a show, compared to the eleven cents regular admission. (Jim Crow laws were strictly honored in Mississippi movie theaters well into the 1960s. Black patrons' money was welcome, but they were always seated in the theater balcony while whites had the ground floor.) Features changed three times a week and usually included a Western on Saturday. In the winter of 1936, for example, local theaters showed films sure to delight young boys' hearts, such as *The Last of the Mohicans* with Randolph Scott and *Border Flight* ("Flying G-Men!" the advertisement proclaimed) with Frances Farmer, John Howard, Roscoe Karns, and Robert Cummings. Movies were another important part of life, then, so much so that for several years in a row "giving up movies" was young Duncan's Lenten discipline.

Major league baseball was also a passion, and the St. Louis Cardinals were the favored team, in part because they were the closest pro team to Columbus. Duncan remembers sitting glued to a new radio during the 1934 World Series as Dizzy Dean pitched the Cardinals to a winning 11–0 shutout over the Detroit Tigers. The elder Gray was also a Cardinals fan and managed to take his son to St. Louis to see the Cardinals play on their own field, thus beginning a father-son tradition that has persisted into the current generation. In 2001, in fact, Duncan Jr.'s sons treated their father, as well as their sons—three generations of Gray fans—to a St. Louis baseball trip.[19]

By the 1930s, automobiles were becoming more common, but still relatively few Mississippi families owned one. The first family car that Duncan remembers was a 1929 Model A Ford that made it easier for his father to carry out his pastoral duties in and around Columbus. And in 1934, not only did the Cardinals win the Series, but that year also brought the family a new car, one much advanced over the Model A.

But then, as now, fathers and mothers couldn't supervise children *all* the time, and for children that fact offers the opportunity for creative mischief. Such was the case when a ten-year-old Duncan made a start on what he refers to as his "police record." That day Duncan and two friends—one, another "preacher's kid," the son of the Methodist minister—decided that climbing the inside of the Methodist Church's steeple would be a good way to pass the time. When they got as far as a set of louvers set in the steeple, they removed one so they could look down and see how far they were above the street below. Peering out, however, they found themselves looking directly into the window of the police station across the street from the church. And when they climbed down, they found two police officers waiting for them. There was no way to escape—at least not to escape the police call to parents to advise them of the boys' escapade.

Although Duncan was only eleven when he was confirmed in the Episcopal Church, he remembers the event as a very meaningful one for him. That year was the parish's hundredth anniversary, and his father wanted a large confirmation class as part of the celebration, so he allowed a few of the parish's more mature children—including his son—to join the group of twelve- and thirteen-year-old confirmands.

Confirmation preparation in the Episcopal Church was in some ways a less structured process than it is in many parishes today, and Duncan remembers the class meeting several times with his father as part of their preparation. But that didn't mean the process was a casual one. In a time before education—including Christian education—was expected to be "fun," St. Paul's Sunday school superintendent spent each Sunday morning with the prospective confirmands, drilling them in the catechism of the Episcopal Church according to the 1928 *Book of Common Prayer.* The catechism consisted of twenty-five set questions and answers that included recitations of the Lord's Prayer, the Apostles' Creed, and the Ten Commandments and a brief description of the Trinity. After the teacher posed the question, he joined the class members in chanting back the prescribed answers.

The process was not all hard work. By late elementary school, Sunday school classes had been divided by gender, and the boys' teacher was a restaurant owner. On occasion, in the middle of a Sunday morning class, he would say to his pupils, "Boys, how would you like a hamburger?" and as one, off the group would go to the restaurant for a Sunday morning treat.

When Duncan entered seventh grade, he moved from the Demonstration School to Lee High School in what turned out to be the Grays' last year in Columbus. There he got to know "a whole new set of friends" who had gone to other elementary schools in town, and he developed some typical adolescent interests—popular music, dancing, and girls.

The summer of the year he was confirmed, Duncan began regular attendance at the diocese's summer camp for children, where his first summer he learned to swim. The camp was held on the campus of what was then All Saints' Junior College in the Mississippi River town of Vicksburg, not far from the "end" of David Cohen's Mississippi Delta ("The Delta begins in the lobby of the Peabody Hotel in Memphis and ends on Catfish Row in Vicksburg.") and in the middle of the Civil War battlefield where Confederate and Union soldiers had fought for control of the town and its access to the river some seventy years earlier.

After 1937, he was a camper every summer until his graduation from high school. The "interest in girls," in general, preceded his meeting a particular girl, Ruth Spivey of Canton, at camp in 1941, but it had certainly prepared the way for what became a particular interest in "Ruthie." The two "stayed in touch" during the intervening school years, but it was not until the Gray family moved closer to Canton that the relationship became a more serious one.

In 1939, Gray moved his family back to the Delta and to Church of the Nativity in Greenwood, where he served as rector until his election and consecration as bishop of Mississippi in 1943.

The date of the move—September 1, 1939—stuck in the almost-thirteen-year-old Duncan's mind because it was on that date that Germany attacked Poland and World War II in effect began. A much younger Duncan had adjusted easily to his family's earlier move to Columbus, but the move to Greenwood was more difficult. He described the first few months there as "one of the few sad and lonely periods" of his life. He remembers those early weeks in a new town and new school as being characterized by a "near obsession" with little more than the current "hit parade," and time out of school spent doing little more than listening to the radio and keeping track of which songs were "up" and which "down" according to the latest measure. Before long, however, his naturally outgoing personality and his interest in athletics had rescued him from the "lonely time," and he found himself with a new set of friends. He also made the varsity football and basketball teams, despite his small size.[20]

By the fall of 1942, he was written up in the local paper as the team's halfback who, although "small in stature," made "his presence felt on the team." The team's coach was quoted as saying, "Duncan is one of the hardest working boys on the squad, and what is even more important, he's never lacking in cooperation."[21]

Thus Duncan spent his eighth- through eleventh-grade years with other white teenagers at Greenwood High School, where, in addition to his athletic activities, he was also a clarinetist in the school band.

Although the war and its end would bring a brief flowering of opportunities for African Americans, in the American South of the 1930s, racism and the violence that often accompanied it were rampant. Most middle- and upper-middle-class white Mississippians seldom had any direct contact with such racism, and their children even less. The racism of middle- and upper-middle-class Mississippians, like that of their many of their compatriots elsewhere in the country, was not even recognized as such. Among this group of Mississippians, it took a "good-mannered," paternalistic form and would all but never sink to the level of violence. The children of these Southerners were taught that the word "nigger" was "low class"; instead, these children were told to use such words as "colored" or "nigra" when speaking of African Americans. From the perspective of seventy years later, Gray says he has no significant memories of being sensitive to the racial injustices that surrounded him as he grew up. "I led a sheltered life," he says. "I certainly knew that segregation was the norm, but. . . it was the *norm*!

"I can remember back in Columbus where there was a black Episcopal priest named Richard Middleton, and he was a rather frequent visitor in our house. Now my dad's study was in the house, so it was all business, I suppose you might say, but it was not unusual to see him come to the house and go upstairs to the study.

"And I can remember sitting on our front porch with our black maid, I guess she was, or cook. You know, everybody had servants in those days. Anyway, we would just sit there rocking on the porch—our house was right downtown—and commenting on what was going on in the street in front of us. On Saturdays, for example, everyone would pull in and park along the street in front of our house—I'm talking about wagons and mules in those days, not automobiles—and we'd just sit there and watch and laugh. I've got some very happy memories of just sitting there, commenting on people and all.

"I mean we all had our black friends that we sort of 'grew away from' as we reached our teenage years, but, yes, I just took it for granted. I don't think it bothered me morally or that I had pangs on conscience at that time, but I did lead a pretty sheltered life."[22]

In the middle of Duncan's junior year at Greenwood High, his father was elected bishop of Mississippi following the death of Bishop Green, the man who had presided at young Duncan's grandfather's funeral. The new bishop was not consecrated, however, until May 12, 1943, and the family waited to move until school was out for the summer.[23]

The Reverend Cecil Jones Jr., whose father served Episcopal parishes in Mississippi throughout his life, and who therefore saw the bishop in his home at least once a year as he was growing up, remembers Gray senior as an outgoing man who also "didn't put up with much folderol."[24]

As an example, Jones tells with pleasure a story about his confirmation. "After the service was over, the bishop said to me, 'Well, Cecil, do you feel any different now than you did before?' I didn't, but this was the bishop, and I didn't know *what* I was supposed to say! Finally though I just told the truth and said, 'no.' Bishop Gray just looked at me and said, 'That's good.'

"I didn't realize it at the time, but he was teaching me something about spirituality, see. In my experience, spiritual growth is not something spooky; it's plodding and everyday. And when I start feeling 'spiritual,' I need to go start cutting grass or something."[25]

Jones made a final decision to go to seminary when he was in college, and he remembers the occasion of his examination as a candidate for seminary as the occasion for another instance of Gray's sometimes antic humor.

Jones had been called to Jackson for the by-then standard psychological examination of seminary candidates and was invited to spend the night before at the bishop's home.

"So that night the bishop said to me, 'Cecil, will you do something for me?' And of course I said, 'Why, yes, sir. Sure.'

"'Cecil,' he said, 'I've always wanted to do this, and you're just the perfect person. I want you to go in there tomorrow and do your best to convince that psychologist that you're crazy. I just want to see what happens. Now don't worry. I'll get you into seminary. But I just want to see what happens.'

"What could I say? Your bishop tells you to do something and you do it. But I didn't sleep much that night—I lay awake just about all night worrying about it.

"And then the next morning before I was supposed to go see the psychologist, the bishop comes in, and he says, 'Cecil, let's forget that. I slept on it last night, and I decided we not go'n do it.'

"Whew! What a relief! So I just went in there to that psychologist and did the best I could and got through O.K. But with Bishop Gray it was just little things like that all the time!"[26]

As Jones's story indicates, although Gray had left behind parish ministry for the greater honor, pomp, and ceremony of a diocesan, he kept both his dry sense of humor and his interest in the people he had gotten to know during his eighteen years as a parish priest in Mississippi.

In the bishop's personal and professional correspondence the tone was warm, but Gray also often adopted the same dryly amusing, sometimes antically humorous stance. In a gently self-mocking way he regularly referred to himself in the third person, by his title, and his vocabulary was likewise often playfully "elevated."

A series of letters written to residents of Greenwood about a planned vacation visit there not long after his consecration well illustrates these characteristics.

In a letter to Sam Williams ("Dear Sam") at the Hotel Irving, Gray wrote that he had "in mind spending two or three weeks in Greenwood, . . . and I want you to quote me a rate for a room with two double beds. I am not seeking for much of a concession during these boom times, but I would appreciate you keeping in mind that I will be with you from fourteen to twenty-one days." Then Gray added, "Let me hear from you, and purge your being of all avarice in making your quotation," and signed himself, "Sincerely your friend."

His correspondent replied in kind, and Gray responded, "I have your good letter of the 22nd, quoting me an outrageously high rate [of $4.50 per night], which you say 'is a drastic decrease from current [wartime] O.P.A. regulations.' If you are going to let your generous impulses be thwarted by Government rules, then I have no option but to accept the contract proffered." He concludes, "Thanking you, old fellow, for the many courtesies you have shown me, and looking forward to living with you for a while. I am, with good wishes for you and those you love, Sincerely yours."[27]

Such letters were not confined to adults. A week later in a letter to a teenage "Miss Louise Simpson" at Camp Deerwoode in Brevard, North Carolina, Gray wrote, "The Bishop of Mississippi is very flattered by your kind thought of him. I hope you are having a good time; and I am looking forward to seeing lots of you during your glamorous Senior year at Jackson High." Gray signed himself, "Your friend and Bishop."[28]

The same summer that Bishop Gray corresponded with Miss Louise Simpson, he also kept up a lively correspondence with his son who had also gone out of state to summer camp, this time as a counselor at Camp Chimney Rock on North Carolina's Lake Lure. Less than a half a dozen exchanges between the two remain, but those few show a close and comfortable relationship between father and seventeen-year-old son, with the earliest letter from Duncan beginning "Dear Daddy, How's the Bishop coming along? Is he working hard?"

The camp's sports competition was a favorite topic in the correspondence. The campers were divided into teams named for American Indian tribes, and as a counselor, Duncan served as leader of the Choctaw team. His father was kept well informed throughout the summer on the team's fortunes in basketball, football, softball, baseball, and volleyball.

Sports were also an issue when it came to gaining weight. Duncan's goal was to reach 150 pounds so he would be eligible to play football at his new high school in the fall, and he reported a starting weight of 136 "stripped" and, in the correspondence, a maximum of 141 later in the summer. The process was slowed at one point by a side injury resulting from a baseball game. Dad replied, tongue slightly in cheek, "I hope your side will soon heal. If you are going to be a hero in stealing home, keep in mind that heroism unaccompanied by skill will frequently bring on painful results."

In the same letter, whose salutation read "Dear Bubber," the bishop and father wrote, "I am so glad to get your letter written on Monday, and I can certainly sympathize with you in the prevalent epidemic of homesickness among your Greenwood crowd. As you say, the weather has probably contributed to their nostalgia (look up that word, son)."

In the 1940s some matters were still "man-to-man": "I couldn't ask Mama for this, and I know you're terribly busy, but I need another jock strap badly. I need a small size, so if you have a chance, send me one. Thanks a lot."[29]

Romance obviously can be very complicated for teenagers, and while Duncan's older sister could be confided in ("Tell Ormond I still had my date Monday night in Greenwood, and we understand each other perfectly now. I think we do anyway."), Dad might be the source of advice: "Alice wrote me and said she had seen you. . . . I kind of got my affairs messed up between Canton [Ruth Spivey] and Greenwood [Alice]. . . . I've only had one letter from [Ruth] since I've been up here. I just don't know how to handle the women. You should have taught me more about 'em!"[30]

The move to Jackson and a new high school for his senior year could have been as difficult a transition as the move to Greenwood had been, but perhaps the summer in North Carolina had helped to ease it. In any case, by now Duncan had friends throughout the state as a result of his summers at the diocesan camp, and there is no indication that he responded rebelliously to the necessity of relocating. In fact, despite the complications of romance, he was happy to be within a short drive of Canton, where Ruthie lived.

The new senior quickly made a place for himself at Jackson's Central High School. A March 1944 school newspaper article headlined "Duncan Gray, Hardworking Senior from Greenwood, Carves Special Niche in *Tiger Talks* Hall of Fame" noted that the "dynamic, green-eyed Duncan Gray has the distinction of being the only student chosen personality of the week who had attended Central for less than a year."[31]

After playing wing-back on the school's football team the previous fall, his first in Jackson, he had been elected vice president of the school's student council and president of his homeroom, as well as serving as assistant editor of *Pegasus* and sports editor of the yearbook. Despite the busy extracurricular schedule, Duncan's teachers said, "He has also found time to keep up a high scholastic average." Sounding like a typical teenager, Duncan claimed to spend his little spare time "loafing" and said that homework was his "pet hate." Physics, however, was his "favorite subject."[32]

In the interview, the soon-to-graduate senior confessed to two ambitions: "My main ambition right now is working for a Navy commission," but his "hidden ambition, which he admits with a grin," was "to be six feet tall." The article concludes, "Duncan is one of the kind that gets voted 'most likely to succeed.'"[33]

The 1944 Central High yearbook confirmed the *Tiger Talks* interview with this entry next to Duncan's picture: "A football player and a scholar *par excellence*, Duncan makes us wonder how he manages to make off with the highest grades available while apparently expending no effort. The crowd you see around him is probably clamoring for his trig (or any other) homework."[34]

The navy commission came through with acceptance at an officer training program at Tulane University, and shortly after his arrival there an unidentified newspaper carried a casual shot of a smiling Duncan in uniform in the Tulane mess hall with the accompanying cutline: "No More Bishops. There won't be a second bishop in the Gray family of Jackson, Miss., according to 17–year-old Duncan M. Gray Jr., newly enrolled naval trainee in Tulane University's V-12 program. Only son of the Right Reverend Duncan

M. Gray, Episcopal bishop of the diocese of Mississippi, young Gray is slated for a deck officer ship in the Navy. After the war he hopes to study engineering. A regular fellow, he is known on the campus as 'Dunk,' plans to go out for sports, and wants to earn his commission 'in a hurry.'"[35]

Despite his youthful disavowal of his father's work, it is clear that Duncan enjoyed an unusually close and harmonious relationship with his parents while growing up. Looking back on his childhood from the perspective of his eighth decade, Gray says he remembers being spanked only once and adds with a chuckle, "I think my parents raised me right, even though I might not always have thought so at the time."[36]

In a day in which children sue parents over alleged mistreatment and psychologists warn of the multiple dangers of child-rearing, Gray readily acknowledged that his view of his relationship with his parents as positive and uncomplicated sounds Pollyannaish. But he insists that it reflects a reality.

His conviction of its truth didn't mean, however, that he was unaware that his experience may be a rare one. In illustration, he told a story of an experience that brought him face to face with that fact after he became bishop of Mississippi himself.

"It was at a House of Bishops meeting, and there were ten or twelve of us [bishops] sitting around and talking about things that had happened to us growing up. And two or three of them were talking about—well, their poor relationships with their fathers, let's put it like that.

"And I said, 'I guess I'm just especially blessed. I thought occasionally that my father might be mistaken about something, but I *never* felt estranged from him or hostile toward him or anything in my life.' And this one guy looked at me and said, 'You're lying.' And he went on and on. He said, 'I don't believe that.'

"I suddenly realized that I was with a group of people there that . . . That what I was saying is really inconceivable to an awful lot of people in the world today. And so I kept my mouth shut. I thought, well, I'm not going to say this anymore. But it's true! I never felt this kind of thing that I hear and read so much about. I guess it struck me maybe how common that sort of thing is—I mean some real serious problems with a parent, and with males particularly with their fathers. I just never had that. And I don't think that I've blocked all that out of my memory. I've just been very blessed. And I realize that."

Gray continued, developing as a theological theme a view of the centrality of the family that echoed his father's: "It sounds corny or sentimental to talk about, but I never had those problems. And I think of that both in psychological *and* theological terms. Because I believe that God's grace is mediated to you through that community of which you're a part from the moment of your birth: your family. And I think that's a part of God's plan, that's the way we learn to love, by being loved. Well, all I'm saying is that I had an extra measure of God's grace in my growing-up years. I don't want to sound self-satisfied or something, but it's *true!* And it just strikes me when I hear so many other people in their difficulties.

"The family, I'm certain, is a primary source of grace. And I think it's by God's design that we are born into that community. At least we're supposed to be born into that community, and, of course, that's one of the difficulties we've got in society today—so often, it seems, children don't have that community. Like I used to say in my sermons, when we're born, we come naturally into a community of at least three from the moment of our birth. And of course that's not the case with so many children. It's two—and then it's not even two for very long sometimes.

"So I realize more and more how truly blessed I have been, and I think that that fact probably had a whole lot to do with what I did in the fifties and sixties [with respect to civil rights], and maybe during that time it kept me from 'coming apart at the seams.'"[37]

CHAPTER 4

"THEY SAID I SHOULD BE AN ENGINEER"

Tulane and Westinghouse, 1944–50

O N JULY 1, 1943, seventy thousand young men reported to 131 different colleges and universities throughout the United States to begin
both their college careers and their training to become naval officers.[1] Eight
hundred and fifty of those young men reported to the Tulane University
campus in New Orleans, Louisiana, where a year later, Duncan and approximately seventy-five others would join them. When the 1943 group arrived
on the Tulane campus, one observer said that the scene reminded him of
an "'outdoor Union Station' with hundreds of men standing in lines, some
sitting on suitcases and others hurrying from one location to another."[2]

James G. Schneider, chronicler of the V-12 program, describes the military situation that led in 1942 to the government's plan to make use of the
nation's colleges and universities for training substantial numbers of army,
navy, marine, and coast guard officers for the battle against the Axis powers: "The war was going badly for the United States and its allies during the
first months of 1942. In the Pacific, Japan was scoring victory after victory,
with every enemy triumph marking one more place to be retaken and each
success of the Japanese navy making our ultimate victory ever more distant.
In the European theater, Hitler's forces had control of nearly the entire con-
tinent, and the prospect of a total Allied triumph seemed remote. Indeed,
while the topic of how long the war would last was a daily conversational
theme all over America, the sobering question of whether America and the
Allies would win it was occasionally raised."[3]

At this low point in the war, and with little sense of how long the conflict
would last, all the services found themselves looking toward the future with
some anxiety as they considered their coming need for leaders. The U.S.
Navy required that its commissioned officers hold a college degree and, in
1940, put in place a naval training program for recent college graduates.
Less than a month after the Japanese attack on Pearl Harbor, the navy had

expanded the program to include college juniors and seniors, who were placed on inactive reserve while they completed their college programs, and a month later, it expanded the program again to include freshmen and sophomores.

This strategy seemed likely to ensure future commissioned officers for the navy as long as the draft age was held at twenty, but in the late summer of 1942, the War Department gave strong signs of plans to cut the age to eighteen, in which case the navy could anticipate the possibility of its supply of officer material substantially evaporating.

At the same time, colleges and universities throughout the country found that a large part of their "contribution" to the war effort was the disappearance of many of their students to the services, a process which would obviously only accelerate if the draft age were lowered. For some time, academic institutions had been offering their services and facilities to the armed forces but had received a generally lukewarm response.

By late 1942, the mutual benefits of an alliance between the services and America's colleges and universities were becoming ever more apparent, and on December 17, 1942, there came the public announcement of the creation of the Army Specialized Training Program and the Navy College Training Program designed to help meet "the demands of a mechanical war and of steadily growing armed forces" that required "a flow into the respective services of young men who require specialized educational technical training which could be provided by the colleges and universities."[4]

The navy's program was designed, as its earlier programs had been, to "provide a continuing supply of officer candidates in the various special fields required by the U.S. Navy, Marine Corps, and Coast Guard." Indeed, the navy went beyond that limited claim to add that its program would allow the selection of "the country's best qualified young men on a broad democratic basis, without regard to financial resources, and thus permit the Navy to induct and train young men of superior ability for officers and specialists." It added that the program trainees would be "selected high school graduates, or others of satisfactory educational qualifications," chosen on the basis of the navy's having established to its satisfaction "their proper mental, physical, and potential officer qualifications by appropriate examinations."[5]

In 1942, it would have occurred to few white Southerners, and, indeed, to few whites throughout the country, to inquire whether selecting "the country's best qualified young men on a broad democratic basis" meant that young black men would also be eligible for the program. In fact, it was only in the middle of 1942 that the navy had opened all its enlisted ranks to

African Americans; until then they were permitted to enlist only as steward's mates or as Seabees responsible for navy construction projects. The navy itself had not seriously addressed the issue of black officers.

When the navy announced the April 2, 1943, scheduling of its V-12 entrance exam, however, the question of African American eligibility to sit for the exam quickly arose in the minds of many blacks, including Dr. Mordecai Johnson, president of Howard University. In late March of that year Johnson wrote the navy, posing the question. On March 30, Secretary of the Navy Frank Knox responded ambiguously to Johnson's question. On April 1, Johnson wrote again, asking for clarification: "My specific question to you on behalf of Howard University and on behalf of students who are preparing to take these examinations, is whether the Navy now has a policy which will admit a Negro student to the real possibility of becoming an officer in the Navy and whether these examinations in reality do as a matter of fact offer such a Negro student a first step toward this end."[6]

Knox's reply was dated April 3, the day after the exam, and read in part: "the Navy College Training Program admits all students selected for this program, including Negroes, to the possibility of becoming officers in the Navy and the examinations offer the first step toward this end."[7]

Although Knox's April letter was the first public statement that blacks would be eligible for the navy's officer program, the decision to allow them entrance had actually been made the month before when those responsible for administering the exams had met in Washington to get final instructions. When they asked if blacks would be allowed to take the test, Lt. Commander Alvin C. Eurich, the navy's director of Curriculum and Standards Section, passed the question to his superior, the navy's chief of personnel, Rear Admiral Randall Jacobs. Jacobs replied that the question was an interesting one and should be studied. Eurich responded that the navy had been studying the question for months and that now a decision needed to be made. Jacobs directed Eurich to write a memo which he forwarded to the Secretary of the Navy, who in turn sent it on to the White House. In short order the memo came back with the notation "Of course Negroes will be tested! FDR."[8]

And so they were, although application forms for the navy program did not include identification by race. As a result, the College Training Section was unaware of how many black men it had accepted until July 1 when they showed up on college campuses, including some campuses in the Deep South where racial integration was forbidden by state law. In response to panicked phone calls from commanding officers on those campuses, the College Training Section directed them to its recently issued V-12 Bulletin

No. 5, which set forth procedures allowing each commander to transfer up to 5 percent of his trainees to another campus for "valid academic reasons." Although the navy apparently never clarified for itself the number of African Americans in the program, navy memos indicate that the first group of trainees probably included no more than a dozen, a number of whom were sent to Oberlin College, which had a long-standing tradition of accepting African Americans as students.[9]

Duncan left Jackson on the train on the morning of July 1, and his family bade him good-bye at the station. He had been to New Orleans a number of times before, including one Sugar Bowl visit, so he didn't feel that he was going into unknown country. "There was the Sugar Bowl stadium right there! That was close to heaven!" Although he discovered later that New Orleans streetcar lines would take him directly either to the front of the campus or right outside the Tulane gym (the building that was home to most of the trainees), this first time, still a little unsure of his bearings, he took a cab to the Tulane campus.

Like other young men entering the V-12 program that day at Tulane and at other colleges and universities across the nation, Gray's first impression of his new situation was one of controlled confusion and chaos. "We were all in the same boat—well, not all, because you had that Navy hierarchy over there—but all us newcomers were. We sort of enjoyed it though, getting to know one another. It was kind of an adventure."[10]

At the same time, however, "I was uneasy about a lot of things. For example, I didn't know who was going to be my bunkmate, and I was so pleased when it turned out to be an older guy who had been there for a while already and knew the routine. He got me oriented as far as the Navy part of the program. And then he turned out to be from Macon, Mississippi! We got to be real good buddies."[11]

Two more of Gray's nearby neighbors had been in the navy since before the outbreak of the war and were taking advantage of the V-12 program as an opportunity to get a college education. They thrilled the younger men with tales of active duty in the Pacific and of navy life in general.

Getting along with your bunkmate was fairly serious business for the Tulane trainees. Most of the nearly nine hundred officer candidates were housed in the university gym. Despite the "second story"—a platform built around the sides of the gym to make room for all the men—the double-decker bunks still had to be placed so closely that the space between them allowed for little more than getting in and out of bed. Yet in spite of the spartan accommodations and the unavoidable closeness, the trainees counted themselves lucky to be housed in the gym in the heat of a New

Orleans summer, since the high ceilings and the overhead fans made it one of the coolest places on campus in a day before air conditioning.

Just as for college freshmen today, the first few days on campus meant meetings and lines, as well as making new friends. Here though, the meetings were often with navy commanders and other officers; the lines were as likely to be for navy physicals, including calisthenics to check for skeletal or muscular weaknesses, as they were for class registration or book buying.[12]

And the lines were also for uniforms, since hundreds of young men had to be completely outfitted as soon as possible. The program's first year had taught the navy a few things about uniforming several hundred men at a time, but even in 1944, it faced some of the same problems as before. Schneider describes the situation:

> Imagine a typical V-12 unit of three hundred trainees, more than 90 per cent of whom were coming from civilian life. They needed to be fully equipped with GI clothing, but the Navy had little information about the sizes necessary to outfit them. Accordingly, it had to estimate appropriate quantities and sizes for everything from jumpers to shoes. Only with blankets, pillows, and towels was it freed from that uncertainty. Shoes provided the biggest headache for the V-12 units. Seldom was a qualified person available to fit them. In V-12 Bulletin No. 16, the Navy had advised the commanding officers that most of the shoes were coming from the factories of the Floresheim Company, and that therefore they should call upon the local Floresheim dealer to obtain some qualified assistance. As in most military organizations, it was convenient to organize activities alphabetically, so those whose names began with letters early in the alphabet had little trouble getting clothing and shoes of the proper size. When the latter part of the alphabet was reached, however, the sizes needed had frequently run out.[13]

Gray, with a name that came early in the alphabet, had no trouble with sizes, but his clearest memory of the uniforming process was the change it wrought in a very personal matter: his underwear. Most men in civilian life at the time wore tank-top style undershirts and many wore briefs. In the navy, however, the uniform was T-shirts and boxer shorts, and Gray recalls, "It was a whole change in underwear for me, and I haven't changed back, not since July 1, 1944!"[14]

In some V-12 locations, especially small towns, keeping sailor whites *white* was a challenge. Before the days of coin-operated laundries, local commercial laundries provided the service, but that service might take three or four days.[15] At Tulane, the university provided washing machines on campus, and many young men learned for the first time what "doing the laundry" meant. After washing their uniforms, Gray recalls, "we learned to roll up those whites to press them, so to speak. We didn't get down an iron or anything like that, but if you rolled them up just right after washing them, then they would roll out as they were supposed to and look pretty good. Maybe not exactly like they should have, but they looked good enough for the navy. They probably had some wrinkles in them, but nobody worried about that."[16]

If the navy relaxed the line on wrinkled uniforms at Tulane, it did not on many other things. One was the use of navy language. "The V-12 officers would not tolerate hearing about floors and walls—they were 'decks' and 'bulkheads.' Windows were to be 'ports,' mops were 'swabs,' stairways were 'ladders,' halls were 'passageways,' restrooms were 'heads,' drinking fountains were 'scuttlebutts,' and the dorms usually became 'ships.'"[17]

Along with changes in language came the schedule changes that were part of the navy discipline. Monday through Friday, reveille came at 6:00 a.m. for the V-12ers at Tulane, and the trainees had to hustle themselves out of bed and into formation for the flag raising and a round of calisthenics. Then they returned to the gym to get their bunk area ready for inspection and themselves ready for "chow," to which they marched in formation—all this in order to be in class by eight o'clock.

Classes consumed the morning, the first couple of semesters bringing a standard fare of freshmen requirements. Then lunch followed in a more relaxed fashion—no marching in formation—and the afternoon was filled with more classes, either academic or ROTC, to fulfill the officer training requirements. The day closed with another march in formation to the flag lowering and then to the chow line again. After supper the required study hall began—in the library or a classroom. Study on bunks was not allowed. But come ten o'clock—curfew—all were required to be in those bunks for bed check. After the war had ended, Tulane V-12ers reportedly managed on occasion to cope with the inconvenience of the early bedtime by paying other Tulane students to sleep in their beds. The going rate was five dollars a night. It was not difficult to find interested sleepers; after all, the gym was the coolest "dorm" on campus.[18]

As the trainees drew near to the completion of their second trimester— the V-12 schedule took no summer break—they were given aptitude tests, and the navy advised Gray that his gift was for electrical engineering. He had always done well in math courses, so the assignment made a certain amount of sense. Besides, at this point in his life his determination to avoid the ministry had been made fairly clear in a public way when the New Orleans *Times-Picayune* had published a photo of him in the chow line and in the cutline had quoted him as saying that as far as he was concerned, there would be "no more bishops" in the Gray family.[19] In fact, he had wrestled off and on since late high school with the idea of going to seminary, but, he joked, "I don't guess the Navy needed any priests! They could *use* engineers," and, proud of the possibility of serving his country in wartime, he proceeded with his engineering courses.

"It was a packed schedule, particularly once we got into engineering. You had classes all morning and lectures all afternoon. Then you had study hall at night, and that was compulsory too. We went to school pretty much around the clock."[20]

Despite the rigors of the program and the loss of personal freedom, participation in V-12 carried with it a certain moral burden for many. As Schneider notes, some participants saw the program as "a 'safe harbor'—a place where they could avoid the shooting war for a time." Some of these, he found, got into the "safe harbor" for reasons of conscience—their pacifist beliefs—but others did so simply to avoid the dangers of the war. "Indeed," he says, "the charge that this was an important motivation was often made against the program by the envious parents of men who were in embattled parts of the world facing real danger."[21]

Other participants had "no such thoughts when they joined but began to doubt the propriety of being in college when they received word of the deaths of friends, neighbors, and classmates on the oceans and battlefronts of the world."[22] This was the situation Gray found himself in, but the decisions of the navy and the progress of the war solved his dilemma for him. He had originally gone to Tulane as part of a second navy program, known as the V-5 program, designed to train navy pilots. The V-5 program gave young men two semesters of college and then sent them on to flight-training school.

"Strictly speaking, when I reported for duty in July of 1944, I was actually in the V-5 program. But then a couple of semesters after that the V-5 program was wiped out completely and all of us were transferred into the V-12 program. Presumably they had all the aviators they needed at that point. And second, the end of the war was in sight, and the V-12 would have provided a more generalized resource for the Navy.

"But, yeah, it bothered my conscience at first. I think all of us felt that way to some degree or another. And see, even after the V-5 program was cancelled, up to a certain point we still had the option of dropping out and just going directly into the fleet. But I tell you one thing that helped us. By the time our class started, D-Day had already happened. Before we got through two semesters, the war in Europe was practically over and the war in the Pacific was moving in the right direction. So I guess we salved our consciences because we felt like 'that's O.K., the thing's going to be over before we get out there anyway.'"[23]

Still, the navy uniform had its impact, even if the sailor wasn't involved in the shooting war. One Sunday evening when Gray was returning to campus from a trimester break, he stopped in the train station cafe and ordered a shrimp po' boy and a cup of coffee. Only then did he think to check his wallet, and discovered that he was short of cash. Embarrassed, he told the waitress to hold the po' boy. A group at the other end of the counter observed this and quickly pulled out their own wallets, telling the waitress, "Give that sailor what he wants!" Gray protested, knowing that his cash shortage could be relieved by a visit to the bank the next morning, but his benefactors insisted. "So I sat there and ate my po' boy. They didn't know I was out at Tulane. I was just a sailor boy sitting there with no money to pay for his food."[24]

Life in the V-12 program at Tulane was not all hard work, early curfews, and moral introspection. The young men were, after all, in the heart of New Orleans. And in addition, when they first arrived in July, fraternities had conducted rush—perhaps not quite as they would in times of peace, since even on weekends the V-12 men had to be in their bunks by eleven o'clock, but with the usual round of parties and dances. Gray quickly made up his mind to pledge the Delta Kappa Epsilon fraternity, familiarly known as Deke, despite the initial preferences of Ruthie's older sister, Tootsie, now a student at Ole Miss and a fan of a competing fraternity. In New Orleans for a visit, Tootsie went as Gray's date to a rush party given by the Tulane chapter of the competing fraternity. When Gray told her of his decision to go Deke rather than pledge her favorite fraternity, to his surprise, she heartily agreed. "I don't blame you," she said. "That other party was one of the dullest I've ever been to!"

Many Dekes were New Orleanians, and so, in addition to Gray's already existing knowledge of the city, his fraternity brothers quickly helped fill in the blanks. Not surprisingly in New Orleans, much of the time on the town revolved around food. Food on the "chow line" in the campus cafeteria wasn't bad, as Gray remembers it, but "it wasn't Arnaud's or Antoine's either."

Schneider reports that early in the V-12 program, some institutions simply didn't serve large enough quantities or provide enough calories for young men of whom a high level of physical activity was required. Although this problem, like others, was pretty well corrected by the second year of the program, "at certain times in the week the pickings could be pretty sparse. You'd make a sandwich with a hot dog or something. It wasn't a full meal," Gray recalls.

"I've always had a pretty good appetite and I've always loved bread, so when we'd go down the cafeteria line I always took a stack of bread. My friends used to kid me about it and say, 'I think that bishop daddy of yours taught you to eat bread so you wouldn't spend all his money on other food!'"[25]

For eating out, Galatoires and the Court of Two Sisters were favorites, as was a place right around the corner from the Deke house that served New Orleans Cajun food as well as po' boys and oysters on the half shell, a favorite of Gray's. "It was run by Henry Rodriguez, and he was great. We had a game we'd play with him—he enjoyed it too. We'd sit at the bar and order a dozen oysters on the half shell. He'd put 'em out, and we'd say, 'Ah, Henry. That one's so small it doesn't count. You owe us another one.' And he'd laugh and give us another one. And every time we ordered oysters on the half shell, we'd play that game. I don't think I ever got less than sixteen for the price of a dozen! He would always give them to us with good humor. And prices then were so low."[26]

Gray and fraternity brother Dick Field, later best man in Gray's wedding, discovered additional ways to have a night on the town that was well within the budget of apprentice seamen. "Dick didn't drink any alcohol, and I didn't drink much. I'd have a beer or something like that.

"Well, one night we tried something. We went to three 'strip joints'— they weren't anything like what all those New Orleans places are like today, any more than the prices are—and he would order a Coke and I'd order a 7–Up and we'd fool around with that. They wouldn't kick you out or anything, particularly with a navy uniform on. So we got through the whole night, and he had spent $1.80 and I'd spent $1.50. A night on the French Quarter for $1.50! That was really, really something!"[27]

In addition to his comradeship with V-12 friends and fraternity brothers, Gray had another place in New Orleans where he could feel at home away from home. "St. Andrew's Episcopal Church on Carrolton Avenue was the closest Episcopal Church to the campus, and the rector there was Girault Jones [later bishop of Louisiana], and of course he and my dad were good friends. He had been in Pass Christian, Mississippi, on the coast, before he went to New Orleans. When I was growing up, during the Depression, we spent several summer vacations at his house in Pass Christian. Girault would go to back home to Woodville, Mississippi, for his vacation, and my dad would take services for him in Pass Christian during August while he was in Woodville. And that was our vacation.

"So with all that connection, I'd often go to Sunday services at St. Andrew's. I didn't go there every Sunday—sometimes I'd go to the cathedral. And Girault was also responsible for work with college students—Canterbury work. I'd occasionally go to those meetings on Sunday evenings.

"But with Girault right there, again that was a touch of home, a touch of Mississippi."[28]

After Gray's freshman year, Ruthie Spivey would occasionally provide another "touch of home," but in a day before "going steady," both she and Gray, despite their seriousness about each other, also continued to "play the field." Gray met girls native to New Orleans through his fraternity brothers, and Sophie Newcomb College, Tulane's sister school, also provided a rich source of dates for parties and dances.

"In my later years at Tulane, Ruthie came down quite a bit for Deke formals and parties. The closer I was to graduation, the more often she came. She didn't come much right in the beginning, because she was still in high school, but her sister moved to New Orleans around 1946, and Ruthie could come down and stay with Tootsie. She also had an aunt and uncle who lived there on Carrolton Avenue, and before Tootsie moved down, she stayed with them."

Later, "Ruthie was at Ole Miss, of course, but I didn't manage to get up there much. First of all, I just didn't have enough time. And second, the passes we got from the Navy meant we weren't supposed to travel more than fifty miles from base—the campus. Now I did stretch the regs on that once or twice. I never went to Ole Miss on a pass like that, but I did go to Jackson a couple of times, and I'd have been in trouble if I'd had to show my pass in Jackson. But nobody ever asked me for it. When I did that, it was coming to see Ruthie, coming up for some special event over a weekend.

"The reason for the Navy's fifty-mile rule was a good one—if there was some emergency or something, they wanted to be sure that you could get back to base quickly, but I figured I could get back to New Orleans from Jackson at least as quickly as I could from Hammond, Louisiana, or some place like that."[29]

Restrictions such as the fifty-mile pass limit eventually loosened when the war officially came to an end. Even before that, V-E Day and V-J Day provided celebratory holidays. "We were allowed to go out, off campus, to celebrate—but we were still supposed to be in our bunks by ten o'clock! A lot of people didn't make that, and nobody frowned too much.

"It seems to me that we heard the news about the end of war when we were in the chow line for lunch. Somebody came in and announced it, and there was a big celebration in the cafeteria. We went downtown, but it was such a madhouse that my Deke buddies and I went back to the house, and we had a few toddies. It was a great day, and, as I recall, we had the next day off too—maybe it was a weekend or something—but once we were back it was the same old routine. Of course everybody was in a gala mood, and even the stern old petty officers that ordered us around had smiles on their faces—and that was different!

"And of course we didn't have television, so we'd go to the movies and watch the newsreels to see the treaties being signed and so on.

"It really wasn't until June of 1946, when we were discharged from active duty, that we were free and could go and do whatever we wanted to. Then ROTC was just an additional activity that was another part of your campus life. You weren't under orders all the time like we'd been since we got there."[30]

After the discharge, Gray still had more than a year and a half of college until graduation, but by the fall of 1947, he was looking seriously toward the future beyond college, and the future, he fervently hoped, included Ruthie Spivey. His formal proposal of marriage to her came in September 1947, in New Orleans' famed Absinthe House in the French Quarter. Fats Paison, a locally well-known pianist, played softly in the background in this "very romantic place" as he proposed, and she agreed that they would marry after his graduation in February of 1948.[31]

But Duncan and Ruthie "nearly didn't get married." After accepting his September proposal, she began to have second thoughts. Although her fiancé would have graduated from college, she, an education major, had three more semesters to go, including the semester of practice teaching that was required for her degree. "I was debating whether to stay at Ole Miss until I graduated," she explained. "I talked mostly to my family about it, and they were very supportive of me. But our families were friends, and in that day a woman wasn't expected to have a career. They loved Duncan, and," she said only half seriously, "they didn't want him to get away!"[32]

Her husband of more than sixty years pointed out, "She was having a grand and glorious time at Ole Miss."

Ruthie was both a good student as an education major and also a popular young woman around campus. She had been tapped for Mortar Board, the academic honorary, for the 1947–48 academic year. The previous spring she had been chosen as "Daisy Mae" for the university's annual Sadie Hawkins Day, and in the fall of 1947 she was a finalist for "Miss Ole Miss," both contests of beauty and popularity on campus. She was a member of Delta Delta Delta sorority and had been elected its president. Gray said, "She was having the time of her life, and she hadn't even finished her junior year. She was just getting started."[33] So in addition to asking Ruthie to marry him, Gray was also asking her to give up an exciting college career for the somewhat less glamorous role of stay-at-home wife. And Ruthie had serious second thoughts.

In tears, she called Gray from Oxford to break the news to him. "It wasn't 'no, never,'" he said. "It was 'no, not now.'"

"Well," he said, with characteristic understatement about such matters, "it kind of got me down." In fact, he added, Ruthie's hesitation was probably the low point of his time at Tulane. But, he said, "I figured, 'That's the way it goes. Win some, lose some,' or something like that."

But to his joy, about a week later, Ruthie's second thoughts became third ones, and she called to let him know that she'd changed her mind again. Not long after she made another trip to New Orleans, and the wedding plans were on again, if now in a somewhat rushed fashion.[34]

After she'd initially agreed to his proposal, Gray had bought her an engagement ring, but because of the intervening uncertainty, he'd never given it to her. Instead, he had left it in Jackson for safekeeping. Since he didn't have it in New Orleans, he called on his father to do the honors for him as Ruthie's train stopped in Jackson on its way back to Oxford.

The train pulled into the station in Jackson, and Ruthie stepped off to be greeted by the bishop. It was a bit awkward for him, standing in for his son at this romantic juncture, but the senior Gray pulled out the engagement ring and placed it on her finger. Then, despite the reserve that the awkwardness brought out, the bishop planted a kiss on the cheek of his daughter-in-law-to-be.[35]

The engagement was now official, and frantic plans got underway for a wedding at Ruthie's home parish of Grace Church, Canton, and a reception at the Spivey home afterwards.

With this important part of his life finally settled, Gray went on to pursue his career plans. Rather than become an active navy officer after graduation, he would become a member of the navy reserve. That left a full-time job to tie down. With the economy retooling itself for peacetime, engineers were in demand, and companies flocked to campuses to interview engineering graduates.

Gray was tempted by the opportunities oil companies offered in the Middle East. In 1948, the year the State of Israel was established, tensions in that part of the world were high, but so was the oil supply, and oil companies lured engineers with large salaries if they were willing to locate in the area. Most of the large salary, however, was banked in the United States, and the new hires had to agree to remain in the Middle East for at least three years in order to actually receive that portion of the salary. Working for an oil company in Texas or Louisiana was also a possibility, but those jobs involved a lot of moving around. Gray considered the oil company jobs, but it was very much on his mind that "I was going to be getting married," and so he finally decided against taking a job in that industry.

Instead, he elected to accept a job with Westinghouse Corporation, in part at the urging of a former Mississippian and family friend in charge of Westinghouse's sales to public utilities.

"Westinghouse certainly offered a comfortable salary for that day and time," Gray recollects, "and it offered a stable sort of home," as well as the possibility of locating in the South. First, however, Westinghouse required its new hires to complete a "graduate student training program" which aimed to expose the engineers to all aspects of the corporation. The program assigned them to work for a month to six weeks in different areas of the company, from assembly lines to the various types of engineering jobs available at Westinghouse. That program meant that the Grays would spend most of their first year in Pittsburgh, where Westinghouse was head-quartered, and in an area where a number of different types of company plants were located.[36]

Before Westinghouse and life in Pittsburgh, however, there was a wedding to be celebrated.

The cliché to the effect that the course of true love never runs smoothly could have been coined for the wedding of Ruthie Spivey and Duncan Gray, if not for their subsequent years of married life. In fact, if they and their families had been given to superstition, this wedding would have been guaranteed to confirm any such belief.

Two weeks before the wedding date, a gas floor furnace in the Spiveys' antebellum home exploded in the middle of the night, and the house caught fire. Ruthie's sister was sleeping downstairs and she quickly awakened the other sleepers to the danger. In the typical small-town fashion of the time, neighbors and friends rushed to the house and began to remove as much of its contents as possible as the house burned. One neighbor made a point of saving Ruthie's wedding veil. But her wedding dress went up in flames, along with all her bridesmaids' dresses, as the old house burned to the ground.

Mr. Spivey was out of town, a delegate to the Episcopal diocese's annual convention, but he was quickly called. With his usual calm and unruffled manner, he simply left Bishop Gray a note: "I better get home. My family needs me." When he reached home, his wife was nearly frantic—she had not only lost her home and much of its contents, but her younger daughter was getting married in two weeks.

Family and friends and neighbors, however, once again pitched in—this time to make the wedding happen, and nearly as planned. The reception was moved to the church. A sorority sister of Ruthie's who had married a few months earlier offered Ruthie her wedding dress, which turned out to fit perfectly without alteration. Ruthie drove with her father the short distance to Jackson to find material for new bridesmaids' dresses, and the seamstress set to work. Everything seemed to be falling into place after all.

The day before the wedding, Mr. Spivey set out for Jackson again, this time to pick up the wedding cake. Before he left home, he created a small platform on the back seat of his car so that the cake would have a level place to rest. When he reached Jackson, he and the baker carefully placed the cake on the platform, and Spivey headed back to Canton with it.

But when he reached home and prepared to take the cake in the house, he confronted another crisis: rather than its original multiple layers, the cake had collapsed into one. Once again, apparently unfazed, he turned the car around and headed back to Jackson, reaching the baker before he closed for the evening. The baker's diagnosis: he had rushed icing the cake while it was still too warm, leading to its collapse. He immediately set to work icing another cake he already had on hand and eventually Spivey reached home with an intact cake.

The next morning, the wedding day, dawned—with sleet falling, always a serious matter in wintertime Mississippi. But this time, as Ruthie stepped out of a neighbor's house and headed toward the church, the sun broke through. Now Mrs. Spivey was prepared to believe in omens and declared this a good one. Indeed, the wedding proceeded without a hitch, as did the reception, and the happy couple climbed into their car, loaded with wedding presents and the bride's trousseau, for their two-week honeymoon trip to Pittsburgh, where Duncan's Westinghouse job awaited.[37]

The couple spent their first night together in Meridian, Mississippi, a few hours drive from Jackson. Ruthie's nerves were still on edge. As she cut into her steak, the whole thing slid off her plate onto her new suit. And as she ate the chocolate pie she had ordered for dessert, bits of it landed in the same place.[38]

The next morning, the two headed for Birmingham, the second night's stop on their journey. They pulled up at the hotel where they had reservations for the night and prepared to park the car in the hotel's garage. When they were told that cars in the garage had to remain unlocked, they decided it would be the better part of wisdom to park their packed car on the street right in front of the hotel. But at 2:00 a.m., they learned that had been a bad decision. Birmingham police informed them that the car had been broken into and their possessions, including most of Ruthie's trousseau, had been stolen. Duncan joked that Ruthie, fond of clothes, has been replacing it ever since![39]

When Duncan and Ruthie arrived in Pittsburgh in 1948, at the end of their honeymoon, they found fellow Mississippians and Episcopalians already there to greet them. One such couple was Pete LeGrone, who had originally encouraged Duncan to take the job with Westinghouse, and his wife, Bonnie. Friends of both Ruthie's and Duncan's parents, they took the new couple under their wing, and Mrs. LeGrone made a point of introducing Ruthie to other Westinghouse wives and thus into the social life of the company.[40]

When Duncan went to work on February 24, he found that one of his fellow new engineers was a young man by the name of Hubert Holmes—a friend from his childhood in Columbus. Holmes had also been a student in the V-12 program; he attended Millsaps College in Jackson—"he spent just about all of his free time at my parents' house," Gray said—and then had gone to the University of South Carolina, where he graduated with a degree in engineering. Although the two hadn't seen each other for some time, they quickly renewed their friendship.[41]

Other old friends came to visit, including Maurice Hattrell, known as "Hattie," a fellow Tulane V-12 student and engineer who had taken a job in the insurance industry. Among the people to whom the LeGrones had introduced the Grays was a vice president of Westinghouse and his wife who, when they went on vacation, asked the Grays if they would housesit. "Ruthie and I of course lived in a rather modest little apartment out in Wilkinsburg," Gray recalls, "but when Hattie came to visit we happened to be house-sitting at this home in a very swanky suburb of Pittsburgh. Well, we didn't say anything to Hattie about it—we just met him at the plane and brought him 'home' with us. And he didn't know *what* to think when we pulled up at this house: 'This guy is three or four months out of college and has a house like *this*!' I just said, 'Yeah, they pay pretty well here.' We finally let him in on it though and even took him by our apartment, but I think until then he was ready to resign his job and go to work for Westinghouse!"[42]

Despite the friends and introductions, the Mississippi Grays found Pittsburgh something of an adjustment, and Ruthie teased her husband about taking the "little magnolia blossom" to a land of ice and snow. In 1948, Pittsburgh, a major steel producer as well as the location of Westinghouse factories, had not yet imposed its first smoke control ordinances. Smoke from the burning of bituminous coal in both factories and homes coated the city with a black blanket. When the Grays rented their apartment, the landlord helpfully handed Ruthie a jug and told her "this is what we wash our walls with," a job that had to be done every few weeks. She remembers Duncan coming home from work dark with soot on his hands, face, and clothing.[43]

The first month of "graduate student training" meant more class work for the newly graduated college students, a month in which they learned about the company, its products, and its policies. Westinghouse tended to move its single "graduate students" from Pittsburgh to Buffalo to Baltimore and elsewhere during their training, but the company tried to keep its married students in one place for most of their introduction to the various aspects of the company. Pittsburgh was not only Westinghouse's headquarters; a number of its plants were located in the area as well, including its "M and R"—manufacturing and repair—plant in East Pittsburgh, the largest Westinghouse plant in the country. After the month of classes was over, Duncan, along with his fellow students, spent several weeks at a time on tasks as varied as working on a factory line assembling water-wheel generators for the Grand Coulee Dam, to working in an office with the company's design engineers, to working with the engineers who were the company's sales force for large customers such as utilities or oil companies, and so on.

Gray remembers the time as "real good experience," but his weeks in the M and R plant stuck most in his mind because of a bond formed with a co-worker that was to play a part in changing his view of the world, and ultimately contribute to his decision to leave Westinghouse for the ministry.

"At the M and R plant they really put you on the line. I was there where we were steam-cleaning motors. Motors came in to be cleaned and rewound, and the guy that I worked with on this was a black guy. As I got to know him, I found out that he had spent years in the Army engineers, including during World War II. He'd reached the rank of major, he was very intelligent, and here he was doing this work—I mean the kind of thing you could take just about anybody off the street and teach them to do in no time at all. And so I talked to him about that, and he just shook his head and said, 'Well, that's just the way it is.'

"He found out I was from Mississippi, and he said, 'You know I was stationed down there on the Gulf Coast during the war.' I said, 'Was it pretty rough?' And he said, 'No, I got along just fine. I spent most of my time on the base, but I didn't have any real bad experiences.' Now he may have just been protecting me, knowing where I was from, but what it said to me was 'things are as bad in the North as they are in the South.' Here's a guy that theoretically is equal, but with all his education and experience he ends up cleaning motors. It didn't make sense."[44]

Gray's experience in East Pittsburgh percolated in his mind as he continued his training. His final assignment in December 1948 took him and Ruthie out of Pittsburgh to the Buffalo plant where Westinghouse built electric motors and where the two found a place to live for the month they would be there. "I won't call it an apartment. It did have three or four rooms and a bathroom, but not much kitchen. There was a little icebox in the kitchen, but not much room for refrigeration. That wasn't a problem though because this was Buffalo in December. We had twenty inches of snow one day, and I mean the *wind* coming off Lake Erie . . .! Inside our closet was a little opening to the attic, and the temperature in that attic was close to freezing, so that was our refrigerator."[45]

The training period came to an end with the end of the year. Duncan had decided that working as a sales engineer was the Westinghouse career choice most attractive to him. He and Ruthie happily returned to the South, an option the company had all but guaranteed to them when he first took the job. After Christmas with their families, they moved to New Orleans, where Duncan reported to work in the sales engineering office there.

"All the salesmen were engineers. We're not talking about the appliance division—what we called Westco. This was not so much electronic engineering, but this was power, generators and motors and transformers, so you were dealing with pros. You had to have an engineering background because the sales engineer was dealing with customers like Mississippi Power and Light. It was a matter of talking engineering language and deciding exactly what you would do for this need or that purpose.

"They called us all 'sales engineers.' Some of us worked more as consultants; we didn't go out and meet with the customers very often, we didn't get contracts signed. We were resources both for customers and for the sales people out in the field. What I was doing was actually a lot of clerical work that had a technical dimension to it. I'd write proposals and that sort of thing. But it wasn't a full-blown sales job because I wasn't contacting the customer. What you wanted to do is move up to the point that you were working directly with the customer."[46]

By the summer of 1949, the Grays, now expecting their first child, were transferred from New Orleans to Shreveport, Louisiana, where a small and overworked sales staff dealt with large customers such as Southwestern Gas and Electric and International Paper. Duncan thought highly of his new boss, himself a Mississippian. The Grays settled happily into their new home and quickly became involved members of St. Mark's Episcopal Church, where Duncan helped work on a stewardship campaign and also with fundraising to establish a new Episcopal congregation in Shreveport.

But during the months they were there, at least two matters weighed from time to time on Gray's mind: one was the pull of the ministry, the second was the treatment of African Americans in the South at the end of the 1940s. And as it turned out, two experiences with the latter helped bring Gray to a decision about the former.

Due in part to Ruthie's pregnancy—the baby was due in September—the Grays hired a black woman to help her around the house. She came to their home once or twice a week to help with laundry and cleaning. "Well, one day she came to our house just all distraught. Her son had been picked up by the police and put in jail for whistling at a white woman, and she was just torn up. She didn't know what they might be doing to him there, and she was actively concerned about lynching.

"And so I said I would see what I could do. I went down to the police station, but of course I was a nobody as far as they were concerned. But they told me in no uncertain terms that he was in trouble, serious trouble, and, no, they weren't about to let him go.

"Well, I thought maybe my boss could help. He had been in Shreveport a lot longer than I had, and I had profound respect for him. He was a great guy, just a decent, wonderful person. So I went to him and told him the story and asked him if he could do anything to help. He said, 'They ought to kill the s.o.b.'"

Gray paused a moment and quickly added that he doesn't tell the story to "run down" his boss. "He was really such a wonderful person. But what it was was a revelation to me that this wonderful human being in so many ways had this kind of racist views. I had been kind of sheltered. I knew about the lynchings and I knew about the racists, but here was somebody I knew, a very good friend, and one for whom I had the most profound respect. And that coming from him really shook me up and in a sense waked me up."[47]

Another incident also contributed to the "awakening." "There was an automobile accident just a half a block away from our house. I was out walking and so I happened to see it. One car was driven by a white man and the other by a black man, and it was pretty clear to me that the white man was at fault. The police came, and I was just standing around thinking they would ask me about the accident. The policeman asked several white people, and they all said the black driver was at fault. So I just said, 'Now wait a minute. I'm not so sure of that.' And the policeman just turned on me and said, 'That's all right. We don't need to hear from you.' And went on with what he was doing."[48]

As for seminary, "I'd been wrestling with that since high school practically and particularly in college, even though I'd said there weren't going to be any more bishops in the Gray family! But the navy told me that I was an engineer, so I said, 'O.K., we'll give it a try.' And of course my dad had always told me, 'Don't go into the priesthood if you can possibly stay out of it.' What he meant by that was that there needs to be an overwhelming sense of calling—it's not just another career choice: lawyer or doctor or engineer. And because of all those things, I kept putting it off. I enjoyed my time at Westinghouse. I didn't enjoy those experiences about black people, but they weren't directly related to my work at Westinghouse. I talked to Ruthie about seminary from time to time, but then I figured she was tired of hearing about it, so I kept a lot to myself."[49]

She remembered that she "watched him struggle. It had to be *his* decision and I didn't want to be a stumbling block. I reported pretty regularly to the bishop every time I saw him. He'd say, 'How's it going?' and I'd say, 'He's still struggling.'"[50]

Although Gray continued to feel the pull to seminary, as he thought about it, the largest stumbling block for him was the idea of preaching. "I'd have to preach at least once a week. How could I ever write a sermon every week? I thought, 'I just can't do that!'"

At Easter of 1949, however, the stumbling block was unexpectedly removed. When Ruthie and Duncan went to Easter services, they heard "the sorriest sermon I've ever heard in my life! We left the church that Easter Sunday, and I thought, 'By George! If that preacher can do it, I can do it!' That really was the turning point. So I told Ruthie, and she said, 'Well, I wondered how long it was going to take!' It wasn't any surprise to her. She knew me better than I knew myself."[51]

Although Duncan had talked less to his wife about his thoughts as time went by, like many women she was a close observer of her husband's moods, and she could tell he was thinking about something. In addition to his involvement in parishes in the various places they'd lived in their short marriage, she also noticed that "he'd do things like lingering on his knees after church was over. No, I wasn't surprised."[52]

"So," Gray says, "it wasn't long after that that I talked to the bishop—who just happened to be my father! And he said, 'Come on!' He knew I'd been wrestling with it, and I think he figured that by then I wrestled with it long enough. I hadn't talked to him much about since I graduated from college, but he knew it was on my mind. I think he probably kept in touch with it through Ruthie. He knew it was a live issue, so he wasn't surprised."[53]

Today the Episcopal Church requires a long period of discernment for potential priests, including service in a parish church, approval by a parish discernment committee, and, after that, assents by various diocesan committees and officials.

"When I went through it, there wasn't any process at all! Well, you had to do two things. The first thing you did was go talk to the bishop, and if he would take you, that was fine. And then you did have to have a parish vestry to sponsor you and the rector to recommend you. We chose Grace Church, Canton, as our home parish. I knew half the vestry there and they knew me, so it was home. But that's the way it worked in those days; it was basically the bishop's decision."[54]

And so in 1950, with his father the bishop's blessing, Ruthie and Duncan and infant Duncan III prepared for another move, this time to the University of the South in Sewanee, Tennessee, where they would spend the three years of Duncan's seminary training at its School of Theology.

CHAPTER 5

"HE IS A NATURAL"

University of the South, 1950–52

S EWANEE, TENNESSEE, is a tiny town located on what is known locally
as "the Mountain," a rise of about fifteen hundred feet above sea level
on the western edge of the Cumberland Plateau. Today, Sewanee is about
an hour's drive northwest by interstate from Chattanooga, the closest small
city. A little more than an hour by interstate further west is Nashville, referred to more frequently in the past than the present as "the Athens of the
South," in large part because of its plethora of colleges and universities,
including Vanderbilt, Fisk, and Meharry Medical College. Today Nashville,
the state capital, is known as a center of country music. In 1950, before the
interstates were built and country music became a national and international attraction, Sewanee was even more isolated than it is today, but still
just as thoroughly dominated by the University of the South, which housed
a then all-male undergraduate college and the School of Theology. Together
they claimed a total student body of just under five hundred.[1] In fact, both
then and today, the university is more commonly referred to by the name of
the town: simply "Sewanee," an American Indian word that means "lost."[2]

The University of the South was founded just before the Civil War by
several southern dioceses of the Episcopal Church. At the time of its founding, its endowment was larger than that of any other American university,
but that wealth was, of course, destroyed by the war. After the war ended,
a group of Southern bishops, clergy, and laymen resolved to rebuild the
university. As the Reverend David Vance Guthrie (first a student in the
university's seminary and then a professor in the early 1950s) puts it, this
effort was intended to "renew their commitment to an educated gentry and
clergy." In characterizing the situation and attitudes of those rebuilders and
their sons, Guthrie observes, "No longer were Southern gentlemen able to
afford an English education; they must needs create an Oxford/Cambridge
in the hills of Tennessee. Harvard, Yale, and Princeton were too remote,

both geographically and ideologically, for the young gentlemen of the defeated South."[3]

"Sewanee," Guthrie says, "moved slowly into the twentieth century. Pass-
able roads came, then automobiles, indoor plumbing, electricity; but Ed-
wardian attitudes stayed fixed. World War II intruded and with it a general
change in racial attitudes for which the Domain was ill prepared. Eleanor
Roosevelt was disdained, Harry Truman feared, and Southerners like Frank
Porter Graham were regarded as well-meaning, but errant."[4]

Duncan Gray had both past and present connections with Sewanee. His
father had graduated from the seminary there, as had his grandfather Mc-
Crady. And in the fall of 1952, his uncle, his mother's brother, Edward Mc-
Crady, familiarly known as Ned, was installed as the university's vice chancellor. (At Sewanee, the university administration is headed by a chancellor,
chosen from among the bishops of the dioceses that own the university.
The bishops of those dioceses also serve as members of the university's
board of trustees. The vice chancellor is the chief administrator in the day-
to-day life of the university; the chancellor is something of a figurehead in
that context, although he chairs the board of trustees and certainly is not
without power.)

As for the seminary, St. Luke's, Gray says that as he grew up he "didn't
know there *were* seminaries besides Sewanee. I thought that was it! If you
went to seminary, you went to Sewanee." That long association with Sewanee and his family's connections with it were among Gray's primary reasons for choosing to go there even after he knew that the Episcopal Church
did have other seminaries besides the one at the University of the South.
In terms of his relationship with his uncle Ned, Gray's decision to attend
Sewanee would be a somewhat ironic one, as it would turn out.[5]

In 1950, five young men from Mississippi entered the School of Theology
at Sewanee. The diocese of Mississippi had financial resources that could be
used to support seminarians at Sewanee, but not at other seminaries, another reason for Gray's choice. All five men had served in the war and were
beneficiaries of the GI Bill, but the additional diocesan resources came in
handy. In addition, Gray and one of his fellow Mississippians were married
with one or more children, and the small town of Sewanee was in many
ways a good place for young children.[6]

Married seminarians were a somewhat new thing for seminaries, part of
a postwar phenomenon that went along with the fact that these students,
war veterans, were older than had been the case in the past. At Sewanee
another postwar phenomenon was the housing provided for those students
and their families: surplus army barracks not many steps removed from

camping out. The army sold them to universities for a dollar each after the war. The two-bedroom "apartments" they contained were full of cracks that let in the winter air; the floors had cracks that allowed a glimpse of the ground below, but the units came supplied with heat: a pot-bellied coal-burning stove that sat in the middle of the front room. The university supplied the coal to feed the stoves, dumping it in piles outside each unit in the area dubbed "Woodland Hills." The piles of coal were a joy to young children, who climbed them for such games as "king of the mountain" and came away, according to Ruthie Gray, looking like Appalachian coal miners. Thanks to Gray's training as an engineer, the Gray family moved to a more technologically advanced method of heating. They bought a large electric heater, and Gray did the necessary wiring of the unit to accommodate it. Since their apartment was in the middle of a three-unit complex, neighbors on both sides also appreciated the additional warmth the Gray's heater supplied through the all but paper-thin walls.[7]

The thin walls also made for more "community" than some might have wished. Family conversations—heated or not—carried easily from one unit to the next, but there was "sort of a lady's and gentleman's agreement that you didn't repeat what you might have heard."[8]

The university advised the incoming families that their apartments included an "icebox," then still a common name for a refrigerator. When the students and families arrived, they discovered that "icebox" was no casual misnomer, but a very exact description. The kitchens were too small to have room for the icebox, so it sat on the tiny front porch, and the university also supplied the blocks of ice that cooled the interior, so "you had to go outside to get your milk in the morning, but then of course you didn't really need the icebox in the winter."[9] Because of its altitude, Sewanee has colder winter weather than the area surrounding it, and snows unusual in Chattanooga or Nashville are not uncommon on the Mountain.

"Everybody was in the same boat though, and there were a lot of children there, so we had a good time, a lot of fun, with maybe a tuna fish sandwich and a cup of coffee. You didn't have to 'put on the dog,'" Ruthie recalls. "Nobody had any money. We were living off the GI Bill, and the groceries and necessities took about all we had. It was a big change from the way we had been living when Duncan was working for Westinghouse."[10]

Child number two, Anne, joined the family in February 1952, just after the end of fall semester exams and while Duncan was still finishing papers for his courses. Before the days of disposable diapers and without a clothes dryer, drying Anne's cloth diapers meant hanging them on the line to freeze or drying them inside on a rack in front of the electric heater.

Despite Sewanee's isolation, the local hospital provided an obstetrician-gynecologist, Dr. Betty Kirby-Smith, whose family also had a long connection to Sewanee, and a pediatrician, Dr. Ruth Cameron, whose husband was a member of the Sewanee faculty. Dr. Kirby- Smith was a tough talker who kept her patients in line with her caring, no-nonsense attitude which might include uttering a few four-letter words in an era when ladies didn't ordinarily do such things. Dr. Cameron didn't advertise it, but in an emergency she'd make house calls to see a sick child.[11]

Mrs. George B. Myers, wife of a retired seminary professor, gave regular teas for seminary students and their families. These were command performances for the adults, but Mrs. Myers didn't forget the children and provided special tables and refreshments for them on her lawn, an unusual consideration for the time.

Another wife of a seminary faculty member saw a different need to be filled. Mrs. Bayard Jones, like others, was aware that the war had produced a number of social changes, which might include a change in family backgrounds of seminary students and their wives. Thus she took upon herself the task of instructing the wives in their future role as the helpmeet of an Episcopal clergyman, providing several weeks of sessions for the wives of seminary seniors on the proper way for a clergyman's spouse to dress to go to the grocery store or a tea party. "She told us, 'It doesn't matter that you will be living in genteel poverty. It doesn't matter that you can't afford the finest beef; as long as you polish your silver and use your best china, it will be a lovely meal.' She loved the propriety and formality of the Episcopal Church, and she wanted to make sure that they were carried on," Ruthie remembers. "She was a scream, but it was all well-intentioned and not so out of step with the way things were then. I liked her a lot."[12]

Although Duncan had been out of school for several years, he took readily to being a student again. Entering "juniors," as first-year seminary students were known, were required to take six courses, a total of seventeen hours of course work. The prescribed classes were Introduction to Christian Doctrine, General Christian History, Introduction to the Old Testament, New Testament Greek, Church Music, and Personal Religion, the only course in which Duncan received a B during his first semester. His work in all his other courses earned him A's.[13]

Relations between seminary students and faculty are often close, and Sewanee's isolation tended to foster that closeness. More than twenty-five years before women were ordained in the Episcopal Church, both seminary faculty and students were all men. And because of war service, the average age of seminary students at the time was mid-thirties, not far removed from the age of a number of faculty members.[14] All this contributed to especially close connections between students and faculty.

Gray looked back on his professors of more than fifty years ago with great fondness and appreciation. "I truly believe that the faculty we had from 1950 through 1953 was one of the best faculties—if not *the* best—that The School of Theology has ever had, and I will always be grateful to them for a very special, and, indeed, *exceptional* theological education," he wrote in 2002.[15] Earlier that same spring, when asked to join members of the current and retired seminary faculty in a series of talks entitled "The Theologian Who Has Most Shaped and Influenced Me" at Sewanee's Otey Parish (the town's Episcopal Church), Gray spoke instead about the nine members of the seminary faculty who had been his teachers there. "Otey was having all these scholars, and one would talk about Kierkegaard and one would talk about William Temple and one would talk about Karl Barth, down the line. I was a little uneasy! These other people were professional theologians, and they could cite chapter and verse and what so-and-so said on such-and-such a date. But I decided that I would just talk about *nine* theologians, those faculty members I had when I was in seminary."[16]

Among the nine, two stood out as most important to Gray: Howard A. Johnson and Robert Malcolm McNair. "Those two," Gray says, "were in some ways so totally different, and yet the two of them together made me see the whole picture. They both had a profound influence on me. Howard Johnson was very neo-orthodox, with a heavy emphasis on original sin, the sinfulness of human beings. But he would be *shocked* by people's little minor infractions despite the fact that he was the one telling you all about human sinfulness. Bob McNair was the opposite and a real theological liberal. His attitude was 'Ah, everybody's basically good,' but when people did bad things, he just looked right over it. Howard was very reserved and dignified, and Bob was anything *but*—he was very easy-going."[17]

Johnson, a Kierkegaard scholar, "gave me my theology," Gray says. Johnson taught a series of classes on Christian theology—the Introduction to Christian Doctrine that Gray had his first semester as well as two semesters of the history of Christian thought and a semester of dogmatic theology. Gray called him "a great lecturer."[18]

For Johnson's History of Christian Doctrine, Gray wrote papers on the subjects of creation, human nature, and salvation. From the beginning, hardly a month into the semester, Gray demonstrated a good grasp of theological niceties, earning an A and a comment of "Admirable" from Johnson for the paper entitled "Creation." Less than a month later, a five-page paper on human nature had Johnson asking for a copy from Gray.[19]

In Johnson's written comments on the "Creation" paper, he exhibited the careful kind of reading professors are prone to give new students. He corrected Gray's "seven-day creation" with "literally: *six* days." He responded to Gray's statement that "Genesis goes on to tell us that God was pleased with what he had created" with the comment "No. God said 'It is very good.' There's a nuance of difference." When Gray's prose begins to take flight with the statement, "We can imagine.that, in the beginning, God, in His infinite love of beauty and creation itself, found the existing nothingness lacking and so created the world and the universe as an expression of this love," Johnson cautioned, "This paragraph and the following one are a bit *too* anthropomorphic for me—who normally relishes a vigorous anthropomorphism! All orthodoxy—Greek, Roman, and Protestant—has been concerned to assert God's absolute self-sufficiency. There's nothing 'lacking.' The creation of the world is an act of sheer divine *freedom* and grace. As Archbishop Temple puts it, 'The world minus God = 0. God minus the world = God.'"[20]

As for Gray's theology, it appears that, unlike some entering seminarians, he had no need to struggle with biblical literalism. He began his "Creation" paper with the assertion: "In an inquisitive approach to any subject, we are always concerned with three inevitable questions: What is it? How is it? and Why is it?" and quickly proceeded to explain that, with reference to the first question, as far as Creation is concerned, "Answering this falls in the realm of the natural sciences. We leave it to science to explain the physical and chemical composition of matter." Description, then, falls within the realm of a secular science. But, Gray goes on to say, "It is in answering the question 'How?' that some have imagined a conflict between science and Christian theology. How can one reconcile the story of . . . creation in Genesis with scientific proof that it took thousands and thousands of years for the world to develop into its present state, they ask? The answer, of course, is that Christian theology makes no claim for the scientific accuracy of the story in Genesis. The writer of Genesis was using an ancient myth as a means of setting forth a profound theological truth, namely that creation was by and of the Will of God. Science could never disprove that."

In response to this last paragraph, Johnson adds, "Nor prove. This is a realm which does not lend itself to verification by empirical method."[21]

Gray's second paper for Johnson, on the subject of human nature, was, in a pre-feminist era, typically entitled "Man." Very properly for a seminary student, he began with a rejection of the eighteenth-century English poet Alexander Pope's admonition, "Know thyself, presume not God to scan / The proper study of mankind is Man," and asserted that "the fallacy here is that Man cannot be explained or understood without an understanding of God. Man apart from God is not Man. We cannot separate the creature from his Creator and expect to explain him." From there Gray moved to assert the Christian doctrine of the *imago Dei*: "What makes Man unique among God's creatures was that he only was created in the image of God," and then, to Johnson's great pleasure, Gray not only rejected the idea that this *imago* has something to do with any physical characteristics; he also de-emphasized the notion that it is to be located in some *faculty*, such as the human ability to reason. Gray allowed that "the fact that Man has a will of his own and is able to reason while other creatures cannot seems to be another aspect of the *imago Dei*," but Johnson ignored the faculty claim entirely and instead seized on Gray's assertion that God's image in humans is "expressed in Man's capability to love God and in his ability to appreciate God's creation." Although Johnson cautioned that he "would want to add something about man's capacity for entering into a personal fellowship and loving his neighbor as well as loving God," he continued, "You are wise to have understood (many theologians to the contrary) that the *imago Dei* is a *relational* and not a *substantial* conception. As soon as we grasp that '*imago Dei*' refers not to a faculty or "part" of man, but consists in the whole man's loving and obedient relation to God, then we also grasp that Jesus Christ, being perfectly obedient to the Will of the Father (a Will that is directed always to the loving of the neighbor) is the 'image of the invisible God' (Col.1:15)—i.e. *perfect man*."[22]

Keeping in mind Gray's much later statement that the element of the Episcopal Church's 1979 revision of the 1928 *Book of Common Prayer* he found most troubling was its de-emphasis of human sinfulness, it is interesting to see the consistency between that statement and his 1950 explanation of the human condition. Gray wrote:

All in all, then, Man, of himself, is in a rather lamentable condition. He has fallen far short of fulfilling God's purpose for him. God loves Man, and He had not intended for Man to be lost. Rather God expected Man to return his love and, literally, to return to Him. However, by the exercise of his own God-given freedom, Man has closed the door to the avenue of return. Through this same freedom of choice Man has actually forfeited his freedom by virtually destroying the image of God within himself, which alone could keep him free. This is not to deny that there is goodness in Man. Certainly there is goodness in him, but it is *relative* goodness, not *saving* goodness. This relative goodness cannot in itself approach the fulfillment of God's purpose in

Man. No, with respect to this purpose, Man has reached the point of no return. God, instead, has to take the initiative and come to Man, if this creature is to be saved from himself.[23]

Gray's final first-semester paper for Johnson dealt with the subject of salvation and began with the statement: "Before anyone can become interested in the Christian doctrine of Salvation, he must be aware of two facts: first, that there is something from which he must be saved, or delivered; and second, that he is unable to attain this deliverance without some outside help."

He went on to claim that "the first of these propositions is easy to grasp" because "Man through the centuries has always been aware of the evil in the world.

"The second of these facts," Gray says, "presents a slightly different problem." Using C. S. Lewis's term "the Universal Moral Law" (from Lewis's *The Case for Christianity*), Gray returned to the problem of "relative goodness" that he had mentioned in his earlier paper on human nature. Some, he wrote, would want to argue that the very fact that humans have moral consciousness and some awareness of the Universal Moral Law is "proof enough that Man himself has the capacity to conquer evil."

Such an assumption, he pointed out, "has to be based on the confidence that human nature, essentially the same for these many thousand years, will, someday, suddenly take a turn for the better and begin the steep ascent toward perfection."

"Improbable" as such an event might be, "even if it did happen, this so-called state of perfection would be limited to the precepts of Lewis' Universal Moral Law." Such "perfection" would still fall short, he notes, of the radical ethic Jesus sets out in the Sermon on the Mount: "But I say to you, Love your enemy and pray for those who persecute you. . . . Be perfect, therefore, as your heavenly Father is perfect" (Matthew 5:43, 48; New Revised Standard Version). In the face of this demand, Gray says, "we are left in despair" as the result of our inability to fulfill it. "Here, and here only," he says, "is where the Christian Gospel can step in. It is only when Man has come to the full realization of his impossible situation that the Gospel is really the 'good news' that he seeks."

The "good news," Gray continued, is that "this God, who is the High and Mighty Ruler of the Universe, is also a God of love" who "offers us the *gift* of deliverance, or salvation . . . since he knows that we can never *earn* this salvation. . . . All that is left for us to do is accept it." It is faith, he says, that makes such acceptance possible; indeed, "the measure of our acceptance is our faith."

But once again, "the root of all our sin is our desire to bridge the gulf between God and Man by exalting Man to the position of God," but by attempting this, "we have only widened the gulf.

"Therefore, it remained for God to build this bridge. This he did by self-humiliation; by becoming man."

Gray continued, "But the bridge was actually built in the Atonement at the Cross. Christ became 'at-one' with us and died for us. Quoting from the 1928 *Book of Common* Prayer, Gray wrote, "He made a 'full, perfect, and sufficient sacrifice, oblation, and satisfaction for the sins of the whole world.' Thus, over 1900 years ago, our sins were forgiven through Christ's death on the Cross. It remains only for us to accept this forgiveness."

But at this point, Johnson, whose interjections into Gray's papers had become rare this late in the semester, perhaps because he had gained confidence in his student's theological acumen, commented, "Christmas is already God identifying Himself with us; the at-one-ment begins here, to reach its culmination in his identifying Himself with us in our sin, our guilt, our estrangement, our fear of death."

Unaware of this theological bobble as he wrote, Gray continued his development of the theme of sin and salvation by stating that it is human acceptance of God's forgiveness "that makes salvation current as well as past. Christ died for us then, but He dies again for us each day that we live. No day passes that we do not need forgiveness. Likewise, no day passes in which it is not available, if we will but accept it"

Gray cautioned, however, that this always-available forgiveness does not imply license, but instead "is based on the assumption that our repentance is sincere and that we will try to grow in holiness." Such growth, he declared, must issue in good works "as the Bible calls them," or as Gray proposes, "Christian activities."

Building toward his conclusion, Gray wrote, "We can see that [the] faith required for acceptance of salvation has tremendous ramifications. How easy it would be for us to lose sight of most of them!" It is for this reason, he continued, that Jesus "commissioned the Church as His divine instrument for keeping the true faith in its full meaning ever before us, as well as for spreading the 'good news.'" And it is the church, Gray reminded his reader, which "was also entrusted with the administration of the Sacraments which Christ had ordained. These Sacraments are the means for Man's spiritual nourishment, which Christ realized was essential for Man's acceptance of the gift of salvation. Sinful Man is not capable of . . . true acceptance [of forgiveness and thus salvation] without the aid of Christ's Spirit within him," and, in the sacramental tradition of which Gray was a part, it is those sacraments that feed that Spirit.

Gray concluded,

> Thus, we have seen that our salvation was offered to us upon the Cross, but the acceptance of it is a continual process. It is certain that regardless of how sincere our daily repentance is and how complete God's daily forgiveness is, we will need both of these again tomorrow. We are perpetual sinners, and, as such, we can never attain full communion with God [in this life].
>
> But salvation implies *deliverance* from sin and evil. This can only mean that those who willingly accept God's gift may expect to achieve this full communion only after death. It means that they can expect to conquer death even as Christ did and rise to the life immortal.
>
> What the exact nature of this life after death may be, no man can say, but Christians feel certain that it is therein that God's ultimate purpose in creating the universe will be fulfilled. There those who have accepted God's gift of salvation will know the full meaning of communion with God.[24]

During the spring of 1952, Johnson continued his dialogue with Gray in Johnson's Dogmatic Theology course. In Gray's paper "The Person and Work of Jesus Christ," he wrote that "the Incarnation was designed to reveal to Man the nature and will of God" and added, "we may break this work down into three categories. 1) We are made to understand what God intended Man to be. 2) We are made to understand what Man actually is. 3) We are shown what God has done and will do to bridge the gap between 1) and 2)."

As he did in his first-semester paper on salvation, Gray argued that "the real 'good news' of the Gospel is that God wills to *accept* Man as perfect, however imperfect he may be. God wills to consider Man as righteous under certain minimal conditions: sincere, heartfelt repentance."

But, he continued, "God's love is such that He is not willing to leave this repentance entirely to Man. Instead through the Incarnation He does all that is possible to elicit this repentance without violating Man's freedom."

It is God's revelation of himself in Jesus, which is meant to show humans what God has intended for us to be and to show us how far short of God's intention we fall, that is designed to elicit the repentance that God desires. "But lest this be insufficient," Gray added, " God reveals His infinite love in the very offer of forgiveness and by that love thus demonstrated [in the Incarnation and crucifixion] serves to bring Man to repentance."

Gray's statement elicited an enthusiastic response from the neo-orthodox Johnson, who, at the end of term, "somewhere between Honolulu and Wake" Island, on his way to Japan to lecture on Kierkegaard, wrote, "Thank you for seeing this point. It is incredible that God should love us, incredible that he should be willing to forgive on so minimal a condition as heartfelt contrition. Still more incredible, then, that he should do that in history which has the power to evoke that contrition! Incredible love; in reality, therefore, God puts up no conditions from His side. The only conditions are those that are implicit in human nature itself. That is, where there is no consciousness of sin, there is no sense of contrition, and where contrition is lacking, God's offer of forgiveness goes unheeded—or else is taken in vain. So God—how wonderful—does everything: in Christ he brings sin into the open, makes it show itself as enmity with God—then God, in spite of this, shows His love, and thus hatred of sin and love of God are all born simultaneously."[25]

Johnson's admiration for Gray's work continued until the end of their academic relationship. On both of Gray's last two papers, Johnson recommended the collection of Gray's essays into a book. In fact, on the penultimate paper, "The Resurrection, Ascension, and Pentecost," Johnson wrote, "The papers you have written for Theology 1, 4, and 5 [Introduction to Theology and Dogmatic Theology] when put together and edited very slightly, would make a valuable book for the laity . . . and for professors of theology."[26]

As we have noted, Gray said it was Howard Johnson who "gave" him his theology, and their student-teacher relationship is well documented in Gray's papers and Johnson's responses to them. But it was probably Robert McNair, the seminary's professor of ethics, who had a greater impact on Gray's ministry in the succeeding years. The Reverend Davis Carter, perhaps Gray's closest friend among his seminary classmates, said of him and McNair, "They were thick as thieves during our second and third years."[27]

McNair was among the seminary professors not far removed from his war veteran students in age. McNair had graduated from Wake Forest College in 1937, and then at Harvard earned a degree in systematic theology in 1941, and a PhD in anthropology in 1948. McNair's anthropological interest was in American Indian culture, particularly Navajo culture. Long before contemporary interest in Native American culture as an alternative to or a valuable supplement to Euro-American culture, McNair frequently presented his students with such comparisons.

But the students' first experience with McNair came their first semester in their first New Testament course. McNair announced to his students at the beginning of the semester that they would read all of that portion of the Bible three times through before the semester was over. "Bob Mc-Nair was certainly not above giving tests—and I mean plain old content tests. Nothing about the meaning or anything, but who did what when and where," Gray recalls. "We kidded him and he kidded us about those tests. We felt like we were being treated like kids! We said, 'Bob, we're not first graders!' He said, 'Let's see how well you do on them before you start complaining.'

"But I'll always be grateful to him though because he really made me *read* the New Testament, quite apart from exegesis or interpretation, just the facts. We thanked him for it in the end, but in the beginning we thought it was terrible."[28]

In addition to the seminary's introductory New Testament course, Mc-Nair also taught Christian ethics and moral theology, which was his field. "We talked quite a bit about the desegregation issue in those courses!" Gray recalls. It was McNair who recommended that Gray read the Swedish sociologist and economist Gunner Myrdal's *An American Dilemma: The Negro Problem and Modern Democracy*, the 1944 groundbreaking study of U.S. race relations. The book had a profound impact on Gray, as it did on other Americans of the time. Myrdal described America's "Negro problem" as, in reality, "the white man's problem" because whites oppressed blacks and then tended to cite statistics on blacks' poor performance on a variety of measures as evidence of their inferiority. Myrdal, however, was relatively optimistic that America could solve its "dilemma" because he thought that American democracy and the "American creed" that all are created equal could eventually result in a triumph over racism as blacks managed to improve their situation and whites were cured of their prejudices.

Much of the most important part of Gray's relationship with McNair took place outside the classroom, however, including visits to the Grays' apartment. Gray says, "When I think of Bob I don't think of him nearly as much as a professor, as a teacher—although he certainly was that—but I think of him more in terms of our relationship working together at Christ Episcopal Church in South Pittsburg and of the sort of pastoral pattern he had for his priestly ministry there and the conversations we'd have driving down and back."[29]

It was because of McNair's South Pittsburg connection that Gray met Judge John T. Raulston, who had presided over the Scopes trial. Raulston was an old and sick man by the early 1950s, and when McNair and Gray paid pastoral visits on the judge and his wife, who were members of Christ Church, it was Mrs. Raulston who did most of the talking. Her observations about the trial had less to do with its legal than its personal aspects. Her view of Clarence Darrow, who represented Scopes in the trial, was not favorable. "She didn't like the way he *dressed*, the way he *acted*—he was *not* a Southern gentleman! Bob and I joked about it afterward: 'No wonder the trial turned out the way it did! She wouldn't have let the judge rule in favor of Darrow!'"[30]

McNair's theological liberalism was matched by his political liberalism. He was a frequent visitor at Myles Horton's Highlander Folk School, then just down the road from Sewanee in Summerfield, Tennessee, and Gray was his frequent companion on these trips. Highlander is best known as the place that helped provide Rosa Parks with the spark she needed to refuse to give up her bus seat in Montgomery, Alabama—an action that, of course, resulted in the Montgomery Bus Boycott, which provided Dr. Martin Luther King Jr. his first opportunity for civil rights leadership. Gray frequently accompanied McNair on his trips to Highlander, and thus was exposed to the ideas and energy of people like Horton who had been strongly influenced by the Christian social gospel movement and theologian Reinhold Niebuhr. In its early decades, Horton and other Highlanders had been active in the labor movement, but as racial issues assumed a higher profile after World War II, they moved in that direction.

During the summer after Gray's first year at Sewanee, he was "lay-reader in charge" at All Saints' Church in Tupelo, Mississippi, a small town in the northeastern part of the state. That gave him a taste of what parish ministry might be like; during his second summer, Gray ranged more widely. He sought experience in the missionary field through a program coordinated by Virginia Theological Seminary (VTS) in Alexandria. Along with five others in the program, Gray was assigned to Cuba. The summer produced a thick notebook of field notes and eventually, at McNair's insistence, a senior-year thesis that earned Gray an *optima merens* ("deserving highest honor") degree.

About the missionary experience, Gray says, "I was thinking about some overseas work. In one sense I had a commitment to the diocese of Mississippi—in a real sense—but there was always a little concern that coming back and being under your dad might not be the best thing. The idea of the program was to help recruit some folks who would go do the missionary work after graduation and ordination."[31]

Besides Cuba, VTS offered placement in other countries such as the Dominican Republic and Mexico, but all were Spanish-speaking cultures and

Gray, unlike his fellow students, had no Spanish. He worked diligently on his Spanish, but his lack of fluency was probably the reason that he was assigned to Santiago, an area with a diverse population composed of Hispanic Cubans, Anglos who worked for the U.S. or British governments and corporations, and Cuban descendents of African slaves brought to the British West Indies, particularly Jamaica, in the early sixteenth century. These last, who prized their ability to speak some English, had immigrated to Cuba, mostly to the Santiago area, because although pre-revolutionary Cuba was a poor and unequal society, it still offered more opportunity for agricultural workers than did the desperately poor and overpopulated Jamaica of the day. In any case, the attitudes of these three groups—Hispanics, Anglos, and Jamaicans—toward each other and the history of their presence in Cuba gave Gray an opportunity to observe racial, ethnic, and cultural prejudice at firsthand outside the United States.

He worked in Santiago under the supervision of the Reverend Milton LeRoy, who served three congregations: one Hispanic, one Anglo, and one British West Indian. He also visited West Indians living in desperate poverty on the plantations of the countryside. In his thesis, Gray observed that racial barriers in Cuba were far more subtle than the Jim Crow of the United States, but he also noted that LeRoy's Anglo congregation was clearly "the white folks' church.

"I'm not going to say that they had a *barrier*, and occasionally a West Indian would come, but these were folks who were in the local consulate or in American or British business—but it probably was because of that congregation that the church could support its work with the other congregations."[32]

The racial/ethnic hierarchy of 1950s Cuba was complicated: whites considered Haitians to be at the bottom of the social pile, while British West Indians were considered to be superior to all other Cuban blacks. Hispanics, in turn, looked down on blacks. Cuba of the day embodied the expression "If you're white, you're all right. If you're brown, stick around. If you're black, get back." Even so, some of Gray's experiences with Santiago's diversity and its inhabitants' attitudes left him puzzled. He remembers one incident in particular in which a Cuban of mixed ancestry sat in LeRoy's study and "lit into Batista," then president of Cuba. "This guy was running Batista down, and he kept calling him '*negro, negro.*' He was opposed to Batista because he said Batista was '*negro,*' and this guy looked like he was half '*negro*' himself. Now that's weird. It wasn't just the whites in that Santiago congregation; it was the native Cubans, the Hispanics too. There was prejudice there—not among everyone, but it was there. I guess that just suggested to me that racism may be at its worst in Mississippi, but it's not limited to Mississippi by any means.

"Oriente, the province where Santiago is, was also the area of Cuba with the highest percentage of blacks. You went to Havana, for example, and it was much different. But you can *see* Jamaica from the coast of Oriente, and many Jamaicans had migrated there. I know this is no excuse, no reason in a sense, but just like in Mississippi and the rest of the South as well, where there was the highest concentration of black people, other peoples' feelings were strongest when it came to integration and civil rights."[33]

Both Gray's supervisors, LeRoy and the Reverend William A. Clebsch, the team leader from VTS, were enthusiastic about his performance in his internship.

Clebsch, in his official appraisal of Gray's work, wrote:

> Everything which might be said in a report on Gray can be summed up in the statement that for the aims and methods of the program, he is a natural. His judgment is considered and sound, his motivations deep and healthy, his understanding of himself and his own reactions incisive but never preoccupying, his adaptation to strange circumstances thorough without loss of purpose, his work steady and constructive, his analysis of difficult situations penetrating and positive; to all of this is added a fine commitment to the Christian Gospel which is coupled with rare abilities to witness imaginatively and effectively. In my associations during the past several years with several hundred theological students, I have met none who so adequately combines the features which our generation and the Christian Message to it demand in ministers. In one area alone does this endorsement need qualification: Gray was adequate, far above average, under the circumstances, in his grasp and use of the Spanish language; yet his failure to speak and understand completely preyed on his mind and conscience unduly to the point that he was led to exorbitant self-incrimination as lazy, slovenly, unintelligent.[34]

Clebsch added that "in several instances" Gray learned more about Cuban life and "gained understanding of certain attitudes more clearly than his supervisor, and this by the supervisor's admission." Clebsch went on to quote from LeRoy's report on Gray:

> "[He shows] tremendous ability to adjust to strange situations. This was the thing that stood out from the rest of his personality from the

moment I met him to the end of the summer. It is not shown by a casual acceptance of the status quo, but recognizing the situation or the person as he is, he also recognizes how they should be. His adjustment is not just acquiescence, but acceptance with a view to change. . . . [T]he only recommendation I have (for help in the future) is that he could stand to have a higher estimate of himself. This will not be a real problem, but he could be helped if he had more confidence in the native ability which he has. . . . This lack of aggressiveness is not dangerous, but it is a definite lack that may mark the effectiveness of his ministry. My judgment is that it is due to a lack of self-confidence."[35]

LeRoy concluded, again with uncommon foresight, "He would be of tremendous service in a situation where the people had never really felt a close pastoral love. It would be interesting to see if his love of God's children could make him fight for them."[36]

Whether Clebsch's and LeRoy's assessment of Gray's self-confidence and its possible consequences for his ministry was the best judgment at the time we cannot know. Clearly it is not the only way to interpret his behavior. We might instead understand it as the natural result of a highly self-aware and conscientious young man trying out his wings in a situation very different in many ways from what he had experienced before. We should also recall the constant biblical emphasis on humility as a virtue and Jesus' words in the parable of the great dinner as told in Luke's gospel: "All who exalt themselves will be humbled and those who humble themselves will be exalted" (Luke 14:11).

In any case, at the end of the summer Gray left Cuba on a flight for Miami and then caught a train to Pensacola. There Ruthie was waiting for him, their children safely stowed with his and Ruthie's parents while the young couple had a few days of reunion after their more than two-month separation.

"I didn't give up the idea of mission work, and I stayed in touch with the folks in Cuba. I was still thinking about the possibility—not going off to Africa, but maybe Central America; Cuba would have been fine. But once I got back to Sewanee and school started, that idea fast faded into the background. I think I would have ended up doing what I did anyway, but once I really found out what had been going on at Sewanee over the summer, I didn't reflect for too long a time about foreign mission work. I decided pretty well early in the semester that I was going back to Mississippi."[37]

CHAPTER 6

"FAITH CAN MOVE MOUNTAINS"

University of the South, 1953

T HE SUMMER OF 1952 had indeed been eventful at Sewanee, and, as Gray indicated, the "events" continued throughout Gray's senior year at the seminary. He was one of those deeply involved in them, and the experience did shape him for the rest of his life, especially during his more than twenty years of parish ministry. Of those events at Sewanee during 1952–53, church historian Donald S. Armentrout writes, "In the history of The School of Theology of The University of the South, no period was more tumultuous or far reaching in its effects than the 'integration crisis' of the nineteen-fifties. . . . The controversy was given national publicity, personal and institutional reputations were tarnished, and eight members of the School of Theology faculty, including the dean, resigned their positions."[1]

What became the "integration crisis" at Sewanee during the 1952–53 academic year had actually had its origins in the fall of 1950, just a few weeks after Gray had started seminary. It began in Jacksonville, Florida, on October 3, 1950, when the Executive Council of the Diocese of Florida met. At that meeting, "the question was raised as to the possibility of securing Negro Clergy to fill existing vacancies in the diocese."[2]

This need for "Negro Clergy" was itself rooted in history. The Episcopal Church was the only major Protestant denomination that did not formally split over the issue of slavery and secession during the Civil War. During the war, a temporary organization known as the Protestant Episcopal Church in the Confederate States was set up to carry out the denomination's work in the South, but once the war was over, it quickly merged back into the national church. Even during the war, Northern bishops and Confederate generals prayed for each other, and in 1862, at the church's General Convention in New York, the names of Southern bishops were included in the roll call.[3]

This historical situation was not, of course, the result of an agreement between Southern church people and their Northern brethren over the issues, but instead largely the result of the power of a common liturgy and a national hierarchy. One somewhat accidental consequence of the history, however, was that up until the latter part of the twentieth century, the Episcopal Church included a significant number of African American parishes, especially in the South, which in the late nineteenth and the first half of the twentieth century were traditionally staffed by African American clergy. While enslaved African Americans had attended their slave masters' parishes before Emancipation, after they became free, some formed their own parishes, which persisted through the Jim Crow era. It was only with the advent of the Civil Rights Movement and a move toward integrating churches that these African American parishes began to die out. As was often the case in other areas of society—for example, public schools—"integration" often meant closing black parishes as a way of encouraging African Americans to attend, and integrate, white parishes. The eventual result of that policy was the loss of many African Americans from the Episcopal Church.

In 1950, when Florida's Executive Council considered the issue of a dwindling supply of black clergy, its Archdeacon for Negro Work James K. Satterville spoke in favor of the creation of a seminary to train black clergy, since the denomination's only such seminary, Bishop Payne Divinity School in Petersburg, Virginia, had closed the previous year.[4] After much discussion, the council adopted a resolution that requested its delegates to the Provincial Synod, meeting later that month, to ask that the Province appoint a committee to consider "the desirability of re-establishing a Theological Seminary in this Province for Negro candidates for the Ministry." When the Synod met October 10 and 11, 1950, it voted to forward the resolution to the Province's Department of Christian Social Relations with a request that they study the matter and report back to next meeting of the synod the following year.[5]

In its report to the 1951 Province meeting, the Department of Christian Social Relations stated, "The Department of Christian Social Relations sums up its thinking that it would not be desirable or advisable to establish a segregated seminary for theological education in our Province. But it thinks it desirable and advisable that it should open existing seminaries in the South to students of all races."[6]

The report and its recommendation were approved by a vote of sixty-six to twenty-five, and the secretary of the province was instructed to inform the University of the South, the only Episcopal seminary in the Province, of its action.[7]

As it turned out, members of the School of Theology community had anticipated the Provincial Synod by several months in their discussion of the issue of desegregating the seminary and had even approved the concept of admitting African Americans to the seminary. Donald Armentrout writes of a meeting between members of the seminary community and the owning bishops that took place during the June 1951 commencement period: "According to the Right Reverend Duncan M. Gray Jr., retired seventh bishop of Mississippi, every member of the seminary present voted approval to the proposition to receive Negroes into The School of Theology. Furthermore, all of the bishops present—with the exception of Bishop Frank A. Juan of Florida, Bishop R. Bland Mitchell of Arkansas, and Bishop John M. Walker of Atlanta—approved the proposition along with the faculty."[8]

About eighteen months later, when the concept of desegregation had come closer to becoming a reality, another view of the same meeting was presented to Vice-Chancellor McCrady. In a letter dated August 19, 1952, Dr. Bayard Hale Jones, an older member of the seminary faculty, wrote,

The session of the Bishops with the Theological Faculty on June 7 [1951] discussed the question of admission of Negro students with considerable outspokenness. Bishop [Charles Colcock Jones] Carpenter [of Alabama] brought out the undeniable point that to admit a Negro to the School of Theology was to admit him to the University. He could not, for example, be debarred from the College dances; and drew a picture of Negro dancing [sic] "cheek to cheek with one of our innocent little girls from Alabama." The picture naturally revolted everybody without exception; though the doctrinaires on the Theological Faculty seem to have elected to blame it all off on the Bishop of Alabama's lack of taste in dwelling relishingly on the "cheek to cheek" concept (which might indeed have been omitted as a somewhat improbable extreme), instead of considering that the bishop was clearly right on his essential position.[9]

By the time Jones wrote his letter to McCrady about the 1951 meeting, debate over the issue of integrating the seminary had heated up considerably in Sewanee and elsewhere. In June 1952, the Province's "Report and Resolution Regarding Negro Theological Education" was brought before a meeting of the university's trustees, at which there was a record attendance of sixty-five of the eligible ninety-six board members, including fifteen of its twenty-seven bishops. The group debated the report and resolution in closed session for three hours, and then approved the following resolution by a vote of forty-five to twelve:

> Resolved, that the Trustees of the University of the South inform the Synod of the Fourth Province that there is nothing in the ordinances of the University to prevent the admission of Negroes, or men of any other race, to the School of Theology, but that the trustees are of the opinion that the encouragement of such students now is inadvisable for the following reasons:
>
> 1. We are informed by several legal authorities that such action would be in violation of the statutes of the State of Tennessee.
> 2. The School of Theology at Sewanee, unlike most of our theological schools, is not a separate and self-controlled institution, but is part of the University both in administration and social life; and therefore must consider the whole life of the University community which is located on an isolated domain.
>
> Therefore, we are of the opinion that furtherance of the Church's work and the happiness and mutual good will of both races will not now be served by the action requested by the Synod.[10]

On the day following the trustees' meeting, the seminary faculty had its annual meeting with the bishops who were present for the trustees' meeting. Jones, McCrady's letter writer later in the year, and Howard Johnson, Gray's theology professor, were absent, Johnson because he was on his way to Japan for his Kierkegaard lectures. Those faculty present, however, strongly objected to the trustees' vote. Two days later, eight of the faculty met again twice, once in the afternoon and again in the evening, to discuss the trustees' action and to frame their response. As Armentrout notes, that response made four major points: the trustees had failed to state any Christian principle to support their decision, which, instead, the faculty said, was based solely on expediency; the trustees' action was untenable in the light of a 1948 statement by the world-wide Anglican Communion meeting at its once-a-decade gathering in England: "The Christian Church . . . demands essential human rights for all, irrespective of race or colour. . . . We pledge ourselves to work for the removal of . . . injustice and oppression"; the trustees' statement implied that ministry to African Americans was of no concern to the university; and finally, that the trustees' action had undermined the faculty's effectiveness as teachers and as priests.[11]

The faculty's response went on to make three requests: a reconsideration of the issue by the trustees; a public acknowledgment of that reconsideration; a trustee statement in support of the 1948 Anglican resolution and an accompanying declaration that the trustees were prepared to admit African Americans to the seminary.

If the trustees were unwilling to meet these requests, the eight (of nine seminary faculty) wrote, they were all prepared "to resign our positions and terminate our connection with the University in June 1953." Those who signed the statement were F. Craighill Brown, dean of the seminary; Robert M. Grant, professor of Old Testament; R. Lansing Hicks, associate professor of New Testament; Robert M. McNair, assistant professor of Christian ethics and moral theology; J. Allen Reddick, assistant professor of church history; Claude E. Guthrie, instructor in practical theology; Richard Wilmer, chaplain and professor of English Bible; and Frederick Q. Shafer, head of the department of religion in the college.[12]

At that point the "crisis" began. Gray, who was president of the seminary student body during his senior year and thus had an up-close view of events as they unfolded, said that when he compared Sewanee's "integration crisis" with his experience in Mississippi during the civil rights struggle of the 1950s and '60s, the only element missing at Sewanee was deadly violence. (There were, however, reports of attacks by Sewanee undergraduates on seminary students.) Gray wrote, "First, during that senior year, I heard every argument possible for preserving *segregation* in all areas of public life, but especially in our schools and our colleges. I was *prepared* for every argument that I every heard in the next twenty years back in Mississippi. There was nothing new.

"Second, during those two decades of racial strife [in Mississippi], I watched the opponents of integration resort over and over again to criticism of the 'methods' and 'motivations' of those advocating change rather than dealing with the issue itself—just as so many of the trustees and regents, and the administration itself, had done in my senior year. And certainly, over and over again, the real issue was evaded by attacking the character and personal behavior of those on the side of integration—just as had happened on 'the Mountain' in 1952–53."[13]

The first clash over "methods" and "motivations" came Tuesday, June 10, the day after the faculty had wired their response to Bishop Mitchell of Arkansas, who was chancellor of the University and one of the bishops who had voted against the proposal to approve in principle the admission of blacks to the School of Theology in 1951. Mitchell had left for his home in Little Rock late in the day on Monday and had driven all night. The faculty sent their statement to his office around 2:30 a.m. on Tuesday. The telegram was in turn delivered to Mitchell's home around 9:00 a.m., but Mitchell was sleeping late after his long drive, and his wife decided not to wake him. Mitchell did not see it until later in the day.

Shortly after the telegram had arrived at Mitchell's house, however, Chaplain Wilmer had telephoned the home of the Very Reverend James Pike, then dean of the Cathedral of St. John the Divine in New York City, and asked him to handle release of the statement in New York. Pike's wife took over the task and contacted the *New York Times*, the *Herald Tribune*, and the Associated Press. A member of the *New York Times* staff quickly contacted the *Chattanooga Times*, owned by the same company that owned the *New York Times*, and talked to Charles Puckette, a *Chattanooga Times* officer and a member of the seminary's Board of Regents. Puckette immediately called Vice-Chancellor McCrady about the statement, which McCrady had received by hand from Lansing Hicks, the seminary's Old Testament professor, a little earlier that morning. McCrady told Puckette that he needed time to "digest" the statement.

Meanwhile, the press contacted Chancellor Mitchell for a response to the faculty's statement. At that point he had not read the telegraphed statement, and he, like McCrady, reacted predictably to reporters contacting him about a statement addressed to him by the seminary faculty that he had not even seen. When the faculty learned of the mishap, they wired Mitchell an apology, and Dean Brown personally apologized to McCrady. But the awkward sequence of events clearly did nothing to bring the disagreeing parties closer together.

The press reported the story on Wednesday, June 11.[14]

By then Mitchell had issued a statement to the Associated Press in which he said that he was in full support of the trustees' June 7 resolution. Noting that the seminary faculty response to the trustees' action "appears to be based on press reports and without benefit of the full text of the resolution," Mitchell went on to say about the situation:

> The Christian principles involved are fairly obvious to my way of thinking, and I feel sure that my thinking is not at variance with that of the faculty members. . . .
>
> It is on the practical application of Christian principles to the particular situation at Sewanee that the faculty take issue with the action of the Board of Trustees. Christian men can agree on the principles and disagree on the method or timeliness of applying those principles; and that seems to be the situation in this instance.

I am mindful of the Christian spirit which moved these men. I think the Board is profoundly aware of the Church's need for training Negro clergy in the South for work in the South and of the great field for work among Negro people. . . .

Nobody could be more anxious for the right answer than I am. And I think the Board of Trustees is just as anxious for the right solution as are the members of the theological faculty.[15]

On the following day, McCrady issued his own statement, which read in part: "None of us can know with absolute certainty what the ultimate solution of the many complicated problems connected with race relations in the United States will be. We can only pray that Divine guidance will help us to better judgments than we by ourselves know how to make. After as conscientious and prayerful consideration of the subject as I was able to make, I feel deeply convinced that the action taken was in the best interests of both races."[16]

It is difficult to judge McCrady's sincerity, both in this statement and in his conduct throughout the controversy over integration of the seminary. One can certainly say that at the very least he was *careful;* none of the surviving documents from this period exhibits the animosity and sharpness of tone that some of Bishop Mitchell's private letters and confidential memos do.[17] At the minimum, McCrady was cool under fire. And there was no doubt as to his intelligence. About McCrady, however, David Vance Guthrie's assessment is sharp: "There is no question as to his loyalty and devotion to the Episcopal Church, nor of the brilliance of his mind." But, he adds, "Nor was there any question of McCrady's white supremacist notions, his ego of no mean proportion, or of his willingness to go to Machiavellian lengths to achieve his and the Trustees' purposes."[18]

Mitchell's and McCrady's statements were duly picked up by the secular press, and, as Armentrout notes, that press "as a whole generally supported the position taken by the faculty."[19] By late June, the Episcopal press had gotten onto the story, and it proceeded to condemn the trustees' action in no uncertain terms. In a June 29 editorial, *Episcopal Churchnews* said the trustees should reconsider their decision. Of the trustees' resolution, the publication's editors said, "Can there be language strong enough to describe the heart-breaking damage that the Sewanee trustees did to the church's position and that of the Episcopal Church in particular on June 6?"[20] In another Episcopal publication, the *Living Church*, a signed editorial by well-known Mississippi editor Hodding Carter, himself an Episcopalian, termed the faculty's action "courageous" and said of the trustees that they were "apparently unwilling to listen to the Church's own words," a reference to both the Lambeth and the Province IV resolutions.

It was from that June 29 issue of the *Living Church* that Gray, working as a summer intern in Santiago, Cuba, first learned of the actions of the trustees and faculty. "I was not totally surprised by either the [trustees'] action or the [faculty's] response, but I was especially proud of the faculty, and I vowed even then to support them in any way that I could [upon return to the seminary in the fall]."[21]

In the meantime, many words were penned and exchanged. In a long letter that Bishop Charles Clingman of Kentucky, the chair of the seminary's Board of Regents, wrote to the School of Theology faculty, he said that "in the friendliest spirit" he "would like to make certain comments," comments which, according to Armentrout, "summarized the thoughts and feelings of many Sewanee people and administrators."[22] First, Clingman accused the seminary faculty of basing their statement "on an erroneous account [of the trustees' actions], derived from irresponsible conversation or garbled newspaper reports." He proceeded to state that he "subscribe[d] heartily to the Lambeth resolution," and did "not feel that my affirmative vote on the Trustees' resolution of June 8th is inconsistent with that position," since he believed that the resolution "did not close the door to future consideration of this whole subject," as he "so stated before the vote was taken."

From there, Clingman did go on to attack the faculty's "methods." He wrote,

> In my opinion, your letter would have been received favorably and with no little support by a majority of the Trustees if it had not been for your closing statement. A threat—especially a threat which actually promises to sabotage a great institution—ill becomes men in your position. This has done far more harm to the School of Theology and to the whole University than the action of the Board of Trustees.
>
> You say, "the action of the Trustees undermines our effectiveness as teachers of the Christian faith and way of life." What about your threat, which virtually says to 80 seminary men and 400 college students, "If you wish to have your way, make a threat, a threat of sabotage"? I am sure you have heard of "the mote and beam."[23]

The university's historiographer Arthur Ben Chitty wrote of the situation: "Life has been difficult for the members of the St. Luke's faculty since their declaration of dissatisfaction with the action of the trustees on June 6. Their taking the protest to the public press was interpreted locally as disloyalty to the institution, and feeling against them mounted accordingly. In private conversation they have referred to 'persecution' and 'character assassination' as censure from their neighbors and from parts of the owning dioceses became more conspicuous. Support for their principles has been less vocal than condemnation of their action."[24]

The exchanges continued throughout July. That month's issue of the *Episcopal Churchnews* carried another long editorial on the subject which began, "Sewanee is going to be in the news for a long time to come. If the Trustees, who voted 45 to 12 to keep the doors of the theological school locked in the face of Negro applicants, thought their timid, arid, and expedient 'solution' would avoid tumult and controversy, they grossly underestimated the vitality of the Christian conscience. The kettle is boiling at Sewanee and boiling beyond the University of the South. There will be no tranquility until the issue is settled and settled right by a complete about-face on the part of the Trustees."[25]

But tranquility seemed within somewhat closer reach when a special meeting of the seminary's Board of Regents was called for July 28–30, at which the regents were to meet with Dean Brown and the seminary's faculty. Although, as it turned out, Brown was unable to attend the meeting because his doctor had ordered him to rest, the meeting produced statements from both groups, regents and faculty, headed by a joint statement declaring that both parties thought that their statements "went far toward" representing "a meeting of minds" and they promised "a continuing study of the subject."[26]

In their statement, the regents said that they had "welcomed the opportunity for full discussion with the faculty members" and that both sides felt "assured of the cooperative and harmonious operation of the School of Theology during the coming academic year." In addition, the statement noted that the Chancellor (Bishop Mitchell) "announced that he is appointing a special committee of the Board of Trustees to study the subject and assemble information and opinions to be put into the hands of the Trustees prior to their next meeting" in June 1953.[27]

Thus what came to be known as the Penick Committee, after its chair Bishop Edwin Penick of North Carolina, was formed.

The faculty responded that they welcomed the news that the admission of African Americans would receive "full study" and the further consideration of the trustees. In addition, they wrote, "We wish to clarify our original statement of June ninth with the explanation that we intended our statement concerning resignations not as an ultimatum of eight people acting as a corporate pressure group threatening the University but as an expression of the deepest personal convictions of eight individuals; and we shall continue to act in the light of individual conscience."[28]

When students returned to the seminary in September, "things seemed remarkably calm," Gray recalled. "Certainly we talked with our professors about the controversy, but this was almost always *outside* the classroom. Classes went on as scheduled, and most of us—faculty and students alike— seemed to be in good spirits. The situation could have been described as 'normal.'"[29]

Gray continued,

> Of course, the overwhelming majority of those of us in the seminary community were not aware in these early days of much that had gone on during the summer months. Certainly, we knew that members of the university administration, as well as many regents and trustees, were much concerned about the way the faculty had gone about their protest—their methodology, if you will—and we had heard much criticism along these lines. But we also knew that the faculty had apologized for the way some of these things had been handled, and we assumed that all this was being worked out.
>
> Then we began to hear rumors, rumors of gross misbehavior on the part of certain faculty members and rumors of seminarians who had left, or were leaving, St. Luke's because of such behavior. Then came word of the ultimatum to Dr. Robert Grant, and the mood of the entire community soon changed radically. An academic year of strife and turmoil had begun.[30]

As McCrady reported confidentially to trustees and regents early in the fall, Grant had been instructed to look for a job elsewhere "on account of repeated public drunkenness, serious enough to make him unable to walk without assistance." Grant, McCrady wrote his boards, "admitted the charges fully."[31]

Seminary students had a somewhat different view of the situation though.

Gray compiled a narrative entitled "On the Sewanee Situation," dated October 31, 1952. In there he wrote,

> The faculty action of June 9 precipitated a violent reaction in certain quarters. Persons who were enraged at the action began to turn up with stories of misconduct on the part of three faculty members: Dr. Grant, Dr. McNair and Dr. Reddick. These stories were brought to the

attention of the vice chancellor by Regent Kemper Williams of New Orleans, suggesting that the three men should be dismissed on the basis of these stories. The vice chancellor asked if the stories could be documented and if the sources could be revealed. Williams replied that he was not at liberty to reveal his source at that time. . . .

Shortly [after Board of Regent's July meeting], Regent Williams' source, Regent-Bishop Juhan, announced that he was willing and ready to testify personally and present documented evidence to substantiate certain of the charges made against Dr. Grant only. . . .

On August 25 Dean Brown returned to Sewanee. Dean Brown was told of the charges and was asked to cooperate in the dismissal action. Though "stunned," he declined. The Vice Chancellor wrote Dr. Grant, in the meantime, and asked to see him as soon as possible on his return to Sewanee. . . . In this meeting, the Vice Chancellor told Dr. Grant of certain charges against him involving "public drunkenness and things that grow out of it." Dr. Grant admitted to two specific charges.

A footnote at this point in the "report" adds, "Of the two charges admitted by Dr. Grant, one had reference to an incident which happened about six years ago. The second charge came from an entry in Bishop Juhan's diary dated sometime during the last academic year."[32]

Thirty years later, Guthrie's assessment of the administration's action accorded with Gray's: "The tactic which McCrady et al. devised was that of dismissing the senior professor and best academically qualified member of the St. Luke's faculty, a recent Guggenheim Fellow, on the somewhat vague and even spurious grounds of 'repeated public drunkenness.' Here it might well be inserted that when a crucial moral issue is at stake, those on the defensive—in this instance the Vice-Chancellor and Board of Trustees—often tend to strike back with some petty shot at the personal character of those who dare threaten the status quo."[33]

Even at the time, Grant's effective firing stirred significant unrest among seminarians. In the same confidential memo to his board, McCrady wrote, "Rumors immediately arose that the [other] protesting professors would all be dismissed one at a time on false charges. The obvious answer to such stories is that the only accusations which have been made were fully confessed by the accused and their seriousness fully admitted by all who heard the charges and the confession."[34]

In any case, Grant did resign as of the beginning of the spring semester, but was quickly offered a position at the University of Chicago, which he took. He asked, however, to continue teaching his classes at Sewanee through the spring semester, and the vice-chancellor agreed. Grant commuted to Sewanee from Chicago and taught his New Testament class on Fridays and Saturdays.[35]

A few weeks later, Allen Reddick, professor of church history, received a letter from Chancellor Mitchell in which the bishop wrote, "I suppose you are aware that you and McNair have been reputedly linked in the drinking and other unseemly parties in which Bob Grant figured. . . . But I think you should know, if you don't already, that you have the reputation of being one who drinks and carouses. . . . My advice then . . . is that you do not consider the possibility of remaining on after this year."[36]

In response to the letter to Reddick, McNair wrote Mitchell asking him for something more definite with respect to himself, a statement that would "either exonerate me or one that you are prepared to substantiate." Mitchell responded by saying that he had made no charges against McNair, but added, "I think the thing to be concerned about is not whether somebody can substantiate the truth of the reports about you but whether you know in your heart that they are or are not true. . . . If your heart honestly tells you that there is no truth in the reported items referred to, let that be your sufficient exoneration as a Christian and a priest of the Church."[37]

McNair replied that he was grateful to Mitchell for the clarification and added that he considered himself exonerated by the bishop's letter.[38]

But the controversy about McNair was not over. He had been recommended for promotion to associate professor by Dean Brown in May 1952. On June 5, the vice-chancellor forwarded the recommendation to the Board of Regents, and they approved it. Four days later the faculty issued their statement protesting the trustees' vote on integrating the seminary. At that time McNair's promotion had not been announced. Indeed, as time went on with no announcement, it became clearer that a decision had apparently been made that the promotion would be withheld. When McNair asked the American Association of University Professors to investigate, its executive committee concluded that "the sole ground for withholding the promotion was Mr. McNair's participation in the action of June 9th" and noted that the university's actions raised serious questions about academic freedom.[39]

It was during the tension surrounding Grant's, Reddick's, and McNair's situation that St. Luke's Society, the seminary student organization of which Gray was president, met and on September 23 approved several resolutions of support for their faculty. The first stated the students' "full confidence in the professional competence and integrity of each member of the faculty" and was approved by a vote of fifty-nine in favor, two opposed, and fifteen abstentions. Just over a week later this resolution was forwarded to the seminary faculty, now with the names of sixty-two students attached, including that of Ed Browning, later to become presiding bishop of the Episcopal Church in the United States.

The second resolution stated that "this society fully favors admission of applicants . . . on the sole basis of merit and preparedness for study leading to the sacred ministry, regardless of the race or color of . . . the applicant." Seventy-two members voted in favor of this resolution, with none opposed and only six abstentions.

The third resolution announced the society's approval of "the published position of the majority of the members of the faculty of the School of Theology concerning the action of the Trustees of the University of the South at the June, 1952, meeting . . . on the question of admitting Negro students to the School of Theology." Here student support was more uncertain. While forty-six members of the group voted in favor and only two voted against, there were thirty abstentions. As a result, there was a demand for a roll call vote in which individuals were forced by name to state their position before the group. The abstainers on this resolution included Browning.[40]

Copies of the resolutions and the votes were sent to members of the board of trustees, and Gray's files preserve two quite different responses, one from a layman and the other from a clergyman.

Morgan Cartledge Williams, personnel director of Commonwealth Life Insurance Company in Louisville and a trustee from the diocese of Kentucky, wrote, "I am glad to see the large majority under Resolution # 2. That happens to be my position unqualifiedly."[41]

On the other hand, the Reverend Prentice Pugh, rector of the Church of the Advent in Nashville, replied, "May I ask whose bright idea this was that you voted on questions 1, 2, or 3. Perhaps No. 4 should be, 'Do you still believe the Bible to be the Word of God?'"[42]

As the controversy deepened throughout the university and positions hardened, the protesting seminary faculty took a more drastic step on October 6: they announced their resignations, to become effective at the end of the academic year. In their letter to the vice-chancellor, they wrote about the controversy over the seminary's integration: "It is our deep concern that this question of Christian principle be restored to its former simplicity so that it can become the subject of full and objective discussion, freed from the essential irrelevance of procedure and personalities. What gets discussed at present is not the issue itself in its clarity but the real or imagined defects of our character and the debatable points in our procedure. So long as *we* are the center of the controversy, and the issue is not, we seem to be in the position of hindering the free facing of the issue by which alone it can be decided on its merits."[43]

At first McCrady, after consulting with his regents who were meeting in Sewanee October 9 and 10, decided not to accept the resignations "because it was a violation of our agreement of last July and would further inflame emotions and interfere with the peaceful pursuit of the proper academic functions of the current year."[44] Two weeks later, however, McCrady received a letter from Dean Brown urging him to accept the resignations, saying, "It is our judgment that no good for anyone involved can be served by any further withholding of the resignation." Brown wrote that "we must insist" that the resignations be accepted and added a request that the full text of the resignation letter be released to the *Living Church, Episcopal Churchnews*, and the *Witness*, a similar publication. By the end of October, McCrady wrote his trustees and regents that following "full discussion with all concerned, I have now decided that it would be foolish and fruitless to continue to refuse to accept the resignations." He refused, however, to release the resignation letter to the media and wrote his boards, "I told them that if *they* release it to the press, instead of leaving it confidential with the Trustees and Regents, whom it concerns, they will be repeating the very mistake which, they confess, has made objective and dispassionate discussion of the original issue so nearly impossible now."[45]

By the next day news of the faculty resignations had leaked, and McCrady and Mitchell once again found themselves in the position of being asked by the media to respond. Although it is hard to know whether McCrady was being sarcastic or was expressing genuine naiveté in a November letter he wrote the trustees and regents, he told them, "No doubt you have all been surprised and puzzled by the fact that within a week after I sent you a confidential account of the resignation of eight members of our faculty and asked you to be as careful as possible to avoid giving it any publicity, the whole matter has appeared in the newspapers and Church magazines." Although the university administration conducted an investigation of the leak, it was unable to uncover the culprit.[46]

A week before his November letter, McCrady had issued a long statement in response to media requests in which he said, "The University learns with deep regret of the announced intention of the Dean of the Seminary and several members of the faculty to resign," and, at the same time, stated that nine new faculty members, including a replacement for Grant, would be hired. He continued, "The authorities of this University, long dedicated to Christian education, and ever cherishing tolerance, sincerely believe that with Christian patience and forbearance on both sides a solution of the differences of opinion on the present issue might have been reached upon which all men of good will could agree with full respect for themselves and their consciences, and for others. We shall continue, with God's help, to seek the path upon which this University must walk to serve the cause of true Christian education."[47]

The faculty's resignations received extensive media coverage. As Armentrout notes, "The faculty, while being roundly condemned on the Mountain, received wide support from within the church and without. Nine deans of Episcopal seminaries came out against segregated education for ministers as a violation of Christian principle. The faculties of three other seminaries—Yale, Union, and General—also issued statements in support of the faculty."[48]

In mid-November, another voice spoke on the Sewanee controversy. Meeting in Atlanta, the bishops of the Fourth Province, headed by North Carolina's Bishop Penick, who also chaired the seminary's special committee to study the issue of integration, voted unanimously to approve what Bishop Clingman referred to as "a statement in which we clearly stated our acceptance of the Christian principle involved [in integrated theological education]." In reflecting on their action, Clingman added, "Our action in Atlanta did not indicate a change of mind, or conviction, since June. I then believed in both things [acceptance of the principle, but refusal of its implementation in 1952]; I still believe in both things. I fail to see why a man may not accept an ethical principle, and at the same time give careful consideration to the time and circumstances of its application."[49]

Early in February, McCrady announced the Board of Regents' approval of five new faculty members for the seminary. McCrady wrote the trustees about the hiring, "It was made perfectly clear to each of these gentlemen that we were not interested in assembling a group prejudiced for or against admission of Negroes to the University of the South now. They will enjoy the same academic freedom accorded to all Sewanee professors. Their right to express their conscientious convictions on this, or any other subject, will be completely uninhibited and genuinely respected. All that we ask of them, as of others on our staff, is a reasonable respect for the opinions of any equally devout Christians who may differ with them, and a corresponding reasonable adherence to democratic procedure in working for the application of their principles in practice."[50]

In response to the news, the *Episcopal Churchnews* editorialized that the fact that the seminary would continue to operate was good news, but stated that the issue of integrating the seminary's student body still remained to be resolved. It also noted that the youngest of the new hires was fifty-two and that the average age of the five, plus Jones, was sixty-two, and added that despite the "glowing terms" in which the university had announced the new faculty (they would bring "a combined sixty-three years of seminary teaching experience"), yet three of the men had no experience at all with seminary teaching.[51]

A stronger reaction came from the Reverend John M. Krumm, chaplain at Columbia University and a letter writer to the *Churchnews.* Krumm wrote, "In the opinion of many of us, no priest ought to accept any position on the faculty at Sewanee until the Penick Committee has reported and the response of the trustees to their recommendations has been ascertained." He concluded, "In the ranks of union labor, there is an ugly word for those who, in a strike situation, capitalize on the bravery and courage of others who fight for the workers' welfare. The word is 'scab,' and it has an uncomfortable relevance to the new situation at Sewanee."[52]

Sometime in the midst of all this, Bishop Penick attempted to intervene with McCrady. According to Guthrie, who was at the time a student at the seminary from Penick's diocese, Penick, "himself a Sewanee alumnus, undertook a strenuous journey to the Mountain by train to intercede with the Vice Chancellor. Dean Brown and two other senior faculty members and several seminarians . . . were under his jurisdiction and pastoral care. He felt he could do no less. As it eventuated, he could do no more. McCrady's mind and that of Chancellor Mitchell were set."[53]

Guthrie suggests that another element in the equation was the influence of Bishop Juhan of Florida and his close ties with members of the duPont family, especially Mrs. Alfred duPont and her brother Edward Ball, who, according to Guthrie, largely controlled Mrs. Dupont's "family interests and largesse." Guthrie adds, "Ball was an old-school segregationist, as well as being a Communist-fearing 'union buster.' . . . Ball's role in [the controversy] cannot be overlooked; the University looked to him for money—endowment, faculty salaries, even, thought some, material survival."[54]

Exactly what Penick hoped to achieve with McCrady, Guthrie does not make clear, but perhaps most telling were Penick's next actions. According to Guthrie, Penick "called his Seminary students together for dinner in nearby Monteagle" and communicated his desire that students from North Carolina transfer to other seminaries.[55]

The University of the South was not yet done with negative publicity. At the same meeting at which the seminary regents had approved the hiring of new faculty, it had also voted to award an honorary Doctor of Divinity degree at the June 1953 commencement to James Pike, dean of the Cathedral of St. John the Divine and the faculty's New York contact the preceding June in its effort to draw media attention to their protest. Pike was also to preach the baccalaureate sermon.

The invitation had some history. Pike and McCrady had met a few weeks after the trustees' 1952 vote at a meeting held at the Episcopal Church's Kanuga Conference Center in western North Carolina, and at that time, in Pike's view, had immediately "hit it off intellectually and personally."[56] In fact, their contact was so cordial that McCrady had discussed with Pike then the possibility of him coming to the university as baccalaureate preacher for the 1953 commencement.[57]

Following their encounter at Kanuga, Pike's July 14 letter to McCrady was actually a confession of his and his wife's role in contacting the press on behalf of the Sewanee faculty six weeks earlier. The controversy had been discussed at Kanuga, but Pike wrote that he did not feel free to inform McCrady of his actions until he had talked with Wilmer, the Sewanee faculty member who had originally contacted the Pike's about the matter. While Pike certainly did not apologize for his role in his letter to McCrady, he did explain it and expressed his "sympathy for the difficult position the action of the two groups [trustees and faculty] has put you in."[58] In a warm reply headed "Dear Jim" and dated five days after Pike's letter, McCrady wrote that he appreciated "very much your taking the trouble to write these details, and I admire your exceptionally conscientious attitude." He added, "In your position I am sure I should have done exactly the same thing." McCrady concluded the letter with a reference to the 1953 baccalaureate, saying, "This letter confirms in writing my invitation to you to be our Commencement Preacher."[59]

By February 1953, however, the situation had changed, at least from Pike's point of view. Although no official announcement of the trustees' vote to award Pike an honorary degree had been made, such a decision was hardly unusual, and Pike had apparently learned of the vote through the grapevine. On February 10, Pike wrote McCrady, addressing him as "Dear Ned." Despite the intimacy of the address, Pike went on to say that he "could not in conscience receive a doctorate in the white divinity which Sewanee is apparently prepared to offer the Church."[60] He added, "Preaching is supposed to have some relevance to what is in people's minds and hence I doubt if my words at the baccalaureate would have contributed to the great harmony of the weekend."[61] On February 12, Pike released his letter to the press, and it was published in the *New York Times* and the *New York Daily News*. The seminary class of 1953 wired him, "Congratulations on your defense of Christ's Church. . . . Faith can move Mountains."[62]

Meanwhile, three days after Pike's "white divinity" letter to McCrady, an Associated Press story appeared which reported that the Vanderbilt University board of trustees had voted unanimously the previous October to admit two African American students to its School of Religion. Vanderbilt's chancellor issued a statement in which he said, "The School of Religion studies and teaches the Christian gospel. Christianity is not the sole or private possession of any one race or nation. . . . We were not willing in this issue to vote against that principle."[63]

Pike's decision and the events surrounding it (referred to by Pike's detractors in Sewanee as "Pike's pique") obviously produced a significant amount of news coverage itself, which in turn prompted Gray's aunt Sabrina Pierce in Nashville to send him a lengthy letter cautioning him about his role. Mrs. Pierce wrote that she did not believe "one should sacrifice his principles for the sake of family loyalty," referring to his uncle Ned, but added, "I do believe that family loyalty is something that should not be considered too lightly." In this context, she said, "some of us would like to know just what are your principles. For example, we would like to know if it is true that you sent a telegram of congratulations to Dean Pike after his recent public denunciation of your Uncle Ned."

She went on: "Now don't misunderstand me. If you are really convinced that the administration has been wrong in the way they have handled this thing, then you certainly have a right to your opinion. But I find it hard to believe that you sincerely think they could have done otherwise under the circumstances. Let's face it, Duncan, you and I know that this is not really a fight for the Negro. . . . [I]t is easy enough to see that this is a battle of prejudices, some of which may or may not be justified, on the part of the faculty and students of the Theological School."

Concluding with a kind of prescience, Mrs. Pierce wrote, "Before I get through meddling, there is one thing I would admonish you: remember, you are about to be ordained, and judging from all accounts you are facing a brilliant future which we shall all follow with interest, but never forget it is the Lord's work to which you have dedicated yourself; take care lest you find yourself up against crises such as this in your own work."[64]

Early in May the university trustees had received the much-awaited Penick Report. A nearly thirty-page document, the report contained a one-page summary of the history of the controversy from the time the question was raised at the Fourth Province synod meeting in Florida in 1950 to the time that the 1951 synod referred it to the University of the South. Then followed information about the numbers of African Americans congregations in the Fourth Province as well as the number of African American clergy and communicants. Included also were the numbers of African American congregations, clergy, and communicants in the twenty-two "owning dioceses" of the university and the number of "Negro theological students" in nine other, mostly Episcopal seminaries. Then followed a legal analysis of the question of integrating the seminary, which concluded that "it is illegal under the Tennessee statutes to allow white and Negro students to attend the School of Theology of the University of the South simultaneously." The legal section of the report did acknowledge, however, that recent and upcoming Supreme Court cases, including *Briggs v. Elliott* (which derived from Clarendon County, South Carolina, and was one of the five cases that would be decided as part of *Brown v. Board* in 1954), raised certain question about whether the prevailing doctrine of "separate but equal" would be upheld in the future. It noted that while the federal appeals court had at that time decided *Briggs* in favor of the defendants, Judge Waites Waring had written in his dissent in that case, "Segregation per se is inequality." But the legal report concluded, "Sewanee is under no legal obligation to admit qualified Negroes to its School of Theology."[65]

Other members of the committee had produced a "report on inquiry made of the seminaries of our church which now admit or have admitted Negro students" and concluded, "All reported satisfactory experiences and pleasant relationships between student body, faculty and Negro students. In no case did there seem to be a large number of students. One or two schools frankly stated that their experience was so limited that it would have to be considered 'special' rather than normal."[66]

In an additional report on the experience of Virginia Theological Seminary, the only other Episcopal seminary in the South, the writers noted, "The first Negro was admitted in the fall of 1951. . . . The Negro candidate, now in attendance, has an unusual background which suited him for the necessary adjustments. He has been accepted by his fellow-students and is making an excellent record. He participates in all seminary activities, including dances and other social events. He brings a Washington negress of comparable cultural background to the dances. He is from Michigan and will probably return there for his ministry."[67]

The same subcommittee also looked at Southern seminaries of other denominations that did not admit African American students. These included Baptist, Lutheran, Methodist, Presbyterian, and Roman Catholic institutions. The members found that

none of the seminaries belonging to the aforementioned groups and operating in the Southern States has any regulations whatever prohibiting the matriculation of Negro students. The representatives of these bodies were able consistently to say, therefore, that none of their institutions function under 'a policy of racial segregation.' However, it has been indicated by at least two of the seminaries (both owned and operated by a large denomination) which have no ordinances prohibiting the matriculation of Negroes, nevertheless, as a matter of *unwritten* policy have not admitted them. In each instance this has been the *working* policy of a board of trustees which does not necessarily reflect the prevailing attitude of the religious group which owns the institutions.[68]

The Penick Report's remaining pages summarized the results of a survey of various university constituencies on the issue of the integration of the seminary: bishops of the owning dioceses, priests who were alumni of St. Luke's, priests who were not alumni, college faculty, seminary faculty, college students, seminary students, members of the Sewanee community, and "lay alumni, friends, and benefactors." The different groups were asked somewhat different questions or given somewhat different choices for replying, but the results were as follows:

	Generally positive	Generally negative
Bishops	16	2
Alumni priests	24	36
Non-alumni priests	256	59
College faculty	12	13
Seminary faculty	5	1
College students	7	23
Seminary students	65	6
Lay alumni	14	54
Friends/benefactors	13	16[69]

Just a few days later, the *Sewanee Alumni News* announced that six of the eight faculty members who had resigned had found other jobs, for the most part at more prestigious universities than Sewanee. Although the news was not announced then, the other two would follow in the same path. The *Alumni News* also reported that of the fifty-six seminary students due to return to Sewanee for one or two more years, twenty-one were returning and thirty-five were transferring to other seminaries. The incoming first-year class would consist of fifteen students, a significant drop in enrollment.[70]

On June 4, 1953, "the largest gathering of trustees in Sewanee's history" met in special session. Penick was asked for his committee's conclusion. He indicated that the committee was divided, but that a majority favored a resolution stating that "no qualified applicant to the School of Theology of the University of the South be denied admission on the basis of race or color." Lay trustee Augustus Graydon of Columbia, South Carolina, presented the committee's minority view in the form of a much longer statement which noted that Sewanee had no "Ordinances limiting acceptance of students on the grounds of race," but added that the trustees were "still of the sincere opinion that the best interests of the White and Negro races will not be served by admitting Negroes at this time." The statement ended, however, by directing the vice-chancellor and the Board of Regents "to give all applications for admission to the School of Theology sincere and thorough consideration regardless of race."[71] Both statements were moved and seconded as resolutions of the board, the minority view as a substitute motion which was voted on first, but rejected. Several more substitute motions that represented various other wordings of the same minority view were made, but also were also voted down. Chancellor Mitchell called the question on the resolution representing the committee's majority view, but it was also rejected. Finally, the Reverend George M. Alexander of Columbia, South Carolina, moved: "Whereas the Constitution and Ordinances of the University of the South do not deny admission of students because of race or color, Be it therefore *Resolved*: That the Board of Trustees instructs the Vice-Chancellor and the authorities charged with admission of students to the School of Theology to give all applications for admission thereto sincere and thorough consideration without regard to race."[72]

This motion passed seventy-eight to six. It had taken the board almost exactly a year and nearly six hours of meeting time on June 4 to reach this point. An application for Sewanee's summer session from the Reverend John M. Moncrief, rector of a parish in Orangeburg, South Carolina, was already waiting in the admissions office. Thus Moncrief, already a graduate of Fisk University and General Theological Seminary, became the first African American to enter the university's School of Theology.[73]

Others followed, but their numbers were small and the area's rural isolation and overwhelmingly white population often made life at Sewanee difficult for them. Apparently, a strong sense of humor helped, and at least one of the early African American students was so equipped. One seminary alumnus recalled, in a discussion that followed the university's annual DuBose Lectures in 2002, that in the 1950s it was a tradition at the university to show *Gone with the Wind* in the student union every year and a custom for students to stand when Scarlett O'Hara shoots an invading Yankee soldier. White students of the college continued to follow custom, but the black seminary student remained seated, only to rise by himself later in the movie when Scarlett falls down the stairs.

In another incident, the Kappa Alpha fraternity had an annual homecoming dance at which its members and their dates dressed in Confederate uniforms and Civil War styles. The same seminary student "put out a rumor" that he had a friend in the fraternity who would supply him with a ticket to the dance. He planned, he said, to come dressed as Robert E. Lee and his date would portray Scarlett. When the word spread, his bishop ordered him home during the homecoming period for the sake of his safety.

Commencement 1953 at St. Luke's came and went, and Duncan received his bachelor of divinity *optima merens* as a result of his thesis about his summer in Cuba. The last year had taken its toll, however, and he was ready to be gone from Sewanee—so much so that he deliberately did not return to the Mountain for nine years. Instead, he looked toward the future: preparing for his canonical exams, his ordination, and his first parish ministry in two small parishes in the heart of the Mississippi Delta.

CHAPTER 7

"LITTLE OLD LADIES AT THREE O'CLOCK IN THE AFTERNOON"

Mississippi Delta, 1953–54

A FTER HIS GRADUATION FROM SEMINARY, Gray was given his first parish assignment: Calvary Church in Cleveland and the smaller but older Grace Church in Rosedale, both in Bolivar County, Mississippi. Bolivar County borders the Mississippi River on its western edge; it is there that Rosedale is located. Cleveland is about twenty miles east, near the county's opposite edge.

The Grays settled in the larger town of Cleveland, the same town in which Gray's grandfather, W. F. Gray, had owned and edited the *Bolivar Commercial* for seven years between 1919 and 1926, and where his father had served as managing editor until 1922.[1] It was in Rosedale during his seminary years that Duncan Gray Sr. met his wife, Isabelle McCrady, while he was working as a summer intern at Grace Church there. They would eventually become the parents of the new Bolivar County rector.[2] So in many ways the new place felt like home to the young Gray family.

The Gray children were left with relatives for a few days as the parents moved into their new home. And it *was* new, just finished for the new family, with hardwood floors, two baths, and a screened back porch. It sat on the lot adjacent to Grace Church and offered plenty of outdoor play space for Duncan, now four, and his sister, Anne, just over one year old. Ruthie Gray says, "It was just like a castle after that barracks covered with tar paper, that tar paper shack at Sewanee."[3]

As Will Campbell writes, the Mississippi Delta in the mid-1950s "was reminiscent of the Gershwin and Heyward *Porgy and Bess* folk opera. Fish were jumping and the cotton was high."[4] As the rest of the *Porgy and Bess* song has it, there was little need for baby to cry as long as "daddy's rich and mamma's good-looking." And for a portion of the white population, at least, such was the case.

Bolivar County is in the Mississippi Delta, that area between the Yazoo and Mississippi rivers that Mississippi writer David Cohn famously described as beginning "in the lobby of the Peabody Hotel in Memphis" and ending "at Catfish Row in Vicksburg." More than a century before Cohn, another observer of the region had predicted great things for the places that eventually became Memphis and Vicksburg, but he found it difficult to imagine much of a future for the area between the two rivers, still covered with primeval forests and "impervious and widespreading cane brakes." In the early eighteenth century, one visitor had described the area as "a seething, lush hell," and by the turn of the next century, a traveler making his way through the region still wrote "all the country, or nearly so between the Yazoo and the Mississippi to the mouth of the Yazoo, overflows annually [with floodwaters from the rivers] and renders it of no value."[5] As James C. Cobb points out, these discouraging prophecies about the Delta proved untrue for the simple reason that their authors "failed to appreciate the importance that the remarkable fertility of [the area's] continually replenished alluvial soil would assume in a regional, national, and international economy grown ravenous for cotton. More than that, however, those who doubted the Delta could ever be cleared, tamed, and farmed efficiently failed to take into account the determination, rapacity, and cruelty that humans could exhibit if the proper incentives were in place. Scarcely three decades after Mississippi joined the Union [in 1817], though still a largely uncleared wilderness, the Yazoo Basin had already emerged as the most attractive new planting region in the Cotton South."[6]

When Mississippi became the twentieth state, the land that came to be known as the Delta was still claimed and inhabited mostly by Choctaw tribes, but the growing demand for cotton and the fertility of the soil soon resulted in their removal, as whites along with their black slaves began to move in and clear the region for cotton planting. The 1820 Treaty of Doak's Stand transferred much of the Choctaw's southwestern Mississippi holdings into white hands, and counties began to be organized in the area. Sixteen years later, the lands were further divided; Bolivar County came into existence in 1836.[7]

More than a century later, the post–World War II boom had its impact on Cleveland. As early as the mid-1930s, Mississippi Governor Hugh White saw the need for diversifying the state's economy beyond agriculture; during the war Cleveland began to implement the plan. When Baxter Laboratories proposed to locate a plant in Cleveland in 1949, the town's leaders were jubilant at having landed a representative of what was described as "the world's largest manufacturers of intravenous solutions and equipment."

Later that year Cleveland voters would overwhelmingly approve the sweet-
eners of land, building, "and certain amenities" that the town had agreed to
provide Baxter. The wisdom of the voters' decision seemed to be confirmed
when in 1951 Baxter announced its decision to expand the facility as long
as the town provided additional inducements. In the same year, Mississippi
Power and Light built "the largest electric generating station ever built in
Mississippi" on Highway 61 leading into the town.[8]

Several decades earlier, the town's booster spirit had also made possible
the creation of another important Cleveland institution: Delta State Teachers College was established in 1925. W. F. Gray had lent his expertise to produce a ninety-four-page booklet entitled *Imperial Bolivar*, designed to convince the state legislature to locate the college in Cleveland rather than in
competing Sunflower County next door. In 1942, Delta State awarded bachelor of arts and bachelor of science degrees for the first time as it changed
its identity from a teachers college to a liberal arts institution. And in 1955
it would become Delta State College with a student body of approximately
five hundred. By that time, Gray had served as chaplain to its few Episcopal
students for two years.[9]

World War II brought changes to blacks' view of themselves in relation
to the white community. Cobb quotes a researcher from the U.S. Department of Agriculture who spent time among Delta blacks in the county immediately north of Bolivar in 1944: "Beneath the surface among the Negroes, an important change is going on; even down to the sharecropper
there is a feeling of discontent and a growing consciousness of exclusion
from social, economic, and political participation. Furthermore, Negro
leaders are becoming more fearless and ready to state what they believe to
be the basic rights of the group."[10]

Sociologist Samuel Adams attributed the growing sense of dis-ease
among blacks during the war to such influences as radio, movie theaters,
and automobile transportation.[11] And, of course, many social historians
have pointed to the impact of African American service in the war, resulting in not only a wider exposure to the outside world but also a growing
cognitive dissonance between fighting Nazi racism in Europe and risking
their lives in segregated units in the Pacific, only to return to Jim Crow racism at home.

One such individual was Amzie Moore, who came to the Delta from
north central Mississippi around 1930, looking for work picking cotton.
Moore picked cotton for a while—crushing work for long hours at low pay
in the Delta's stunning heat and humidity—but then moved to an eight-
dollar-a-week job in a Cleveland hotel. As the Depression became worse,

however, Moore lost that job and found "harder work for less pay" at the Southern Gin Company. A friend remembers that "his salary there was so small that he and a group of his co-workers had to go to the Red Cross for food. They gave him a piece of meat and some flour in a paper bag."[12]

In 1935, Moore took and passed the Civil Service exam for the post office, but in Bolivar County he was not offered a job as a postman, but rather hired as the post office janitor. When war came, Moore volunteered.

After his Bolivar County experiences, army service might seem like a reprieve, but during World War II Moore found himself in one of those segregated units in the Pacific and given the army assignment of helping to counter Japanese propaganda aimed at black soldiers by assuring them in speeches that life for them would be better back home when the war was over.[13] He reacted strongly to the experience and formed a secret society of black soldiers to resist oppression in the armed forces.[14] "Here I'm being shipped overseas, and I been segregated from this man whom I might have to save or he save my life. I didn't fail to tell it," Moore said later.[15]

Moore's first reaction when he arrived back in Bolivar County after the war was to protect himself as much as possible from white oppression by achieving economic independence; he acquired a store, a gas station, and a brick house, while resuming his post office job. But Moore's attitude changed dramatically after a trip to the nearby all-black town of Mound Bayou to look at some property. He found a house occupied by a woman with fourteen children, all naked from the waist down. It was winter, and the family was burning dried cotton stalks in a barrel in an attempt to keep warm. They had no bed and no food. "Just looking at that I think really changed my outlook on life. I kinda figured it was a sin to think in terms of trying to get rich in view of what I'd seen, and it wasn't over seven miles from me," Moore remembered later.[16]

It would not be long after Gray arrived that he and Moore would find each other.

* * *

Gray had been ordained to the church's transitional deaconate in April before his graduation from seminary, but that meant, according to the church's canons, that he was not yet able to preside over the Eucharist. "In those days the number of clergy in the diocese was so small, and there were a number of small congregations all around, and my dad said he didn't have much use for a deacon. He needed a priest who could celebrate the Eucharist and the other sacraments.

"So what he would do—and the seminary wasn't always happy with this—but he would ordain us to the deaconate before we graduated, so then we could be ordained to the priesthood not too long after that. The norm in those days, as it is today, was a year in the deaconate, but the canons provided for the possibility of cutting it shorter than that, although it had to be a minimum of six months.

"So the five of us from Mississippi who had graduated from seminary that year were ordained to the priesthood together at St. Andrew's in Jackson on the feast of St. Simon and St. Jude, October 28, 1953."[17]

The five quickly agreed on the single preacher for their ordination. "It was just instantaneous and unanimous: Duncan Hobart. That's who we wanted. He had been very supportive of the Sewanee faculty, and that meant a lot to us. I guess from that point on, I identified him with those in the church who were concerned about racial justice and integration. And he was an alumnus of the college. He went to General [Theological Seminary in New York City], but, as for college, he graduated from Sewanee," Gray recalled.[18]

Hobart, the son of an Episcopal priest and a native of New York State, had moved to South Carolina as a child with his father and the rest of his family. He had come to the diocese of Mississippi in 1943 from Atlanta to be rector of St. Paul's in Meridian, a position he held for nineteen years until he left to become rector of the parish of St. James' in Jackson.

"I had really only known him for about a year before I graduated from high school, but I kept running into him at Camp Bratton-Green. I remember his first summer there he taught a course on marriage for us older campers. Ruthie and I took that course together, and at one point he had us divide up, two by two, and do things like put together a budget. I still kid Ruthie about that, because I remember so vividly when we started putting this budget together. I also remember the figure: one hundred dollars a month. And when we got to clothes, Ruthie had spent practically the whole amount on clothes! I said, 'Unh, unh!' She said, 'That's what I spend!' So it was an eye-opener to me! But we both got to feeling close to Duncan."[19]

The two Duncans could hardly know that in a little more than six months they would be involved together in a controversial writing project that would bring them both under attack.

After the ordination, the four young Grays began to really settle into their new home. Despite its newness, it was a small house with only two bedrooms for parents, brother Duncan, and sister Anne, so the parents turned the dining room into a third bedroom.

The Grays remember only one design flaw in their new home: one bathroom was in a direct line with the front door. "This was in the days before air conditioning, but we had a wonderful big old attic fan, but you needed to have the front door open for it to work, so every time you walked in or out of the bathroom, you had to worry about whether someone was walking by on the sidewalk," remembered Ruthie.[20]

With one parishioner the problem wasn't just "walking by." Carrie Byrd Russell was "a wonderful, wonderful lady, but she was kind of nosey. Carrie Byrd was going to be into everything. Everything was her business."[21]

"Everything" had included the rectory during its construction; Mrs. Russell had been the butt of some joking over her close inspections of the process—at least until her voluntary supervision of the builders uncovered a pile of insulation that had been left out of a wall. Thanks to Mrs. Russell, the wall was rebuilt with insulation added.

After the Grays moved in, Mrs. Russell continued to stop by, since the place was new and there were little things remaining to be finished up or corrected. Because of her close involvement in the construction process Mrs. Russell had a key to the new rectory; early one morning she used it to let herself in as the family was preparing to go about its day. As she walked in the front door, Gray walked out of the bathroom door—in his underwear. "She was such a proper Victorian lady, she just said 'Ooooooo' and covered her eyes and turned around and ran. But she never came back again unannounced!" Ruthie said.[22]

With the beginning of Gray's life as a parish priest also began a pattern that would follow the family for the rest of his life and was the result of his understanding of the Christian gospel: those who knocked on the door found it opened to them.

Ruthie recalls at least two extended examples of that during the Cleveland years, one initially frightening, but then comforting, and the second a bit funny but finally at least somewhat helpful to a woman in need.

The first came soon after the family moved to Cleveland. A young man appeared at the door saying he was tired, and "Duncan invited him in. He said his name was Andrew Jackson, and Duncan was tempted to say that his was George Washington! We didn't know at first whether he had a drug problem or just a real serious emotional problem. It turned out that his father was an Episcopal priest out West somewhere, and we learned later from him that 'Andrew' had had an emotional breakdown of some kind and just wandered around, drifting.

"Well, he and Duncan talked all afternoon. And he really had the most gentle manner! He had walked on country roads, and he had worn the soles of his shoes out. His feet were blistered and he had kind of raw, sore places on his feet, so we cleaned up his feet and fixed them all up. He stayed ten days or two weeks or something like that.

"He made me very nervous at first. He was so quiet and he would just *sit*. But anything you did for him, he would just thank you so profusely. But then his quietness began to have an effect on us. He was a quieting influence on all of us. We all just sort of settled down while he was there, and after he had been fed for a while and rested up and his feet were better, we found a pair of shoes for him, and he left. If there is such a thing as 'an angel unawares,' he was ours! He had us all so *calm* and *soft-spoken* by the time he left."[23]

"And then later there was the woman who banged on the door of Duncan's study at the church. She was just frantic when she came to see him, and she had these two little boys, about four and two with her.

"We found out fairly quickly that she was desperate for drugs, and we learned later that she went all over the Delta with this story she told us about these horrible headaches she had and how she had to get something for them. But Duncan wasn't sure what to do with her. He wanted to get on the phone and find out who her relatives were and maybe get our doctor and see if he could give her something to quiet her down for a while.

"And so he brought her home. I heard all this scuffling on the front porch. I was about eight and three-quarters months' pregnant, but I opened the door and there stood Duncan with this woman in her twenties or early thirties all draped around him and these two little boys beside her pulling on her skirt. The first thing I wanted to do was just to shuffle them inside as quickly as possible and *then* find out what was going on!

"By then she was in a terrible state, and you know you didn't see much of that kind of thing back then. So I said I would call the doctor and Duncan started to take her back to the bedroom to try to get her to lie down. But then she started pulling off all her clothes! So we quickly agreed to swap places, and I helped her get undressed and got her in bed.

"And bless his heart, the doctor came and gave her something to make her sleep.

"But during the night the little boy got a bad nosebleed—it was just gushing! I got up with him and started to get a ice pack, but his brother said, 'Oh, he does that all the time. We just do this,' and he pushed his fingers up against his brother's nose and, sure enough, he stopped it.

"But it made me understand," she concluded with a smile, "why the Roman church thinks they ought to have celibacy. Not everyone has a wife who can stay up all night!"[24]

In addition to Gray's regular Sunday services in Rosedale, on Thursdays he would drive the twenty-some miles there to visit with his parishioners. Looking back, he remembers fondly as "fun" going to see "little old ladies at three o'clock in the afternoon." Other parts of the day he might spend wandering around Rosedale's small business district. "That was in the days before we had 'dial' telephones. It was still central: 'Operator, give me number so-and-so.' And if Ruthie needed me when I was over in Rosedale, she'd just call up the operator and say she was trying to find me, and the operator would say, 'My goodness! You know I think I just saw him walking across the street a minute ago. I think he was going to Michael's Café. Let's try him over there.'

"And then during Lent, we'd have Thursday evening services and if there was a confirmation class, that would be on Thursdays. They just knew I'd be there in town if it was Thursday."[25]

Gray had not been in Bolivar County long before he heard about a doctor in nearby all-black Mound Bayou said to be an Episcopalian. "So I went up there—it was just eight miles away—and sure enough, there *was* a doctor who was an Episcopalian, he and his wife and a couple of kids."

But the visit to Mound Bayou also meant meeting another doctor: T.R.M. Howard. "He was a fascinating guy. He had started a clinic with several other doctors and they were trying to serve the medical needs of poor blacks in the Delta. He was also chairing something called the Regional Council of Negro Leadership (RCNL), and it was the big social action operation in the Delta among blacks. I invited him to come to church in Cleveland, but he never did. He was a Seventh-Day Adventist and it was strictly a missionary operation that he was carrying out in Mound Bayou. He made a tremendous contribution to the whole life of the town."[26]

Dr. Howard was a native of Kentucky who had come to Mound Bayou from southern California in the early 1940s as chief surgeon at the town's Knights and Daughters of Tabor Hospital. In some ways he seemed an unlikely civil rights activist. He was a successful businessman who, in addition to his medical duties at the hospital and his clinic, had founded the Magnolia Mutual Life Insurance Company. He had bought a plantation on the edge of town and staffed it with servants in order to entertain in the best planter tradition. In the same tradition, he raised pheasant, quail, and hunting dogs, and he liked to gamble on the horses. Myrlie Evers, whose husband, Medgar, began his career as an agent for Howard's insurance company and would later serve as field secretary of the Mississippi NAACP, remembered the doctor well. Author John Dittmer quotes her as recalling

Howard "sailing down the highway in a red Buick convertible on his way to visit a patient." Evers also remembered Howard's "friendly smile and hearty handshake. . . . One look told you that he was a leader; kind, affluent, and intelligent, that rare Negro in Mississippi who had somehow beaten the system."[27]

Gray agreed, searching for words to describe Howard's energy and impact. "He was very serious about the work he was involved in, but he had such a happy nature. He was so good-spirited. He was sort of an extrovert and he was so welcoming. It was just 'y'all come.' He *was* a remarkable person."[28]

Howard's Regional Council probably never had more than five hundred members in twenty-nine Mississippi counties, but with him at its head, the group could attract crowds, as Gray would learn a few months later. It was perhaps for that reason that the NAACP fretted about the competition that the RCNL represented in Mississippi. The larger, older organization's regional secretary told NAACP president Walter White that "the Council is a threat which I have recognized and tried to combat on my several visits to the state."[29] Amzie Moore was one of the RCNL members, and, as a local history of Cleveland puts it, together he and Howard "railed against poll taxes and they fought for increased voter registration. One of their slogans was 'Don't buy gas where you can't use the bathroom,'" a situation that would not be applicable to Moore's station, of course.[30]

When the parish men's club next met after Gray's visit to Mound Bayou he dutifully reported his invitation to the doctors to visit Calvary Church since he was well aware of the impact a surprise visit might have on his congregation in segregated Mississippi. "The men's club met once a month, and we occasionally had a speaker, but most of the time I would just lift up some issue or some proposition for us to deal with. This time I never will forget. I had two issues: one was my invitation to Dr. Howard and the other was that a union that was trying to organize employees at Baxter Laboratories wanted to use the parish house for a meeting with the workers, and I had told the organizers that it was okay.

"Well, when I told them about Dr. Howard, they said, 'Well, sure. Okay.' but when it came to the union, I mean the whole roof fell in! 'You said *what?*' I mean we had an all-night session over that! The labor issue, the union issue raised a lot more cain in Mississippi in the winter of 1953 than the integration issue."[31]

In 1953, most white Mississippians were accustomed to a status quo in which blacks and whites could, they believed, mingle freely because white dominance was so secure that it could not be threatened. That situation would change within a few months time, but meanwhile there was the busy season of Advent and Christmas looming for the new, young rector.

On the first Sunday of Advent 1953, Gray delivered to his congregations a sermon that showed the marks of a recent seminary graduate, including a certain amount of information about the relationship of Christianity to its Hebrew roots; it was also a sermon that included a message which would have a significant relevance for his hearers in the near future.

Gray began by speaking of Christmas preparations in the same vein that many twentieth-century American preachers have: "How many times have we heard already and how many more times will we hear before December 25 that desperate cry 'My goodness, Christmas is just around the corner, and I haven't done half the things I need to do to get ready for it.' Of course when we say this, . . . we are thinking of our Christmas shopping, of buying and mailing Christmas cards, of preparing decorations and fancy meals for a festive occasion, of the one hundred and one things that need to be done to make the holiday a big success for ourselves and our loved ones."

While allowing that "all these things have to be done, I'm sure," Gray went on to speak of the more "spiritual" preparation for Christmas that the church looks for, asked "what is the nature of this preparation?" and answered his question by pointing his hearers to John the Baptist's call to "Repent, for the Kingdom of God is at hand," and went on to explore the meaning of that repentance. "Repentance in John's preaching is a thorough-going change. . . . The word in Greek is a particularly strong one. It means literally 'a new mind.' Repentance—true repentance—is a 'right about face.' It is the act of turning our wills in an entirely different direction. Repentance is much more than just penitence. It means far more than remorse or a feeling of being sorry for what we have done; it means more than just admitting mistakes.

"You know," he continued, "it is easy for us to admit mistakes from time to time. It is relatively easy for us to indulge in self-condemnation after we have made obvious mistakes. It is easy for me to tell myself at times 'I have been a fool.' Which one of us has not recited such rituals as this from time to time? This is easy, but repentance involves so much more. It is more even than being 'sorry' for one's sins. It is nothing less than a moral and spiritual revolution. It is a complete change of heart and will. It is the giving of new direction to all our thoughts, words, and deeds."[32]

Four weeks later on Christmas Day, Gray took his text from the gospel reading of John's prologue, "the Word was made flesh and dwelt among us," pointing out to his listeners the significance of the Incarnation: "Christmas is an event almost beyond human comprehension. No wonder it is a day of such joy and gratitude! What glad tidings the angel did bring to that band of shepherds on that first Christmas night! Tidings that God himself had united himself with sinful humanity for the redemption of his lost creation."

He concluded, "'Joy to the world! The Lord is come.' Are our hearts open to receive him?"—a question that his parishioners, fellow townspeople, and fellow Mississippians might well have asked themselves less than six months later.[33]

January came, and with it not only the new year of 1954, but also an invitation from Howard to come to Mound Bayou for the RCNL's annual rally. Two years earlier, Mahalia Jackson had entertained the crowd at the rally that took place on Howard's plantation; this year the speaker would be Thurgood Marshall, chief counsel for the NAACP's Legal Defense Fund.[34] In December of 1953, during the period when Gray and his congregations had been observing Advent, Marshall had been focused on arguing before the U.S. Supreme Court the five school desegregation cases that were bundled into a group known by the name of the first case on the list: *Brown v. the Board of Education of Topeka.* The late 1953 arguments were the court's second hearing on the cases, and black leaders in Mississippi and throughout the South were well aware that the court's decision in the cases was likely to be handed down very soon. On the other hand, Gray's sense was that most white Mississippians were generally oblivious and indifferent to the coming decision.

If ordinary white Mississippians weren't paying close attention, Mississippi's elected officials were keeping a close eye on the court situation, as were leaders in other Southern states where segregation was *de jure.* At its regular meeting in January 1954, the Mississippi legislature appropriated school funds for only one year, although it was normally a biennial body, thereby assuring that it would meet in special session to consider education again once the court had ruled. It also originated a strategy that other states would adopt: a pupil placement law that made possible individual assignment of students to particular schools and created a series of administrative reviews for any student who objected to his or her placement.[35]

In late April of 1954, Gray took Howard up on his invitation to the RNLC gathering at which Marshall would speak, and the meeting turned out to be an important one for Gray: it was there that he was introduced for the first time to Amzie Moore and Aaron Henry, then an NAACP leader in nearby Coahoma County.

When Gray reached Howard's plantation, he was amazed at what he saw: "There were ten thousand people up there in Mound Bayou, in the heart of the Delta, and only two other whites besides myself that I saw. It was an impressive thing."[36]

The other two white men were reporters from Hodding Carter's *Delta Democrat-Times* of Greenville, Mississippi, a newspaper liberal by contemporary Mississippi standards since Carter editorialized in favor of fair and equal treatment for the state's black citizens, if not for their integration into white Mississippi society. Despite the fact that Howard's affair was an annual one, and despite the speaker's significance, the *Democrat-Times* was the only newspaper in the state to cover the event, and it published only a few paragraphs.

Gray recalls an "inspirational" speech from Marshall, who returned that afternoon to Washington. Howard announced a panel discussion of Marshall's speech and related issues in the evening, and Gray returned to find a group that had dwindled to around three hundred.

"Dr. Howard was presiding, and he looked out into the audience and he asked me to come up and be part of the panel. I was the only white person there at that point; the reporters had left.

"The discussion was largely about anticipating and dealing with the *Brown* decision. It was pretty clear to them, especially after hearing Marshall, which way it was going to go. So they were talking about things like 'What's going to happen to black teachers? Will they lose their jobs?' It was pretty clear that there was agreement that a lot of the black teachers weren't up to snuff compared to the white teachers. They hadn't had the opportunity for education that white teachers had had. I remember one panel member in particular who said, 'If they're not qualified to teach white students, then they shouldn't be teaching black students.'

"Of course there were questions directed at me about how whites were going to react. I remember being pretty defensive about the white brothers and sisters. I said, 'I know it looks pretty bad, but, believe me, there really are a lot of folks who really do care.' I was pretty sanguine about it, I think, but I'm not so sure I believed with all my heart and soul what I said that evening, but I felt like I needed to say it to try and give them hope. . . .

"And it's true. There was more good intention and latent good will among so many whites in Mississippi—and I'm talking about even those dark, dark days—that never really came out and was not given expression. People talked about it in private, in their homes with friends, but you didn't come out and say it in public. I can still look right now out on that congregation in the heart of the Delta."[37]

Gray uttered these words with complete sincerity and with absolutely no indication that the old expression about "good intentions paving the road to hell" had crossed his mind, and it almost certainly had not. He remembered instead those among his parishioners whose hearts, he knew, had been in the right place, even if those feelings were never expressed in public word or deed.

More than fifty years later, he remained convinced that May 17, 1954, the day a unanimous Court delivered its opinion that "separate is inherently unequal," began a period that became a watershed in the perspective of white Mississippians, and social historians generally agree with him about Mississippi and the South as a whole. Indeed, at about the same time that Gray spoke hopefully in Mound Bayou, Jonathan Daniels, editor of the Raleigh *News and Observer*, expressed a similar kind of hopefulness in a speech to the National Urban League, relying on what he took to be "the good sense and goodwill of the people of both races [to act] in a manner which will serve the children and honor America."[38]

Gray recalled two occasions after the Court spoke that illustrated for him the initial calm with which Bolivar County whites greeted the decision.

"About a week after May 17, we had a funeral at Calvary Church. Margaret Green, whose husband was a judge there in Bolivar County, died. She was a wonderful, wonderful human being, and she was ahead of her time. She had been so helpful in terms of black-white relations, and one of the black schools there in town was named for her. She was a member of the Southern Regional Council [a group formed in the 1940s to promote racial understanding], and there weren't many SRC members in Cleveland!

"Well, we had the funeral, and there were several blacks who came. She was originally from Rosedale, and we had the interment over there. I rode over there with some of the pall bearers, and among them was the president of the school board. He brought the subject up. He had seen those black folks in church, and he said it was all right with him. He said, 'You know, we're going to work this thing out. . . .'

"And then a couple of weeks later I was in Rosedale at a Rotary Club 'ladies night' party, and I was talking to the man who was superintendent of schools in Cleveland. A local optometrist came up and said to him, 'Well, are we going to have niggers in school next fall?' And the superintendent said, 'Not this fall, but I imagine that we will in four or five years.' Well, the other guy calmed down and entered into a rational discussion of the matter.

"But then four or five months later, some of those men were yelling from Citizens Council platforms that we would *never* integrate. Segregation forever!"[39]

Gray recalled two more examples of the shift in attitudes that took place in Mississippi in 1954. His former seminary classmate Elmer Boykin, posted to two parishes to the southeast of Bolivar just outside the Delta, preached a sermon on the parable of the Good Samaritan in September of 1953 that was well-received by his congregations. "About a year later he got caught short one Sunday, and he preached the same sermon—he swears it was the exact same sermon. It asked 'who is my neighbor?' and the answer, of course, was 'everybody is your neighbor.' That was okay in 1953, but he caught holy hell for it a year later. Nobody made the connection in 1953, but by 1954—*Brown versus the Board of Education*, Citizens Councils were rising up. His vestry was on the bishop's doorstep pretty quick complaining about his saying everybody was your neighbor and you had to love everybody equally.

"And then Hal Crisler in Indianola where the Citizens Council was organized—he didn't mince many words in his sermons and I guess he probably had members of the Citizens Council in his parish. He was processing out after one service in 1954, and a local planter grabbed him by the collar out of the procession. Didn't beat him up or anything, but he let him know in no uncertain terms what he thought of Hal's sermon."[40]

The Citizens' Council was "respectable" white Mississippians' response to the *Brown* decision and its alternative to the "low-class," violent Ku Klux Klan. Numan Bartley succinctly sums up the council's origins:

> The first Citizens' Council was formed in July, 1954, in Indianola, Sunflower County, Mississippi, near the heart of the Delta. Robert B. Patterson, a plantation manager, and several local businessmen and political officials were searching for a method to counter the threat posed by the Supreme Court decision when Circuit Judge Tom P. Brady of Brookhaven focused their thinking with a speech delivered in Greenwood in late May. Brady pointed to the need for organized southern resistance, and, following his address, he discussed the project with the Indianola group. Shortly afterward Brady formalized his message in *Black Monday*, a pamphlet that became the handbook of the movement. In July, Patterson and thirteen associates created the original Citizens' Council and developed the organizational structure that served as a model for future local groups. From Indianola an energetic core of proselytizers spread into neighboring counties.[41]

By the fall of 1954, about twenty Mississippi counties had Citizens' Council groups. The organizers maintained their initial energy so that the council's chapters spread across the Deep South in the following years.

Neil McMillen explains the organization's ideology in his book *The Citizens' Council.*

> Primarily the ideology of the Citizens' Council was the ideology of white supremacy. Like Negrophobes of an earlier age the Councilors rested their case for white dominance on the postulate that Negroes were inherently different from Caucasians and that this difference, this hereditary inferiority, rendered them unsuitable for free association with white society. In the Councils' view, the black man's presence could be tolerated only so long as the range of his economic, political, and social interaction with the white man's world could be systematically defined. In the Councils' syllogism of white supremacy, then, segregation was the conclusion that necessarily followed the premise that human worth is calculable in terms of apparent physical characteristics.[42]

The council's success or lack thereof was generally inversely proportional to the ratio of black-white population in a particular location. As McMillen says, "The best single index of the problem of adjustment required in a given southern community by the decree of May 17, 1954, was the communities' own Negro-Caucasian ratio. Almost invariably, racial tensions ran highest and white intransigence was greatest in areas where the Negro population was most dense. Conversely, in areas where blacks comprised a relatively small minority, white compliance was very often achieved with comparative ease." He adds, however, that "many other factors of no ethnological relevance could and did serve to modify racial attitudes. . . . A community's urbanization, the character of its leadership, its political and economic structure, and its local customs frequently influenced its response to school desegregation."[43] Thus, in Mississippi, the counties "most thoroughly organized" by the Citizens' Council, Bartley notes, were those "which border the Mississippi River and constitute the western one-third of the state where a majority of its Negroes reside," in other words, the Delta.[44]

Business leaders were perhaps about equally divided in their views of the council. Like Mississippi politicians, many of them were supporters, even in relatively urban areas such as Jackson. There the president of the city's chamber of commerce and the son of one of the city's most prominent bankers provided the leadership for organizing Jackson's council chapter.

In addition to social and business pressures to join a local Citizens' Council, the group also relied on an appeal to class. The Ku Klux Klan had been the Reconstruction-era creation of Mississippi's upper classes, but by the mid-twentieth century its membership was primarily "redneck" or lower class, and the group openly advocated violence as a means of dealing with "the race problem." Thus, in the 1950s, the middle- and upper-middle-class members of the councils could distinguish themselves from the Klan not only by socioeconomics, but also by their avowed commitment to "legal" means to prevent desegregation and by their official anti-violence policy. But the racist positions and proclamations issued by council members who were also community leaders undoubtedly gave others the encouragement they needed to commit racist violence.

Pressure to join a local Citizens' Council could be intense. In Canton, for example, where Ruthie Gray's brother practiced law, Lloyd Spivey's refusal to join the local chapter of the Citizens' Council resulted in his banishment from the firm founded by their father. In other cases, such refusals might mean economic ruin and even the necessity of leaving the state because of the pressure from council-led business boycotts.

Economic pressure from the council was by no means confined to re-calcitrant whites. "The people who suffered most" from such tactics, Gray points out, "were blacks because they were the most vulnerable. Take Amzie Moore for example. He lost his service station because of the Citizens' Council, not because council members did business with him, but they had employees who did business with him or they had maids who did business with him, and they could say to them, 'Don't go down to that service station anymore or you won't be working for me.' Amzie had the post office job so he was somewhat shielded.

"Where council pressure on blacks was most evident was when they signed a petition asking for a school to be integrated. That list of people who signed was distributed automatically: 'if any of you know any of these people. . . .' I mean it might be an employee and he might be fired unless he withdrew his name. Or if there was some other economic leverage that could be used—like with Amzie—then it was used. It was used," Gray recalled.[45]

As Bartley points out, some white members of the power structure "considered a temporary sacrifice of school children an eminently acceptable alternative to desegregation." He quotes one Louisiana council leader who argued publicly that whites "would prefer that our youth grow up in ignorance than . . . permit them to attend integrated schools." And sounding rather like many contemporary conservatives, a Georgian who had been head of the Georgia States' Rights Council argued that a shift away from public schools to private ones "would contribute twenty years to the advancement of education in this state."[46] In time and in some places in the

South these arguments had a real impact: after the 1957 turmoil centered around the integration of Little Rock's Central High School, Arkansas Governor Orval Faubus simply closed all of Little Rock's high schools the . following year. Seventy percent of Little Rock's voters approved keeping the schools closed rather than integrate them. In the same year, Virginia Governor J. Lindsay Almond closed the high schools in Warren County, Charlottesville, and Norfolk that were under court order to desegregate. Such was the impact of years of incitement and propaganda by Southern white racists in both private and public positions.

Gray found such positions to be not only unjust but undemocratic and would soon go to work refuting them.

CHAPTER 8

"SEGREGATION IS INCOMPATIBLE WITH THE CHRISTIAN GOSPEL"

Mississippi, 1955–56

G RAY'S VIEWS were diametrically opposed to these private and public racists who supported closing public schools, and he could not sit idly by while leaders throughout the South, but especially in Mississippi, espoused such sentiments. The Department of Christian Social Relations for the Fourth Province of the Episcopal Church (which includes all southeastern states from North Carolina to Louisiana) had declared the court's decision "just and right" the day after the *Brown* opinion was issued. Gray was a member of the diocese's Department of Christian Social Relations, which Duncan Hobart chaired, so he soon contacted Hobart and suggested the committee meet to formulate its own response to the Court's decision.

In addition to Gray and Hobart, the diocesan committee members included James Raspberry, professor at Okolona College in Okolona, Mississippi, and father of later nationally syndicated columnist William Raspberry; and Dudy Noble, the wife of the athletic director at Mississippi State. ("I liked to point out that we were a very representative body," said Gray with a chuckle. "We had clergy and lay people, black and white, and male and female.") The group agreed that Gray should draft a statement, which he did.[1]

The committee met again on July 1 in the Cleveland rectory, this time with Bishop Gray in attendance. Ruthie Gray, very pregnant with their third child, served the group a light lunch. (Son Lloyd was born the next day, July 2.) Committee members considered the draft, while the bishop mostly listened and then approved the statement.

The statement began with what was, in effect, a direct refutation of the views expressed by segregationist leaders.

In many ways the public schools form the very cornerstone of our great democracy. In order for democracy to work, the people must be educated. They must be prepared for the exercise of honest and intelligent citizenship, and this irrespective of race, creed, or color. Nor must the opportunity for a good education be dependent on one's economic or social status. Basic to the very theory of public schools is the assumption that one's opportunity for an education is not to be determined by his ability to pay for it, whether in the form of tuition, or in the form of taxes. The poverty-stricken who pay no direct taxes at all are just as much entitled to an education in the public schools as are the sons and daughters of the more fortunate who bear the major part of the tax burden for public institutions. This is a basic premise of a Christian democracy. If we find ourselves resenting this, then we should examine our attitude toward democracy itself.[2]

In a section entitled "The Issues at Stake," Gray noted the labeling of the Court decision as "political" by those who opposed it, but went on to say, "The Supreme Court's decision has to do with human beings. The great ethical principles of the New Testament proclaim the sanctity of the human personality as that which takes precedence over every other human consideration. Man, be he white or black, is made in the image of God. This is fundamental to the Biblical concept of the Fatherhood of God and the brotherhood of Man. Our attitude toward the Supreme Court's decision is, therefore, essentially a religious question, since it concerns what we really believe about God and His creation. It concerns what we believe ourselves to be in relation to God and in relation to other human beings."[3]

Concluding the section, he wrote, "Thus, from the standpoint of Christian principle, we cannot believe that the Supreme Court's decision was anything but just and right. In our Christian faith, as well as in our political creed, we are committed to the principle of all men's equality before God and before the law. How, then, could we have expected any other verdict from the highest court of a professedly Christian and democratic country?"[4]

Gray went on to recognize "the problem of application." Segregation, he noted, was a tradition of long standing and "customs and traditions of such long standing are not overthrown overnight." In addition, however, "Christian principles are not always easy to face" and "life is often easier for most of us if questions of Christian principle are never raised."[5]

"Yet when such a question is raised, there can be only one answer for the true Christian. The truth is often hard to take; a bitter pill, a harsh prescription. Yet in the long run, the truth will never hurt us. This must be the conviction of any follower of that road that led to the Cross. As bitter as the pill may be, as difficult as the task may appear, the only enduring foundation for the kingdom of God, and a strong democracy as well, is the truth as we have received it in Jesus Christ, 'come whence it may, cost what it will.'"[6]

Gray concluded with a section entitled "What We Can Do" and listed four points: first, recognition of the fact that "each race rejects the other" and of the responsibility of both to work toward a "Christian solution" to the problem of "mutual antagonism and distrust"; second, the necessity that whites "not assume that they alone are concerned with a peaceful solution to the problem" or that "they alone have the wisdom to work toward" a solution, but instead involve "local Negro leaders at every level"; third, parents must raise their children in such a way that they "grow up free of prejudice and ill-will toward members of the other race"; and finally, each Episcopal parish should welcome "any Churchman who wishes to attend, without regard for his race or color."[7]

At the time, such recommendations may have seemed to be excessively optimistic; however, the pamphlet concluded, "We affirm once more that we do not underestimate the herculean task that confronts us. . . . In spite of the dangers which the Court's decision may present, the opportunity it affords us is far more important. . . . It can be the beginning of a long stride toward the consummation of Christ's ideal of brotherhood among men everywhere. We who live in this age may see little of that consummation, for it is our lot to live with the crisis, not after it. Yet our faith and our hope are not dimmed."[8]

The statement was printed in full in the August issue of the diocese's newspaper, the *Church News.*

Gray had already talked with a Cleveland print shop about reprinting the statement as a six-by-three-and-a-half-inch pamphlet and had gotten price estimates. When he returned to the printer with "The Church Considers the Supreme Court Decision," however, the owner of the shop very nearly changed his mind. "He was furious," Gray recalls. "He said he didn't know it was going to be *that* kind of stuff! He finally agreed to go ahead and print it though, as long as his or his shop's name didn't appear anywhere on it. And it didn't. It just says "Reprinted from *The Church News.*"[9]

The statement in pamphlet form was widely available and copies were mailed to key individuals in the state. The reaction from white Mississippi Episcopalians was predictably mixed.

Greenville editor Hodding Carter wrote, "I concur in everything [the pamphlet] says most heartily" and asked for fifty more copies to distribute. Carter, however, added, "I hope you are right in thinking I am pessimistic about the length of time required in the matter. I do believe it will vary in different states and Mississippi will be the one least prone to change."[10]

Gray's former seminary professor Craighill Brown wrote, "Your father, with characteristic thoughtfulness, has shared with me information about your authorship of the pamphlet 'The Church Considers the Supreme Court Decision.' . . . It is a very fine piece of work, Dunc, and I am indeed proud that it is the work of one of 'my boys.'"[11]

On the other hand, two months later the vestry of Trinity Church in Yazoo City sent out a letter addressed to "Dear Fellow Episcopalian" requesting that other parishes hold a special vestry meeting to discuss the contents of the pamphlet, explaining, "We have already met and held such a discussion and are in complete disagreement with much that is said therein." The parish's junior warden, signing for the vestry as a whole, added, "We feel that the publication is not representative of our Diocese and that it should have been discussed with the membership of the entire Diocese before publication."[12] Although there were undoubtedly other parishes and vestries in the state which were likewise "in complete disagreement" with the statement, the vestry of Trinity Church apparently failed to get the kind of response they had hoped for, because a little over a month later, a second letter followed to those who had not responded to the first, advising the recipients that "this article will be discussed at our annual diocesan meeting in January. We feel that this matter is of such importance that we are asking the churches nearest Yazoo City to meet with us to have a preliminary discussion."[13]

Gray made a point of sending copies of the pamphlet to members of the Bolivar County delegation to the Mississippi legislature: not only his parishioner Charles Jacobs, but also Jacob's uncle, Speaker of the House Walter Sillers, and state senator W. D. Alexander. The copies were accompanied by a letter in which Gray wrote the men, all lawyers, "The Church does not pretend to be an expert on constitutional law, but she certainly does consider herself qualified to speak on moral and religious questions."[14]

Sillers didn't bother to reply, but Jacobs and Alexander did. Both letters are worth quoting at some length since they give a good snapshot of the position of most elected officials in Mississippi at the time.

In what Gray characterizes as "a steaming letter," Jacobs addressed his rector as "Dear Sir," and began by wondering "just whose views these are that were expressed? Were they the views of the Bishop or all of the clergy or part of the clergy?" He continued:

> I look at the matter of segregation from the practical angle and the idea of integration is out of the question so far as I am concerned, and this applies both to schools and churches. Because of the wide gulf between the races in morals, background and culture, any attempt at integration would lead to the gravest kind of difficulties, particularly where the blacks outnumber the whites 2 to 1 as in Bolivar County.
>
> I feel that this is a time when the white people should stand together in Mississippi, and my observations are that that is pretty well the feeling of the people in Mississippi. I would hate to think that in this time of crisis the church took a different view from that of its people. My personal view is that the church should have its hands full administering [sic] to the needs of the sick and needy in the community without doing anything to tear a congregation apart by taking such a stand on segregation.

Jacobs concluded by restating his original query: "I would like to know who wrote this pamphlet which you forwarded to me if you could give me that information."[15]

Gray didn't hesitate to inform him of his role in drafting the document and of the work of the diocese's Department of Christian Social Relations and its meetings with the bishop in finalizing and approving it.

Alexander's letter was longer and more conciliatory towards Gray, if not about the issue. Addressing Gray as "Dear Friend," he wrote, "I appreciate your letter of September 1. I realize that you are utterly sincere in everything you say. However, I disagree with the conclusions reached in the pamphlet you mailed me. As a member of the State Senate, I shall do everything humanly possible to insure permanent segregation in the public schools of this state."

He continued by informing Gray, "Although I am certainly not a wealthy man," he had requested that his wife, in the event of his death, spend up to half of the value of his estate making sure that his grandchildren, nieces, and nephews never attend an integrated public school, "I feel that it would be utterly disloyal to my constituents in this county and to the people of the state generally if I did not fight to the last ditch to preserve segregation in our public schools." In one long, continuous paragraph, Alexander wrote:

I think there is ample scripture upon which to base a belief in segregation. I feel further that I am not under the slightest obligation to uphold this decree of the Supreme Court, which I personally intend to disregard entirely. I do not think that the question has any religious aspects at all. I do not see how anyone could consider this decision of the court other than as one rendered by a stacked court at the behest of the NAACP and other allied organizations, most of which are treasonable and subversive. I think that the schools for the races should be separate. I also think that we should improve our negro [*sic*] public schools as rapidly as we can within the limit of our ability to pay. I intend to vote for the resolution to amend the Mississippi constitution so as to give the legislature by three fifths vote the right to abolish the public school system in any county or school district, but I do not intend to vote to actually abolish any of these districts except upon a petition of the majority of the voters in that county or district. After we have voted in these amendments, I certainly do intend to vote to rapidly improve the negro school system. I shall cast these votes deliberately and prayerfully and with an absolutely clear conscience, because I know this is best for both the white and colored citizens of Mississippi.

Alexander concluded his letter to Gray by expressing his regret at their disagreement and his view that "the churches, including the Baptist Church, of which I am a member, have made a drastic mistake in taking any stand on this matter" since in his view it was "primarily" a political and economic matter rather than a religious one. He concluded by telling Gray, "You have a perfect right to your opinion and I know you are perfectly sincere and I respect you and have the deepest admiration for you."[16]

Although leaders in mainline denominations, including Southern leaders, tended to speak and write in favor of the decision, individual clergy were often a different matter. For example, in November, Gray received a letter from Bernard Munger, pastor of the First Presbyterian Church in Corinth, Mississippi, thanking his Episcopal colleague for the pamphlet and his work on it and adding, "I was especially glad to hear from you under the circumstances! My remarks at the Synod of Mississippi, on two occasions, concerning the very same thing, were not appreciated by any considerable number of my brethren. However, I have never felt that numbers on my side was a good criterion for judgment as to the truth of my witness. I will continue to make it, even if the number with me decreases!"[17]

Gray had by no means confined his comments on the decision to his relatively anonymous work on the pamphlet. Although most of his sermons to his congregations in the weeks following the court decision continued to address the preacher's usual themes of theology and personal piety, on the first Sunday in September, following the appearance of the diocesan statement in the August *Church News* and after sending copies of the pamphlet to Bolivar County legislators, Gray spoke from his pulpit directly to the issue at hand. Pointing out that there were copies of both the diocesan newspaper and the pamphlet in the church vestibule, he commended them to his parishioners for their reading. But in the process, he also took the opportunity to speak more broadly to his congregants on the role of the church in the world. Taking as his text Paul's words in I Corinthians 14:8— "For if the bugle give an uncertain sound, who shall prepare himself for the battle?"—part of the lectionary prescribed for the day, Gray reminded his hearers that Paul had posed his rhetorical question in the context of a concern about the usefulness of "speaking in tongues." He acknowledged the unlikelihood of the "tongues" phenomenon being an issue in an Episcopal church in the 1950s, undoubtedly drawing a chuckle from his listeners, but went on to suggest that Paul's objection was not so much to the phenomenon itself, but with whether it distracted from what should be the true goal of Christian speaking: instruction and inspiration. "What St. Paul is arguing for," he said, "is *relevance* and *meaning* in the worship of the Church and in its life as a whole."

> Christianity, to be true to itself, must be meaningful and helpful to its adherents and to the world at large. It is not just the occasion for an emotional binge or a flurry of meaningless words. We should pause to consider this as we examine the state of the Church today. . . . [W]hat is the Church doing to give a clear and unmistakable leadership in the battle against evil and injustice? How distinct and how certain is the call which we give to call the world to spiritual warfare?
>
> These are questions which we should take very seriously, for it is of the very nature of the Church for that body to give *leadership*— leadership not just in times of personal crisis in private lives, but in every phase of the world-wide and age-long struggle against every form of evil in the world. . . . We want the Church close by in times of personal tragedy or misfortune, but we do not expect it to be immediately relevant to the practical problems of everyday existence.
>
> In short, we have lost the concept of the Church as a corporate body leading the fight against evil in the world. We do not ask that

our religion give meaningful and relevant answers or insights into the social, economic, and political problems which confront us. We would prefer to handle these on our own and let the Church deal only with personal piety and the denunciation of evil in terms of vague generalities; to be against sin and let it go at that. But to accept the Church as this and nothing more is to reduce Christianity to a triviality.

After reviewing for his congregation the church's history as the earliest provider of charity and other social services for the needy, Gray noted that that role had been largely taken over by governments, "which, for the most part, are doing a good job." He went on by turning once more to the church's contemporary responsibilities and the diocese's statement on the issue of segregation. After urging his parishioners to read that message "closely and prayerfully," Gray concluded, "The Court's decision poses tremendous problems for us here in the South. We all recognize this, and certainly we should make no attempt to minimize those problems. Yet the Church reminds us that we cannot compromise the basic Christian principles at stake and still be worthy of the name Christian. Whatever the final solution to the many problems may be, the Christian cannot evade or avoid the conclusion that the Supreme Court's decision is just and right, and the Christian conscience can never rest easy until we make this the starting point for all our deliberations and legislation on the subject."[18]

Looking back on the occasion, Gray recalls that "the first major resistance came after that sermon. The most serious was from Charlie Jacobs, who was a very active member of the mission committee [equivalent to vestry]. After he read that pamphlet, he never came back to church. His wife and his children kept on coming to church. I imagine there were some tensions in that household, because she was never a crusader and wasn't out making speeches, but in my private conversations with her I know she sympathized with my position.

"Charlie had many a quite nasty thing to say about me in the months that followed, but of course he was a politician at that time and he was held responsible for that preacher that's out of whack down there at Calvary Church, and I think that's the reason he was so outspoken. He was sincere; he really believed in segregation, but he probably made more of an issue of it than most of them because he was in politics.

"On the other hand, Jack Russell, my senior warden, was supportive."[19] Russell was the son of Carrie Byrd Russell and also the Gray's family physician—"we've been very lucky in our doctors," said Ruthie Gray.[20]

Mrs. Russell, although distressed by the controversy among her neighbors and friends, was also supportive in her own way, Gray remembers. "She certainly wasn't any flaming liberal or out crusading, but she came storming into my office one day. And my office was *the* office—the whole church wasn't big! There was hardly room to get in there. She came storming in and went to the church files and got out the parish register, just muttering and mumbling. I didn't know what in the world was wrong with her.

"Well, it turned out that she'd been in conversation with some unhappy members of the congregation who were on my case and really going after me about how terrible all this was. But, bless her heart, she was in her seventies and had been around long enough to remember a time when blacks were members of the congregation at Calvary and their babies were baptized there. So she went back to those old parish registers and she said, 'There, there it is!' And I said, 'There's *what*, Miz Russell?' And she showed it to me where the babies were actually identified as 'col.' and she said, 'My goodness, we baptized folks. . . .' She wanted to show them that it wasn't anything all that new.

"But we had some folks drop out at that point. We had some pledges reduced, but quite honestly, on a percentage basis, it was not nearly as much as we had in Oxford later on. By that time we were in a climate that was really charged. In Cleveland this was more or less just within the congregation. It didn't seem as serious in 1954 as it did later in Oxford."[21]

However mixed the local reaction to Gray's words, both written and spoken, his work on the pamphlet caught the attention of staff members at the national church's headquarters in New York City. In early October, Duncan Hobart, as chair of the diocesan Department of Christian Social Relations, received a letter from his counterpart on the national level inquiring about copies of "The Church Considers the Supreme Court Decision." Hobart replied that he had doubts about the pamphlet's usefulness for wider distribution without some changes, but that if the church wanted to distribute it more widely, it had the diocesan committee's permission to do so. In the event, Hobart and Gray became members of the thirteen-member Committee of Advice to the national group and helped shape a draft report and statement entitled "Just, Right, and Necessary: A Study of Reactions to the Supreme Court Decision on Segregation With a Statement of Guiding Principles, Policies and Practical Suggestions." As a young priest in charge of two small parishes in two small towns in Mississippi, Gray stood out among a group that included two bishops, a state Supreme Court justice, the executive director of the National Urban League, and rectors and congregants from parishes in a number of large cities along the East Coast.

The draft received the approval of the church's National Council in December 1954, and the council commended it "for study to all Churchmen . . . with the hope that this report of facts and this statement of guiding principles and policies may assist parochial and diocesan authorities in their efforts to promote a wise, wholehearted, and genuine realization of the principles set forth by the Court and supported so widely by Churchmen in all parts of the country."[22] The council's statement about members' support of the decision was, in hindsight, overly optimistic, but there were indications that it was so even at the time. After the church's 1952 General Convention had approved a resolution on justice and equal opportunity (largely in response to the conflict over integration at the University of the South), the church commissioned a study of its leaders' and members' views on segregation. That showed that about 10 percent of the church's bishops and 25 percent of its lay people "still believed in the validity of segregation."[23]

A few weeks before the National Council issued "Just, Right, and Necessary," the Fourth Province bishops meeting in synod in New Orleans voted to direct its province's Department of Christian Social Relations "to develop an extensive guide for the extensive study of the problems of desegregation, such as might be effectively used on the parish level . . . in order to create a positive and receptive atmosphere for the recent Supreme Court decision and its forthcoming enactments."[24] This Provincial committee was also chaired by Hobart. It membership was composed of Gray; the rector of an Episcopal parish in Macon, Georgia; a black priest from the diocese of Atlanta; and Hodding Carter. That document was approved and issued in 1955, and this time Gray wrote the portion that argued that support for segregation was incompatible with the Bible's teachings. He pointed out that the Bible has no concept of race "except to refer to an athletic event." In a section entitled "The Ethics of Jesus," Gray wrote, "That which was most fundamental to all of our Lord's ethical teaching was His belief in the dignity and worth of the individual as a child of God made in his Father's image."[25] He concluded his portion, "Ultimately, this complicated problem will be resolved in a Christian manner only when we can accept every human being as a child of God, equally precious in his sight and equally the object of his love and concern. We must never forget that in Christ, God identified himself with every human being, be he great or small, powerful or weak, white or black. . . . Our treatment of our fellow man, whoever he may be, is an action directed toward God Himself. Christ dwells in each and every one of us. Our attitude toward another human being, whatever his race or status, involves our attitude toward God. Thus the Bible teaches.

"Will we take such teaching seriously?"[26]

The prospect for a positive response to Gray's question did not look good in Mississippi. White men were charged with the killing of four black men in Mississippi in 1955, but none was convicted despite the fact that one killing occurred on the lawn of the Lincoln County Courthouse in the daytime.[27] A second man, the Reverend George Lee from Belzoni, approximately fifty miles southeast of Cleveland, was shot on the night of May 7 as he drove down the street in his hometown. A few days earlier, Lee had become the first African American to register to vote in the county.[28] Lee had also been a "spell-binder" of a speaker at Howard's 1955 Mound Bayou rally where he told his hearers that if they registered and voted "someday the Delta would send a Negro to Congress."[29] No one was ever charged with Lee's murder.

Nationally, the best-known murder of a black person in Mississippi that year was, of course, the killing of Emmett Till in August. Till, a fourteen-year-old Chicagoan, was in Mississippi visiting his great uncle, a share-cropper in the tiny Delta town of Money. Till boasted to a group of his Mississippi contemporaries outside an area country store that he had a white girlfriend back in Chicago. Doubtful of Till's story, the other youths responded by daring him to go inside the store and ask the white woman behind the counter, Carolyn Bryant, for a date. Till took the dare, but exactly how he acted on it is still a matter of dispute. Bryant testified later that a black man, whom she did not identify on the stand, came in the store and asked for two cents worth of bubble gum. When she gave him the gum, she said, he grabbed her hand and squeezed it and asked her for a date. Then as he turned and left the store, he gave her a wolf whistle.

Two days later, when Mrs. Bryant's husband returned from a truck-driving run and learned of the incident, he went to his half-brother J. W. Milam and the two planned how to respond to it. In the very early hours of Sunday morning, Bryant and Milam arrived at Till's great uncle's house and demanded that he turn over his nephew. The uncle protested and in effect apologized for Till, but the men forced Till into Milam's pickup and left. Three days later, Till's mutilated body was recovered from the Tallahatchie River tied to a cotton gin fan.[30] Bryant and Milam were tried for the crime in federal court, but an all-white jury found them not guilty after deliberating slightly more than an hour. In 1956, Milam admitted to writer

William Bradford Huie and *Look* magazine that he and Bryant were guilty, but to have tried them again would have represented "double jeopardy." (The U.S. Department of Justice reopened its investigation of the Till murder in 2004, and Mississippi officials cooperated with them. In February 2007, the Jackson *Clarion Ledger* reported that a grand jury impaneled by a black prosecutor in majority-black LeFlore County, Mississippi, found no basis for charges against any possible living defendants. Milam died in 1980 and Bryant in 1994.)

Gray, his hands full with his efforts to persuade white Mississippians, especially those who were Episcopalians, of the rightness and desirability of desegregation, remembers the Till murder and its aftermath as "one additional blow." He said, "When Bryant and Milam were arrested, you kept hearing over and over from so many people in Cleveland, 'Ah, they didn't do it! That's just a lie. Those folks are good people' and all this sort of thing. Then after the trial began, it was 'They're being persecuted!' So many people were so defensive and on the side of the murderers."[31]

As author Cobb notes, however, once the Huie article had been published, "the white community that had tried its best to act as though Milam and Bryant could be innocent found itself 'sold out.' Neither man found Tallahatchie County hospitable thereafter."[32] Indeed, at least one of them began to talk of moving to Bolivar County. Then, Gray remembered, those same Bolivar County whites who had defended the murderers earlier began to sing a different tune: "Then everybody was all upset: 'We don't want them folks around here!' Now you were hearing from the same people who had been saying 'those men are being persecuted,' 'We don't want those folks around here! We don't want *him* living in Cleveland!'"[33]

But the murder of Emmett Till by no means ended violence against blacks that year, and Milam's and Bryant's acquittal presumably emboldened others. Gus Courts, a Belzoni activist who was a target of Citizens' Council economic pressure, contacted a lawyer about bringing a damage suit against the council. After Reverend Lee's death, the NAACP heard that Courts was "next on the list." By November, he had been shot in his own store. The county sheriff told the press that "some damn nigger just drove there and shot him." Although the F.B.I. was called in to investigate, no arrests were made.[34]

In December, again in Tallahatchie County, a white man, who reportedly had been drinking, shot and killed a black gas station attendant. The victim was so well-regarded by Tallahatchie whites that the local Lions Club approved a resolution expressing regret at the loss of "one of the finest members of the Negro race in this community," but although some jury members reportedly voted "guilty" on the first ballot, after four hours of deliberation, the jury voted to acquit.[35]

Amzie Moore wrote a friend in Chicago, "A man's life isn't worth a penny with a hole in it. I shall try to stay here as long as I can, but I might have to run away up there."[36] But Moore later pointed to the Till murder as "the beginning of the modern civil rights movement in Mississippi."[37]

And so that same year, 1955, Moore organized and became president of a Cleveland branch of the NAACP. As an additional part of his activism, he became involved with a group known as the National Sharecropper's Fund, which attempted to provide financial assistance to black sharecroppers under pressure from whites. By now Gray and Moore saw each other daily when Gray went to the post office to pick up his mail. Moore had already lost his service station as a result of council pressure, but had retained his federal job as post office janitor.

"Amzie would be sweeping the floor when I went in and we'd talk. One day he asked me about my willingness to do investigations of potential recipients for the National Sharecroppers Fund. They wanted me to check 'em out. They wanted to be sure, of course, that the applicants' needs were genuine and that they actually were under pressure.

"Now they called the money these farmers got a 'loan' even though they said they really didn't expect to get the money back, but because it was supposedly a loan, they had to have a lawyer to draw up the loan instruments for them.

"I said, 'Amzie, where are you going to get a lawyer in Cleveland to draw up the loan instruments for you? There aren't any black lawyers in Cleveland.' Amzie said, 'Joe Feduccia.' I said, 'What? Joe Feduccia? Do you know what you're talking about? W. B. Alexander's law partner?' He said, 'You just go talk to Joe.'

"Well, sure enough. Now Joe was a Roman Catholic and he ended up doing all this work for me in relation to the loans, and he never intimated that he knew what it was all about, but I know darned well he knew what he was doing. Eventually the Sharecroppers Fund ran out of money after a year or eighteen months, but Joe processed many a loan like that. And all the time his law partner was out there screaming and yelling from the Citizens' Council podium. But Amzie knew what he was doing; he had already made connections with Joe and knew he was a friend."[38]

But blacks like Moore didn't have many such friends in Mississippi, and whites like Gray would soon find additional evidence that their white skin guaranteed only a limited degree of tolerance from their white brethren. Indeed, it was during the next year, 1956, that Gray began to earn widespread opprobrium among Mississippi segregationists outside the Episcopal Church.

In the 1950s, it was the practice of Mississippi's public colleges and universities to set aside a week during the school year that was designated as "Religious Emphasis Week." During this week, speakers were brought to campuses to address public audiences and classes, to conduct seminars, and to lead discussion groups in dormitories and sorority and fraternity houses on a variety of religious topics.

At the University of Mississippi, the university's chaplain, Will Campbell, decided that its 1956 REW should deal with matters of racial justice, but he knew that he could not address the topic head-on. Instead he made sure that the speakers who were invited were "sympathetic to racial justice."[39] When one of those speakers, Episcopal priest Alvin Kershaw, whose knowledge of jazz won him $32,000 in November 1955 on the popular TV quiz show "The $64,000 Question," was asked what he intended to do with his winnings, he replied that he hadn't given it much thought, but would probably give more money to causes he already donated to, including the NAACP. When Kershaw's comments were reported in Mississippi newspapers, a firestorm broke out, and the chancellor at the University of Mississippi received a flood of letters from Mississippians. Although not all the letters were negative about Kershaw (including one very supportive one from Duncan M. Gray Sr. and another from his son), the pressure in Mississippi built to a point that the chancellor withdrew the invitation to Kershaw. At that, the other invited speakers withdrew, and Campbell turned the week into one of daily silent meditation in the university's main auditorium.[40]

However, the Mississippi brouhaha over Religious Emphasis Week was not over. Approximately two weeks after the scheduled event at Ole Miss, Mississippi State College in nearby Starkville planned to have its own observance, and the young Cleveland rector had been invited to speak its first night on the topic "The Social Implications of the Christian Gospel" and two days later to chair a seminar called "The Changing South."[41]

As he observed what his friend Will Campbell in Oxford was enduring, Gray called Hodding Carter for advice about whether he should keep the speaking engagement. Carter immediately said, "If I were you, I'd pull out." Gray replied, "Wait a minute now. Let me tell you what they asked me to talk about." Carter reiterated: "I wouldn't go." Gray interrupted Carter long enough to tell him the topic for the first night. Carter said, "What?!" Then Gray told him the seminar topic. By then Carter's mind had been quickly changed. "You go," he said.[42]

So Gray went and in his first-night address stated that segregation was incompatible with the Christian gospel. When his statement was reported in the Mississippi press the following day, Mississippi State's president quickly called Gray in and told him he had three options: he could say he'd been misquoted, he could promise not to mention race or segregation again or any related topic while he was there (Gray exclaimed, "How was I supposed to talk about 'The Changing South' and not mention race!"), or he could leave. Gray refused all three choices. He instead remained in Starkville for a couple of days, hoping to find a way back into the university's event, but that did not happen.

When he returned to Cleveland, he soon found that his notoriety made a difference there. "The police started following me everywhere. Particularly if I went to the black part of town, they'd be right behind me. One night I went to Amzie Moore's house—that was the night I met Medgar Evers [by then, field secretary for the NAACP in Mississippi]. I had dessert with them and then we sat out on the porch, and I'll never forget that police car pulling up and just sitting there with its lights on blinding us. Of course we got up and went inside, but they stayed there with their lights on until I came out and got into my car and went home.

"The next day they went to see my senior warden, Dr. Jack Russell, and told him where I had been the night before. They said something like 'you better straighten your preacher out,' but Jack, who was not an integrationist by any means, told them it wasn't any of their business. 'Furthermore,' he said, 'I don't want you following him around any more.'

"Well, he was a big man in the county, so that solved that problem. But Jack's an example of someone who wasn't really sympathetic to what I was trying to do, but he felt like I was doing this in good conscience and so he was going to protect me."[43]

As further evidence of support among his parishioners, Gray points to the Sunday after his return from Mississippi State. "Coincidentally, the Sunday after I got back was the annual bishop's visit for confirmation. And we were doing pretty well in a little congregation like that—I had ten adults who were being confirmed. But with all that had been in the papers, I didn't know what was going to happen. But lo and behold, on Sunday morning all ten adults showed up to be confirmed. Now three of them pulled out the next week, but I remember how gratified I was that in spite of that, they had showed up and were confirmed.

"I had a good friend, a member of the congregation, Clark Boyd. He and his wife had come to Cleveland from up North, so they were sympathetic, but I remember he came by to see me Monday afternoon and said, 'You don't know how reassuring this is to me, to have ten people stand up and make that commitment in the wake of all that publicity about you at Mississippi State.' That was a moment of rejoicing, I think; we really thought that was a kind of high point. It suggested that there was acceptance of this out in the community. People who had not been Episcopalians before were coming in and they were under no illusions about me and the church; their eyes were wide open, so to speak."[44]

As for those members of the parish who did remain, they could hardly help but hear Gray's Good Friday sermon with a particular poignancy. Congregations often hear preachers speak of Christ's suffering and of his admonition to turn the other cheek and return good for evil, but seldom are they forced to hear it from the mouth of one who had recently practiced it so publicly.

Although Gray himself was far too humble a man to identify his sufferings with those of Christ, it would have been difficult to listen to the vivid description of that suffering as he spoke on Good Friday 1956, in Calvary Church, Cleveland, without thinking of what the preacher had recently endured. And when he quoted Anglican Archbishop William Temple, speaking of Christ, to the effect that "here in this courage that bears the worst that hate can do and still is unfalteringly calm; here, in this love that is unquenched and undiminished by the desertion of friends, by the blows and jeers of enemies—here we see Man fulfilling his true destiny and manifested as superior to circumstances," presumably at least some of those who heard Gray utter those words must have thought of their applicability to him.

Later in the sermon, he offered as an illustration of his point an example of a contemporary person attacked and betrayed by a friend who, rather than vowing to "get even," resolves not to let the blow make him "bitter and resentful," and Gray told his listeners, "What then will be the result? The man will have taken the pain which is the result of sin and made of it not the parent of further evil, but rather he will treat that pain as the raw material for increasing the total output of goodness in this world. There will be no rippling circles of evil spreading out from the original sin, but rather he will have absorbed the sin's power for evil within himself and cut short a possible further infection of evil in this world in which we live."[45]

About his situation in Cleveland, Gray acknowledges, however, that soon enough "things went a little downhill" from the high points of confirmation

Sunday and Easter. Episcopalians throughout the state contacted their bishop to express displeasure with his son's views. In addition, some members of Gray's own parish went to his father to complain about him. "Unbeknownst to me, some very unhappy people, including some very respectable people, even some people who agreed with me, made an appointment with the bishop, and said, in effect, 'Young Duncan has either got to cool it a little bit or he's going to have to leave.' And the way my dad decided to handle it was to tell them, 'I will communicate this to young Duncan, but I'm not going to tell him what to do.' And that's all he did—pass on to me their comments. But the fact that he was having to deal with that sort of thing did put me on the spot in a way. There I was creating trouble for him.

"But he never, ever put any pressure on me to do anything other than what I felt I ought to do. And if you rate his enthusiasm of really wanting to fight for integration. . . . He was of a different generation, and although he thought segregation was wrong and that it had to be eliminated, he would have been a lot more patient with doing it than I was."[46]

However, pressure of a very different kind came not long afterwards, once again in part because of Gray's contact with Amzie Moore. "I had stopped to talk to Amzie right there on the main street of Cleveland. Now in Cleveland the railroad track runs right down the middle of the main street, as it does [in] some of those Mississippi towns. And this man who ran what in those days we called a 'drayage' business—he hauled coal and other materials that arrived on the freight train to wherever they were going—he came up to me and cussed me out and said, in effect, 'You better watch out because you're not long for this world.'

"Well, I guess I took that more seriously than any of the other threats I've gotten because this man was actually known for having killed two black men and having got away with it. Now I think that the fact that he threatened me in such a public manner—there were people all up and down the street—probably kept him from ever carrying it out, but I took it seriously.

"I got a lot of anonymous phone calls over the years, and you don't know how to measure those. But most of them we just had to go on and assume they were nuts who didn't intend to carry out their threats. So this incident in Cleveland was the only one that I really kind of worried about."[47]

Although after these events, Gray did perhaps "cool it" to a certain extent, during Advent his parishioners heard him preaching against "self righteousness, or spiritual pride" for which, he said, "our Lord reserved his strongest condemnation." Gray told them, "Maybe we think we are free from this sin, at least, for we know our faults and imperfections. But our complacency and indifference with respect to duty and discipline in our religious life is, by and large, nothing more than a subtle expression of this very sin of self-righteousness. For apathy and complacency can only mean that we are satisfied, by and large, with things as they are; with ourselves as individuals and with the society in which we live. We feel no real compulsion for moral change and progress, for we feel we are doing quite all right as it is."[48]

Although Gray never mentioned the contemporary political situation in this sermon, one can understand how some parishioners may have felt that "young Duncan" was still not "cooling it" sufficiently.

Another example of Gray's persistence with racial issues was his involvement in the founding of the Mississippi Council on Human Relations the same year. The MCHR, like its counterparts in several other Southern states, was an outgrowth of the Southern Regional Council, an organization formed in 1944. At that time the SRC, whose membership was "heavily white" and composed primarily of journalists, ministers, and educators who were "moderate liberals," was unwilling to oppose segregation.[49] Instead, it committed itself "to fight racist propaganda and prepare southern opinion for gradual amelioration of black social conditions."[50] It thus alienated key Southern white liberals such as Lillian Smith, author of *Killers of the Dream*, and also some black leaders.[51] In 1951, the SRC changed its position and stated that its new goal was indeed racial desegregation.[52]

The 1950s MCHR was, however, short-lived as the result not only of a lack of funds ("We ran out of [SRC] subsidy money and we couldn't raise our own," Gray said), but also because of accusations of Communist influence, the pairing of race and "Red" that Southern politicians were finding very fruitful.

In this instance, one consequence of that pairing resulted in violence that Gray and others attributed to Byron de la Beckwith, later the murderer of Medgar Evers.

As Gray recalls, the Louisiana legislature had held a recent hearing during which the SRC was labeled as a "communist front." On the following weekend, the *Jackson Daily News*, a strong voice for racism throughout the 1950s and '60s, ran an article identifying the connection between the MCHR and the SRC and making similar claims of Communist links. In addition, the newspaper ran a list of the names of the MCHR board members, including that of Seth Wheatley, a Greenwood cotton broker.

The next night, a shot rang out and a bullet pierced the Greenwood home of Wheatley and his wife, the daughter of an Episcopal priest. Gray, who had of course spent several of his young years in Greenwood, "got in the car right away and drove up there to see what service we could be.

"Well, they seemed in pretty good spirits. They said that obviously the shot was intended to intimidate, not to kill them since the bullet had been fired at an angle, up towards the ceiling. I said, 'Do you have an idea who did this?'" They just looked at each other and then at me and said 'Delay,'" meaning de la Beckwith. Those who had grown up with him had, with intended humor, given him the nickname as a commentary on his tendency to "talk big" but not act.

Gray elaborated: "Now nobody ever proved that it was Delay, but I tell that story because it illustrates how we thought about him at the time. By then, Delay, who was an Episcopalian, was on a segregationist, racist crusade against the Episcopal Church. He finally left the Episcopal Church, but at that time I was getting letters from him, hate mail right and left, and threats. But nobody took Delay very seriously. He was just a nut, poor fellow. He was always trying to talk big about his 'aristocratic heritage' and so on. Everybody just kind of felt sorry for Delay or laughed at him. No one took him seriously. Of course later we found out we should have been taking him seriously, but by then it was too late.

"Another story about Delay that illustrates what I'm trying to say about him. I'd been getting these awful letters, and he also wrote letters to the Jackson papers, calling on the bishop to depose his son.

"Well, while we were still in Cleveland, they dedicated a new rectory in Greenwood, and I went over for the occasion. It was a beautiful Sunday afternoon and they had a big crowd—everybody was out in the yard.

"I remember seeing Delay across the yard and thinking, 'I don't want to see him,' and obviously he didn't want to see me. But all of a sudden, there we were face to face with each other, we couldn't get away, and I was just as mean as I could be. Delay said, 'Ah, you know I didn't mean that. I'm sorry.' He started apologizing and he was practically groveling. I didn't say much of anything else and that was the end of our conversation. But I hadn't been back in Cleveland three days before the letters started coming again, hate mail."[53]

Mississippi was certainly full of racist hatred in 1956. In addition to the activities of individuals and such groups as the Citizens' Councils, the state legislature itself took several steps that year to preserve and even celebrate the institutionalized racism that constituted what many of the state's leaders referred to as "the Mississippi way of life." First, the legislature repealed Mississippi's compulsory school attendance laws as preparation for abolishing its public school system if it found itself unable to avoid desegregation. Governor James P. Coleman, a "moderate" by Mississippi standards because, among other things, he had refused to join the Citizens' Council or speak at council meetings, signed the bill into law. Its immediate impact was that fewer poor children, white and black, attended school.[54]

The legislature also approved other measures that tightened enforcement of segregation in public transportation, authorized investigation of any organization operating in the state that officials considered subversive, and made it a crime, worth up to six months in jail and a thousand dollar fine, to advocate or encourage "disobedience to any of the laws of the State of Mississippi, and nonconformance with the established traditions, customs, usages of the State of Mississippi." In addition, Mississippi legislators approved, as other states had, a "resolution of interposition" that declared the *Brown* decision to be "invalid, unconstitutional, and of not lawful effect in the state." As Dittmer notes, after state House members passed the resolution 136 to nothing, the body cheered when a quartet of its members broke into a chorus of "Dixie."[55]

Well aware of this and other similar facts, Gray, like his friend Will Campbell, was willing to listen to job offers when they were made. In 1956, the National Council of Churches offered Campbell the job of working on race relations in the South. He accepted and moved to Nashville.[56] The same year the national Episcopal Church offered a similar job to Gray. He considered it, but finally said no.

When, however, Emile Joffrion, the rector of St. Peter's Episcopal Church in Oxford, decided to leave for a parish in Alabama, he suggested Gray as his successor to his vestry. Several vestry members were immediately doubtful—"What about all that ruckus he raised at Mississippi State?"—but another vestry member said, "Ah well, you know [Mississippi State president] Ben Hilburn!" and the discussion turned to Hilburn. Not long afterwards, three members of the Oxford vestry paid a call on Gray and the four quickly came to an agreement. In August 1957, the Gray family moved to Oxford.

CHAPTER 9

"*WE* ARE RESPONSIBLE"

Oxford, 1957–62

W HEN MOVING TO OXFORD had first come up as a possibility, Ruthie
was less than enthusiastic. "It wasn't Oxford. Oxford was fine. I'd
been in college there. It was leaving Cleveland. We were so settled in there.
I was born in the same house that my mother was born in, and I just hadn't
been raised with this moving around. Since we'd gotten married, we'd lived
in New Orleans, Shreveport, Pittsburgh, and Sewanee. I'd rather not have
moved again. Once we got there, it was fine, of course."[1]

In 1957, the Gray children—Duncan, eight; Anne, five; and Lloyd, three—
were too young to have much feeling one way or another about the move.
As it turned out, they found life in the town of a few thousand to be "idyl-
lic" for a child.[2] Their house in Oxford was on a short dead-end street with
woods to play in behind it. The town's business district, which centered
around the courthouse square, was within walking or biking distance for a
school-aged child. The square included drug stores that still had soda fountains, dime stores with candy and toys, and, just off the square, two movie
theaters with regular features. The church itself shared a parking lot with
one of the theaters. The public library was in the courthouse. The university
campus offered a swimming pool. In a day when girls were less likely to
participate in organized sports, Little League was popular with boys and
pick-up games were easy to find.

People who grew up in Oxford and return after some years as adults are
often struck by the narrowness of its older streets and the shortness of their
blocks. In some ways it was a child-sized town where most people knew
each other and where adults usually knew who a child's parents were and
could be counted on to both look out for a child's safety and, if not always
directly correct a misbehaving child, at least inform the child's parents if
misbehavior occurred. More than forty years later, Lloyd recalls, "Oxford
was such a great place for a kid. We could wander anywhere we wanted to

go. I loved Oxford. I loved my life there as a kid, separate and apart from the fact that I had wonderful parents and a happy home. Every time I drive over to Oxford even now, there wells up in me this good feeling."³

In Oxford, as in Cleveland, Pastor Gray continued his habit of bringing "lost sheep" home. Son Duncan remembers an extended visit from "Teegar" when he himself was nine or ten. He was part of a youth sports league that played on Saturday mornings on the playground of the town's single white elementary school, which stood across a street that ran by the side of St. Peter's. "We were playing football," he recalls, "and I looked around and Dad was standing on the sidelines with a guy who had sideburns, a leather motorcycle cap, leather pants and a leather jacket. The other guys said, 'Ooh! Your dad's hanging around good company!'

"Well, it turned out that this guy was a carnival worker. Now the carnival workers had many scams, and one of them was to shake down people on the rides and use it as a chance to pick their pockets. But for some reason, one particular day Teegar felt bad about this, and that it wasn't the right thing to do, so he went over to a man who'd lost his wallet and gave it back to him.

"Well, of course he'd broken the carnival workers' code of conduct, so these guys were out to get him, and he ran into the church to hide out. Dad found him, and he brought Teegar back to the house. He lived with us for a couple of weeks. On Sundays he came to church with us.

"Finally he left. He was going to get a job, go straight. He told us it was 'the end of one part of my life and the beginning of another.' And we all cried. He gave me his leather cap before he left. About a week later, however, we got a call: Teegar was in jail! So his resolutions didn't last long.

"That experience was really sort of a pattern though. In fact, Dad brought so many people home that when a few years later [sister] Catherine was on the way and they told us, 'You're going to have a new brother or sister,' my first response was 'we're adopting one of those folks that Dad brings home.' That was what I thought."⁴

At Gray's new parish things were going smoothly. Because of its size and financial resources, St. Peter's was still a mission church, which meant that some of its funding was supplied by the diocese, but the little mission continued to grow in a town and a state dominated by Baptists. In Gray's first full year, membership at St. Peter's increased from 273 to 303, and contributions increased by nearly 10 percent. The growth continued in the following years, so that by 1961 the congregational membership stood at 359, and their contributions had more than doubled their 1958 level to an amount over twenty-two thousand dollars.⁵ Part of the growth was almost certainly the result of continued postwar expansion and the slow but steady growth of the university, but a substantial amount was also surely due to the rector's pastoral skills as well as his appreciation for sharing with his church's members such everyday pleasures as Ole Miss football, an occasional "toddy," and good food and conversation.

At any rate, at the parish's annual meeting in February 1961, Gray had several pieces of cheering news to report. First, he reminded the congregation of their upcoming elevation to parish status, a diocesan confirmation of the church's health and growth. Next, he called attention to the addition to the parish's staff of an Episcopal chaplain to university students, the Rev. Wofford K. Smith, a month earlier. Finally, he formally announced the upcoming installation of a new organ for the church. Planning for the organ had begun in earnest a year earlier, but its acquisition had been speeded up considerably when Mrs. Robert M. Carrier, a member of the parish and the widow of an heir to the Carrier air-conditioning fortune, presented the parish with a check that made an immediate purchase possible. The new Dutch organ was installed in the summer and dedicated in November 1961.[6]

During the summer of 1961, Gray had also made some peace with a part of his past. As the family made its plans to go on a camping vacation in state parks in east Tennessee, Ruthie suggested they spend the first night of their trip at the Sewanee Inn, which had recently opened on the edge of the University of the South campus. "Well," Gray recalls, "I hadn't set foot back on that campus since I graduated and hadn't wanted to. But we did go there, and of course my uncle Ned was still the vice chancellor. And Ruthie said, 'Well, if we're going to be there, we'd better look in on the McCradys,' and I said, 'Yeah, I guess so.' So we did look in on the McCradys, and we all acted like nothing had ever happened, we were well received, and then we went on our vacation.

"It was probably because of that visit that about a year or two later I got a call from the university development office asking if I would be willing to serve as class representative for my seminary class to try and get contributions to the university's annual fund. Boy! You talk about a challenge! But then I got to thinking: well, whether we like it or not, an awful lot of our clergy are being trained there, and the university *did* do what we wanted them to do by integrating the seminary, and that's seven or eight years ago now, and we have to give them the benefit of the doubt.

"Anyway, the long and the short of it was that I rationalized it and came around. 'Yeah, I'll do it.' And I wrote, and, by George, I got response! Let's say our class had thirty members. I imagine I had ten of them who contributed, which was a big surprise to me. I didn't think we were going to do that well. And that included my old buddy Davis Carter, who when he left Sewanee, man! he wasn't *ever* coming back anywhere close! But that got me going again, and I wrote the rest of them a letter with the rationale that 'we've won our battle, and this place is going to be training our clergy and lay folk for a long time to come. We'd better help 'em out and support 'em. And we did."[7]

Of course it had been earlier in 1961—in January—that James Meredith had first contacted the University of Mississippi about admission. His initial letter had received a prompt and positive reply with an enclosure of admission application materials. In response to that, Meredith sent a second letter informing university officials, "I am an American-Mississippi-Negro citizen," and the admissions process ground to a halt as the court battles began, consuming all of 1961, and continuing into the new year. Almost a year to the day after Meredith's first letter to the university, a Mississippi federal judge denied Meredith's petition, and his attorneys took their case to the federal appeals court in New Orleans. Gray had been watching the process all year, and on February 11, 1962, which had been designated "Race Relations Sunday" nationally, he preached his first sermon to his congregation about their duties as Christians with respect to Meredith's admission, since he anticipated that the appeals court would rule in Meredith's favor and allow his registration for the spring 1962 semester. Gray's assumption that right would so readily prevail turned out to be mistaken, however. The appeals court panel ruled two to one against Meredith. In his dissenting opinion, Judge Elbert Tuttle warned that since Meredith was almost certain to win his case eventually, delaying his admission would only allow time for tensions to build and "massive resistance" to be organized. As we have seen, Tuttle's prediction was correct. In addition to the increase in community tensions, Gray's sermon also resulted in at least two families leaving St. Peter's.

But race relations weren't the only things on Gray's mind during the summer of 1962. Vacations for the Grays were usually simple affairs such as the camping trip the summer before or, more often, a trip south to "Tithelo," a property near Canton that Ruthie's father and several other men had purchased and developed as a rustic family gathering place. On visits to Tithelo, there would be swimming and fishing in the lake or playing cowboys and Indians in the surrounding woods. The fish caught during the day—brim and bass—would be served for dinner.[8]

On Friday, July 6, Gray's pastoral skills were called upon when Oxford's most famous citizen—Nobel prize–winning author William Faulkner—died, and his family contacted Gray to request that he perform the funeral,

just as he had done for Faulkner's mother nearly two years earlier. Faulkner
and his wife, Estelle, were what Gray referred to as "nominal" members of
St. Peter's. Neither was a frequent communicant at the parish, and Faulkner
less so than his wife, but it was where she and he went to church when they
went. As Gray put it, by the time he came to Oxford, the Faulkners were
most likely to show up for special services: Christmas Eve, Easter, or a bap-
tism, wedding, or funeral. It was Gray's impression that, like many parents,
the Faulkners had been more active earlier when their daughter Jill, who
sang in the church choir, was growing up. But after his mother's death in
1960, Faulkner had expressed a wish for funeral like hers—a funeral that
Gray had conducted at the family's request. Maude Butler Faulkner was
not a member of St. Peter's—in fact, she had been a Methodist, the denomination that Faulkner himself had grown up in. Her funeral had been
held at Rowan Oak, her son's home, and consisted simply of "The Order
for the Burial of the Dead" according to the 1928 Book of Common Prayer.
Gray's files contain a postcard dated "Oct 21," five days after Mrs. Faulkner's
death, that was addressed simply to "Rev. Duncan Gray, City." On the re-
verse, in Faulkner's small, difficult handwriting, is the message, "I thank
you, not only as spokesperson for my family, but for myself personally, for
your kindness and sympathy in our recent bereavement. Sincerely, William
Faulkner."[9]

Gray proceeded to do his best to fulfill the novelist's wishes for his own
funeral. Given the deceased's fame, however, reporters quickly began to
pour into town, and family members met them Friday evening to tell them
that they would not be allowed at the funeral, but would have their opportunity for photographs when the procession made its way from the Faulkner
home to the town cemetery for burial.[10] One such photograph made at that
time shows Gray conducting the graveside burial service in his long black
cassock and white surplice.

In the years after Faulkner's death, Gray was called on many times to
comment on his relationship with the author and discuss his understanding of Faulkner's religion. In 1997, for example, he was invited to speak at
the University of Mississippi for the centennial honoring Faulkner's birth.
One of the points he made there, as he had elsewhere in other talks about
Faulkner, was that he understood Faulkner as a man who considered himself a Christian—at least in the broadest sense of that word. Gray told his
audience, "He would not have passed any test of theological orthodoxy, nor
would he have wanted to; nor did he have any close ties with organized religion. . . . He thought of himself as a somewhat unorthodox, or even a mav-
erick Christian; but he said grace at meals—at least in my presence—and he

believed in a God who cared about the world that He had made and about the people in it."[11]

In that same address, Gray approvingly quoted Walker Percy, another novelist with Mississippi connections, who described Faulkner as "a theologian in spite of himself." Based on Gray's own reading of Faulkner's work, a process that had begun for him in high school, Gray elaborated on Percy's point to note that Faulkner "certainly had a strong belief in what the Church has always called Original Sin. He saw that human beings have in common a basic self-centeredness that tends to dominate our outlook on life and that is the root of so much of the evil and injustice with which the world is filled. He understood sin and guilt as profoundly *corporate* as well as individual in nature; and he knew how profoundly individual behavior could be influenced by corporate sin and guilt."[12]

In other contexts Gray was asked to provide a variety of other information about the person whom the historical marker outside St. Peter's refers to as "a distinguished member." He notes that his first serious exposure to Faulkner was in 1951, during his second year in seminary, when he made a study of *The Sound and the Fury* and *As I Lay Dying* as an independent study with Robert McNair, who taught Christian Ethics at Sewanee and who probably influenced Gray more than any of his other professors.

In two conversations with Sally Wolff King in 1996 and 1997, Gray said his first awareness of Faulkner's existence came when he was eight or nine and visited his grandfather McCrady, who was then priest-in-charge of the mission church of St. Peter's. Gray's uncle John McCrady, a painter of some regional renown, also visited periodically in Oxford at the time, and it is Gray's understanding that his uncle and Faulkner "stayed in fairly close touch with each other in those days," since they were both artists in an environment not especially friendly to men who pursued such "effete" occupations. As Gray notes, one of McCrady's better-known paintings, *Political Rally*, set on the Oxford Square, shows Faulkner with McCrady behind him, standing at the edge of a crowd listening to a candidate speak. Gray recalled that as a young boy, either his uncle or his grandfather pointed out Faulkner to him as a local writer who had a connection to St. Peter's.[13]

Gray's recollection of first meeting the novelist was at a party given by St. Peter's senior warden Billy Ross Brown soon after the Grays moved to Oxford.[14] Brown was a close sailing friend of Faulkner's.[15] In an address to an English class at Emory University in November 1996, Gray observed that "most of Mr. Faulkner's friends and associates were somewhat compartmentalized in relation to his own life. That is to say, his deer-hunting friends knew him primarily as a deer hunter, his fox-hunting friends as a fox hunter, his social friends as a charming gentleman and host, observing all of the social amenities when he chose to do so; but few, if any, of these knew him as a writer or thinker."[16]

In two addresses that he gave at St. Philip's Cathedral in Atlanta when he was theologian in residence there in the fall of 1996, Gray spoke of his experiences with Faulkner.

As rector of St. Peter's, Gray performed the wedding ceremony for Faulkner's niece Dean in 1958. Dean's father had been Faulkner's younger brother, but when the brother died a few months before Dean's birth, Faulkner acted as a father figure to her as she grew up and at her wedding gave her away. Gray recalls that as "father of the bride," Faulkner "filled the role with great pleasure and much gusto. We saw lots of him in connection with the pre-nuptials and the wedding itself, during all of which time he was at his courtly-gentleman best!"[17] As Gray and others in Oxford knew, Faulkner could be difficult and unpleasant, especially when he had been drinking.

Gray told his audiences at St. Philip's that much of his insight into Faulkner as a person came from Brown and another member of St. Peter's, Phil Stone, an attorney who had functioned as a mentor to Faulkner in his early years and to whom Faulkner dedicated his Snopes trilogy. Faulkner's formal education was limited—he failed to finish high school—and "Phil was a well-educated man with a deep interest in things literary." Stone had spent his late adolescence and early adulthood as something of a professional student: he had earned undergraduate and law degrees from both Ole Miss and Yale University, so, as Gray noted, "it was Mr. Stone who encouraged and guided Mr. Faulkner in those early years. He guided his reading, giving him many books and suggesting others." Faulkner aficionados are familiar with the stories that Stone had particularly recommended to Faulkner for their use of language, the King James translation of the Bible and the works of Shakespeare, but Gray told his St. Philip's audience that "Phil once told me that there was a third book that he put right at the top of the list for Faulkner: the 1928 Book of Common Prayer!"[18]

Outside of church, the Grays' and Faulkners' other connection was one of "back door neighbors." Their homes were separated by a wooded area, but particularly on one occasion the woods became a thing that drew the two families together. As Gray recalled, "some hunters would go into the [wooded] ravine hunting for squirrels. As they began to shoot into the trees, some of the bullets would go right through the trees into our backyard, and something very similar happened to the Faulkners. . . . In any event, Bill Faulkner put an end to all this with a letter to the Oxford *Eagle* in which he spoke sarcastically of what great sport it must be for those hunters down in the ravine behind his house who were shooting at 'tame' squirrels, squirrels who were more like pets to the children who played in the woods from time to time. As best I can recall, we had very little trouble with such hunters after that letter ran in the *Eagle*."[19]

In addition to this neighborly concern, Gray's daughter Ann was also a visitor to the Faulkner's place. By the early 1960s, she and a friend of hers who was related to Faulkner were entering the "horse crazy" stage that many girls go through. Faulkner, of course, had a stable full of hunters too high strung for Ann and her friend to ride, but the girls enjoyed cutting through the woods to Faulkner's stable where, with his permission, they helped care for his horses.[20]

The late summer of 1962 added a second daughter to the Gray household with the birth of Catherine—the child whom brother Duncan had thought would be an adopted visitor. Catherine was born on August 30, and Gray missed a diocesan conference he had been scheduled to attend as a result. The baby wasn't expected for another month—the official due date was September 30.

In September, Gray's friend Will Campbell, by then working for the National Council of Churches as a peacemaker in situations of racial tension, visited his friend in Oxford as they both saw the dispute about Meredith's admission continue to build toward a crisis. When Gray said to him, "Will, you're the expert. You're supposed to know what to do in these situations. Tell me, if you were in my spot, what would you do?" Gray recalls, "He puffed on his pipe, and he said, 'I'd get out of town *soon* and not come back.'" Gray insists that Campbell wasn't serious: "Will would have been the last one to say, 'You ought to do *this*.' The way I read it, I think what he was really trying to say was that 'I really don't know. I don't know what you ought to do. I'm here to give you moral support or do whatever I can to be helpful.' But what he said was, 'I'd get out of town fast!'"[21]

Gray, of course, did *not* get out of town, but continued his quiet work of attempting to influence his congregation's attitudes and the town's climate as events moved forward and Meredith's admission to the university became a surer and surer thing. The rector's efforts were to a certain degree successful—no members of St. Peter's and few, if any, residents of Oxford participated in the violence of September 30–October 1, but they were unlikely to have become rioters, in any case. And, of course, a full-scale riot— "an insurrection," according to one federal marshal—was what occurred on the Ole Miss campus that night. Once again, as we have seen, Gray almost certainly risked his life in trying to do his part to stop it, but as the night wore on, the situation deteriorated. Gray was forced to recognize his help-lessness and finally left for home.

After he left, things continued to go from bad to worse around the University Lyceum. More and more people who were not students infiltrated the campus, some undoubtedly drawn by area radio and television stations' recruiting tactics. WJDX and WLBT, the state capitol's leading radio and TV stations, for example, broadcast Confederate war songs and the new ditty recently composed for the crisis: "Never, never, never, never! No, never! / Ross is standing like Gibraltar, we shall never, never falter."[22] Although north Mississippi was ordinarily outside the Jackson stations' range, its segregationist management helpfully provided a remote radio broadcast from an entrance to the campus.[23] The broadcasts helped attract potential rioters from the southern part of the state, as did similar ones in surrounding states. As the night passed, eventually cars with license plates from as far away as California would appear in Lafayette County, their occupants ready to do battle against federal forces.

William Doyle, in *An American Insurrection: The Battle of Oxford, Mississippi, 1962,* captures part of the mood of many who appeared on the Ole Miss campus on the night of September 30–October 1: "The years melted away, and suddenly it was 1861 again and Jeff Davis was president, and the Confederate army was unvanquished, and the dream of an independent Southern republic was almost as alive as tomorrow morning, consecrated in blood and bullets and the glory of gallant, golden-haired young heroes. The transistor radios cheered the rioters on with songs of vengeance: 'I can take the hide off the Yankee that stole ol' Abner's shoes. . . . The Yankee took me prisoner, and if I get parole, I'll go right back and fight 'em, I will upon my soul.'"[24]

And indeed, like Rebel soldiers before them, the rioters persisted against the power of the federal government. Just before 10:00 p.m., a group of them broke into the university's fire station, commandeered its one fire engine, and drove it to the street known as the Circle in front of the Lyceum where federal marshals, armed with tear gas, were stationed. After a pass toward the marshals with the truck, its driver headed toward a nearby fire hydrant, and others hooked the hydrant to the engines' hoses, directing a powerful stream of water at the Lyceum's defenders. The marshals responded with pistol fire, aimed not at the fire truck's occupants, but at its hoses, which soon leaked profusely. Other marshals used their clubs to rip up the engine's wiring.

As the clock on the Lyceum approached 10:00 p.m., Deputy Marshal Gene Same aimed his tear gas gun at some rioters about to charge a group of marshals. Just after he fired his tear gas, he was hit by a sniper's bullet that severed his jugular vein. Three of his comrades hastily carried him inside the Lyceum, where one, Border Patrol Inspector William Dunn, pressed on the wound, managing to stop the hemorrhaging. Blood drained into Same's trachea, however, making his breathing difficult. When Same's heart stopped, Dunn gave him mouth-to-mouth respiration and external heart massage. Same's heart stopped twice, but Dunn and others managed to get it started again each time before an ambulance finally reached the back of the Lyceum and transported Same the several miles to the Oxford-University airport for a flight to Millington Naval Air Station in Memphis, where doctors finally managed to save his life.[25]

When the marshals saw what had happened to Same, they were infuriated. One demanded of Deputy Attorney General Nicholas Katzenbach, the Kennedys' man on the scene, permission to return fire on the rioters. Katzenbach refused, however, and the marshals continued to defend themselves and the building with tear gas alone.[26]

At about the same time a deputy marshal reported to Katzenbach, "Mr. Katzenbach, that's not a riot out there anymore. It's an armed insurrection." In addition to the noise of shotgun blasts, the marshals could now hear the sound of an automatic weapon. Soon they seemed surrounded by gunfire. Quickly there were other injuries: an Associated Press reporter, a federal prison guard, and a Border Patrolman. And the supply of tear gas was beginning to run low. Katzenbach got on the phone to the White House and urgently requested soldiers be sent to the campus.[27] With presidential permission, Katzenbach quickly put in a call to the Oxford National Guard Armory, where Captain Murray C. Falkner, a nephew of the Nobel prize–winning author (who had retained the family's original spelling of its name), answered. Kennedy had federalized the guard earlier, and now these local men were ordered to proceed to the Circle to defend the federal marshals at the Lyceum. Although "Chooky" Falkner strongly disagreed with the federal goal of integrating the university, in this situation he was first and foremost a soldier under the orders of his commander-in-chief, and so he gathered the men under his command and passed on their orders. While some of them initially resisted, Falkner quickly made clear to them that they were risking court martial by doing so, and they fell into line. By the time Troop E reached the Lyceum, a distance of less than two miles from their armory, they had been so violently attacked by rioters that seven of them were wounded, one by gunfire. Falkner's arm was broken by a projectile. As a result, by the time they reached their destination, they were willing to throw in their lot with the marshals, at least for the sake of

safety. But they were few in number and had only fifteen bayonets, no ammunition, and only a few hours of riot training. They did what they could,
however, filling in the ranks of marshals standing on the porch of the Lyceum, as their fellow Southerners attacked them physically and verbally for
their "treason."[28]

Around 11:00 p.m., the rioters had sufficiently repaired the fire engine
that the marshals had earlier disabled to use it again as a weapon, again
charging toward the Lyceum, only to veer away at the last minute. When
the truck headed toward the Lyceum for the third time, marshals heard the
order from one of their number to "shoot the tires." Several of them pulled
their pistols, aiming them at the tires, the hood, and the gas tank. At least
fourteen shots were fired; one of them apparently ricocheted and claimed
the second fatality of the night: Ray Gunter of nearby Como, Mississippi,
who had been standing to one side for hours, observing the rioting with
his childhood buddy Charlie Berryhill. Gunter and his wife, Virginia, were
expecting their first child within days.[29]

As the hands of the Lyceum clock moved forward and the marshals continued firing tear gas at the crowd, their supplies continued to dwindle.
Finally, sometime after eleven, they fired their remaining canisters towards
the mob, and a marshal turned to National Guard Sergeant Buford Babb
of Oxford. "O.K., Sarge, it's all yours," he said. Babb called to his men, "Fix
bayonets." As they obeyed, they let out an ear-piercing yell, a tactic they
had learned in their brief riot-control training. Their M-1 rifles loaded only
with bayonets, the twenty guardsmen marched aggressively forward a few
steps and then stood shoulder-to-shoulder with their bayoneted rifles extended at arm's length before them. At first the mob surged forward, but
the soldiers held firm, staring at the crowd through their gas masks. The
crowd hesitated, then fell back. Each time they began to charge, the guards-
mens' bayonets gave them pause. Babb thought, "We're not playing. You
can come across that street if you want, but we're not playing. We're not
going to stand here and let you hurt us or the marshals. We're not going to
let you burn down the Lyceum or tear it up."[30]

Nearly two hours earlier in Memphis, Brigadier General Charles Billingslea, who had been designated commander of all army troops and guardsmen assigned to the Oxford situation, had finally received clear orders to
prepare to transport his men to the scene of the riot. Billingslea decided to
send his men south in two groups. Company A of the 503rd Military Police
Battalion would be airlifted to Oxford to quickly reinforce the men at the
Lyceum, while the remaining two companies would travel by land. By midnight, Company A was on its way and began landing at the Oxford airport

about half an hour later. About an hour after that, they arrived at the edge of the campus, but at the wrong entrance. Plans were to have them enter the campus through a route that would have taken them to the back of the Lyceum, where crowds remained light; instead, they were deposited at the end of Sorority Row, a street that would require them to move uphill and then down another street that ran past the "Y" building, where Gray and others had occasionally found refuge from the tear gas earlier in the evening. Then the soldiers would turn onto the Circle and have to make their way through the midst of the rioters in front of the Lyceum.

At about 2:00 a.m. they reached the first turn, where the university chancellor's residence stood and where an emergency meeting of the school's board of trustees was convening. As its members paused to watch, a blaze of gasoline suddenly sprang up in front of the troops. At their lieutenant's command, the soldiers marched straight through the flames, barely breaking stride while brickbats and Molotov cocktails rained down upon them. As they held formation, some of the soldiers marveled to themselves that what they saw in front of them was happening in the United States of America. A battalion commander thought it was inevitable that the MPs would have to shoot in order to control the chaos, but at the moment he simply urged his men to "take it" and keep marching forward. They finally reached the Lyceum at 2:15 a.m., but as one company of just over a hundred men, they were hardly in a position to stop the mob—the defenders were still outnumbered by the hundreds of rioters.[31]

Over the next two hours, however, additional Mississippi National Guardsmen began to make their way to the university campus from other small towns in the state. Like Falkner's group, many of them struggled with the prospect of supporting federal troops against some of their own townspeople with whom they tended to agree, but there is no record of any Mississippi guardsman refusing to obey orders. The military command structure held.[32]

By presidential order, other troops were also on their way to Oxford in convoy from Memphis, and just before 4:00 a.m., B and C Companies of the 503rd arrived at the town's northern limit. As they made their way south toward the town square, they were attacked by men who had by now moved east from the campus into the heart of Oxford itself. On the square, as the rioters became more aggressive, the soldiers' commander barked out, "Load shotguns." As the order traveled down the convoy and MPs rose to carry it out, the mob backed off. Just before 5:00 a.m., the two companies reached the Lyceum. By then, much of the crowd had been chased away from the campus by the more than five hundred troops, mostly Mississippi guardsmen from the 108th Armored Cavalry. The remainder of the 503rd joined them to completely line the Circle in front of the Lyceum.[33]

Thus, after more than eight hours of rioting, the campus was finally under control. Gray's colleague, Episcopal chaplain Wofford Smith, who had much earlier joined Gray in taking weapons away from students, had been forced to spend much of the night in the basement of the Lyceum. Now as he emerged and looked down the Circle, he saw that the Confederate battle flag the rioters had hoisted onto the flagpole in the middle of it was still flying. He walked up to the pole and took down the flag.

The U.S. Justice Department's press spokesman turned to Katzenbach and asked what was next. Katzenbach replied, "We're going to register Mr. Meredith at 8 a.m."[34]

Meredith had spent the night under federal guard in his new dorm room several blocks west of the Lyceum, somewhat miraculously attracting little attention from the rioters, who instead contented themselves with attacking the troops. Somehow he had managed to sleep through most of the violence. He awoke at 6:30 a.m., dressed neatly, and at 7:55, accompanied by Chief U.S. Marshal John Doar and a group of marshals still wearing battle helmets, he arrived at the back door of the Lyceum, entered and registered for classes: algebra, English, foreign language, American Political Parties, and American Colonial History.[35]

* * *

When Gray had returned home from the campus around 11:30 the night before, he found that in addition to the student he had taken there earlier, several others had found refuge for the night. Ruthie, with these unexpected guests, her four children, including month-old Catherine, and a husband who had spent a good part of the evening in the midst of violence that had ended the lives of two persons, had retained as much of her customary calm as possible under the circumstances. Her brother Lloyd, then a law student at Ole Miss, had also come and spent the evening at the house out of concern for his sister.

And there certainly seemed reason to be concerned. The woods between the Grays' and the Faulkners' houses also bordered the university campus; rioters used it during the night as a passage to escape from troops and tear gas. About an hour after Gray arrived home, he heard their shouting and looked out to see a group of ten to fifteen armed men in his front yard. His first thought was, "Oh-oh, they're after me!" but as the group moved on he realized that their presence in the yard of the man who had earlier attempted to dissuade their compatriots was coincidental. In fact, he decided later that they may well have been in search of a cache of .45 caliber ammunition and hand grenades that he and a neighbor found in the garage of a vacant house near theirs later that day.[36]

After little sleep, Gray got up Monday and followed his usual morning routine: first a trip to the town post office, located on the courthouse square, to pick up his mail. He arrived there between 8:30 and 9:00 a.m. "I don't know what I was thinking about; my goodness, there were crowds all over the square there, and by then the regular army people were coming in great droves. They were coming right through the Square, and there were people still throwing rocks at the trucks when they came through the Square. And actually there was a helicopter coming down on the Square, and some guys with Mississippi State [University] jackets were throwing things at it.

"I went on down to St. Peter's [three short blocks west], not knowing any better, and went into the office, and I suddenly realized that a crowd had gathered behind the church in the parking lot. And of course the army trucks were coming right down the street on the side of the church on their way to the campus. But because of the building on the other side of the parking lot, the soldiers couldn't see these people until they were actually passing them, and when they did, the folks would run out and throw stuff at the soldiers and their trucks.

"Nicholas Katzenbach, who, by the way, was an Episcopalian, had made contact with me earlier, and he called me that morning, and I told him about this group behind the church. He sent the army folks in and cleared them out. So we were really part of the battleground for a little while, and I had some anxious moments. I thought they'd be turning on the church with rocks and breaking out windows and so on.

"I remember I got a call around 9:30 from Phil Zabriskie at 815 [national church headquarters] in New York. He had visited us the spring before, and he was worried about us and wanted to know what was going on. Just as I was talking to him, the army was coming in with tear gas after the guys in the parking lot, and you could hear 'pop, pop, pop.' He said, 'My goodness, are they shooting?' and I said, 'Well, they're shooting tear gas and I'm glad to see them. That's the right kind of shooting!'"[37]

Duncan's and Ruthie's parents were of course concerned about the well-being of their children and grandchildren, especially when they learned about Duncan's involvement on campus the night before, and they were soon on the phone to Oxford. Mrs. Spivey quickly made her way to the town itself.

"Now Mrs. Spivey was just the sweetest lady there ever was, but she wasn't exactly in favor of integration. So there we were in the middle of all this—telephone ringing off the wall, a lot of threatening calls already, and military police everywhere you went. You could hardly go through an intersection without getting your car searched. And Mrs. Spivey never said a word about all that; you would go up to where you had to stop and have the soldiers look in your car, and still no mention or acknowledgement of what was going on. She'd just talk about the baby and that sort of thing. Obviously she was worried sick, but she wouldn't say anything about the cause of all this. It was kind of funny. There *were* some light moments!"[38]

Although the traffic stops and auto inspections would continue for several weeks, by Tuesday, October 2, it was clear that the "insurrection" had been defeated. But while it raged, the *New York Times* estimated, more than 350 people had been injured. Another 300 persons were taken prisoner by the federal troops and marshals; only 25 of them were Ole Miss students and another 15 were enrolled at Mississippi State. The Ole Miss students were brought before the university's student judicial board and disciplined, although none was expelled. By October 3, after FBI interviews, most of the prisoners were released for lack of evidence.[39]

In the week that followed, several of Oxford's ministers called on Christians throughout the state to observe Sunday, October 7, as a "Day of Repentance," and they preached sermons in their respective churches on that topic. Gray's text, again from the prescribed lectionary, was from an Old Testament lesson: "If my people, who are called by my name, shall humble themselves and pray, and seek my face, and turn from their wicked ways, then will I hear them from heaven, and will forgive their sin and heal their land" (II Chronicles 7:14).

After reminding his congregation of the events of the previous weekend, Gray began by saying, "I'm sure that all of us here today—a week after the tragedy—feel depressed, burdened, and sorrowful; as, indeed, we should. But, as Christians, we cannot let our reaction stop at this point. Fundamental to the Christian faith is the profound conviction that even out of the worst tragedy, some good can come; that light can be born out of darkness; that there can be an Easter for every Good Friday. It is in the light of this faith that we call on you this morning to reflect prayerfully upon the past so that we may look creatively to the future. What can we *learn* from our tragic experience? (And God help us if we do *not* learn, for we will only have it to go through again.) What can we do *now?* This is the real question."

He continued, "The first thing we can do is face up to our own *guilt* in the situation. You and I didn't go out and throw the bricks and the bottles. You and I didn't go out there and fire the guns. Yet, you and I, along with every other Mississippian, are responsible in one degree or another for what happened. For we are responsible for the moral and political *climate* in our state which made such a tragedy possible. Maybe you and I didn't actually create this climate, but, if we didn't, it is certainly evident that we did all too little to dispel it or change it."

Quoting from the Confession of Sin in the *Book of Common Prayer*, Gray told his congregation, "The things that we have 'left undone . . . that we ought to have done' should bother us every bit as much as 'the things we have done that we ought *not* to have done.' The decent, respectable, and responsible people of Mississippi have *failed* when events like those of last Sunday night can take place within our state."

Gray went on to acknowledge the importance of the role of Mississippi's elected leaders in misleading many Mississippians about the likelihood that the federal government and its courts could be successfully defied. He asked his listeners to "think of the freshmen—and upperclassmen as well—who were out there throwing bricks and bottles the other night. Who could really blame them when the Governor of the state himself was in open rebellion against the law; a living symbol of lawlessness?" (The last phrase was one his critics would later fasten on as inappropriate and disrespectful of Barnett.)

He also reminded his listeners that Ole Miss freshmen in 1962 were ten years old when the Supreme Court had handed down its decision in *Brown*, and that they had grown up in an atmosphere "of textbook censorship, mandatory essay contests on white supremacy, and a massive propaganda campaign against the federal courts. . . . Seldom, if ever, has he been reminded that half of the people in Mississippi are Negroes and that they are people, too, with rights of their own."

He spoke also of "the thugs and the toughs from near and far who did the most damage Sunday night and nearly all of the damage Monday morning. What could you expect when supposedly responsible legislators were saying 'We will never surrender,' and 'The people of Mississippi know what to do!' What could you expect when so much of the Mississippi press was voicing the same sentiments. It was an open invitation for every thug and tough within three hundred miles to come pouring into Oxford, for they had every reason to believe that the decent, responsible people of Mississippi would back up their actions one hundred per cent. There are thugs and toughs everywhere, but they come in such numbers and with such violence only where they think they are wanted.

"The major part of the blame," Gray told his hearers, should be placed not only on the state's leaders, but also "upon you and me and all the other decent and responsible citizens of the state of Mississippi, who have allowed this impossible climate to prevail. It is *we* who have failed. We have failed our children, our University, and our state. It is for this that we pray God's forgiveness this morning."

Gray returned to his theme of Christian theodicy—that the role of Christians is to strive to bring good out of evil, thereby imitating God:

> But true repentance is more than just remorse. It includes also a re-direction of our will and our efforts. We must now give our all to salvaging the situation; to bringing order out of chaos, peace out of strife. We must come to grips with reality, throw off the old climate and put on the new. In short, we must accept the fact that the color of a person's skin is no longer a barrier to his admission to the University of Mississippi. I would hope that, as Christians, we could accept this as just and right, whether we like it or not. But if we are not yet to the point where we can do this, we, at least, can be realistic and patriotic enough to accept it as the law of the land. In any event, we should know by now that this is the only happy and reasonable issue out of all our afflictions. To think and act otherwise—to continue to breathe defiance and disobedience—will only bring more suffering and anguish. It will only mean more of the same violence and horror that has shocked us so deeply since we last came together at this altar of the Lord.

Gray ended his sermon by telling the story of Robert E. Lee in his parish church after the Civil War: When, during a celebration of the Eucharist, a black man made his way to the altar rail, the congregation hung back and left the man at the rail alone. Lee rose, walked to the rail, and knelt beside him to receive the bread and wine. Gray concluded, "This great man set a standard which has never quite been forgotten by the South. It is to this standard that we must now repair. For it will be through countless small words and deeds, done in the name of Christ by Christians, that this University, this community, and this state will yet redeem themselves for the tragic events of last Sunday and Monday."[40]

One parish member, Patricia Young, remembered the sermon well. "It was the most wonderful I've ever heard," she said. "It changed my whole perspective on things. It made me realize a lot of what the prayer book means when it talks about sins of *omission* as well as sins of commission.

"I was busy raising my children then, so there wasn't much else I could do. But I remember one time not long after that, I was in the [*Oxford*] *Eagle* office and Duncan walked out of the elementary school across the street. Somebody in the office said something ugly about him. I just got up and walked out and went and hugged him right there on the street. I tried to tell him several times what that sermon meant to me, but when I tried, I always just broke down crying. He must have thought I was some kind of an idiot."[41]

But for some in the university community and Mississippi, such redemption and repentance were of little interest.

Meredith's successful registration for classes marked only the beginning of a difficult semester for him. For the rest of October, he endured regular taunting and name-calling from students as well as occasional physical attacks. On the other hand, several faculty members and even a few students made a point of trying to welcome him and even to introduce elements of normality to his life: he had a regular weekly date to play golf with several faculty members. He was, however, constantly guarded by federal marshals who also shared his dormitory living quarters.

After Christmas and after a drive-by shotgun attack on Meredith's parents' home on Christmas Eve, he threatened to withdraw from the university unless conditions improved. Three days later, as Meredith attempted to study for exams in the library, over five hundred students followed him there to harass him. Despite such incidents, on January 20, Meredith announced that he would remain at the university, and in his second semester he hunkered down for the long haul and hit his stride academically, thereby raising his grades significantly.[42]

For the Grays too, the fall of 1962 was not an easy one. Oxford and the university campus had swarmed with reporters, so many Americans and all Mississippians were well aware of the events of September 30–October 1, as well as those of the surrounding periods. The phone calls to the Grays' home began almost immediately. With Duncan at work, Ruthie was often the one to answer the phone and be treated to a torrent of curses and other verbal abuse of her husband as well as threats against his life because of his views and actions. Duncan couldn't help but admire her self-control; she'd listen until the caller finished his tirade and then reply in her best Mississippi belle voice, "Thank you for calling. I'll give him the message," and hang up the phone.[43]

Gray said he found himself able to do something similar "some," but "obviously there were times when I was *very* angry, very *mad*. I *tried* to control it. Ruthie saw more of it than other people. You come home and you have to get it out of your system. I don't mean I was taking it out on her or taking it out on anybody else, but she had to listen to me 'express my anger,' so to speak," Gray said with a chuckle. "I think I was reasonably successful at not losing my cool in public, with individuals. But I certainly got mad."[44]

But sometimes the roles were reversed. As adults, Gray's children were well aware of the dynamics of their parents' marriage. Son Duncan described it thusly: "I sometimes think that some of Mom's role was to be valve for my dad's anger. It was sort of a good cop/bad cop thing. He'd be trying to be real nice about these people, but Mom would tell us the *real* story. And when she'd sometimes say things, he would just say, 'Ah, Ruthie,' but emotionally some of it would come out. Of course she was also his biggest cheerleader. She was always 'beating his drum,' so to speak, and he never had to beat his own drum."[45]

Ruthie's methods of coping with the situation were not always verbal. The three oldest Gray children remembered one persistent caller they refer to as "the breathing man" for his practice of simply breathing into the phone rather than saying anything. After many calls from him, Ruthie had finally had enough. "He kept calling until one day Mom got hold of one of those horns like you have at football games. The next time he called, Mom got Lloyd to hold the phone and she went "WHOOOO!" into the phone and all this cussing came out of the other end. He didn't call again after that."[46]

Duncan remembers that the calls would often come when his father was out of town, which suggested that callers knew Gray's travel schedule, a fact that made the family wonder if some of the callers could have been parishioners. "I think the ones that scared Mom most were the real specific ones where the caller would do things like mention one of our names and what they were 'gonna do' to us."[47]

Gray with his mother, Isabel McCrady Gray, and his sister, Ormond Gray (Caldwell), in the early 1930s.

Gray at age four.

Gray at age four.

Central High School football team, Jackson, MS, in the fall of 1942. Gray is in the top row, his number 26 partially obscured, second from the left of the player raising his hand. Gray played halfback. The team held its practices at the Mississippi State Fairgrounds, about two miles from the downtown school, which had no field.

Gray in his U.S. Navy ROTC uniform at Tulane University in fall 1947.

Ruthie and Duncan Gray following their marriage at Grace Church, Canton, MS, on February 9, 1948.

Gray and Ruthie as newlyweds in 1948, after their move to Pittsburgh, PA, where Gray had taken a job as an engineer with Westinghouse Corporation following his graduation from Tulane University.

Newlyweds Ruthie and Duncan in 1948, outside their Wilkinsburg, PA, apartment.

Gray, following his ordination to the transitional diaconate, Grace Church, Canton, MS, on April 8, 1953.

Gray with his father, Bishop Duncan M. Gray, following Gray's ordination to the transitional diaconate, Grace Church, Canton, MS, April 8, 1953.

In the Name of the Father and of the Son
and of the Holy Ghost. Amen.

✠

The Ordering of

The Rev. Elmer Monroe Boykin
A. B., B. D.

The Rev. Henry H. Crisler, III
A. B., B. D.

The Rev. Michael Thomas Engle
A. B., B. D.

The Rev. Duncan M. Gray, Jr.
B. E. in E. E., B. D.

The Rev. Peyton E. Splane
B. S., B. D.

Deacons
to the
Office of Priest
by

The Right Reverend
Duncan Montgomery Gray, D. D.
The Fifth Bishop of Mississippi

✠

Feast of Saint Simon and Saint Jude, Apostles
October 28, 1953

The Church of Saint Andrew
Jackson, Mississippi

Cover of the order of service booklet for the ordination to the priesthood of Gray and his fellow seminary graduates at St. Andrew's Cathedral, Jackson, MS, October 28, 1953, the date of the Feast of St. Simon and St. Jude.

Gray with fellow graduates from the School of Theology, University of the South, just before their ordination to the priesthood. The ordination took place at St. Andrew's Cathedral, Jackson, MS, on October 28, 1953, the date of the Feast of St. Simon and St. Jude. *Left to right:* Elmer Boykin, Mike Engle, Hal Chrisler, Gray, and Peyton Splane.

Three generations of Duncan Grays outside St. Peter's Episcopal Church in Oxford, MS. *Left to right:* Duncan M. Gray III, vested to serve as acolyte; Bishop Duncan M. Gray Sr.; and Duncan M. Gray Jr. while he served as rector of St. Peter's. The photo was taken in 1965 when Gray Sr. was already bishop of Mississippi. His son would become bishop in 1974 and his grandson in 2000.

Gray in St. Peter's Episcopal Church, Oxford, MS, in 1962. Gray served as rector of St. Peter's from August 1957 to August 1965, when he left St. Peter's to become rector of St. Paul's Episcopal Church in Meridian, MS. It was during Gray's years in Oxford that he became nationally and internationally known for his support of civil rights, especially because of his actions in support of James H. Meredith's integration of the University of Mississippi in 1962. Martin J. Dain Collection, Southern Media Archive, Special Collections, University of Mississippi Libraries

The Gray children at St. Paul's, Meridian, MS, 1967. *Front*, Catherine Gray (Clark), and *behind*, Anne Gray (Finley), Duncan M. Gray III, Lloyd Spivey Gray.

A formal portrait of Gray as the seventh bishop of Mississippi. Gray was elected bishop in 1974 and served until his retirement in 1993.

By special invitation of the Vatican, Gray meets with Pope John Paul II at his summer home in Castel Gandolpho on August 7, 1983, following a service at the papal villa.

Gray on the campus of the University of the South, TN, in 1993 during his service as Chancellor to the University.

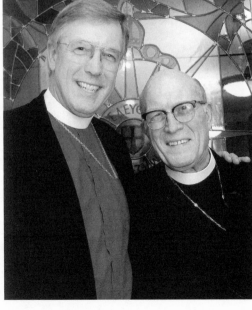

Duncan M. Gray Jr. with his son Duncan M. Gray III after his consecration as ninth bishop of Mississippi on June 17, 2000. The son's consecration marked the third Gray to serve as bishop of Mississippi. In each case, there was one intervening bishop of Mississippi between each Gray bishopric.

Children, spouses, and grandchildren gather for the Grays' fiftieth wedding anniversary in 1998. *Seated in front, left to right:* Lloyd Gray Jr., Mary Gray. *First row:* Isabel Gray, (son) Lloyd Gray, (daughter) Anne Gray Finley, Duncan Gray Jr., Ruth Spivey Gray, (son) Duncan Gray III, Shelton Clark Jr., (daughter) Catherine Gray Clark. *Second row:* Sally Gray (wife of Lloyd), Tillman Finley, Mack Finley, Ruth Finley, Peter Gray, Kathy Gray (wife of Duncan III), Duncan Gray IV, Shelton Clark.

Duncan and Ruthie Gray on the occasion of their fiftieth wedding anniversary, February 1998.

CHAPTER 10

"THEY WOULDN'T FEEL COMFORTABLE UNTIL I WAS GONE"

Oxford, 1963–65

BEFORE LONG THE LETTERS BEGAN ARRIVING TOO. Ruthie, determined to keep some lightness in a difficult time, filed them in fold-
ers labeled "in-state goodies" and "in-state baddies" as well as "out-of-state
goodies" and "out-of-state baddies." Three of the four files remain. As Will
Campbell has observed, it is almost emblematic of Gray and his loving,
forgiving attitude toward his fellow Mississippians that it is the "in-state
baddies" file that has mysteriously disappeared. "I lent it to somebody, I
can't remember who, and I just never got it back," Gray said. Both the Grays
remembered, however, that the "in-state baddies" file was significantly
thicker than the "in-state goodies" one.

Among the correspondents from Mississippi who attacked him in writing, Gray remembered most clearly one from an acquaintance who, with
his wife, had been students at Ole Miss with Ruthie. "I got this wire from
him just *blasting* me, calling me the worst kinds of things you could think
of! And then he ended it with 'Love to Ruthie!' I think that's so typical of
Mississippi relationships—people would scream bloody murder, but then,
okay, 'love to Ruthie.'"[1]

Mississippi correspondents who praised Gray and thanked him for his
words and actions included two elected officials, one a state legislator from
Greenville and the other Gray's congressman, Rep. Frank E. Smith, a moderate who had already lost the state's Democratic primary as a result of the
state legislature's redistricting; legislative leaders who objected to Smith's
moderate stands had been careful to draw the new district lines in a way
that Smith was bound to lose.

Another supporter was Aaron Henry, president of the state NAACP,
with whom Gray had visited on Amzie Moore's front porch in Cleveland
several years earlier. Henry wrote in response to Gray's October 7 sermon,

"Yes, I agree with you that we all must take our rightful share for the tragic consequences of the last week. The Negroes for not letting our white brothers know much sooner that we were desirous of implementing the legal gains made over the past few years. The Whites for being so reactionary toward those gains and the Federal Government for taking our complaining to them so lightly for almost too long. Yes, the Church has to accept its share of the blame for its silence for almost too long." Henry concluded his letter, "Please accept the thanks of a grateful people for your forthright stand now as in the past. . . . With you we will work to bring a better day to all," and signed it "Gratefully yours."[2]

A. D. Beittel, president of all-black Tougaloo College near Jackson, wrote to thank Gray "for the splendid statement you made recently concerning the violence which erupted in Oxford" and invited him to join the effort to revitalize the Mississippi Council on Human Relations, of which Gray had earlier been a part when he was in Cleveland. Beittel wrote, "We need your prophetic leadership," adding, "There was a little flurry of excitement last spring when we reorganized the Mississippi Council, and the Citizens' Council proceeded to point out its Communist affiliation. [The allegation was unfounded.] The pressure from the Citizens' Council was enough to prevent three of the proposed officers from taking office. The chairman was to have been a retired businessman in Jackson and two of the vice-chairmen were [Roman Catholic] Bishop [Joseph] Brunini of Jackson and Rabbi [Charles] Mantinband of Hattiesburg."[3]

Gray also heard also from the Wheatleys in Greenwood, whose house he had visited after it had been shot into by, they believed, Byron de la Beckwith. Several residents of Oxford who were not members of his church also wrote to express their thanks, including Mrs. Calvin Brown, one of the most powerful doyennes of Oxford University society. Oscar Carr, a former king of Memphis' annual Cotton Carnival and the otherwise socially prominent owner of Mascot Plantation in the Delta near Clarksdale, sent "a note of encouragement in regard to your sermon . . . on which I congratulate you." Carr wrote, "If the church fails to speak up on the side of law and order, we might as well disband," and added, "I for one feel repentant for all of us in Mississippi who have failed in leadership."[4] Carr would soon offer more substantial support to Gray and his parish.

A mother in Sardis, about thirty minutes' drive from Oxford, wrote Gray that her daughter was one of his parishioners and told him, "I am thankful and honored that she has such a man as you for her spiritual guide."[5]

A student who had camped out in the Gray's home the night of the riot wrote a thank-you to both Grays, adding, "Witnessing a man standing up for right and order in the midst of chaos helps restore the faith of man in his fellow man. It is refreshing to see you call for sanity and reason in the times that have come, and it is even more refreshing to see a lesson in practical Christianity practiced where it is sorely needed. God bless and keep you, good Christian people!"[6]

More poignantly, Gray received letters from two Mississippians who thanked him for his willingness to speak out, but confessed their own lack of courage to do so. A businessman in Natchez wrote simply, "I wanted to speak out, but I was afraid." A man in Starkville wrote, "I still cannot speak as I should. I am a coward. Just the other day I was invited to a conference at Tougaloo. I had to refuse because I dare not let it be known abroad where my sympathies lie. My son is a freshman at the medical school in Jackson and you get the idea."[7]

Outside Mississippi, supportive and appreciative letters came from as far away as Spain, Korea, Japan, Indonesia, Hawaii, and the Canal Zone. Gray heard from members of the army, navy, and air force. Letters came from all over the United States. A number came from lawyers, a few from university professors, a couple from U.S. congressmen and a couple from journalists, as well as many from people who didn't otherwise identify themselves except to thank Gray for his stand and his October 7 sermon. From Durham, North Carolina, J. B. Rhine, well-known for his work in the field of extra-sensory perception and other paranormal phenomena, wrote that he and his wife were "deeply moved by the insight of your sermon," and he included "a small check."[8]

A number of letter writers identified themselves as Episcopalians, often lapsed. One such, a seventy-three-year-old man in Connecticut wrote, "It was my intention to stay away from church until I went in feet first. Maybe now I better go *once* to see if some cobwebs have been brushed out of the high corners." A woman in Raleigh wrote, "I am an Episcopalian, although an unenthusiastic one, for ever since my college days I have felt that the Church temporized toward all pressing problems," but she added that she and her husband "send you our grateful respect for your goodness and courage. We thank you as Churchmen and even more as Americans."[9]

A New York attorney, a Jew, wrote, "If all the clergy of your state, and I include the Rabbis who constitute the spiritual advisors of my own faith, were only to speak out as you have, I believe that such men as Governor Barnett would not long be in public office." He added, "As I have been taught in my own religion, we are all the children of one Father and to the extent that we live up to this ideal we can make and will make this a better world in which to live."[10]

Others who lived outside the South wrote to express not only their thanks, but an awareness that racism also existed in their communities. A woman from Buffalo wrote, "It is ironic that we all go to church, synagogue, or cathedral once a week and then, after hearing about the brotherhood of man, go right out and persecute the Negro," adding, "When I speak to some of my associates in this way, they respond with, 'Would you want to marry a Negro?'"[11]

A correspondent from East Lansing, Michigan, wrote on October 10, "May I join the large body of people who applaud your sermon of last Sunday on race relations and the police state? You have made it easier for many of us who feel as you do and yet are reluctant, at ease in a northern Zion, to take a stand that is easy enough to take in safety. You express our sentiments, but you do so in an ambience of personal peril. One has compunction, as a northerner, to lambaste the south. We have not the right, with our own sins on our shoulders—even the memory of the Detroit race riot some years back."[12]

Roger Treat, a resident of Virginia and the editor of the *Encyclopedia of Football*, wrote energetically, "I am a native of Connecticut, and I watch the disgraceful performance of the people there with the uneasy feeling that back home we are just about as bad although in different ways. I have no respect whatsoever for a clergyman who fails to come out punching for what is right and decent, who hides behind a comfortable dogma and bleats about sins, and goes along with 'local custom.' . . . On the other hand, I love a guy with guts and you qualified gloriously."[13]

Gray also heard from two Little Rock women, both involved in efforts to integrate and support the city's public schools. One was Vivian Brewer, in 1958, the first chair of the Women's Emergency Committee to Open Our Schools following the 1957 crisis over the desegregation of Little Rock's Central High School, and the other was Pat House, in 1962, the chair of the same group. Both expressed hope that Gray's words and actions and the events at Ole Miss would encourage "responsible people" to speak out. Mrs. Brewer wrote hopefully, "Wouldn't it be wonderful if these foolish, tragic attempts to impede social progress could be finished now and forever by the brave ones in Mississippi!"[14]

Gray's seminary classmate and friend Davis Carter, who a year earlier had surprised Gray with his contribution to Sewanee and who by then was on the staff of U.S. Representative Jack Brooks of Texas, wrote from Washington, "All your friends here knew you'd be doing the right thing at the right time, but we've had our fingers crossed about your offering that shiny head as a target. Whoever said that Trinity Season was dull?" His boss, Representative Brooks, sent a clipping from the *Washington Post* which had covered Gray's October 7 sermon. Brooks wrote, "Not many sermons make the front page!" and thanked Gray for the "fine job" he was doing.[15]

Early the next year, Brooks wrote a letter to Attorney General Robert Kennedy commending Gray's ongoing efforts in Oxford and adding, "Incidentally, it was in September 1960, that I personally helped Mr. Gray put a Kennedy sticker on his bumper while we were on our way to campaign for the President in the Second Congressional District of Texas."[16]

Two months before that, however, Gray had received a letter from Ralph Dungan, special assistant to the president, in response to the media coverage of the October 7 sermon. He wrote, "The President has asked me to express his deep appreciation for your public spirit and concern for our national principles. Equal opportunity will be achieved in all parts of our public life only through the action and cooperation of both the Government and private citizens. Your continued constructive leadership in this will be important."[17]

The writers of "out-of-state baddies" were a much less exalted group, and many of them, judging by their penmanship and grammar, also far less educated. But their number did include some professionals, among them a Chicago lawyer, a South Carolina doctor, and a professor at a large state university in the Deep South. The majority of the baddies came from the Deep South, but in addition to the Chicago attorney, Gray had correspondents from California, Illinois, Maryland, Massachusetts, Missouri, New Mexico, New York, Pennsylvania, and Washington, D.C., who attacked him and his stand. The writers' most prominent themes were to accuse Gray of Communism because of his support for integration, with the view, well known at the time, that the NAACP was simply a Communist front. As one letter writer put it, "I want to tell you the NAACP is dominated by Russia, they are calling the signals and we have no better sense than to jump every time they call. Where is our backbone? And pinheads like you and a few other so-called Ministers are taking time out to knock their own people because they are not afraid to stand up and be counted."[18]

Another popular theme was that Gray had strayed from the proper ministerial role. One letter writer admonished him to "confine your efforts to the morals of your congregation, as you should, and leave governmental, political, and economic affairs to those more qualified." Another wrote, "As long as you and so-called Ministers like you rave about social issues and neglect the Gospel, the Church will continue to go downhill."[19]

Several correspondents urged Gray to consult his Bible for evidence that separation of races was God's plan. Combining several themes, one wrote, "Since you didn't quote any Scripture in your sermon as reported in the [Memphis] *Commercial Appeal*, one wonders where you got so much authority to speak from a religious point of view on the Oxford-University crisis, or could one guess it was from the N.C.C. [National Council of Churches] who are following the same *peace line* as Khrushchev and Castro—'peaceful coexistence,'" and she urged Gray to "*study*" Genesis 10 for evidence that "it was God that separated the races."[20]

Another correspondent simply urged Gray to "quit preaching niggerism."[21]

Gray also received a folder full of supportive letters from fellow clergy, including a number of Episcopal bishops. Many clergy letters came from Mississippians and other Southerners, but others came from places as far away as California, Ohio, and Connecticut.

Arthur Lichtenberger, then presiding bishop of the Episcopal Church, telegraphed Gray his support following the October 7 sermon, but two months later also wrote him, enclosing a copy of an article on the Ole Miss rioting and Gray's role that had appeared in an Anglican publication in Uganda.[22]

Gray heard too from John Hines, then Episcopal bishop of the diocese of Texas, but later to be elected presiding bishop following Lichtenberger, and from John Shelby Spong, then in his first parish in Tarboro, North Carolina, but later bishop of the diocese of Trenton, New Jersey, and famed as a popular liberal theologian addressing such matters as biblical literalism and sexual orientation.[23]

Gray's old theology professor at Sewanee, Howard Johnson, wrote, "I could easily have predicted how you would distinguish yourself—and have to suffer for it—because in 1953 you proved your mettle and showed yourself to be courageous and prophetic but also a rational and stabilizing influence, devoid of fanaticism even while fighting fanaticism in the opposite camp. . . . You cannot imagine with what pride and thankfulness I have pointed to articles about you in the newspapers and have said to my friends, 'I was one of his teachers.' If that sounds like a boastful remark, I can temper it by adding, 'All I did was teach. He *acted*.'"[24]

Gray's friend and predecessor at St. Peter's, Emile Joffrien, wrote, "For my money, you have . . . taken a position with the prophets of Israel and the daring figures of the New Testament, and this I say, knowing full well that you will reject it, of course, but . . . I am proud to be wearing the Anglican collar."[25]

On October 10, the National Council of the Episcopal Church issued a statement in which it quoted approvingly Gray's words in his September 30 sermon: "None of us can stand in the presence of Jesus of Nazareth, look him squarely in the eye, and say, we will not admit a Negro to the University of Mississippi." The council went on to call on all Episcopalians to abide by the church's 1961 General Convention resolution "to conform to federal and Supreme Court orders in regard to giving all students equal access to our public schools."[26]

Gray also heard from Methodist, Presbyterian, American and National Baptist, Roman Catholic, Disciples of Christ, and Congregational clergy. The director of the Commission on Social Action of Reform Judaism wrote, "In reading of your attempt to quell the riots and bloodshed at the University of Mississippi, I am compelled to express to you my deep admiration for your courage in witnessing religious truth at a time of testing and crisis." He added, "May God give you the strength to continue to stand for dignity and brotherhood."[27]

Several Northern clergymen sent letters that not only expressed appreciation of Gray's stand, but also included confessions of their own communities' racism. A Presbyterian pastor in Vandalia, Illinois, site of an early state capital, wrote, "Abraham Lincoln was in the House of Representatives here. He got his start in politics here in Vandalia. We are proud of that. But yet in a town of 5,500, there is not one Negro in residence. In a county of 20,000, there is one family of 8 Negroes. Perhaps we are even further separated from our brothers in Christ. At least the South is not hypocritical about its true feelings."[28]

An Episcopal clergyman in New Jersey wrote, "It so happens that we have had racial problems here in Englewood, for 27.4% of the population is Negro. The controversy has centered on education, but the real problem is civil rights and housing."[29]

The rector of an Episcopal church in Bronxville, New York, sent a copy of a letter to members of his parish which was headlined "WHO THROWS STONES AT MISSISSIPPI?" To his congregation he wrote, "We are appalled, but how righteous is our indignation? How clean are our hands and how solid is our position? Can any Northern community that might hesitate to welcome Ralph Bunche or Leonard Bernstein or Marian Anderson as citizens and neighbors sit in complacent judgment upon a state claiming to possess problems unknown to us?"[30]

Of course not all church correspondence was supportive. The vestry of Trinity Episcopal Church in Natchez, Mississippi, sent Gray's father a nearly three-page letter, complaining of his son's words and actions, that gives clear evidence of what some Mississippi Episcopalians, who would surely be considered "responsible people," were saying and thinking at the time. On behalf of the vestry, its clerk wrote:

> Our concern lies in our fear not only that [Gray and Smith] are creating misunderstanding and distrust among the lay people of the Diocese toward members of the clergy, but also that they are creating among the people of Mississippi and the South generally a feeling of ill will toward the Episcopal church and its members.
>
> What is perhaps more important, these two men, because of their present positions in Oxford and the University, have a particular opportunity to influence the thoughts and feelings of inexperienced young people who are away from home and who are in an unusually sensitive and impressionable stage of development. When they are instilled by ministers of their own church with ideas repugnant to those of their parents, the result must, in many cases, be unpleasantness, discord and strained family relationships among the people of our diocese.
>
> We are led to believe that the Reverend Smith and the Reverend Gray are opposed to segregation of the races. We are also led to believe that they, as a matter of principle, did not approve of the resistance offered by the State of Mississippi and its officials to the forcible placing of James Meredith in Ole Miss by the Federal government. As to these matters, we are in complete disagreement with them.
>
> We are tiring rapidly of apologists for the Southern White people, particularly among members of our own clergy. Those of us who have lived among Negroes and associated with them throughout our lives are not burdened with any guilt complex about our treatment of them. There are not many people of our acquaintance who have not contributed freely their time, effort and money toward the improvement of the Negro race and to the raising of their standards of education, living conditions, and general welfare. . . .
>
> It is indeed true that we take a realistic view of the Negro race. Although we did not create their difference, we recognize that they are different from the White race. We do not think that as a race they have yet reached the stage of accomplishment which entitles them to complete social acceptance or which makes integration either desirable or practical. We think that their future welfare and happiness, as well as ours, will be best served by affording them every opportunity for development along their own lines, among their own race.

The letter concluded, "We . . . accord completely to [Gray and Smith] the right to have and express their own opinions. Where these opinions are so diametrically opposed to those of a majority of their churchmen within the diocese, however, we think that they should seek a more congenial climate in which to express them."[31]

Of course not all who opposed Gray's actions were content with such relatively tempered appeals to their bishop. Gray's family was also the target for verbal abuse. Later that fall when Ruthie was shopping at an Oxford fabric store just off the town square, a woman shouted "Nigger-lover!" at her across the aisles.[32] Son Lloyd remembers that his mother "got a lot of social snubs and had clerks in stores being rude to her when they found out who she was."[33]

Gray's older son, Duncan III, then in eighth grade, was labeled by some of his contemporaries with the same epithet that had been shouted at his mother, but unlike her, it was never said to his face. He thought that his participation on the school football team and the comradeship that the team provided protected him against such name-calling, even among some teammates who held views like those of the woman in the fabric store. He added, "There was plenty said in my presence like 'nigger-this' and 'nigger-that' and 'the damn Kennedys'—but I was too 'chicken' to say anything about that!

"Nobody ever said anything directly to me about my dad. There may have been some friendships that faded that I chalked up to other things—in those days I wasn't drinking and smoking like some of my buddies were. But my friends pretty much stayed the course.

"My folks seemed to be so much in charge and so stable that we kind of *rested* in the security that they provided. They weren't falling apart, so we didn't see any need to either. What I remember that should have probably bothered me more than it did were the phone calls. But a couple of years later, in 1964, I remember that the thing that upset me most was the football team, which wasn't good. *That* really made it a *terrible* year!"[34]

Duncan's brother Lloyd's memories were similar. "I *knew* what was going on in Oxford, at least to a limited extent, as much as a ten- or eleven-year-old can. I knew what my dad was going through. And I *knew* we were different in a sense. I had arguments with kids at school. I remember arguing over 'who caused the riot.' My friend said James Meredith caused it, and I said Ross Barnett caused it! But we would have our arguments and then we would go on. I *never* felt alienated from the community or isolated. I suppose our parents shielded us from some of that, but what's most amazing, given the circumstances, was how *normal* our childhood was.

"I have very vivid memories of the night of the riot and what followed. That was something that was *important*, of course, but not consuming to me as a child. I loved baseball and I played in the woods behind the house with my friends. As a child, those were things that were important to me too.

"Like Duncan, I didn't have to deal directly with attacks on my dad from other kids. Sometimes Mama would tell us that somebody had said such-and-such about Dad, but that was always in the context of helping us understand what was going on. I was never *aware* of being excluded from any birthday parties or any kind of gathering. I was never confronted by an adult or a teacher. I think a lot of that was that people maintained that Southern politeness and gentility—at least to us. They might cuss my dad to his face—or even my mother. But people seemed to draw the line when it came to the children."[35]

Sister Anne's recollection was different, however, perhaps because she was a girl—perhaps more socially attuned than her brothers to such slights or perhaps because girls tend to deal with conflict differently. In any case, she recalled birthday parties to which she was not invited and conversations with her mother that were intended to soothe the hurt feelings that resulted from such incidents.[36]

Many in the community certainly held to views very different from the Grays. When Will Campbell returned to Oxford in October, he said to his friend, "This is so different from the rest of the country. Most places that you go when you see a profusion of American flags, you know it's the John Birchers and the rest of the far right. But when you go into Oxford, Mississippi, and you see an American flag, you know that that's a wild-eyed liberal!"[37]

Gray confirmed Campbell's observation: "I mean people didn't *want* to see an American flag! You made people *mad* putting an American flag in front of your house because that meant that you were sympathizing, fraternizing with the *enemy*. The enemy *was* the United States government. An American flag in Oxford meant you were a 'wild-eyed liberal' instead of a John Bircher!"[38]

In this atmosphere, the threats and telephone calls continued ("We never had a cross burned, but you know the Klan was not really active in north Mississippi"), but so did Gray's ministry to his parish, and, as a pastor at heart, it was the opposition within his congregation that produced the most pain for him. Even as he talked about that opposition, however, he prefaced his account by saying, "Let me say right at the outset that I don't want to dwell on those things too much without saying that there was a lot of support. That's the positive side of it that you need to keep in mind."[39]

But a number of parishioners left the parish, some for a so- called Anglican Orthodox Church that formed in town, but didn't last long. Perhaps most damaging was the departure of members of the Ole Miss athletic department. Nearly every member of the department except legendary head football coach Johnny Vaught was a member of St. Peter's. Their departure "had a severe economic impact on the parish, because they were some pretty substantial pledgers," Gray said, but then immediately recalled the support of those who stayed: Junie Hovious, coach of the Ole Miss football team's offensive backfield, and his wife, Kitty, as well as athletic trainer "Doc" Knight. "Some of the coaches and their spouses were pretty rough on me. That hurt," he acknowledged, but "on the other hand, I again want to say how much it meant to me that Junie and Kitty supported me because they were under pressure out there in the department."[40]

But another member of the parish, Frank Peddle, whose wife, Marge, was a member of the Godchaux sugar family, disagreed strongly with Gray and was instrumental in helping to found and support the new Anglican Orthodox congregation. "Folks like that hurt the parish financially when they left," Gray recalled.

As the years passed, however, Peddle had a change of heart that he attributed to his readings in philosophy. Trained as an engineer, physicist, and educational psychologist, he described himself in his younger years as "a died-in-the-wool materialist whose religion was technology."

Peddle recalled that in the fall of 1962 he "had some rough words with Duncan personally—face to face, eyeball to eyeball. I was upset about his stand out there in the Grove. I wasn't upset about Meredith—I was a Yankee. I believed in integration—but I was very, very upset with Duncan at the time. I told him, 'You're going to attract those crazies [the rioters] here to the church. They're going to break out those stained glass windows.' I realize now that I was putting my priorities in a different order from Duncan's. I thought it was *my* church."

Thirty-five years later, Peddle recalled that several years after the riot "at communion, I put my hand on his and asked for forgiveness. I love that man. I know now what he represents. I think he represents Christ, both as a priest and as an individual. Doing what he did, getting out there on that statue, placing himself in personal danger." His voice trailed off.[41]

Although many in Oxford did not welcome Gray's presence, Episcopalians elsewhere wanted to hear his message. Late in 1962, Gray was invited to speak at a series called "The Church and Race" at St. Mark's Episcopal Church in Houston. In his address, he began with modesty and gentle humor by telling his hearers, "Judging from the first two programs in this series and the persons who participated, you expect to hear from an expert. The only claim that I have to such a status is the fact that I am nearly a thousand miles away from home, and this, I understand is what makes one an expert! The trouble is that the problem of which we speak this evening is *not* a thousand miles away, but as close as your own front doorstep. Therefore *you* are as much of an 'expert' as I am, and I am here only to pass along some thoughts of my own for your consideration."

After addressing the question, "What is the church's stand in regard to race?" by directing his hearers' attention to copies of "The Church Speaks on Race," the pamphlet which Gray had helped draft in the 1950s, and the issue of "What has the church *done* in this area?" Gray moved on to address the question, "What should our role be as individual Christians *and* as a parish of the Episcopal Church?"

Again, he began modestly by saying, "I hope that you will note that in this section I speak from the first-person plural. I do not want to say what *you* should do, lest I imply somehow that I, or we at St. Peter's, Oxford, have done these things. Certainly we have not."

Speaking to the question of "What should *we* do," Gray first suggested such obvious steps as making sure that worship services were open to all, forming study or discussion groups that crossed racial lines and might or might not focus on race, and having parish leaders take public stands on particular community issues. Then he went on to say, "But ultimately, whatever the parish as a whole is able to do will depend on what you and I as individuals are willing and ready to do. Remember that you and I *are* the Church. Where then do we begin?"

Gray suggested that his listeners first examine their own attitudes toward African Americans and read and inform themselves about scientific studies of race and prejudice. Second, "having done this, no matter how much our ideas may have changed, if we are still taking about '*the* Negro,' then we must take another step. We must remember that there is no such thing as '*the* Negro,' but only *individual* Negro men, women, and children, just as there is no such thing as '*the* white man,' but only individual white men, women, and children. As Christians, we must learn to look at each human being as an individual *person* without characterizing or pre-judging him in our own minds because of some group to which he belongs. It is, perhaps, at this point that the greatest difficulty occurs in the process of desegregation in the South. Many Southerners, having little or no meaningful contact with Negroes of similar educational and cultural opportunity, tend to attribute to Negroes as a race characteristics and behavior which, in fact, belong only to *some* Negroes, just as some of these same characteristics and behavior belong to *some* white people."

Then Gray said, "Having come to terms with ourselves, as Christians, we must be prepared to serve as leaders in the struggle against racial prejudice and discrimination." Long before the phrase became a catchword, Gray told his listeners that as they determined in what sphere they could best act, they should use as their guidepost for action "the single criterion, 'What would *Jesus* do?'"

"But," he cautioned, "in all our efforts, there is one thing we must keep uppermost in our minds. Even our *best* efforts are tainted with sin, and we all bear the burden of guilt. No one of us can speak to another from some self-righteous pedestal, for the integrationist is no less a sinner than the segregationist."[42]

At this point he went on to quote a passage from his friend Will Campbell's book *Forty Acres and a Goat*, a passage that remained a favorite of his over the years:

I have seen and known the resentment of the racist, his hostility, his frustration, his need for someone on whom to lay the blame and to punish. I know he is mistaken, misguided, and willfully disobedient, but, somehow, *I am not able to distinguish between him and myself.* My sins may not be his, but they are no less real and no less serious. Perhaps I have been too close to this man. Perhaps if I had not heard his anguished cry when the rains didn't come in time to save his cotton, if I had not felt the severity of his economic deprivation, if I had not shared his joys and his sorrows in birth and in death, in success and in failure; if I had not been one with him in so many gales of tragedy, I would be able to condemn him without hesitation. If I had not shared his plight; if I had not lived with him in an atmosphere of suspicion, distrust, ignorance, misinformation, and nefarious political leadership, surely my heart would break *less* when I see him fomenting violence in front of *his* school and *his* church. Perhaps I would not pity him and love him as much if I were not a part of him. But pity and love him I do.[43]

As his commentary on the passage, Gray said, "We must speak God's word of judgment with relevance and with power; but not unless we realize that this judgment falls upon *us* as well as upon those to whom it is addressed; and not unless there is love, compassion and understanding for all on the other side of that judgment."

He acknowledged, "These things I have suggested do not come easy. Indeed, we cannot do them on our own. So the essential thing that *all* of us must do is to *grow* in the knowledge and love of God. Without His grace and His mercy, His power and His strength, our words and our deeds are of no effect."

Acknowledging also that "sermons and speeches will not go very far toward solving our racial problems" and that "education and instruction are not the final answer either," Gray told his hearers that "in the means of grace to be found within the worship of the Church lies the real potential for a significant change in the human heart."

In conclusion, he told his audience, "We cannot expect to be very effective in this struggle for racial justice . . . so long as our attention is centered upon Man rather than on God. So long as we think only in terms of human standards, our consciences will always be at the mercy of the kind of people we happen to know. . . . To perform our duty as Christians . . . we must keep our eyes fixed upon Christ Himself, and not even upon the best of his human disciples."[43]

As 1962 became 1963, the tension in the larger Oxford community continued and sometimes manifested itself in almost comical ways.

Early in 1963, a special meeting of the St. Peter's vestry was called after Meredith met with a Japanese reporter at the church. During Meredith's second semester, the university administration had barred reporters from interviewing Meredith on campus, so when the reporter arrived in Oxford, he had made contact with the Wesley Foundation chaplain, and the two of them came by St. Peter's to ask for Gray's assistance in arranging interviews with the university chancellor and Meredith. Gray contacted the chancellor, who refused to be interviewed but agreed to the Meredith interview if it was conducted off campus. At that point in the day, Gray's responsibilities called him away from the church.

Later that afternoon, the editor of the *Eagle*, which had offices just behind the church, frantically called the police to report that Meredith was holding a meeting at St. Peter's. Police contacted church leaders, and Senior Warden Bob Holley rushed to the church, where he found Meredith, his guarding marshals and MP's, and the Japanese reporter. Holley located Gray at his home and the two of them returned to the church, where Meredith and the reporter were just concluding the interview. According to vestry minutes, Gray had known nothing of the meeting; apparently, after their earlier conversation, the reporter had simply assumed that meeting Meredith at St. Peter's would be acceptable. Minutes from the vestry meeting state that "after discussion, no action was taken," since the vestry was apparently convinced that the incident had simply been the result of a misunderstanding. The minutes also state: "The reporter left Oxford on the next bus."[44]

As the year went on, both Gray's supporters and his opponents were active, and in at least one case, those who opposed his stands and actions acknowledged his right to take them. Son Duncan recalls his father anticipating a visit from several men who were members of the parish. "When they said they were coming, he just sort of braced for the worst. But they came and said to him, 'We just want to tell you that we really disagree with what you're doing, but we believe you need to do it.'"[45]

According to Gray, Holley, a physician, was very supportive—"We couldn't have made it without him"—as were other members of his vestry. One, Will Hicks, who served as clerk of the vestry, made a point of enclosing a personal note to Gray's father in a letter from the entire vestry congratulating the bishop on the twentieth anniversary of his consecration. Eight months after the riot, Hicks wrote, "Your son Duncan holds the admiration and love of almost every communicant. In the emotional upheaval we are going through, he has demonstrated that rare gift of the ability to remold and redirect conflicting and deep-seated convictions. You have cause to be proud of him, and we are proud to have him as our Rector."[46]

Despite Hicks's words, a significant number of parishioners had left St. Peter's, some for the Anglican Orthodox congregation and others to form a second Methodist congregation in town. And even among those who didn't leave, there was the issue of their financial support for a parish with a rector with whom they disagreed.

"February 1963 was a critical time," Gray recalled. "We had our stewardship dinner in February, and given the feelings of some people, we didn't know if we were going to make it. We had achieved parish status, we were self-supporting, but it looked like this could be the end—we didn't know if we were going to be able to keep that up."[47]

But Delta planter Oscar Carr followed up his earlier supportive letter with a phone call, asking what he could do to help. Gray responded, "Man, have I got a job for you! We've got a stewardship dinner coming up!" Gray had known Carr since childhood. When another Deltan, Farley Salmon, called with a similar question, he got a similar answer. Salmon was a former Ole Miss star quarterback and had dated Ruthie when both were students at the university. "So Oscar Carr, a former Cotton Carnival king, and Farley Salmon, a former Ole Miss football star, were our speakers at the stewardship dinner in February. I mean the Lord was good to me through these two friends! The bottom line was that we made our budget, just about where it was the year before, and we remained afloat.

"But that was also due to Bob Holley and some others like him who doubled and tripled their pledges. Really it was an unhealthy budget. Bob Holley and his wife were carrying more than 25 percent of it. But we were very, very fortunate and blessed in terms of that kind of support, since we had a lot of pledges cancelled because people disagreed, and it was a rough time for several years after that."[48]

One family's opposition that caused Gray real pain was that which came from members of the Falkner family—and the pain was not because they were relatives of the famous late novelist, but because of the nature of his pastoral relationship with some of them before the Meredith crisis.

Like Faulkner's wife, Estelle, the writer's brother John, his wife, Lucille, and their sons James (known as Jimmy) and Chooky (the National Guardsman who had led his men onto the campus during the riot) were all members of St. Peter's. Although John seldom came to church, he had spent time talking with Gray "in the wee small hours, when he was drinking and so forth," and had given him "the instructions for his funeral, what he wanted done and how he wanted it done."

Although John never achieved anything like his older brother's fame, he had published several novels and also dabbled in painting, as his mother Maude had done before him. John had given Gray the original of one of his paintings (he regularly made copies of his paintings for friends who admired them) called "Going Home," which portrayed a black preacher riding on a mule toward the center of a cross on the horizon as the sun set behind it. Gray had hung it in the parish hall's front parlor and considered it not his personal possession, but the church's.

After the riot and Gray's stand, however, all the members of this branch of the Faulkner family ceased coming to St. Peter's except Chooky.

Gray recalls, "Chooky, bless his heart, didn't agree with me. He got placed in the business of leading the National Guard, and he wasn't in sympathy with what was going on, but he did his duty. And he never missed a Sunday at church. Now he might glare at you or jump on you, but he never quit coming to church."[49]

Years later, Chooky Falkner agreed that his differences with Gray were substantial, but in his view, "He ain't the church. He was a rector. I been in that church longer'n he is and that church is not him. It's not mine either. It's *God's* church. I go to church for God."

Falkner, who was christened at St. Peter's in 1931 and confirmed there in 1942, added about Gray, "He was a good rector though, even if I didn't agree with some of the things he did. He took care of his flock." Asked if he thought of Gray as "a real Christian," Falkner replied with emphasis, "Oh, yeah! Lord, yeah!"[50]

But he added, "He can say what he wants to, but I ain't got to pay no attention to it. He can be standing up in the pulpit preaching, but I can just pick up the hymnal and read that. We got some beautiful hymns if you just look at 'em. I go to church to take communion."[51]

Brother Jimmy, however, had a different response. Along with Peddle, he had been one of the organizers of the Anglican Orthodox congregation and Gray saw him as the "militant" in the family. When John Faulkner died in the spring of 1963, Jimmy visited Gray at St. Peter's and asked for the funeral directions that John had given Gray previously. He also asked for the return of his father's painting. Gray complied with both requests, but over forty years later he said, "That was one of the things that hurt me the most I think—that they wouldn't let me have his funeral. When he was in the hospital in Memphis, I went up there to see him and they wouldn't let me in. I went back before he died, and they still wouldn't let me see him. Jimmy told me to stay away, that I couldn't see him."[52]

Thirty-five years later, Jimmy Faulkner was still unwilling to talk about his and Gray's differences: "There's no need to open up old wounds."[53]

In the midst of the continued fallout from Gray's words and actions, the parish had received a financial windfall early in September with the final settlement of the estate of Kate Skipwith, a longtime member of the community. Oxford attorney Phil Stone, himself a former St. Peter's vestry member, had drawn Miss Skipwith's will, and the amount of her estate was substantial, including a sizable bequest to St. Peter's. Relatives, however, challenged the will, and the case went to trial during the week following the riot. When the trial ended on September 11, 1962, the judge upheld the will as drawn, and St. Peter's received Miss Skipwith's bequest, a sum of $300,000.[54]

Although the bequest was obviously a financial blessing for the parish— "It was a lot of money in those days and we could use the income," Gray recalled—in another way it represented complications for the rector. Once the money was actually received, Gray recalled, "Nobody ever said it, but you could sort of get the feel that there was a reluctance to spend any of that money, or much of it, because they were anticipating the day when the folks who had left the parish came back. Then they'd want to know, 'Where's that money?' And the vestry didn't want to have to say, 'We spent it while you were gone.' Nobody was making it explicit, but I got the strong feeling that they wouldn't feel comfortable spending that money until I was gone."[55]

Reluctance to make use of the bequest was by no means the sum of the new parish's financial problems. For each of the years that Gray remained as rector of St. Peter's, both giving and membership continued to drop. Despite the efforts of Oscar Carr and Farley Salmon and despite the generosity of Holley and a few other members, in 1963, the amount pledged by the congregation dropped to $23,918.73, $2,000 less than the year before. Forty-nine persons had already left the parish in 1962, and another forty-eight followed them in 1963. The number of communicants in good standing (a designation for those who both pledge and take communion regularly) dropped from 221 in 1962 to 179 in 1963. The drain in both money and members continued in 1964 and 1965. The amount pledged each year was about $2,000 less than the preceding year. In 1964, another forty-six persons transferred their membership to other churches and the number of communicants in good standing fell again to 164. During these years other members simply became inactive.[56]

In the midst of this, despite the financial and membership drains and the occasional minor crises such as the Meredith interview, not all of Gray's energies were spent on his parish. As the president of Tougaloo College had written in the letter he sent Gray immediately after the riot, in 1962, a group of committed Mississippians did manage to revive the Mississippi Council on Human Relations (MCHR), which had died in the late 1950s for lack of funds. Gray joined its board in late 1962, becoming board president the following year. Gray recalls it as "a meaningfully integrated group," an obvious achievement in Mississippi in the early sixties. "It was one of the few places that blacks and whites really did get together in Mississippi in those days. [Mississippi NAACP president] Aaron Henry was on our board as one of the vice presidents, and I guess there were more blacks on the board than whites. Of course the only place we could meet was on the Tougaloo campus, and we didn't get too many whites out there."[57]

As 1963 became 1964, Mississippi continued to be a locus for civil rights activity, including Freedom Summer, which began with the June murder of three civil rights workers in Philadelphia, Mississippi. Gray would find himself involved in the aftermath of the murders the following year.

The summer passage of the 1964 Civil Rights Act, which occurred at almost the same time the civil rights workers were murdered, had made states' Jim Crow laws covering public accommodations null and void. The NAACP had conducted a few tests of the law in Mississippi motels, but in November 1964, the MCHR held its annual meeting in one of Jackson's downtown hotels—the first such integrated event in the city since Reconstruction.

"That meeting was at the King Edward Hotel," Gray recalls, "and it may have been the kiss of death for the King Edward! It was right near the railroad station, and at one time it was *the* place. It was where all the legislators stayed in the old days, and it was a sumptuous place then, but it was going downhill. The other downtown hotels—the Heidelberg, the Robert E. Lee, the Walthall—were doing better. When we tried to find a place in Jackson to meet, everybody had an excuse but the King Edward. They took us, maybe because they needed the money bad!

"We had 200, maybe 250 people, about evenly divided whites and blacks. That meeting was a great, great time, momentous on a symbolic level."[58]

Summer 1964 also brought the Episcopal Church's annual convention, held that year in St. Louis. Gray had been elected an alternate deputy to the church's previous convention in 1961—"not too bad for a young guy, but I couldn't have been elected dogcatcher in 1964!" In addition to the church meeting, however, for Gray the added attraction of St. Louis was that his beloved St. Louis Cardinals were playing that year in the World Series at about the same time as the convention. Once again, Holley stepped in with support for his rector: "He said, 'Would you like to go to the General Convention?' I said, 'Sure!' So he gave me a hundred dollars and said, 'See how long you can stay on this.' Well, you could stay in the downtown Y for four dollars a night then, so I went to the General Convention, and a friend actually gave me a ticket to a World Series game while I was there, so I saw that too. And they beat the New York Yankees!"[59]

After he had returned from St. Louis in the summer, Gray found himself rethinking his position. "Now as a matter of principle, I had made up my mind that I wasn't going to leave Oxford for a year or two after the riot, because I didn't want for it to even appear like I was running away. But as I began to see that attitude in the parish about Miss Kate's bequest, I said to myself, 'Well, I really believe it's time to move on.'"[60]

Son Duncan's recollection was that the Grays assumed that "moving on" in 1965 would mean moving out of Mississippi.[61] But then the rectorship of St. Paul's Episcopal Church in Meridian, Mississippi, became vacant. St. Paul's had had a vacancy only three years earlier and had approached Gray then about filling it, but that was July of 1962, and Gray had declined because he saw the storm clouds building in Oxford.

"I wrestled with it, but I finally said 'no,' and one of my reasons was that I knew the Meredith thing was coming. I didn't have any idea we were talking about *rioting,* but I felt like it would be real difficult for some new person coming in and having to go through all that. I had been there for five years by 1962 and had established relationships, so I felt like I *couldn't* go at that point," Gray recalled.[62]

But in the summer of 1965, Gray accepted the renewed call from St. Paul's, where Duncan Hobart, one of the Episcopal ministers whom Gray had admired since high school and who had preached at his ordination to the priesthood, had earlier served as rector for over thirty years. In August, the family moved the approximately 150 miles southeast to Meridian, located near the state's border with Alabama in Lauderdale County. Immediately northwest lay Neshoba County, where a year earlier the murders of Freedom Summer workers Michael Schwerner, Andrew Goodman, and James Chaney had occurred. Once again, the Grays were moving into a hot spot.

CHAPTER 11

THE PHILADELPHIA MURDERS

Mississippi, 1964

JULIAN BOND, who served as communications director for the 1964 Freedom Summer effort, writes, "My job for Freedom Summer would be to spread the word that the Civil Rights Movement was staging a confrontation with the nation's most recalcitrant state. The summer's events provided more than enough opportunity to contrast democracy's dream with its reality in Mississippi."[1]

Democracy's reality for African Americans in Mississippi was certainly grim enough. When the 1960s began, only 7 percent of black Mississippians who were eligible had managed to register to vote. Five majority-black counties had no registered black voters. Intimidation by whites had made this situation possible, and blacks were well aware that the dangers they ran from white registrars if they attempted to register could go well beyond humiliation and ridicule.

In addition to the political realities that blacks faced, economic and educational realities were equally daunting. Black Mississippians' incomes were the lowest of any state and 86 percent lived below the federal poverty level. Infant mortality among African American babies was twice that of whites, and two-thirds of housing occupied by blacks in Mississippi was designated either "deteriorated" or "dilapidated." Half of that housing lacked water and two-thirds of it lacked a flush toilet. In 1964, Mississippi school districts spent an average of $81.86 per year on a white child's education and $21.77 on each black child's. In 1960, the median number of years of schooling completed by white Mississippians was eleven; for blacks it was six.[2]

When word of Bond's coming "confrontation" spread among Mississippi's white leaders, that was exactly what they began to prepare for. Bond writes, "In preparation for the summer, the city of Jackson, Mississippi, increased its police force from 390 to 450; they added two horses, six dogs, and two hundred new shotguns; stockpiled tear gas; and issued gas masks to every policeman. They amassed three canvas-topped troop carriers, two half-ton searchlight trucks, and three giant trailer trucks to haul demonstrators to two large detention compounds at the state's fairgrounds. The city's pride was 'Thompson's Tank,' named after the incumbent mayor—a thirteen-thousand-pound armored battle wagon built to the city's specifications at a dollar a pound."[3]

Many white Mississippians were nearly hysterical at the prospect of the "outside agitators" coming into their state to interfere with the Mississippi "way of life." Gray, on the other hand, recalls not only meeting with some of the "agitators'" leaders, but also working to help arrange dialogue between them and black and white Mississippians through the auspices of the Mississippi Council on Human Relations (MCHR).

Gray had been involved in council activities in the 1950s, and when in the fall of 1961 a biracial group of Mississippians met to resurrect the group, he had joined again. By May of the following year, council members met at Tougaloo College and approved a "statement of purpose" which called for "promoting respect for all men regardless of race, color, or creed." In the 1960s, this apparently mild statement was not accepted as such by all Mississippians, however, and the Jackson Citizens' Council quickly responded with a three-page letter sent to its members which ended with the ominous words, "We are confident that members of the Jackson Citizens' Council will know how to deal with this threat to our community." Since this was the Citizens' Council and not the Klan, its members were content with such tactics as recording license plate numbers and taking photographs of those who attended Human Relations Council meetings, but these and other methods of intimidation were successful in convincing those who had agreed to serve as officers of the organization to change their minds.[4]

Despite the veiled threats and other forms of intimidation from the Citizens' Council, MCHR succeeded in getting on its feet and soon began to meet quarterly. In addition to Gray, its board included a number of Mississippians active for racial justice in the state: Aaron Henry, president of the state NAACP; Rabbi Perry Nussbaum, the leader of Temple Beth Israel in Jackson, whose synagogue would later be bombed by the Klan; the then Reverend Bernard Law, only three years a priest and then assistant to the Catholic bishop in Jackson, but later cardinal of Boston; and Dr. A. D. Beittel, president of private Tougaloo College near Jackson—almost the only place in the state that the biracial group could meet prior to the passage of the 1964 Civil Rights Act.

Early in 1963, Gray addressed the gathering in a talk titled "Religion and Race in Mississippi." The February meeting particularly stuck in his mind because it was, as it turned out, the last time he saw Medgar Evers alive. In his talk, he spoke of how "Christian theology knows nothing of the category of race," and added, "race is a human category, not a divine one, and, as St. Paul says, we should no longer 'regard any man from a *human* point of view.'" He acknowledged that Christian churches as organizations had done too little in Mississippi to fight racial injustice, but reminded his hearers that "the Church is first and foremost *people;* and whenever and wherever individual Christians have been active in the struggle for racial justice, the Church has also been active *in and through them."* Later that year, the group elected him as its president.[5]

Describing itself as "not primarily an action group, although there is nothing in its charter to prevent its taking action," the MCHR claimed to provide "an opportunity for men and women of good will, of both racial groups, to meet together and to work for better understanding and better human relations in Mississippi." In pursuit of this purpose, members of the Council on Human Relations met again at Tougaloo in March 1964 with five representatives of COFO—the Congress of Federated Organizations— which had been created as the umbrella organization of various civil rights groups to organize and implement Freedom Summer. Those present to talk about the summer plans were representatives of major civil rights organizations: Robert Moses of the Student Nonviolent Coordinating Committee, David Dennis of the Congress of Racial Equality, Arnell Ponder of the Southern Christian Leadership Conference, Johnny Frazier and Aaron Henry of the National Association for the Advancement of Colored People, and also Pearlena Lewis, a Tougaloo student who had been involved in the May 1963 lunch counter sit-ins in Jackson. Henry addressed them about plans for the summer.[6]

Such meetings as the one at Tougaloo attracted little attention, but Julian Bond's promise of summer "confrontation" and the presence of the white students were sufficient to bring national media attention to Mississippi once again. One more reason for that media presence in the state was an event that occurred early in the summer. In late June, just as 250 of the Freedom Summer student volunteers who had trained in Ohio were preparing to leave for Mississippi, three civil rights workers, two of them white Northerners and one a black Mississippian, were murdered in Neshoba County in east central Mississippi near the state's border with Alabama. On June 21, Robert Moses, now acting as director of voter registration for the summer effort, told the volunteers training in Ohio, "Yesterday three of our people left Meridian to investigate a church burning in Neshoba County. They haven't come back and we haven't had any word from them."

As Bond notes, Mickey Schwerner, Andrew Goodman, and James Chaney "were already dead when Moses made his announcement."[7]

Schwerner, twenty-four, and his wife, Rita, had moved from New York City to Meridian, Mississippi, in Lauderdale County in January as paid organizers for CORE. Chaney, twenty-one and a Meridian native, joined them as a volunteer and had invested so much of his time and energy in the effort to encourage local blacks to vote and participate in Freedom Summer activities that by the time the three were killed, Schwerner had received approval from state CORE leaders to add Chaney to the local office's very limited payroll. Goodman, twenty, a student volunteer from City University of New York, had arrived in Meridian the day before his murder.

Although Schwerner and Chaney had spent most of their time in Meridian, and although Lauderdale County had a chapter of the Klan which included some of the county's law enforcement officers among its members, sources agree it was no accident that the murders occurred in neighboring Neshoba County. William Bradford Huie, who covered the search for the three bodies and the ensuing trial for the *New York Herald Tribune*, wrote shortly after the murders:

> The power structure in Meridian controls the police. The police are *told*, and they do as they are told, or they get fired and have trouble getting other jobs. Moreover, they have trouble renting houses or getting their own water and electricity turned on. . . .
>
> The smart way to resist "agitators" in Mississippi is not to break their heads but to protect them and let time and circumstance break their hearts. The men with the power in Mississippi know this. Only the peckerwood politicians and the jerks in the backwoods don't know it. This is why the prosperous growing cities of Jackson, Meridian, and Biloxi are relatively safe for "agitators"—and why most of the violence occurs in places like Philadelphia and McComb. Violence is bad business.
>
> Mickey Schwerner lived five months in Meridian without a hand being raised against him. He walked and rode down dark streets unmolested. Had he remained in Lauderdale County and not ventured into the rural counties, he'd be alive today.[8]

At the time of the Neshoba County murders, Meridian, where the Grays would move in 1965, was the second largest city in the state after the capital of Jackson. In its heyday, it had been a center for rail transportation of timber and cotton, but with the decline of the railroads, Meridian had also declined from its peak. But in the 1960s, it was still relatively healthy and relatively progressive. It had an interesting population mix. In addition to its core of Protestants, the citizenry included a significant number of Irish Catholics whose families had come south to build the railroad and never left. Like Irish Catholics elsewhere in America, they played an important role in local politics. Meridian also possessed a substantial Jewish community, mostly the descendents of German immigrants who had fled anti-Semitism in Bohemia in the mid-nineteenth century, and they had established a strong business presence in Meridian. Although the descendents of these German immigrants were not invited to join local private clubs or organizations like the Junior League, they often went into business with gentiles and served on local boards of directors, and there was little overt anti-Semitism in the town. In general, in fact, these three groups—all white—mingled fairly freely, supporting each other in their civic endeavors. One Irish Catholic attorney observed, only half-jokingly, "Meridian was a weird place because it was populated by Baptists and other illiterates, financed and owned by the Jewish community, but the government was always run by the Catholics. The only people excluded were the blacks."[9] African Americans represented about 40 percent of the population, significantly lower than in some other parts of Mississippi.

Exactly what life in Meridian was like for its black citizens in the 1960s depends on whom you listen to. Mickey Schwerner's wife, Rita, observed shortly after her husband's murder, "There was a good reason why Mickey wanted to do more in the outlying counties. The Negroes in Meridian were *relatively* well off. They suffered from a minimum of police brutality. They were not herded into a ghetto. About seventeen hundred of them voted. The schools, although much inferior to the national average and segregated, were better off than elsewhere in Mississippi. Many Negroes lived comfortably. Therefore most of them, particularly the adults, were unwilling to take risks. So in Meridian our support was chiefly teenagers. But in the outlying counties life was much harder for Negroes, they had less to lose, so the adults were ready to take more risks."[10]

Los Angeles Times Atlanta bureau chief Jack Nelson, who covered Meridian later in the 1960s, points out that "until the late 1940s, Meridian was the only city in east Mississippi where a black student could go to a four year high school," and that, in fact, the county had two such schools for blacks. But because there were relatively few good economic opportunities for blacks in Meridian, many young people looking to get ahead left for

Northern cities, just as they did in other parts of the South. Despite this exodus, the community had "strong local leadership" among its pastors and businessmen, according to Nelson.[11]

But not all members of the black community agreed with Nelson's assessment of the town's black leadership. Obie Clark, a community activist who had moved to Meridian from the more rural Kemper County to the north, thought many of the black leaders were too accomodationist and too inclined to look out only for their middle-class interests.[12] But Meridian had hosted a visit from Freedom Riders in 1961, which, in part because of black leaders' contacts with Meridian law enforcement, occurred without serious incident.[13] When Martin Luther King and his aide Andrew Young came to town, the pastor of First Union Baptist Church had them stay at his home; his church was a center for civil rights activity and the location of an early Head Start center, despite the opposition of more than half his congregation, who were afraid of their church being targeted by the Klan.[14]

That fear was reasonable. In the summer of 1964, forty-four black churches in Mississippi were either bombed or burned. In the first six months of 1968, six black churches in the Meridian area were burned.[15] Clark, a member of First Union Baptist, recalled the "many nights" of pulling armed "shift with other deacons and other people in the community to guard that church from being bombed."[16] Charles Young Sr., later elected to Mississippi legislature in 1980, recalled similar guard duty in his neighborhood when residents learned that a neighbor's home had been targeted for Klan bombing.[17]

Gray's view of Meridian was a positive one, despite the Klan activity in the area. "Yes, the Klan was there—not parading down the street, but you knew they were there. Among other things, they'd make phone calls to people who disagreed with them. But in spite of the fact that I'd never lived there, I must have known fifty people there, leaders in the community, who were real open-minded in their views of racial issues. A lot of them were connected with St. Paul's [Episcopal Church] there."[18]

Whatever one's exact assessment of the racial climate in Meridian and surrounding Lauderdale County, most agree, as we have seen, that it was no accident that the murders of the three civil rights workers occurred elsewhere. Although the "causes" of the crime were multiple, in one sense the murders had their origin in the June 16 burning of a black church in the Longdale community, a small, black farming settlement eight miles east of Philadelphia, the county seat of Neshoba County. Two weeks earlier, Schwerner and Chaney had visited Mt. Zion Methodist Church in Longdale to talk to the congregation about holding a Freedom School at the church during the summer for the purpose of preparing blacks to register to vote. The majority of the congregation agreed, and as one woman present said later, "I guess the word got out that we was going to have a Freedom School."[19]

"The word" did indeed quickly reach the ears of a group of Mississippians organized as the White Knights of the Ku Klux Klan. Its founder, a Mississippian by the name of Sam Bowers, had first joined another Klan group, headquartered in Lousiana and known as the Original Knights of the Ku Klux Klan, in 1955. A few years later, as the Civil Rights Movement grew, Bowers came to the conclusion that the Original Knights were not sufficiently active in combating the challenge to "the Mississippi way of life" and formed the White Knights, with headquarters in Laurel, Mississippi, where Bowers lived.

Bowers was an interesting figure in his own right, and bits of his biography are startlingly like Gray's: both came from prominent Mississippi families; both were students at Jackson's Central High School in the 1940s (Bowers was two years older than Gray and left Jackson before his senior year at Central, so the two did not know each other in high school); both studied engineering at Tulane University, although Bowers did not receive a degree; both served in the navy during World War II, although Bowers served in the Pacific; and both identified themselves as Christian. In fact, Bowers was fond of describing himself as a priest, although, as with his Christianity, that meant something different to him than it did to Gray. Bowers' priest was a "warrior priest," and in a 1994 interview with theology professor Charles Marsh, Bowers laid out his understanding of his role: "There are two really powerful figures in the world: the priest and the preacher. I think I came here as a priest, though not a preacher. A priest is interested in visible, public power relations; this is what makes him powerful as a warrior. A preacher is an evangelist; he will tell people what to do. But the priest will arrange the means and operations to implement this into concrete action. When the priest sees the heretic, he can do only one thing: he eliminates him."[20]

As Marsh notes, between 1964 and 1967, Bowers, as Imperial Wizard of the White Knights, "was suspected of orchestrating at least nine murders, seventy-five bombings of black churches, and three hundred assaults, bombings, and beatings."[21]

Although Mt. Zion's impending Freedom School probably did play a role in the Klan's decision to burn the church, the burning turned out to serve the double purpose several days later of attracting Schwerner and Chaney back to Mt. Zion, where they could be prey for their murderers.

With Chaney and his other volunteers, Schwerner had been busy since January in Meridian and the surrounding area integrating churches, organizing boycotts, and running a community center in the black neighborhood in which he and his wife lived. As a result, he quickly became the symbol of "outside agitation" to area racists.

At the same time Schwerner was at work in Meridian and the surrounding area, the U.S. Congress was debating what would become the 1964 Civil Rights Act, and Mississippi politicians did not lose the opportunity to whip up emotions in the state with their claims about the cataclysmic effects the bill would have if it passed. It was as if, as journalist William Bradford Huie notes, "Satan was battling God."[22] In this climate, it was all too easy for Bowers to get his followers' enthusiastic agreement to "eliminate" Schwerner as the symbol for all that was "wrong" in the nation and the state.

The murder seems to have been initially planned for the night of June 16, when the White Knights in Lauderdale and Neshoba County apparently expected Schwerner to visit Mt. Zion again. Leaders of the congregation did indeed gather at the church late in that evening, but for the purpose of conducting other church business rather than meeting with Schwerner. In fact, early that morning, Schwerner, his wife, and Chaney had left Meridian for Ohio, where the training for Freedom Summer volunteers would take place.[23] So on the night of Tuesday, the sixteenth, the White Knights who gathered at Mt. Zion, cheated out of their opportunity to get Schwerner, instead contented themselves with forcing the church leaders out of the building, beating several of them, and then burning the church. According to Huie's account, the arson was a spur-of-the-moment decision on the part of the Lauderdale County contingent of the White Knights.[24]

It took several days for the Mississippi civil rights workers in Ohio to learn about the fate of Mt. Zion and its leaders. A Philadelphia businessman had managed to get Jackson newspapers to refrain from publishing anything about the arson while representatives of a New Jersey firm who were considering locating a plant in Neshoba County were visiting, and it was several days later that Bill Minor, the Mississippi correspondent for the New Orleans *Times-Picayune*, got wind of the events and broke the story.[25] When Schwerner did learn what had happened, apparently on June 20, he made immediate plans to return to Mississippi with Chaney and a number of student volunteers, including Goodman.[26] Because Schwerner and Chaney assumed that the church burning was the result of their visits to Mt. Zion and their urging the congregation to hold a Freedom School there, they felt responsible for its fate and that of its leaders.[27] Rita Schwerner was convinced to remain in Ohio another week to help train the next group of volunteers. Schwerner, Chaney, and the students left Ohio around 3:00 a.m. on Saturday, June 20. As they drove south that day, the U.S. Senate finally gave its approval to the civil rights bill that Southern senators had filibustered for months.[28]

Schwerner and the others arrived in Meridian around 8:30 Saturday evening.[29] The next day, the date of the summer equinox as well as Father's Day, Schwerner, Chaney, and Goodman piled into the COFO station wagon for the trip to Longdale. Given the dangers they knew they could face, they agreed that if they had not returned by 4:30 p.m., volunteers in the Meridian office should begin telephoning concerning their whereabouts.[30]

They reached Longdale, surveyed the damage, and visited with several church leaders who told Schwerner that the men who had come to the church were looking for him. In the early afternoon, the three headed back to Meridian, but soon afterwards their car was stopped for speeding by Neshoba County Deputy Sheriff Cecil Price.[31] Price radioed two Mississippi Highway Patrolmen in a nearby car for assistance in transporting the three to the county jail, ostensibly so he could find a magistrate to deal with the ticket he had issued, certainly not a normal procedure for dealing with speeders.

Unknown to the three, Price was a member of the local chapter of the White Knights, and once he had the three jailed, he contacted his boss, Sheriff Lawrence Rainey, who was in Meridian visiting his wife in the hospital, and Edgar Ray Killen, an ordained Baptist minister and the man in charge of the Lauderdale-Neshoba Klavern, to tell them that he would hold the civil rights workers until around ten that night.[32] When CORE staffers contacted Price in search of the three, Price denied that they were prisoners in the jail.[33]

Killen got busy rounding up his Klansmen. Around 10:30 p.m., after the speeding fine had been paid, Price released his prisoners, and once again, they headed back toward Meridian. Price, on the pretext of accompanying them to the county line, followed, and soon stopped the station wagon again. Although by this time the three were undoubtedly suspicious enough to be in fear for their safety, they were unarmed and apparently felt they had little choice but to obey a law officer's commands. Price ordered the three into his car and quickly drove them the four miles to the site of their murder—a side road off the highway to Meridian. Before midnight the three were dead, shot by the assembled White Knights; by dawn their bodies had been buried in a farm pond dam under construction about six miles from the murder site. Six weeks later, as a result of information from an informant, the F.B.I. uncovered the bodies.[34]

John Dittmer summarizes the impact of the killings in this way: "The Neshoba lynchings provoked international outrage and provided the Mississippi movement with the visibility it needed to force a reluctant federal government to take action against the Klan. The killings were decisive in persuading the state's white elite that continued violent resistance to federal law would lead to political anarchy and economic devastation. Within the movement, however, the tragedy only left feelings of grief and rage. Publicly, the anger focused on the federal government's failure to prevent the killings; privately, veteran activists also blamed themselves for the deaths of their three comrades."[35]

Despite the grief, anger, and self-blame, the murders did not stop Freedom Summer. Something like a thousand volunteers came to the state during the summer. At least half of them were college students; the other half were doctors, lawyers, and ministers who contributed their summer vacation time to assist the student volunteers and their leaders. The summer's efforts went first into voter registration training and attempts to register voters and into fifty "Freedom Schools" throughout the state that offered remedial education, literacy training, citizenship training, and black history to over two thousand students in the state whose ages ranged from preschool to elderly adults.[36]

Late in 1964, Gray offered his own assessment of the impact of Freedom Summer in a nine-page, single-spaced memorandum addressed to Leslie Dunbar, executive director of the Southern Regional Council in Atlanta. The memorandum was organized around a series of questions that Dunbar had sent to Gray and covered a variety of topics such as "General Effects of the COFO Summer Program on White Mississippi," "Effects on Negro Mississippi," and "Effects of COFO Program on Citizens' Councils, Klan, and APWR [Americans for the Preservation of the White Race]," as well as "Does the COFO program help create or does it inhibit opportunities for moderate or liberal opinions to develop in Mississippi?"

On the first issue, Gray began by pointing out that "in general, White Mississippi has responded to the COFO program with hostility and resentment." He attributed a large amount of the negative reaction to ignorance of the program's goals and to "the biased and sensationalized advance publicity given to the program by most of the Mississippi press." While pointing out that few of the volunteers and movement leaders lived up to the "'horror' stories of drunken brawls, Negro-white dating [something that CORE leadership had actively discouraged], and pregnancies among visiting students," he also noted that there had been a few instances of COFO workers who had seemed "to make a point of staying dirty and wearing dirty clothes as part of their revolt against bourgeois standards in general." Gray wrote that the behavior of these few individuals had offended whites and that "some elements of the Negro community" and "some of the COFO workers themselves" had expressed their concern to him about the matter. He observed that "as 'revolutionaries,' a number of the COFO people tend to equate conformity with *any* of the customs of middle class respectability with weakness, and there is a studied effort on the part of some to make this point."

Looking beyond this relatively minor issue, he turned to a wider analysis. "Comments thus far have dealt with the obvious and more or less measurable effects on the white community, but something should be said of the more subtle and indirect effects, which I, for one, feel have been considerable. One thing the outsiders have done, if nothing else, is to focus the attention of the whole country on the racial problems in Mississippi. This has produced resentment, of course, but it has forced white Mississippians to *face* the problem day in and day out. Very little *creative* response has yet been evident, but the confrontation continues, so that it becomes increasingly difficult for one to pretend that there is no problem and refuse to talk about it."[37]

He went on by acknowledging the violence of "the white extremist element" and the growth of racist organizations like the Klan and Americans for the Preservation of the White Race, but continued on a more hopeful note. The "terrible" violence of the white extremists, he suggested, "seems to be producing a reaction among the more responsible elements in some communities at least which may mark the first faint signs of a new day. More and more whites are becoming increasingly fearful of the road down which the racial extremists are taking us, and they are beginning in some small way to assume responsibilities which they would have shunned not too long ago." As evidence he pointed to the "peaceful desegregation" of schools that fall in several Mississippi school districts and to the public expressions of support for compliance with civil rights laws by the mayor of Jackson and the Jackson Chamber of Commerce board of directors.

He concluded, "In short, as regrettable as the cause may be, the fact remains that the violent reaction precipitated by the COFO program among one element of white Mississippians has in turned produced the first signs of a creative and constructive approach on the part of many responsible whites to the whole question of civil rights. I would emphasize that there has been only the slightest beginning and much of this, perhaps, only out of desperation, but I do think that much of what has happened, even if indirectly, has been the result of the summer program."[38]

As for the effects of Freedom Summer on black Mississippians, Gray noted, "There is no question but that the summer program was received enthusiastically by the overwhelming majority of Mississippi Negroes. Even those who were too timid, too vulnerable, or too remote to have direct contact with it got a psychological shot in the arm from it.

"Of particular significance," he added, "was the active involvement and participation of the white students and other COFO workers. Whether or not any measurable gains were made in a given community, the very fact that these whites were willing to identify so completely with their cause gave a great boost to Negro morale."[39]

CHAPTER 12

"WE MUST RETURN TO THE *DREAM*"

Meridian, 1965–68

I N THE MEMORIES of many outside of Mississippi, the 1964 murders of Mickey Schwerner, James Chaney, and Andrew Goodman near Meridian marked the peak of white Mississippians' resistance to the integration of their society and gave the state a well-deserved reputation as the most racist part of America in the mid-twentieth century. But while those murders received the greatest amount of attention then, as well as today, they represent neither the beginning, nor the end, nor even the peak of Klan violence in the state.

It is also the case that the violence in no way represented the majority of white Mississippians. In the case of most of them, their sin was not violence but the failure to resist it. Duncan Gray was an exception to both these categories.

As for the violence, a total of six black civil rights workers were killed in Mississippi between January and May 1964 as they were planning the summer project.[1] But their deaths did not receive the kind of notice that the media and the nation gave to the June deaths in Neshoba County. By the end of the summer, in addition to the then nine murders, thirty homes occupied by African Americans had been bombed, thirty-seven black churches had been burned, and at least eighty civil rights workers, both black and white, had been beaten by Klan members and sympathizers. The White Knights of the Ku Klux Klan increased its membership in Mississippi from about three hundred to more than six thousand between February and October of 1964. But Klan membership would eventually rise to about seven thousand, and the scope of its violence in east central Mississippi would increase dramatically before it was finally brought to an end.[2]

Gray, however, knew a different Mississippi and a different Meridian from that portrayed in the news media, and he told a story to illustrate that difference. After the 1964 Civil Rights Bill was passed, the federal

government organized throughout the South what were known as community relations advisory committees to help implement the provisions
of the law. Gray, along with the president of Tougaloo College and then
Monsignor Bernard Law, were the only whites on Mississippi's committee.
After Gray announced his decision to go to St. Paul's, he was contacted by
the director of the closest community relations committee office, located
in Memphis, Tennessee, eighty miles north of Oxford. The director told
him, "Man, I'm glad you're moving to Meridian! I'll have at least *one* person
I can talk to there." Gray recalled his response: "Joe, I can give you at least
one hundred names right now of people in Meridian who'd be glad to talk
to you! And I don't even live there.

"My point was the people *I* knew in Meridian were really very open,
very liberal, very committed to doing the right thing. And yet this guy, who
was supposed to be an authority, feeling the pulse all over, he didn't know
that part of Meridian at all. All he knew was the Klan—which certainly was
there, but I bet you the Klan in Meridian didn't include a 150 people. They
did control the city to a large degree at that time and that was certainly the
image of Meridian, but it was not the Meridian that I knew."[3]

Many of the people Gray had in mind when he spoke of "open, liberal"
inhabitants of Meridian were members of St. Paul's, the church that had
welcomed Schwerner, Chaney, Goodman, and other civil rights workers to
worship with them when other churches turned them away.

The congregation had a long history of tolerance and acceptance of those
different from itself, even though not all of its members always conformed
to that history. It first organized in 1901, and until it completed its own
building in 1902, the group held its services at Meridian's Temple Beth El,
which that congregation made available to them rent-free. St. Paul's returned the favor three years later while the synagogue was building a new
facility.[4]

In 1950, the church's Women's Auxiliary sponsored a performance by
soprano Leontyne Price, a native of nearby Laurel and later one of the first
African Americans to become a world-famous opera star.[5]

In 1952, St. Paul's vestry responded to the "integration crisis" at Sewanee
by passing a resolution condemning the decision of the university's trustees
not to admit black applicants to its seminary.[6] At the time, St. Paul's rector
was the Reverend Duncan Hobart. It was Hobart whom Gray and his fellow seminary graduates asked to preach at their ordination because they so
admired his support for the seminary faculty during the "crisis." In 1954, he
and Gray had collaborated on the diocesan response to *Brown* decision.

Hobart came to St. Paul's in 1943 and remained until 1961, clearly a man well-liked by the members of his congregation. Indeed, those who were members of St. Paul's when Hobart was rector still remembered him fondly almost fifty years later. Parishioner Tile Howell said, "It would have taken an angel to replace Duncan Hobart."[7] When Hobart left, the parish issued a call to Gray, but that was when he refused because of the impending storm over the integration of Ole Miss.

After Gray turned the parish down, the vestry called the Reverend James McKeown of Jacksonville, Texas.[8] Long-time St. Paul's member Gil Carmichael said, "You can't talk about Duncan Gray's time here without talking about Jim."[9]

While following a long-time, well-beloved minister can always be tricky, McKeown had problems with the parish that went beyond that. His positions on racial issues weren't substantially different from Hobart's, but he apparently lacked the latter's finesse. Howell, a self-described conservative, remembered her doctor-husband's introduction to McKeown: "My husband's office was across the street from the church and so very soon after Father McKeown arrived in town, my husband went across the street to welcome him. He walked into McKeown's office and the man was wearing black cowboy boots with his feet on top of the desk. Father McKeown did not take his feet off the desk, and he never even got up to greet my husband. He finally did extend his hand. George came home absolutely livid and said to me, 'That man is no gentleman!'"[10]

Although many in the congregation agreed with Dr. Howell, not all did. Deanie Carmichael remembered about McKeown that she "loved him to death," but agreed "a lot of people didn't. They thought he was too pushy. *I* think Jim was ahead of his time, but he was *not* appreciated by many, many people in this parish. Many of the pledges were stopped and that kind of thing."[11]

As an example of McKeown's uncompromising bluntness, she recalled a class with him in which "he said that his grandmother was definitely *not* going to heaven. And I thought, 'What in the world is he saying!' And I said, 'Jim?' And he said, 'Well, she's never recognized . . . whatever [theological concept] it was!' And I said, 'But Jim, you don't mean that she's not going to heaven!' And he said, 'Indeed I do.'"[12]

Her husband, Gil, recalls McKeown talking about his view of Meridian and his response to it. "He said, 'I'm facing evil here. There's no way to face the evil we've got in Meridian sweetly. You can't be kind to evil. You've got to be tough with it.'"[13]

By 1964, a number of McKeown's congregation had had about enough of what they considered to be his injudicious maladroitness. They had tolerated his welcome of Schwerner, Chaney, Goodman, and the other civil rights workers to their Sunday service, but when McKeown later went to the local airport to welcome the families of the murdered civil rights workers to Meridian and, as Meridian residents noted, "*hugged* Chaney's mother," they took note. When the scene was shown on local television, that was about the last straw for some members of the parish.

Less than a year later McKeown was gone and the second call to Gray was issued and accepted.

How could a parish that had had such difficulty with McKeown's stands on matters related to civil rights call as its next rector the man who had received national and international publicity for his own stands on integration and racial reconciliation?

Tile Howell recalled that when Gray was a student at Tulane, she was a student at its sister school, Sophie Newcomb, and was dating one of Gray's fraternity brothers. "Our paths crossed a lot. I was just elated when he came here. George was not as happy about it. He wasn't always very fond of Duncan because of his ideas, but I could accept the fact that priests are supposed to be open-minded. It did not bother me personally. Duncan was outstanding."[14]

It was Gil Carmichael's view that McKeown's tenure helped "vent the fire and anger of the racists. So when Duncan shows up, he's the great peacemaker."

"And he *was*," chimed in his wife, Deanie.

Carmichael agreed, "He was. He did a great job helping us transition from the confrontation we had had with the civil rights thing." But he insisted, "If it hadn't been for McKeown, he would have had a harder time."[15]

Both Carmichaels made explicit what Tile Howell's comments suggested: the fact that Gray was a Mississippi Episcopalian, that his father was bishop, that he already knew many of St. Paul's congregants, and that they knew him all helped contribute to his success in Meridian. But beyond that, the Carmichaels and others agreed, of paramount importance was the kind of person Gray was. Deanie said about McKeown and Gray, "At least the door had been opened before Duncan got here. And he was such a *tender* person and he didn't come on strong like Jim did."

Her husband added, "All the priests in the Church, especially in the South, at that time were confronted with 'What's the *Christian* response to this thing [of integration]?' And a lot of them were wishy-washy about it. Well, McKeown wasn't and Duncan wasn't."

But again, Gray's personal history and his gentle manner made the difference. Because of that, Carmichael said, "some of the arch-racists in this church at the time—men I knew real well and a couple of women too—could say, 'You see, we don't mind having communion with the blacks.' Duncan, just by his nature and his relationship to this parish, was a godsend."[16]

St. Paul's vestry minutes show that the 1966 Every Member Canvass that followed Gray's arrival a little over a year earlier showed a 10 percent increase in pledges over the previous year.

For the Gray children, the move to Meridian was in some ways a difficult one. For all of them it meant leaving friends of eight years standing, and for most of them the only ones they could remember.

For son Duncan the move was particularly hard; he was preparing to enter his senior year of high school where he was a valued member of the football team.

Anne, who had just entered her teens, remembered anticipating the move with excitement. "It was a new adventure, a new place. I don't think I really had an understanding of what moving meant: starting all over again."[17] As it turned out, for her, "eighth grade was horrible. All the classes in Meridian were tracked, so I got put in the low level because I hadn't been there for the testing. I didn't understand that coming from Oxford where we all went to school together. I was in a group of very slow learners in all my classes, and their values were just totally different from mine; there was no value for education. And sort of the crowning point, by the end of that year, three of my good friends were pregnant. After that my mother made *sure* that in ninth grade I was in classes with people I had more in common with!"[18]

Token integration had begun in some Meridian schools by the time the Grays moved there. A few African American boys, often football players, and a few girls whom Anne described as "very academically oriented and very quiet and shy" attended the town's formerly all-white schools under a "freedom of choice" plan.[19]

Although the murders of Schwerner, Chaney, and Goodman had happened more than a year before the Grays moved to the area, and their bodies located almost a year to the day before the Grays relocated in Meridian, it was not until 1967 that the trial of nineteen defendants began in the small city.

At the time, no white person had ever been convicted of murdering a black person in Mississippi. Federal authorities were well aware of this fact and also of the view many Mississippians had of civil rights workers, and for these reasons they decided to try the accused in federal rather than state court. In fact, in the fall of 1964, the F.B.I. even refused to turn over information from its investigation to Neshoba County prosecutors for use in a state trial.[20] At the time, however, there was no federal law against murder, so that meant that in federal court the defendants could only be charged with the lesser crime of conspiring to violate the civil rights of the victims. On December 4, 1964, such charges were duly filed against nineteen men. But reminiscent of the legal wrangling over James Meredith's admission to Ole Miss a few years earlier, the Mississippi justice system's first response to the charges was to dismiss them. At a preliminary hearing in her Meridian courtroom on December 10, U.S. Commissioner Esther Carter accepted the defense's argument that the government's use of a written confession obtained from a Klansman who had been involved in the murders was hearsay because the author of the signed confession was not present in the courtroom. Since hearsay evidence is inadmissible, so the logic ran, the federal government had no evidence to support its charges. Thus the dismissal.[21]

But Justice Department lawyers, floored as they were by Carter's "unprecedented" ruling, moved quickly to convene a grand jury in Jackson, and on January 15, 1965, it returned indictments against eighteen men. This time Commissioner Carter had no choice but to arraign them, although she also released each of them on a bond of $5,750. The case against the Klansmen appeared headed for U.S. District Court. However, once again, as with Meredith, the plaintiffs faced the familiar Mississippi phenomenon of a judge friendly to the defense. For decades, the rumor was that Judge Harold Cox had been appointed a federal judge by John Kennedy as part of a trade with Mississippi's senators in which they agreed not to block Thurgood Marshall's appointment as a federal appeals court judge in return for Cox's appointment, although those knowledgeable about the matter deny it. Justice Department lawyer John Doar later recalled a hearing before Judge Cox in a Mississippi voting rights case in which Cox referred to black voter applicants as "a bunch of chimpanzees."[22]

So in late February 1965, when Cox ruled favorably on several defense motions and dismissed charges against all but three of the defendants— Neshoba County Deputy Sheriff Cecil Price, Sheriff Lawrence Rainey, and Philadelphia Policeman Richard Willis—on the basis of an odd reading of the federal law as applicable only to law enforcement officers, the ruling was no great surprise. Justice Department lawyers quickly asked the Supreme Court for an expedited appeal. The Court denied that request, but placed the case on its calendar to be heard in the 1965–66 term.[23] In March 1966, a year and a month after Cox's ruling, the Supreme Court overturned it and reinstated the charges against eighteen defendants.[24] When the parties appeared before Cox again in October, this time for trial, he once again dismissed the charges when he ruled favorably on the defense's cynical motion that their clients could not receive a fair trial because the jury pool did not include enough minorities and women.[25]

Early in 1967, seventeen of the eighteen defendants were indicted once again by a federal grand jury in Jackson, and on October 9, their trial finally began in Judge Cox's courtroom in Meridian. One of the prosecution's witnesses was Delmar Dennis, a twenty-four-year-old minister who had been the Klan's "Kludd," or chaplain. Dennis, however, was bothered by much of the Klan's activity, and when he heard about its plan to murder Goodman, Chaney, and Schwerner, he quit, making him an easy recruit for the F.B.I.

Gil Carmichael, who owned the town's Volkswagen dealership, remembered Dennis because he owned a Volkswagen. "The F.B.I. would regularly meet with him there at my dealership. And then during the trials for the murders, it turned out that one pair of gloves from the killings belonged to a man that had a little store there right across from my dealership. Often you didn't know who the good guys and the bad guys were."

Deanie Carmichael recalls that "Delmar came to church with us one time. Scared everybody to death." Gil adds, "He was looking to be an Episcopalian."[26]

Whether or not Dennis was serious about becoming an Episcopalian, it was certainly the case that he admired Gray and, indeed, came to him for counseling about his role as a Klan informant. Dennis was a minister in a breakaway denomination known as the Southern Methodist Church, which had split from the Methodist Church South because that body was not sufficiently segregationist. Gray recalls that Dennis was "a very vocal, outspoken segregationist. I had no idea that he was involved with the Klan though until he came to see me one day needing pastoral counsel, direction, advice. He had already become an informant for the F.B.I., but he didn't have anyone to talk to except the F.B.I., and he just needed someone else. I helped him as best I could."[27] However much Dennis admired Gray, the counseling did not part Dennis from his right-wing views; he spent a number of years as Mississippi coordinator for the John Birch Society and at his death in 1996, its national publication eulogized him.[28]

On October 18, the Philadelphia case went to the jury. They deliberated for two full days, nearly deadlocking, but finally returned a verdict of "guilty" against seven of the defendants, including Cecil Price and Sam Bowers. Seven were acquitted, including Sheriff Rainey and Richard Willis. Cox declared three mistrials, including one for "Preacher" Edgar Ray Killen, an ordained Baptist minister whom witnesses testified was the planner and organizer of the murders, because one female juror famously held out on the grounds that "she could never convict a preacher."[29]

In 1967, however, when Cox sentenced the seven found guilty, only two men, including Sam Bowers, received the maximum ten-year sentence. The others were given sentences of either three or six years in prison. After the sentencing, Cox commented, "They killed one nigger, one Jew, and a white man. I gave them what I thought they deserved."[30] The appeals process delayed their imprisonment for another three years.

Two days after the jury's verdict, Gray had a message different from Cox's for his congregation at St. Paul's. Taking his text from the Gospel for the day, "And [Jesus] said unto them, 'Why are you so fearful? Have you no faith?'" (Mark 4:40), Gray began his sermon with a discussion of rational and irrational fears and noted how many once apparently rational fears had become irrational as a result of growing human knowledge and experience. He also called his congregation's attention to the fact that "there is seldom, if ever, an instance of social conflict in which fear does not play a principal role," and added, "As someone has said, fear 'is the acid that corrodes the natural bonds that tie society together.'" He told his listeners, "If fear is not controlled by *reason* and *will*, it can seize a human life and ruin it; and it can just as well take hold of a community, or a society, and destroy it for all practical purposes. And it is these fears that we must guard against and purge from our souls and from the society in which we live."

But then he turned to the particular issue at hand: fear of the Klan and the impact of the jury's verdict on that fear. He told his listeners,

Here in Meridian during this past week, a giant step has been taken toward eliminating one more fear from our social order; a fear that has so often in the past plagued and paralyzed our community and our state. In their precedent-shattering verdict of last Friday, the all-white jury in the Neshoba case has served notice, I believe, that we of this state will no longer tolerate or turn our heads away from crimes of violence related to race and civil rights. And in doing so, it seems to me that they have made you and me and the other citizens of our community and state much *freer* human beings. In recent years, the Klan in this community and county has never been large. It may have included a maximum of some seventy-five or so *active* members at its peak. And yet this microscopic fraction of the total population has had a certain power over the lives of the rest of us altogether out of proportion to any rational assessment of its true strength and influence. Think, first of all, how damaging has been their influence on the image of our community in the eyes of the nation and how much effect this may have had on our community. But more importantly, think of how many times you have heard people say, 'We mustn't do this or that because of what the *Klan* might do.'

How many times have you seen people hesitate and turn back from progressive or humane proposals for our community, not because of lack of conviction or motivation, but due to *fear* of Klan reaction and retribution? So very many words and deeds have been so carefully weighed and considered, not so much as to their rightness or wrongness but as to what response they will evoke from the Klan. This tiny group has limited the freedom of the whole community to a degree all out of proportion to its numbers or influence because of the medium of fear through which it has worked.

And, tragically enough, some of the fears were valid and legitimate; because we had in our midst a tiny group of people who felt that they could quite literally get away with murder—or bombings, or burnings—if they were associated in some way with race or civil rights. And as long as they felt immune to punishment for such things as these, they *were* a danger—a very *real* danger—so that many of our fears were quite valid. But this past week's action ought to put an entirely different light on the matter. Notice has been served to the Klan that they can no longer indulge in their tactics of terror and still remain immune to punishment. And this in itself should serve as the most powerful deterrent possible for any such acts in the future. Once these people understand clearly and unequivocally that the community in which they live will not put up with such things, then they will be much less inclined to do them. And the rest of the community should be and will be much more *free* as a result. The fear has begun to be extracted.

As we listened to or read the sordid tale that came out of this trial, I think we realized how far we have come since the summer of 1964. Such things are not nearly as credible now as they would have been three years ago; and we owe a tremendous debt of gratitude to all those who during these past three years have worked so hard to make the Klan so impotent and ineffective as it is in our community today. But it still took last week's verdict to sound the death knell of the fears which the Klan had instilled. As the Psalmist says, we may have been "afraid where no fear was," but the fear was still there; and it would always be there until we felt that the Klan had "gotten the message," the message that they would have to answer at the bar of justice for their acts of terror and violence.

Certainly, the fear is not yet entirely gone. Even as recently as last week, I talked with no less than four persons in a space of four days, each of whom was in the progress of making a decision that was influenced, at least in part, by fear of the Klan. But the days when such a restriction on our freedom can still exist must surely be numbered. Indeed, I trust that we are just about at the day when we can relegate this particular fear to the category of the irrational and the anachronistic. But the exact time that we can do this will be determined very largely by you and by me and all the other decent, law-abiding citizens who constitute the overwhelming majority of this community. It will be determined by our putting our fears behind us and resolving that no tiny band of violence-prone hoodlums is going to limit or restrict our freedom and the freedom of the community in which we live.

Gray concluded, "We can do it. All it takes is the will and the faith. . . . There is no better task to which [the] Church can devote herself than to the dissipation of the fears that hinder and handcuff a community and keep it from doing and being its best. St. Paul reminds us that God has not given us a spirit of timidity and fear, but a spirit of power and love and self-control. The early disciples, after the Resurrection, found their fears conquered and overcome in Jesus Christ. He can do the same for you and for me. And we can do the same for this community in which we live."[31]

Others also found the jury's decision momentous. Like Gray, the *New York Times* saw it as a turning point: a "measure of the quiet revolution that is taking place in Southern attitudes—a slow, still faltering, but inexorable conversion to the concept that a single standard of justice must cover whites and Negroes alike." The F.B.I. came to a similar conclusion, hoping that the jury's verdict indicated the destruction of the White Knights.[32]

While it was true that Klan membership declined precipitously after the trial, the hope that, as Gray put it, the jury's verdict sounded a "death knell" for the Klan was overly optimistic. From the vantage of forty years, he acknowledged that instead the verdict probably helped fuel the White Knights' further violence, which continued even as the Philadelphia murder defendants went through the judicial process.

In 1965, Bowers had ordered his Klansmen to kill Vernon Dahmer and burn his house. Dahmer was a black man who lived near Bowers' home in

Laurel and who had helped other blacks to register to vote. Bowers' minions responded to his order on January 10 by shooting into Dahmer's home and setting it ablaze with Molotov cocktails. Dahmer's wife and three children escaped the house through a back window, but Dahmer remained behind to defend them against their attackers, firing his shotgun through the flames that raged in the front of his house. He died several hours later from the effects of the fire and smoke.[33]

By 1966, the F.B.I. had obvious reason for watching Bowers and his associates closely, and within less than three months had warrants against them for the Dahmer crime. But all-white Mississippi juries failed to find those defendants guilty; two federal trials and one state trial all ended with hung juries. Yet as Gray and others hoped, pressure on the Klan was building.[34]

But that pressure was not yet enough to stop a new type of Klan campaign, this time against Mississippi Jews. This campaign also featured a change in tactics and a new type of perpetrator. The new tactic was bombing, and the new perpetrators were a young, middle-class white man, Thomas Tarrants, and his elementary-school-teacher girlfriend, Kathy Ainsworth.

Tarrants, twenty-four when he began his work for Bowers, was a native of Mobile. When his high school there was desegregated by federal court order in 1963, he helped lead violent student demonstrations against the move. The next year he dropped out of his junior year in high school in order to pursue full time his desire to work with right-wing hate groups that targeted blacks and Jews. That same year he was stopped twice by law enforcement officers who seized weapons from him. The second time he was charged under federal law with possessing an illegal weapon. The judge let him off with probation and a stern warning against any kind of weapon possession. By 1967, Tarrants was in Laurel offering to work for Sam Bowers. Jack Nelson, author of *Terror in the Night: The Klan's Campaign against the Jews*, says of Tarrants that he "saw himself as something far different from an ordinary Klansman; he had a theoretical framework—a belief in an all-embracing international Communist-Jewish conspiracy. In his own eyes, at least, he had come to Laurel a professional radical, a terrorist prepared, even eager, to make personal sacrifices for his cause."[35]

With F.B.I. infiltration of the Klan at a peak, Bowers was naturally suspicious of this young stranger, but Tarrants was persistent and eventually he won Bowers over. Bowers' confidence in Tarrants was finally sealed when Tarrants proposed a violent strike against Jackson Jews at a time that Bowers could establish an air-tight alibi. As Nelson observes, "To Bowers, Tarrants and [girlfriend Kathy] Ainsworth seemed the perfect instruments, and not only because they were prepared to take violent action—the White Knights had other members willing to do that. What made these two special was that they operated in such secrecy that the F.B.I. and police knew almost nothing about them."[36]

Nelson adds that at first, no one outside of Bowers' small inner circle even knew about them. "In their personal backgrounds, in their right-wing radicalism and in their associates, Kathy and Tommy were a different species from the Klan members the F.B.I. and local police were focusing on. The lawmen's formidable network of informants would be of little help."[37]

So on September 18, 1967, Tarrants and Ainsworth launched what Nelson dubbed "the Klan's campaign against the Jews." Around 10:00 p.m., with Ainsworth beside him in the car, Tarrants drove through a quiet Jackson neighborhood to Temple Beth Israel, a building that had been dedicated only seven months earlier, stepped out of the car with a bundle of dynamite, placed it by the wall of the synagogue, and lit its fuse with a cigarette lighter. Fifteen minutes later, the blast was so powerful that the two heard it as they reached the outskirts of Jackson, and temple member Al Binder, who lived about half a mile from the building, was literally lifted out of his bed.[38]

Binder guessed instantly that the synagogue was the target of the blast. The Klan had already made threats against Jews, and his rabbi, Perry Nussbaum, had been an active force for civil rights since he had arrived in Mississippi from Massachusetts in 1954.[39] Many who knew Nussbaum found him difficult, but Gray, who knew him from both the Committee of Concern and the MCHR, thought Nussbaum a good man to work with.[40]

F.B.I. response to the synagogue bombing was massive. For some black Mississippians that fact itself was telling. As Meridian resident Obie Clark would say later about similar incidents there, "After they bombed or burned . . . black churches . . . we would go to the F.B.I., police, and they would tell us they were doing all they could to apprehend those who were burning and bombing the churches, but there was nothing they could do. But then, when the Klan shifted its focus from the *black* community to the Jewish community . . . that's when the law enforcement community and the white politicians got serious about that kind of violence."[41]

Aside from racism, one difference between the situation of blacks Mississippians enduring Klan violence and Jews in the same situation was *money*. Jews had it and blacks didn't, and that fact made it possible for the F.B.I. to buy Klan informants with knowledge of the anti-Jewish violence to an extent that was not possible in the case of the violence against blacks. As top Mississippi F.B.I. agent Roy Moore told Binder, bombings are difficult crimes to solve because the crime itself destroys much, if not all, of the physical evidence. The best way to identify such terrorists, he said, was to pay informants.[42]

Despite the new front against Jews, Klan violence against blacks did not let up. But with so many Klan members under intense surveillance, it was now Tarrants, in consultation with Bowers, who carried out the attacks. Three weeks after the synagogue bombing, Tarrants placed a bomb next to a residence on the Tougaloo campus. As was the case with the temple bombing, no one was injured, but again, F.B.I. investigation was frustrated by the fact that agents had no knowledge of Tarrants. Another bomb exploded just over a month later at the Laurel home of the Reverend Allen Johnson, whose church was the home church of Leontyne Price. Johnson, an NAACP leader, had long been active in civil rights. Once again, there were no serious injuries.[43]

The next bomb went off only four nights later, just after a Klan informant testified in the Philadelphia trial and less than a week before the case went to the jury. Tarrants, this time with Ainsworth accompanying him, placed this bomb at the Jackson home of Robert Kochtitzsky. Kochtitzsky and his wife were both active in civil rights activities, and he had urged the minister at his Methodist church to be more outspoken on the issue of racial violence. As in the other bombings, because the house's occupants had gone to bed a short time before the bomb went off, no one was injured. Despite the fact of his civil rights activity, Kochtitzsky later concluded that the perpetrators may have come to the conclusion that, because of his name, he was Jewish.[44]

Not long after that bombing, an F.B.I. agent played a tape recording for Temple Beth Israel member Al Binder. On the tape two Klansmen discussed the possibility of placing a firebomb in the synagogue's air-conditioning system, timed to go off at 8:30 p.m. on a Sabbath evening. The effect would be to kill the entire congregation. Binder and other young men in the congregation began carrying pistols to temple services.[45]

Two nights before Thanksgiving, Tarrants and Ainsworth planted another bomb, this time at the home of Rabbi Nussbaum. This explosion was a powerful one, hurling a window air-conditioner in the dining room into the living room and collapsing the ceilings in the Nussbaums' bedrooms, where they were in bed. Miraculously, neither was seriously hurt. Nussbaum's house had been under protective police surveillance since the temple bombing in September, but after the Philadelphia defendants were found guilty in late October, Nussbaum had asked that the surveillance end.[46]

After this event, Rabbi Milton Schlager at Meridian's temple—also Beth Israel—tried to warn his congregation that they might be in danger too. They dismissed his warnings, pointing out how much they were a part of the fabric of Meridian and how completely they were accepted by their fellow townspeople. Like Nussbaum, Schlager was an "outsider," a native of Massachusetts who had come to Meridian only five years earlier, and, as a result, his congregation dismissed his fears. But Schlager listened in horror as he heard survivors of Nazi concentration camps argue that "it won't happen here." And as Nelson points out, Bowers and Tarrants weren't inhabitants of Meridian; for them, Meridian Jews were simply *Jews.*[47]

And, in fact, by 1968, as the F.B.I. pressed hard on the Jackson bombings, agents in Meridian began to receive information from their informants that the Klan was preparing to shift its campaign against the Jews to that town. Soon an agent received a hit list of Meridian residents, not all of them Jews.

One example was the Carmichaels. He was a native of Columbia, Mississippi, the county seat of Marion County in south Mississippi along its border with Louisiana, and she was from Memphis. He had spent many years working with businesses as a circulation salesman for the *Wall Street Journal*, and they had lived in urban centers throughout the United States. But in 1961, the Carmichaels decided to settle in Meridian, where he bought a Volkswagen dealership. From the point of view of the Klan, they had reason to be suspicious of Carmichael, a longtime moderate Republican. An example would be his aid to Mickey Schwerner, who owned a Volkswagen during his time in Meridian. "I liked Mickey," Carmichael recalls. "He was not a very impressive looking figure. He was probably about five eight and a little chubby. But he was very devoted to voter registration. He probably got paid about thirty dollars a week for what he did.

"Now the police would regularly knock the windows out of Mickey's Volkswagen and then give him a ticket for having an improper car. And Mickey would bring the car down to my place to have the windshield put back in. Of course Mickey didn't have the money to pay me—I think the windshields were eighteen dollars or something like that. So I'd fix the windshield for him and just not charge him. My employees were scared to death of this boy. Klansmen were all around us, so my men were scared to work on his car."[48]

Once the Klan turned its attention to Meridian, acts like Carmichael's aid to Schwerner were sufficient to put Carmichael and others like him on the organization's hit list, which became known in Meridian as the "Klan's black list." The Carmichaels recall that as the Klan gained strength and confidence in Meridian, the black list was dropped weekly from the window of a downtown Meridian law firm.[49]

Carmichael especially remembered one example of living with the threat of Klan violence and a police department compromised by it. "We had a maid that worked for us named Mary. Our son Scott was real young, maybe two or three, something like that. Anyway, one day the phone rang and Mary answered it. I think I know who it was, but he said to her, 'Mary, you tell that son-of-a-bitch that you work for that we're going to kill *him, you, Deanie, and Scott.*' Scared Mary to death. Scared me to death when I got home and found out about it. I didn't know what to do because you couldn't just call up the police and report something like that. You didn't know who you might be talking to. So I called my lawyer and said, 'Tom, what do I do?' And he said, 'Well, don't call the police. Call the F.B.I.' So we did that."[50]

But early in 1968, Klan violence around Meridian was still dominated by actions against blacks. There were two bombings of black churches in the Meridian area in January and one in February. Later that month, Klansmen torched New Hope Baptist Church, site of a Head Start center. The next night Klansmen shot into the house of J. R. Moore, a Head Start school bus driver, and set fire to another Head Start center.

Much of this violence passed unnoticed by most Mississippians, but not so with the Grays. Gray was president of the Lauderdale County Head Start board and Ruthie Gray taught music in one of the Head Start centers that was bombed. Daughter Anne says, "Probably one of the most vivid memories I have of that time was when Mom picked me up from school one day, which was not real common. And she was just visibly shaken and almost crying. She said, 'You've *got* to see this,' and she drove me to where this black church had been bombed and she stopped. And I remember so vividly, she said, 'Now you get your *white* face out and walk over there!' I said, 'What am I supposed to say, Mama?' And she said, 'You just *say* something.' It was the church where she had helped with the Head Start program, and so it was real personal. It was people she knew. I remember all I could say to them was 'I'm just so sorry.' It wasn't a conversation; everybody was just in shock. I remember walking up to an old man who was crying. I was more emotionally wracked by that than by just about anything up to that point."[51]

Anne recalled that her school friends were either ignorant of or oblivious to the violence going on around them. "This had happened during the night, but nobody said a word about it at school. When I tried to talk to my friends about my experience, they were in denial. They said it didn't happen. People wouldn't do things like that. Nobody could be that mean. They said it was an accident. They said things like, 'Well, you know that church was old. It had bad wiring' or 'Why would anybody do anything like that? They're just trying to get sympathy.' But it wasn't in their part of town.[52]

The F.B.I. and local police continued their investigation of Klan violence, but with few results. As Roy Moore had told Binder after the Jackson synagogue bombing, informants were the best means of uncovering terrorists. Frank Watts, who headed the F.B.I.'s Meridian office, knew that this was true and began reflecting on who in the Klan's inner circle was most likely to gain Bowers' confidence enough to penetrate the secrecy surrounding Klan bombings. He quickly came to the conclusion that two brothers, Raymond and Alton Wayne Roberts, were the obvious choice. Alton Wayne was one of the seven defendants found guilty of the Philadelphia murders and was believed to be the person who actually shot Mickey Schwerner and Andy Goodman. He was free on appeal bond. His brother Raymond had not been among the Philadelphia defendants and was perhaps less violent than Alton Wayne, but he had been involved in enough Klan activity that Watts concluded that both men were susceptible to both pressure and the promise of money. But Watts still didn't know where the amount of money that might be needed would come from. F.B.I. funds to pay informants were limited and were already stretched thin.[53]

The weeks passed and Mississippi's mild winter turned to spring. Christians were observing Lent and Jews were looking forward to celebrating Passover. Early in April, Meridian got a visit from J. B. Stoner, head of the National States Rights Party, a right-wing group also committed to racial and anti-Semitic violence. On April 4, Stoner held an organizational meeting at a barbershop across the street from the F.B.I.'s offices. Watts and several other agents sat in their office with the lights turned off and observed the meeting in progress, noting the presence of Raymond Roberts and several other Klansmen. As they watched, their radio broadcast the news: Martin Luther King Jr. had been killed in Memphis. Stoner, Roberts, and the others soon got the same news across the street and shouted and jumped for joy. Watching, one of the F.B.I. agents swore, "Damn. J. B. Stoner's got an alibi."[54]

The following Sunday, three days later, was Palm Sunday. Gray reminded his congregation that the day was for Christians the first day of Holy Week,

> the most sacred and most solemn time in the Church's calendar. We commemorate this week those tragic events of the last days of the earthly life of Jesus of Nazareth; our mood is expected to be subdued

and solemn. Ordinarily, this is not easy for us. Holy Week comes in the spring when the weather is getting pretty and warm, the flowers are blooming, and the trees are budding. Furthermore, we can't help but anticipate to some degree at least the great festival of Easter that brings this week to an end. So it is not always easy to maintain a mood and a frame of mind appropriate to the events we commemorate. But such is not the case this year; for this first day of Holy Week, Palm Sunday, has been proclaimed by the President of the United States a *day of national mourning* for Dr. Martin Luther King, the tragic victim of a senseless murder this past Thursday. Under such circumstances, our mood cannot help but be one of solemnity and sadness.

Gray continued by acknowledging that many Southerners, including some of his hearers, thought nothing good about King.

The fact is that he was *hated* by many; and we in this community are provided with constant reminders of this by malicious and grotesque signs along the highway and by numerous letters to the editor in our local newspaper. But what you and I need to do today is to stand back and look at this man from the long-term perspective. . . . Because I believe that there is nothing more certain . . . than that your children, your grandchildren, and your great-grandchildren will read about this man and regard him as one of the truly great prophets and saints of the twentieth century. . . .

If it is difficult for you to see this at this time, maybe it is because you and I are too close to the man himself and the evils against which he fought. Remember that it often takes the perspective of distance and detachment to recognize true greatness. . . . Was it not our Lord Himself who said, "A prophet is not without honor except in his own country . . . ?" And was not His life itself a testimony to the truth of this . . . ? The people of Nazareth would not accept him. And the people of Jerusalem finally killed him.

Gray continued by speaking of King's dream: "a dream of justice and brotherhood among all the sons of men, a dream worthy of the support of all men and women of goodwill in these critical times." He cautioned, however, that "the difficulty is that cynics don't think much of dreams; and there are many other people who tend to be impatient with them. They point out that the goals of idealists are seldom fully realized. Dreams don't come true, as a rule. So at this very moment there are those who have given up on dreams, those who have forsaken hope, and those who are responding now in bitterness and hate."

Speaking of the urban riots that occurred in many American cities after King's assassination, Gray noted, "Violence erupts in city after city. Frustration and despair break out in ugly revenge, and common criminality follows close behind. We reap now the bitter fruits of four hundred years of history. . . . What do we *do* in a situation like this? Where is a Christian to take his stand and do his bit?"

He continued by pointing out the need for restoring law and order, and then added, "But having seen to this, we must then make sure that we return to the *dream;* that we devote and commit ourselves to erase every trace of racism; every trace of discrimination, injustice, and bigotry in this wonderful land of ours. We must return to that dream and make it our own, not only for the sake of this nation, but for the sake of our own souls!"

As an example of what his congregation should do, Gray referred to Stoner's recent organizational efforts in Meridian and said, "We must see to it that hate groups such as the National States Rights Party . . . get no help or support or encouragement. Furthermore, we should make certain that vicious statements such as those attributed to the vice chairman of this group do not go unanswered. We should make it perfectly clear that such a man speaks only for a tiny handful of very sick people, and *not* for the community in which we live—and not, I trust, for the newspaper in which these remarks appeared."

Building to his conclusion, he quoted a line from Alan Paton's novel dealing with South African racism, *Cry the Beloved Country,* in which an African priest addresses a white man: "What I fear most is that before *your* people turn to loving, *my* people will have turned to hating." Gray acknowledged, "It seems painfully obvious that we have already come to that point in many parts of our own country today. But it also seems evident that we have *not* yet reached this point in our own community. On this day of national mourning, this fact about Meridian, Mississippi, should move us to do two things: First, to give humble thanks to Almighty God for the grace and the time that we yet have; and second, to get busy with the fulfillment of that *dream* that will spare us what others have had to endure and make of our own community a model of what this great nation is really meant to be."[55]

CHAPTER 13

"WE ARE INEVITABLY INVOLVED"

Meridian, 1968–74

O NCE AGAIN, Gray did not content himself with sermons on the local situation. Later in April, he joined with his friend Bill Johnson, director of economic development at the Meridian Chamber of Commerce, and other clergy and business leaders to form an interracial group called the Committee of Conscience, which took as its mission the rebuilding of black churches that had been torched. Johnson placed the group's origins in a speech he made to the Lauderdale County Baptist Pastors Association.

"I finally got completely outdone with the burning of black churches around here. I was scheduled to make a talk to the county-wide organization of Baptist ministers. And I threw away the speech I had planned to give, and I said to them, 'I'm in charge of economic development for the Meridian area, and I want you to know that we will not get any economic development as long as these black churches continue to be burned. You can forget it! It's over! We're going to wither away. And we will be the outcastes of the nation, rightfully so.'

"And out of that, the fellow who was pastor at Poplar Springs Baptist Church, Harold O'Chester, came to me afterwards and said, 'I'm willing to help. What can we do?' So he and I and others formed what we called the Committee of Conscience." O'Chester agreed to head the group. (His congregation later fired him for his activities.)

Johnson recalled, "We started out with thirty people—businessmen, preachers, kind of a cross-section of people that saw that we had just gone beyond the pale. That we *had* to do something."[1]

The group had as its epigram a paraphrase of Deuteronomy 22:1–3, which read, "Thou shalt not see thy brother's church or House of Worship destroyed and hide thyself from them. Thou shalt restore it to him." In its statement of purpose, the group wrote, "The Committee wishes to make it possible for men, women, and children of goodwill to respond to violence, hatred, and destruction with concern, compassion, and construction. So, we are initiating a community effort for concrete and personal action in response to physical losses and personal injustices and indignities suffered by congregations whose buildings have been set afire by arsonists." The statement went on to say, "We accept the losses and suffering as our own," and invited contributions by "individuals, churches, synagogues, and businesses."[2] The group was eventually responsible for the rebuilding of a number of African American churches in the county that had been bombed or burned.

Gray himself became public relations chairman of the group. In a letter dated April 30 and addressed to Lauderdale County clergy, he invited them to become members of the Committee of Conscience and to participate in a "Day of Restoration" which was to be held in June. Gray closed the letter by telling his correspondents that "we want this to be a *local* response to a *local* need," adding that none of the money raised through contributions would be "dispersed until a thorough investigation has been made and the Committee is convinced that that congregation's situation falls within the aim and scope of the Committee's concern."[3]

Late in May, Al Binder of Jackson had been invited to Meridian to speak to a B'nai B'rith meeting. In his talk to the group, he seconded Rabbi Schlager's earlier warnings to his congregation of Jewish vulnerability to Klan violence, but the members continued to dismiss such concerns. Schlager then did his best to get them to agree to hire a guard for the synagogue, but the temple's board rejected even that.[4]

On the following Tuesday, Schlager and his wife arrived home late in the evening after visiting a young couple who planned to be married soon. The Schlager children, ranging in age from four to eleven, were all asleep, as was Mrs. Schlager's mother, who lived with the family. The rabbi and his wife were getting ready for bed themselves when, just after midnight, they heard a powerful explosion. Schlager burst out, "I knew it. I knew it. They've blown up the synagogue." He was correct.[5]

He and his wife were still dressing when they heard a knock at the door. It was Gray, who lived nearby. Years later, Schlager recalled, "My friend appeared to try to speak but words did not come. Only a profusion of tears. I had never seen tears flow in a rushing stream like that before. Certainly not in a grown man. . . . His heart was truly broken. His tears spoke so much more than mere words could have. I will never forget that expression of authentic love of a Christian for his Jewish neighbors." He, his wife, and Gray silently embraced until the police arrived. Then Gray accompanied them to the ruins of the synagogue.[6]

Tarrants, this time with another Klansman, had planted fifteen sticks of dynamite by the door of the synagogue's education building. The blast shredded the building's walls, blew a hole in the roof, and shattered the windows of the adjoining sanctuary. Scraps of cloth from the building's curtains hung from the tops of tall pine trees around the property. The building's foundation was warped by the blast.[7]

The following Sunday, June 2, was Pentecost, fifty days after Easter and the day that, as Christians believe, God sent the Holy Spirit on Jesus' disciples to aid them in the spread of the Gospel. At St. Paul's, it was also the Sunday set aside to honor seniors graduating from high school. Combining the significance of these two occasions with the tragedy of the synagogue bombing would be a tall order for any preacher, but Gray found a way.

Speaking first to the seniors, he urged them to become involved in the lives of others. "The self-centered life, the life that is concerned only with one's own comfort and happiness, represents the final rejection of the spirit and message of Jesus Christ. We *are* our brother's keeper," he told them, echoing both the biblical story of Cain and Abel and the inscription on a monument at Temple Beth Israel which had been given by Meridian Christians in memory of those killed in the Holocaust. Gray continued, "His pain must be our pain, his sorrow our sorrow. We are responsible for one another and responsible for the community in which we live. Those are the facts of our existence under God, and we cannot make them otherwise."

Quoting lines from Anglican poet John Donne's meditation, "No man is an island," anthologized in many a high school literature textbook, Gray went on to sound what was for him a familiar theme as he spoke of the churches bombed and burned and now the attack on Beth Israel, where the St. Paul's graduates would have had friends. "You and I didn't set the fires or place the bombs. Furthermore, you and I abhor and condemn such despicable acts of violence, and we wish with all our hearts and souls that such things had never happened. And yet, because we live in this community, we are inevitably *involved* in these things. We share a portion of the responsibility for them." Just as he had told his congregation in Oxford after the riot at Ole Miss, now he told those in his Meridian parish that the perpetrators of violence there had assumed "some measure of community sanction" for their deeds and had counted on "the apathy and indifference" of others. "In short, they assume a moral climate in which such acts would go unpunished, if not unnoticed, by most of the community."

"After all," he went on, "apathy, indifference, and silence are the unwitting allies of the burners and the bombers; and so long as we limit our concern to wringing our hands in the privacy of our own homes or in the presence of those who agree with us, then we will have to bear a measure of guilt for the acts of violence which occur. To the burner or the bomber, silence is consent; and until we have given meaningful *public* expression to our indignation and our determination, we have been silent, we have consented."

Once again, as he had eight months earlier when the Philadelphia defendants were found guilty, Gray expressed his hope and belief that the atmosphere in Meridian was changing, citing the work of the Committee of Conscience and the public statements from city leaders and elected officials condemning the bombing of Beth Israel. He warned, however, that the change could not be accomplished overnight and added, "Furthermore, it takes *all* of us. One man cannot do it. A group of men cannot do it. It takes us *all*, and it takes a willingness to give liberally of our time, our energy, and our resources."

Then he reminded his listeners again of the holy day they celebrated. "Pentecost," he told them, "was a symbol for the early Christians of the essential *unity* of all mankind and of God's attempt to make that unity real in Jesus Christ. . . . The message of today is that we are members one of another. We *are* our brother's keeper."

In conclusion, he told his listeners that the unity that Pentecost promised and that their community required in order to stop the violence would "*not* get done without the guidance, direction, and power of God's spirit at work within and among us. 'Unless the Lord builds the house, those who build labor in vain.'"[8]

As for Meridian's Jews, they had needed a wake-up call, and now they obviously had one. They quickly appointed temple member Meyer Davidson chairman of a committee to raise money to pay informants, and Davidson stated that his goal was one hundred thousand dollars. Binder and other Jackson Jews had already raised forty-five thousand, and they contributed this to the fund. Now F.B.I. agents Roy Moore and Frank Watts had the answer to their money problem.

The temple bombing functioned as a wake-up call for white Meridian Christians too since the Klan was now operating in *their* neighborhoods. That fact undoubtedly contributed to the success of the Committee of Conscience as well. By June the group had three hundred members, thirty of them clergymen. The "Day of Restoration" became a "Day of Conscience" designed to "provide the people of goodwill in our community an opportunity to give public expression to the common sorrow and sadness we feel as a result of the burnings and bombings of eight church buildings in our county during recent months." The flyer for the Day of Conscience service, held Sunday, June 9, at 7:30 a.m. in Ray Stadium, urged its readers to "show your compassion and concern by being with us at this community-wide service this Sunday morning!" The service was an overwhelmingly Christian one, including several Christian hymns, but the invocation was offered by a member of Temple Beth Israel. Gray presided and O'Chester preached the sermon. African American ministers read from Isaiah 6:1–8 and offered the benediction. Between two and three hundred Meridian residents turned out for the event.[9]

Both the F.B.I. and the Meridian police were drawing closer to identifying Tarrants, known to most Klansmen only as "the Man," as they made use of their existing informants. In fact, since March, Tarrants had been a fugitive on federal weapons charges and had operated from an underground hideout in the mountains of North Carolina. Just before Christmas 1967, a policeman in a small Mississippi town had checked a car sitting at a closed service station and had found Tarrants and Bowers sitting in it for one of their periodic conferences. On the seat between them was a .45 caliber machine gun. Police called in the F.B.I. and Tarrants was charged with possessing an illegal weapon. So the F.B.I. had information about a link between Tarrants and Bowers as of late 1967, but it took them several months to put the pieces together and realize the significance of what they knew.[10] By May, that significance was becoming clear, and Watts decided it was time "to fight fire with fire." As it turned out, the "fire" would mean laying a trap for Tarrants, and Watts planned to use the Roberts brothers as part of the bait.[11]

After some weeks, the verbal and psychological pressure that the agents used on the Robertses was finally successful, despite some tough talk on the brothers' part. When their lawyer went to them in June with a strong message from the agents, the Robertses finally said, yes, they'd meet with the F.B.I. So late one night, their lawyer drove the brothers to Watts's home, where Watts warned them that a failure to cooperate would result in vigorous investigation and prosecution of the incidents that law enforcement officers already knew they were involved in. Cooperation, on the other hand, would mean reward money and a recommendation to judges for leniency. The brothers refused to give the agents a yes-or-no answer, and the negotiations went on. Finally on June 8, the Roberts brothers made what they claimed was their final offer, which included a tip that the two who had bombed the synagogue were planning a murder in Meridian two days later. In exchange for all the reward money collected—eighty-five thousand at that point—they would be willing to identify the terrorists.[12]

But by the morning of June 10, the two sides still had not reached an agreement. Worried about the murder warning, Meridian police detective Luke Scarborough, the only Meridian law enforcement officer that both the Roberts brothers' lawyer and the F.B.I. were willing to deal with, gave the lawyer an earful. He in turn contacted the Roberts brothers with Scarborough's message, and by mid-afternoon, they had an agreement to meet at an old trailer Watts owned and had parked on some property in the woods of Lauderdale County. Watts, Rucker, Scarborough, both Roberts brothers, and their lawyer met that evening for several hours, and finally the Roberts brothers confirmed law officers' suspicions: Tarrants and Klansman Danny Joe Hawkins had placed the dynamite that had done such damage at the Meridian synagogue. The Roberts were adamant, however, that they would not testify to this information in court; in their view, no amount of reward money was worth their lives, and they were certain that if they did testify, the Klan would kill them. But they did agree to become informants and to participate in setting a trap for the terrorists. The murder that the Robertses had predicted for that date apparently did not occur.

Jack Nelson writes, "Somewhere along the line between the Philadelphia murders and the Meridian synagogue bombing, the F.B.I. started playing by different rules." Noting the effects on the agents of continuing Klan violence, their failure to stop it, and the continuing pressure for results, Nelson quotes Watts's description of the situation:

> My name was on the [Klan black]list and my house was being watched or protected because I had my wife and three small sons there—and that got my attention. Every time I looked at one of the Roberts brothers I would think that one of the places targeted to be blown up was my house with my wife and children. And [Meridan businessman and Temple Beth Israel member] Meyer Davidson, one of the finest guys anyone would ever want to meet, targeted too. And [Meridian Police] Chief [Roy] Gunn, of course. People's sons and daughters who weren't harming anybody. And these animals, these mad dog killers, want to eliminate them. That gives you enough strength to look them in the eye and say, "You son of a bitch, you're going to tell me or I'm going to get rid of you."
>
> It changes your personality when you realize what you can do. You're sitting there and you know in your own mind that you may have the key to aborting a multiple murder. And when you realize that you can accomplish what you set out to do, it's just a matter of making them understand that you're capable of doing it.[13]

In a post-9-11 (September 11, 2001) world and in the midst of the twenty-first-century war on international terrorism, what the F.B.I. and Meridian police proceeded to do may seem tame, but by the public standards of the time it was extreme. The shift in tactics was part of the F.B.I.'s COINTELPRO operation, which had originated in 1956 in J. Edgar Hoover's Bureau as a covert effort to investigate and disrupt the Communist Party in the United States.[14] Consistent with COINTELPRO methods, law enforcement officers in Meridian adopted something close to the tactics of the Klan in order to defeat the group; as Watts had said, the F.B.I. began to "fight fire with fire." With the help of Raymond and Alton Wayne, who cooperated in return for an eventual sum of more than twenty thousand dollars, law enforcement officers set a trap for Tarrants that ended with a chase and shoot-out worthy of anything Hollywood could produce.

The meeting at which the Roberts brothers agreed to become F.B.I. informants was on June 10, 1968. Over the next two and a half weeks, Raymond and Alton Wayne kept a busy schedule, meeting with both Klansmen and the F.B.I. agents and Scarborough regularly. In meetings with his fellow Klansman Danny Hawkins, who had helped Tarrants with the Meridian synagogue bombing, Raymond Roberts' argument was that he was worried that a Meridian grand jury was about to indict him on charges of setting black churches on fire, and he needed an alibi. He asked Hawkins that he and Tarrants let him in on plans for a Meridian bombing so Roberts could be sure to be in a public place with witnesses at the time the bomb went off. He told Hawkins that he hoped the result of the plan would be at least to delay the indictments. Hawkins agreed as a favor to Roberts and the plan proceeded. On the night of June 28, Hawkins told Roberts, Tarrants and Hawkins would plant twenty-nine sticks of dynamite at the home of Meyer Davidson. Roberts informed Scarborough and his F.B.I. handlers.[15]

On the evening of Friday, June 27, the Gray family was enjoying a quiet evening at home, but Gray knew to expect a visit from Ken Dean, an ordained Baptist minister and the executive director of the Mississippi Council on Human Relations of which Gray was now president. Dean was headquartered in Jackson, but in his phone call to Gray earlier, he had stressed that he needed to see his boss right away and was headed toward Meridian. When Dean arrived and told Gray his story, the priest was incredulous. Dean said that he had reliable sources who had told him that the money Mississippi Jews had raised was going toward arranging the attempted bombing of the home of a Meridian Jew, but that the attempt was a trap in which the bombers, whom he expected to be Tarrants and Hawkins, would be killed. Although the two were Klansmen, Dean's Christian principles were offended by such summary justice. He wanted Gray's help in stopping the set-up. Gray found Dean's tale of a trap hard to credit, but he knew and trusted Dean, so on the chance that his story was correct, Gray agreed that they couldn't contact the F.B.I., because if the story were true, they were likely to be involved in the planned ambush. The two decided that they would drive around north Meridian, where the Grays, as well as prominent Jews, lived to see if they saw any signs of such an impending event. They drove by the Davidsons' house, as well as the Schlagers' and several other homes, but saw nothing that aroused their suspicion. Gray suspected that Dean had been working too hard and that that had led him to take such a rumor too seriously, so he urged his friend to get away for the weekend and get some relaxation. Dean agreed and Gray returned home.[16]

As it turned out, the only thing wrong with Dean's story was the date. But the next night, at the last minute, there was a change in the Klan's plan. It was decided that Kathy Ainsworth rather than Hawkins would be the one to accompany Tarrants on his mission. Hawkins knew his movements were closely watched by the F.B.I., and he and Tarrants assumed that the agency had no knowledge of Tarrants' and Ainsworth's existence and activities. But there they were wrong, of course, and Raymond Roberts informed his contacts that one member of that night's team was a woman. Those waiting for Tarrants' arrival at Davidson's house were warned of Ainsworth's presence and, to their irritation, were cautioned to "be careful."[17]

The recent summer equinox meant that darkness fell late, but once it had fallen, F.B.I. agents, select members of the Meridian police department, and a U.S. Army bomb demolition team took their positions at the stake-out around Davidson's property. Davidson and his wife had been evacuated to a local motel. Watts and Rucker were lookouts in the home across the street from Davidson's, which had also been evacuated. Other agents and the Meridian policemen were stationed at various points on the property and at other nearby spots on the street. All worried that if gunfire hit the bomb before the demolition team could retrieve it, a resulting explosion might kill most of them.[18]

At 12:45 a.m., very early on Sunday morning, Watts and Rucker saw a dark Buick cruising down the street, and they alerted the other men by radio. With lights off and Tarrants driving, the car pulled quietly to the curb about fifty feet from Davidson's driveway. The door opened and Tarrants emerged, carrying the bundle of dynamite attached to a timer set to go off at 2 a.m. and a small automatic pistol. He moved carefully across the lawn and driveway of the house, heading for a window of the Davidson's bedroom. Rucker quietly commanded his men to stop Tarrants there.

Scarborough, who had been hidden with some of his men on a bank planted with shrubs not far from the street, stood up suddenly and shouted, "Stop! Police!" Tarrants whirled and let go with two shots. Scarborough returned the fire with his shotgun. Then a burst of gunfire erupted from the other men. Tarrants dropped his dynamite and pistol and zig-zagged back toward his car. As he reached it, Scarborough struck Tarrants' thigh with a load of buckshot. Tarrants staggered, but managed to grab hold of the side of the car. Ainsworth leaned across the seat and opened the driver's door. Two loads of buckshot hit her in the shoulder and then a rifle bullet at the base of her neck. She fell back on the seat, dying. Tarrants, bleeding from the leg wound, managed to push her to one side, get in the car, and turn the ignition. With bullets still striking the car, he floored it down the street. A police car parked several doors down pulled out into the street to block his escape, but Tarrants swerved around it into the yard of Judge Ben Cameron, the appeals court judge who, several years earlier, had managed temporarily to block Meredith's admission to Ole Miss. The driver of the patrol car took off after Tarrants. The policeman's partner leaned out his window, firing his shotgun at the fleeing Buick. He hit the back windshield, which shattered, and then the front tires as the two vehicles turned corner after corner. With two flat tires, Tarrants' vehicle finally skidded to a stop more than fifteen blocks from the Davidsons' home. The patrol car rammed the back of the Buick, pushing it into a fire hydrant and slamming Tarrants into the steering wheel.[19]

After a moment, Tarrants emerged from the car with a submachine gun, which he began firing at the police car. He hit one of its occupants, but the other got off a shot with his .38, hitting Tarrants in the other thigh. But somehow Tarrants managed to keep moving in the direction of a nearby house. He frantically limped about fifty yards before he came to a chain link fence, which he tried to climb. The top of the fence was electrified, though, and finally Tarrants fell. As he lay on the grass, officers continued firing their shotguns at him from a distance of no more than fifteen feet. As the men reached Tarrants, blood gushing from his wounds, one aimed his gun at the man's head. "Shoot him, shoot him," someone yelled. But another said, "Don't shoot. The neighbors are here."[20]

Once Tarrants was out of the picture, violence in and around Meridian dropped sharply. Although those convicted in the Philadelphia murders remained free until March 1970, as their appeals progressed through the courts, they and others like them knew that the F.B.I. and local police had them under such close surveillance that further violence in the area was a practical impossibility. And after the shock of learning that the Roberts brothers had become informants, they realized fully to what extent law enforcement had penetrated their organization.

Meridian had not finished paying the costs of racism and segregation, however. Just over fifteen years after the Supreme Court's first *Brown* ruling that had declared racially separate schools inherently unequal, and after years of token integration of Mississippi's public schools, the courts finally ruled in November 1969 that its school systems must become unitary—thoroughly desegregated—beginning in January with the new semester.

Just after the courts spoke, Gray addressed the situation in his sermon on November 9. The Old Testament lesson for the day was from the prophet Jeremiah, who is customarily associated with lamentation and complaint. As Gray told his listeners, Jeremiah's prophecies span the period of a low point in Hebrew history when the Jews had been conquered by the Babylonian Empire and were forced to spend a generation in exile in Babylon. In this passage from Jeremiah (29:5–6), however, the prophet's tone is different from the lamentation customarily associated with him. He writes to the exiles telling them to make the best of their situation there: "Build houses, and live in them; plant gardens, and eat their produce. Take wives and have sons and daughters; take wives for your sons, and give your daughters in marriage that they may have sons and daughters" (Jeremiah 29:5).

Gray assured his listeners that while their situation was far from as dire as that of the Jewish exiles, he found the mood of the community similar to that the exiles. "There is anger, resentment, and bitterness—even some suggestion of despair—as we see the panic button being pushed as a result of the [court's school] decision," he acknowledged. But he warned his hearers, as Jeremiah did, to beware of "'false prophets' who would hold out to us the vain hope of evading these Court decisions, or, at least, hopes of evading the consequences for ourselves. We have heard too many of these voices over the past fifteen years; and listening to them has been one of the major factors we face in making the situation today even more difficult than it should be."

Then, on a far more personal note than he usually took in his sermons, he reminded his congregation that impending change was not "an academic matter" for him. He still had three children in Meridian's schools: Anne in the twelfth grade, Lloyd in the tenth, and Catherine in the second. He acknowledged that "my children and thousands like them, black and white, will have a heavy burden to bear. The educational process will suffer for a time, and there will be a certain emotional trauma associated with changing schools in the middle of the year." But he assured his listeners that Meridian schools were strong, as were its leaders, and he told them that their "primary duty" was to support the schools by asking what they could do to help with the transition and not by "looking for ways to avoid personal involvement and responsibility."

In words reminiscent of those he had written for the diocesan pamphlet supporting *Brown* in 1954, Gray told his hearers that sound public education is essential to a democracy and added, "The fate of the public schools concerns us *all.*"

As he built toward his conclusion, he said,

> You and I face today a situation the seeds of which have been sown over a period of many, many years, from the institution of slavery through the years of separate but very unequal education, up through the resistance and evasion of the past fifteen years. And now we come to a point that any thinking person knew *must* come, sooner or later, in a professedly Christian and democratic country. We don't like the timing and the form in which this crisis has come. We wish with all our hearts that it had been met and resolved by some previous generation—or that it could be postponed to sometime in the future. . . . But *somebody* was going to have to do it, sooner or later, and maybe we ought to thank God that he has called *us* to such an important and essential task. . . . In a very real sense, God has *chosen* us, you and me, to live in this difficult, but very significant time. True, it is a time of crisis, but times of crisis are times for greatness. . . . And I know in my heart that the people of this community, white and black alike, children and adults, have the talents and the resources, the patience and the wisdom, to get through this difficult period of transition, to support our school board and our school system, and to create for the future an even *better* education for our children and a whole new understanding of human relations. We have the talents and the human resources, the patience and the wisdom, *and* the grace and power of Almighty God. What we need is the *will*, the *faith*, and the *confidence*, and it is for these that we pray today.[21]

Like many others at St. Paul's and in the community, Gray's family took him up on his challenge. Forty years later, he and others in Meridian were proud of the success with which they managed the crisis. Since like many segregated school systems, Meridian had two high schools, one white and one black, school leaders decided to desegregate the two by sending black eleventh and twelfth graders to the white school and white tenth graders to the black school.

Anticipating the decision, Meridian's superintendent of schools had asked Ruthie Gray to offer herself as a candidate for president of the city-wide P.T.A., a position for which she was chosen. She quickly organized a series of meetings and other sources of information to answer parents' inevitable questions and respond to their accompanying fears.

Daughter Anne remembers that the Christmas vacation, the time between semesters, was an especially busy one. Student leaders from both high schools were brought together during the break not only to get to know each other, but also to help with registering the new black students.[22]

Lloyd's reaction to the situation was perhaps most poignant. He had been born two months after the *Brown* decision, and now he asked his father, "Dad, why didn't you folks solve this years ago?" But he was also president of the sophomore class at the white high school, and the administration had made the decision to have black and white co-presidents for the remainder of the school year. The president of the sophomore class at the black high school was Obie Clayton, named after his father, who was a leader for civil rights in Meridian and whom one of the black students involved in the earlier token integration of Meridian High later compared to Malcolm X as "black America's manhood."[23] Although Gray knew and had worked with the senior Clayton, Lloyd and son Obie had not met before they took on their new task. They became good friends, however, and later both attended Millsaps College in Jackson.

A year later, Lloyd found himself the only white candidate for student body president for their twelfth-grade year. In his speech to the assembled students, Lloyd, who was already fascinated by all things political, speculated on whether that fact was indicative of student apathy or a desire to avoid splitting white students' votes. He told his fellow students, "I can assure you that I would rather stand before you today representing Lloyd Gray rather than the white race, and I am sure my opponents would prefer to be representing themselves as individuals rather than their own race."[24] In any case, he was elected president.

In Mississippi, the Civil Rights Movement and the violence associated with it really did end after 1970. The F.B.I. had broken the White Knights of the Ku Klux Klan and had put its leaders in prison. Mississippi schools were integrated and, like public schools in other Southern states, remained so to a remarkable extent for decades, far more than those in other parts of the country. And Mississippi business and political leaders had finally realized the harm that racist violence did to their state throughout the nation and the world.

For Gray, these changes in Mississippi and the years of peace in the state undoubtedly contributed to the next turn his life would take: in 1974 a majority of the overwhelmingly white laypeople and clergy of the Episcopal Diocese of Mississippi elected him as their bishop coadjutor.

CHAPTER 14

"THE BISHOP'S ROLE IS TO BE A PASTOR"

Jackson, 1974–93

I N THE EPISCOPAL CHURCH, a bishop coadjutor is elected by a combi-
nation of clerical and lay delegates in a specially called convention. The
coadjutor's role is to assist the diocesan bishop, and the assumption is that
when the diocesan bishop leaves his post, the coadjutor will succeed him.

In Mississippi in 1974, it was clear that the bishop coadjutor whom the
convention elected would succeed the diocesan bishop almost immediately.
The previous October, the national House of Bishops had selected Mississippi's diocesan, John Maury Allin, to become the new presiding bishop of
the Episcopal Church in the United States.[1] Allin would assume that role at
the church's national headquarters in New York City on June 1, 1974.

Mississippi Episcopalians called their special council to elect Allin's successor as short-term coadjutor on January 12, 1974, at the diocese's cathedral, St. Andrew's, in Jackson. Following a celebration of the Eucharist, the
council faced a daunting slate of thirty-two nominees.[2] That number was
quickly narrowed to eight, all of them priests in the diocese of Mississippi.
In order to be elected, a nominee had to receive at least thirty-seven of
the clergy's votes and seventy-three of the laity's. Gray had strong support
among the clergy of the diocese, many of whom admired the stands he had
taken on racial issues. Many lay delegates were less admiring.

At the council meeting, Gray led the other seven nominees in both clerical and lay votes on the first ballot, but he was still short of the number
needed in both orders' votes. On the second ballot he achieved the required
number of clergy votes, but still needed an additional twenty-five votes
from lay delegates. The Reverend Clifton McInnis, rector of Holy Trinity
Church in Vicksburg, had emerged as his clear competitor for laymen's
votes. Voting continued throughout the day, and by the fifth ballot, McInnis
received the number of lay votes needed for election, but still fell far short
of the number of clergy votes needed; however, on succeeding ballots the

number of clergy votes he received grew slightly, as did the number of votes from lay delegates. On the next four ballots, Gray's total in both the clergy and lay orders began to shrink as the day wore on and delegates began to yearn simply for *an election*. By the time the council reached its ninth ballot, it was late afternoon and the group adjourned without a decision. The delegates would not meet again until March 9.

During the intervening two months, several things occurred. In addition to some informal "politicking" on the part of Gray's supporters, the diocese revised its selection process by creating something much closer to the method by which nominees for bishop are chosen by dioceses today. It downsized its large procedural committee into a five-member "research and recommendation committee." That group was charged with "collecting in-depth information on no more than ten possible nominees."[3] Ruthie Gray had something to do with the changes.

Gray recalls, "Ruthie went and talked to Bishop Allin. She told him, 'You need to put together biographical data on these people.' Of course she was a bit biased. She thought my biography would look better than Clifton's [McInnis]! Clifton had done a great job as parish priest, but he hadn't been as involved on the diocesan level or the national level or in activities both inside the church and outside."[4]

Gray's "biography" included both an assessment of his ministry at St. Paul's and a statement from him on his vision of the bishop's role. The assessment noted the growth in St. Paul's physical plant and its budget during Gray's rectorship. It also remarked on "his ability to preach, his sharing of leadership in the parish, and his concern for the ever expanding of the ministry of our faith [*sic*]." Parishioners called him "intellectually honest," but also said that "he has unified our parish." They praised him as "a respected leader in the community" and called him "outstanding." The assessment concluded, "A conversation with Duncan Gray is free and relaxed and quickly reveals that here is a man with deep convictions and an acute awareness of the problems confronting mankind and our church."[5]

Gray's own statement showed that he already had a strong sense of the tone and direction of his ministry as bishop. He noted a bishop's responsibility for ordaining clergy and administering Confirmation; for recruiting, screening, and training individuals for ordained ministry; for administering the diocese; and for leading church members within the diocese. He concluded, however, with the following: "Above all, I believe the Bishop's role is to be a *pastor* to the people within his diocese, both clerical and lay. Indeed, all of the duties mentioned above, from ordination to the most mundane of administrative details, need to be carried out in a pastoral manner; in a manner reflecting a creative concern for all the persons affected or involved."[6]

More than twenty-five years later, reflecting on a bishop's responsibilities—visitations ("That's a full-time job with ninety-one congregations in Mississippi and only fifty-two Sundays, and you got to take a little vacation sometime!), meetings, and administrative functions—Gray said, "Administratively, it was a pretty big operation, and that was the part I liked least. I liked the pastoral part. You want to spend as much time as you can with the clergy—you're *their* pastor—but then with the congregations too. I tried hard to be in close touch with the clergy, but certainly with the congregations too. That meant a lot of visitations, more than just an annual visit for confirmations."[7]

When the special council was reconvened on March 9, some laity from the Mississippi Delta had ensured the nomination of a strong candidate from outside Mississippi, Moultrie Moore, then suffragan bishop of the diocese of North Carolina. But even so, the movement was clearly in Gray's direction this time. On the council's first ballot he received thirty-one clergy votes and a total of forty-six lay votes. By the second ballot, he got thirty-seven clergy votes, a majority in that order. Three more ballots were required for Gray to pick up the lay votes he needed, but by early afternoon the selection had been made, and he was now bishop coadjutor-elect.[8] On a motion by the Rev. Benjamin F. Bell, rector of Trinity Church in Hattiesburg, Gray's selection was made unanimous by the council, and its members gave Gray an extended standing ovation.[9]

Reflecting on the long-drawn-out process of his election, Gray said, "I think the real issue there was still the race issue. A lot of the votes were *for* Clifton, but some of them were just against me. It had to do with the race issue."[10]

Gray was consecrated bishop on May 1, again at St. Andrew's. He remembers that Allin "left the office here the day after I was consecrated! He was available to me and we talked, but it was pretty fast. He had to get up there to New York, and he had even more to get accustomed to than I did!"

Gray recalled, "My biggest problem in those early years [of his episcopate] was just trying to make peace with or settle things with those who were very much opposed to my having been elected."[11]

In this, if one clergyman's testimony is any indication, Gray was successful. About a year after Gray's consecration, a Delta rector, a supporter and seminary classmate of Gray's, sent him a copy of a letter from a north Mississippi rector in which he wrote, "About Duncan Gray, you were right and I was wrong. I felt the diocese was in such shape it would take someone from outside to get it together, but he seems to be doing the job very well. You were right, too, about his being honest and truthful—and I've found him to be so. A good man!"[12]

But in both the national Episcopal Church and in the diocese of Mississippi, the year 1974 fell in the middle of a period of turmoil over issues other than race, and that turmoil would continue for at least fifteen years. In fact, to some extent the turmoil has not been fully resolved today. The two issues that created the greatest division at the time were revision of the prayer book that more than a generation of Episcopalians had used since 1928 and the question of the role of women in the church, especially the matter of their ordination to the priesthood. The issue of sexuality, the most prominent one in the Anglican communion in the twenty-first century, came up as early as the 1970s, but did not emerge as a major controversy until the 1990s.

In the decades following World War II, the Episcopal Church had experienced impressive growth, especially of its suburban parishes. But by 1965, the picture had begun to change. Robert Prichard observes, "In terms of baptized membership, the fifteen years between 1965 and 1980 were the most devastating for the Episcopal Church since the American Revolution."[13] Other Protestant denominations experienced similar declines, but in the Episcopal Church, Prichard attributes the membership loss not only to a very significant drop in the U.S. birthrate as baby boomers came of age, a fact that affected all denominations, but also to the Episcopal Church's "theological reorientation." Prichard writes,

> The theological reorientation was both necessary and painful. The obvious successes in the suburbs in the 1950s had narrowed the perspective of many Christians. They began to see new buildings and growing Sunday schools of white middle-class children as the sole goal of the church. When the birthrate dropped and black and other ethnic groups that had been excluded from the new suburban center of American life began to demand more equitable treatment, such Christians were forced to reexamine their premises. Some responded to the challenge in positive ways; they attempted to make the liturgy more accessible to the laity, removed limitations on the participation of women in the church, called for greater responsibility to minorities, and adjusted the pastoral ministry of the church for the problems of a new decade. Others, troubled by a rate of change that they believed was either too rapid or too slow, left the Episcopal Church.[14]

Indeed, Allin's election as Presiding Bishop was a symptom of Episcopalians' reaction to this "theological reorientation." His predecessor, John Hines, a Texas bishop before his election as presiding bishop in 1965, had convinced the 1967 General Convention to approve a program known as the General Convention Special Program (GCSP). Following the urban rioting that began in Los Angeles in 1965, Hines came to believe that the Episcopal Church must take a larger role in attempting to right the injustices of American society, and GCSP was the program he advanced to work toward that goal. The 1967 General Convention approved an outlay of $9 million to fund the program. Prichard writes,

> Hines turned to [Leon] Modeste to administer the fund. Modeste, an Episcopal layman who had grown up in Brooklyn slums, was convinced that the fund would be effective if the minority groups to whom grants were made were free to make their own decisions. He recruited minority staff members and began to make grants, most of which went to organizations outside the Episcopal Church. This created some tension, especially when Modeste and his staff made grants to organizations other Episcopalians viewed as violent or hostile. Grants to Malcolm X University in Durham; to the Black Awareness Coordinating Committee in Denmark, South Carolina; and to the Alianza Federale de los Mercedes in New Mexico over the explicit objections of bishops Thomas Fraser of North Carolina, Gray Temple of South Carolina, John Pinkney of Upper South Carolina, and Charles Kinsolving of New Mexico resulted in unfavorable publicity for the program. By 1969, some Episcopalians were calling for the termination of GCSP.[15]

GCSP was discontinued by the 1973 General Convention. In the meantime, however, Episcopalians, especially in more conservative areas, including the South, were very much outraged by GCSP's decisions, and the ethnicity of the program's recipients was certainly a factor in that outrage. In large part because of the division that GCSP had created, Hines resigned a year before his term ended, and a new presiding bishop from Mississippi looked like a good choice to succeed him. Although Allin was by no means a racist, he was a theological conservative, and his signature program as presiding bishop, Venture in Mission (VIM), marked a return to more traditional and more acceptable forms of ministry, evangelizing to spread the Gospel both nationally and internationally.

Characteristically, Gray spoke highly of both Hines and Allin. "I had profound respect for Bishop Hines and what he tried to do, but I think Bishop Allin handled things mighty well himself. GCSP was not only well intentioned, it was well designed for the time. It was just going to inevitably create opposition. But I think it was very helpful and helped the church take a step in the right direction. There was going to be criticism of it, but I was fully supportive of it and I think it was a good idea. I'm sorry Bishop Hines had to pay for it. Venture in Mission was much more acceptable because it was clearly evangelism. We were moving out and trying to reach out to people, spread the Good News, the Gospel. It didn't focus on social issues or social action or social justice as GCSP did, which was a specific effort to respond to racial injustice, economic injustice. But Venture in Mission was a good program too. I don't want to put words into Bishop Allin's mouth, but I think he thought that VIM was a way to pull the church together and get it focused on the basic mission of the church. He wasn't saying, 'Forget about social justice,' but more 'Let this be our focus right now.'"[16]

But the election of Allin could not halt other changes taking place within the church. As noted above, the two most prominent ones were liturgical change, which was most disturbing to lay persons, and the ordination of women to the priesthood, which provoked some in both the clergy and lay orders.

The most obvious change in the new trial liturgies was their shift from Elizabethan language to a more contemporary English, a fact that bothered many who held that Elizabethan English, as embodied in such great works as the King James translation of the Bible and Shakespeare, marked a significant high point in the development of the English language. Others simply found the use of such language in church services familiar and comfortable.

Other changes were designed to make the prayer book's language and message more inclusive, most notably in the shift from such words as "man" and "men" to more gender-inclusive language. The new liturgies also prescribed more participation on the part of the congregation, and included the priest celebrating the Eucharist facing the congregation at a table near them, rather than at an altar at the very front of the church with the priest's back turned.

There were also more subtle theological shifts that some were explicitly aware of and that others probably sensed without, perhaps, being able to articulate them fully. One such shift, probably inevitable given the times, was a lessened emphasis on human sinfulness and a greater emphasis on the positive aspects of humans' relationship with God and God's with them. An eventually unsuccessful attempt to omit the prayer of confession during the Eucharist was an instance of this shift. This de-emphasis on human sinfulness was one aspect of the revision that Gray found himself less comfortable with.

Nevertheless, as a loyal son of the church, he did his best to encourage and educate his flock in the use of trial liturgies and then, after the 1979 General Convention approved a revised prayer book, to make sure that the parishes in his diocese fell in line with the change. He recalls about the shift that "there was more opposition from the laity than the clergy on that one. There certainly were clergy who were opposed, but they were more familiar with the process and understood that this was going to happen."[17]

As it turned out, prayer book revision did not spark as much controversy during this period as did the issue of women's role in the church. After all, members of the other significantly liturgical branch of the western church, Roman Catholics, had been dealing with liturgical change since Vatican II in the 1960s. But although other mainline Protestant denominations in the United States had been ordaining women to congregational ministry for some years, they made no claim of apostolic succession for their clergy, as did Anglicans and Roman Catholics.[18] Of course, in the line of apostolic succession back to the time of Jesus' apostles, all clergy had been male. And for both the Roman and Anglican communions, tradition, in the form of church history and practice, is of enormous importance, second only to scripture.

Between 1964 and 1976, the Episcopal Church, meeting in General Convention, had gradually begun to remove the barriers to women's participation in the church. It recognized the right of female deacons to marry, just as male deacons could, in 1964. In 1965, Presiding Bishop John Hines appointed the Committee to Study the Proper Place of Women in the Ministry of the Church. In 1966, the committee presented the House of Bishops with a recommendation that they seriously consider the ordination of women to the priesthood, but that resulted in no real action of the part of the bishops. In 1967, the General Convention approved women's service as lay readers during church services and began the process of allowing women to serve as deputies to General Convention.[19]

In 1973, a resolution to permit women's ordination had actually passed in the House of Deputies, but not in the House of Bishops. In any case, once again the pace of change was too slow for some women. In July 1974, in Philadelphia, eleven women who had already been ordained as transitional deacons (a position preliminary to ordination to the priesthood) were ordained to the priesthood by three retired bishops but without the permission of their home dioceses or bishops. Six weeks later, another four women in similar circumstances were ordained to the priesthood by another retired bishop.

Gray cautiously favored women's ordination. Mississippi's delegates to the 1973 convention discussed the issue before the convention. Gray recalls, "I'm ashamed to admit it now, but I remember saying in that meeting, 'I'd just as soon the issue didn't come up, but now it's come up, there's only one way we can go.' I knew it was going to be a real fight!"[20]

Gray's predecessor thought differently about the matter. Gray said, "Allin opposed women's ordination—there's no question about that. But I remember that he made a very significant statement in Mississippi that changed some votes on this. It was at Diocesan Council just before the 1976 convention. He said something like, 'I'm not in favor of it, but I think under the circumstances we'll have to go ahead and pass it.' Alex Dickson [at the time rector or headmaster at the diocese's only school for girls, All Saints' Episcopal in Vicksburg], I remember, was very much opposed to women's ordination, standing with Bishop Allin. But when Bishop Allin said that, I think it changed Alex Dickson's vote. That made an impression on me because everybody knew that Bishop Allin was opposed, but he thought maybe the church needed to go ahead and do it. And that surprised everybody, and it surprised Alex Dickson so much that he changed his vote."[21]

According to a 1974 article in the *Christian Century*, Allin believed "the problem [with women's ordination] is essentially a theological one; he says it is not enough to find no theological reason *against* ordaining women; the church must search for cogent theological reasons *for* doing it."[22]

Gray's understanding of the issue was exactly the opposite: he saw nothing in scripture as he read it that should prove a barrier to women's ordination to the priesthood and, as a member of the House of Deputies, voted in favor of it in 1973. By the 1976 convention he played a more central role, since part of the debate centered on the crucial procedural question of whether allowing women's ordination required a change in the church's constitution or merely its canons. The former would necessitate the approval of two consecutive conventions, allowing three years in between for lobbying. The latter allowed the decision to be made on a single vote in 1976. Supporters of women's ordination knew that they had the votes in 1976 and were already, as we have noted, impatient with further delays. And in the meantime, Allin had appointed Gray as chair of the Committee on Constitution and Canons.

Gray downplays his qualifications for the appointment. "Bishop Allin and I had had a canonical argument at some point in a council meeting, and I ended up being right. I wasn't any expert on canons, but *he* decided that made me a canonical expert because I had proved him wrong one time! I got my experience after I was appointed."[23]

At the 1976 convention, the committee, with Gray as chair, chose the canonical argument. "I think I was right about that—at least the church accepted it as right. Of course some people never did accept that decision. They thought it should have been a constitutional change requiring two conventions." Once the church had made its decision in 1976, revision of the church's canons became necessary as part of the effort to make the church more inclusive. "We wanted to make sure that there was minority representation on all the committees. And the other thing: pronouns! 'He's' and 'she's'! Getting that straight. Women priests were as eligible as men."[24]

Like other bishops, when Gray returned to his diocese he faced significant opposition to the convention's decision, as he knew he would. "As bishop, I didn't get any real militant opposition until the women's ordination issue surfaced. We had eight or ten clergymen in the diocese who were very much opposed and made a big issue of it at council and elsewhere. *That* suddenly became the big issue rather than race. Now again, this wasn't a majority by any means, but it was a *very* vocal minority who felt *very* strongly. There were lots of laymen who felt very strongly about women's ordination, but in terms of militant opposition, it was altogether clergy. That made it a little tense and difficult at clergy conference and at council. And several just pulled out of the Episcopal Church altogether and some went to other dioceses."[25]

A group of twenty-two priests and three lay brothers quickly formed an organization to oppose women's ordination in Mississippi, naming themselves "Churchmen for Apostolic Faith and Order" (CAFO).[26] The members composed and signed a "Statement of Conviction" in which they argued,

> General Convention cannot, of its own will and by its own act, decide to change the fundamental principle of a male priesthood held by the Universal Church. It follows that the limitation of the priesthood and the espiscopate to men can be changed only by heavy consensus (approaching unanimity) of the Catholic Church ["Catholic" here as in "universal," but, practically speaking, applying only to branches of the church that claim apostolic succession], under the clear and unmistakable direction of the Holy Ghost. God's Spirit must speak to his CHURCH, not just to a majority of the General Convention of the Episcopal Church. . . . Therefore, we, the undersigned, will not participate in or recognize any "ordinations" of women to the priesthood

or the epsicopate; nor will we attend, participate in, or recognize any priestly act performed by such a woman.[27]

Gray's correspondence on the matter included letters from two Mississippi clergymen, both of whom pledged their loyalty to him as bishop, but who had slightly different "takes" on the CAFO statement. One in east central Mississippi wrote, "I likely would have supported ordination for women had I voted, but I have to wonder if all this is going to be worth the trauma, and I have to wonder how real reconciliation can be if it has strings on it and knocks down one group of people in order to bring another one up." On the other hand, a clergyman in Meridian wrote of the CAFO statement that he considered it "so far beyond the bounds of discretion and propriety as to prompt this complaint to the Ordinary [bishop] of the diocese," on the grounds that all clergy sign a document promising "to uphold the Doctrine, Discipline, and Worship of the Protestant Episcopal Church." With warmth, the writer concluded, "It is my hope that you will not equivocate in clarifying that matter [of discipline] for all of us. Furthermore, I should like to go on record as being opposed to any priest or layman holding office in this diocese who cannot recognize the legitimacy of the decision making process in which he participates."[28]

Rejecting a quick resort to discipline, Gray instead agreed to let a representative from CAFO address Diocesan Council in January 1977. But before their representative spoke, Gray, as bishop, delivered his annual address to the meeting. He began by observing, "We have just completed an eventful year in the history of the Episcopal Church—a year marked by crucial decisions—and we move now into a year in which we will be dealing more and more with the consequences of those decisions. This means, of course, that we will have difficulties." He continued, "In a letter I addressed to you through *The Church News* back in October, I said that the General Convention in Minneapolis and the national Church as a whole had set for us our agenda for the coming year. Those words have proved to be even more true than I might have anticipated at that time, and I daresay that the things that are uppermost in your minds tonight are things which have to do with the *whole* Church, not just the Diocese of Mississippi." In an optimistic vein, he said, "Basically this is a good thing; a welcome sign that we know ourselves to be part of a community of faith that transcends all parochial, diocesan, and even national boundaries. We are not preoccupied only with that which goes on within the four walls of our own church. We are part of a much larger community, and we are becoming increasingly aware of this. But," he noted, "such an awareness also brings problems."[29]

First addressing the convention's endorsement of the revised prayer book, Gray told the meeting that he had asked the clergy and vestry wardens of each congregation in the diocese to develop a local plan for phasing in use of the new book over the designated three-year period. "All, I trust, will be in operation by the beginning of the summer so that, at the very least, we will all be thoroughly familiar with Rite I [the more traditional version of services] by the end of 1977," he said.

Turning then to women's ordination, Gray noted that January 1 had been the effective date of the convention's action and reminded his audience that the women who would be ordained that year "had been serving as deacons for several years . . . and they were simply waiting for General Convention to act before they could be advanced to the priesthood." He noted that there were no female deacons, seminarians, postulates, or even applicants to the process in Mississippi, "so we are at least several years removed from any ordinations in this diocese."[30]

Assuring the assembled delegates, "I firmly believe that our General Convention made the right decision" about women's ordination, Gray acknowledged, "I know that some of you are deeply troubled by this decision," and promised them, "Your conscientious convictions will be respected. We will not force a female priest on any congregation, and we will understand if there are those who feel, in conscience, that they cannot accept the sacramental ministrations of such a priest." He added, "We ask simply that those on both sides of this crucial issue respect the consciences of those with whom they differ and approach one another in a spirit of mutual love and trust and reconciliation."[31]

His request was ignored by CAFO's spokesman.

The Rev. Thomas Waggener spoke at some length to the council on behalf of CAFO's position. He began with the heated declaration, "Oh woeful day when we must cry out in protest! We come before you with a grim message in a dark hour. Your house is on fire. Do not be deceived with smooth words." Waggener continued by saying, "In the General Convention in Minneapolis, we see the triumph of secular humanism over Christianity in the Episcopal Church. We see the abandonment of two thousand years of Apostolic faith and practice. We see the adoption of a novel 'gospel of liberation,' which is another way of saying accommodation with the world."

After reviewing other issues that concerned the group, including homosexuality, the prayer book, and abortion, Waggener concluded with a message to the church's bishops: "If you cannot order the life of this Church in accordance with the Word of God, the teaching of the Fathers, the ancient Creeds and Ecumenical Councils, then we shall be obliged to turn to those who can." To Gray, who was presiding over the meeting, he said, "The presence of a woman functioning as a priest in this Diocese will be an absolute block to reconciliation."[32]

Letters in Gray's files reflect the deep division among clergy, and the issue of women's ordination quickly became entangled with other issues. One letter from a Delta rector to a clergyman in Hattiesburg focused first on what he saw as the church's lax contemporary attitudes toward homosexuality as opposed to its earlier ones ("When I was in seminary, only 25 years ago, a fellow seminarian was expelled when his homosexual *tendencies* were discovered . . . [and] he hadn't even committed an overt act as far as anyone knew"). Clearly his concerns about homosexuality were only one aspect of his general anxiety about the direction of the church, because he concluded by writing, "the saddest of all though is that Tom Waggener's last sentence in the second paragraph of page four ["What dear and precious friendships have been ground up in this precious mill."] is no doubt true and may become even more so in the future."[33]

At about the same time, another Hattiesburg clergyman wrote Gray, "Ever since Council I have been hurting over the most irresponsible and divisive statements produced by the Faith and Order folks. I really could not believe that after asking for 'understanding and sympathy,' they leveled such a ridiculous shot at the whole Church, and particularly at you. . . . To tell a Bishop, in effect, 'if you follow the Canons of this Church you have broken faith with us' has got to be the most self-righteous thing I have ever heard from any group."[34]

A year later at the 151st Diocesan Council meeting, those in Mississippi who supported or at least tolerated the idea of women's ordination and those who opposed it had come to a parting of the ways. In his address to council, Gray acknowledged to the assembled delegates what they already knew. He said,

> This past year has been a difficult one in many respects. The Episcopal Church throughout this land has been beset with controversy and unrest, and we have had our share of this in Mississippi. There have been some painful and agonizing moments, not the least of which was the departure of four of our clergy, two mission priests and two monastics, to the American Orthodox Church [one of several relatively short-lived groups that broke away over such issues as women's ordination]. This is something we deeply regret; but, at the same time, we respect the decisions of these men, and we wish them well. Others of us, both clergy and lay, have shared our disagreements on such

things as women's ordination and Prayer Book revision, and there
have been some tense and trying moments in the process.[35]

Waggener and three other priests involved in CAFO were deposed, or
dismissed, from priesthood in the Episcopal Church for renouncing their
ministry in the denomination.[36] But by 1980, when Mississippi Episcopalians gained their first female priest, Mary MacSherry (Molly) McBride,
who transferred from the Diocese of Central New York to Jackson as an
assistant to the Dean of St. Andrew's Cathedral, furor over the issue had
quieted, and Gray's address to council that year focused instead on natural
disasters such as flooding and hurricanes in Mississippi, on Allin's VIM
program, and on national and international issues such as Vietnamese
refugees, some of whom had been sponsored as immigrants by Episcopal
congregations in Mississippi. At the 1981 meeting, the only official mention of McBride was as one of a dozen new clergy whom Gray introduced
to delegates to council.[37] The same year the diocese gained its first female
postulant as Annwn Leigh Hawkins, a communicant of St. Andrew's, enrolled at Episcopal Theological Seminary in Virginia. She was ordained to
the priesthood by Gray in 1985.

In 1978, Gray got a break from his immediate diocesan responsibilities
as a participant in that year's Lambeth Conference in England. The Lambeth Conference, named for the Archbishop of Canterbury's residence,
meets at the University of Kent on the outskirts of Canterbury and is the
once-a-decade gathering of Anglican primates from throughout the world.
The archbishops and bishops meet for almost three weeks for Bible study,
worship, conversation, and consultation. Gray, his wife, and their younger
daughter, Catherine, left Mississippi for Paris on July 3 and spent almost
three weeks visiting various sites in France and in England before settling
in Canterbury in preparation for the conference. As they left France for
London after experiences such as Eucharist at the American Cathedral in
Paris; visits to Notre Dame, the Louvre, and the Eiffel Tower; exploration
of churches in the Latin Quarter; and "dinner, dancing, and a show" at the
Lido ("Lots of fun, but expensive! Once is enough!"), and arrived to settle
in a flat near the Thames, Gray commented in his official journal, "Hard to
believe that all this is happening to us!"[38]

While for a little more than another week they enjoyed being tourists
in England with activities such as visits to Buckingham Palace and the
changing of the guard, 10 Downing Street, Greenwich, and a performance
of "Measure for Measure" in Stratford, Gray settled down in Canterbury
with equal enthusiasm. At his first sight of Canterbury from the university

campus, Gray wrote, "The University is on a hill overlooking Canterbury and the view is magnificent! The cathedral towering over the town down in the valley takes on added beauty with floodlights focused on it."[39] At the conference, days began with a celebration of the Eucharist according to the rites of such Anglican provinces as Tanzania, Australia, Ireland, Central Africa, and Japan. On a number of days there were morning addresses by such figures as British economist Barbara Ward. In the afternoon the bishops met in their small groups; Gray's focused on the ministry of bishops, and he noted that the group included representatives from eleven different countries.[40]

Lambeth did not mean a complete break from the issues surrounding women's ordination, however. That year the conference approved thirty-seven resolutions, including three on women's ministry. During the second week of the conference, the attendees met in plenary session, first to hear an address on the issue from the Rev. Dr. John MacQuarrie, Lady Margaret Professor at Christ Church, Oxford, and one of the most eminent Anglican theologians of the time. Then the floor was open for discussion. Gray made no comment in his journal on MacQuarrie's address or the hearing, but years later he remembered how impressed he was with MacQuarrie, as he had been earlier with the theologian's writings.[41]

Between the second and third week of the conference, the Grays took advantage of a weekend break to do a little more sightseeing with a day-trip to Oxford. Exploring the campus of Christ Church, they ran into MacQuarrie, and Gray took the opportunity to tell him how much he had appreciated the theologian's address on women's ordination. Following a brief conversation, MacQuarrie offered to show them around Christ Church Cathedral, and they took advantage of the offer, beginning a personal relationship that would last the rest of McQuarrie's life. They were back in London by evening for a performance of "Chorus Line."[42]

The Grays returned home from England on August 14. Gray took one day at home "enjoying [his] grandson," but returned to the office the next, finding "re-entry a bit difficult." He soon resumed his normal routine, however, and the rest of the month involved a series of visitations to parishes, including to his first clerical assignment in Rosedale and Cleveland, Mississippi, where there was a clerical vacancy and where he preached and celebrated the Eucharist. His weekdays were full of conferences and meetings with various clergy and laypeople as well as a number of hospital visits. The month also included two "annual consultations" with diocesan clergy.[43]

The annual consultation program, which involved giving each of the well over one hundred active clergy in the diocese a half-day meeting with the bishop during the month of his or her birthday, was one that Gray initiated and which reflected his view of the importance of a pastoral focus in the episcopate. "I'd just set aside a couple of hours to talk about whatever they wanted to talk about, although of course sometimes I might have a little agenda myself depending on what was going on in their congregations. But it was mostly just sort of spend some time together and talk about 'How's your ministry? What are the highs and lows? How's your marriage? Are you interested in a move?' Then we'd have lunch. There were some who didn't want to do it, and I didn't make any of them do it, but most of them jumped at the opportunity to spend a few hours with the bishop and talk about anything they wanted to. And those meetings were real important to me too because it was an opportunity to relate to the clergy on a level somewhat similar to the way I related to individual parishioners. I think it was 'quality time' with the bishop that you didn't get on the run, coming into a service and confirming, and moving on to another meeting. With a bishop's schedule there aren't many times you can spend three hours with someone, but I just set aside those blocks of time, and I felt like that *may* have been the most important thing I did as bishop."[44]

In 1990, as Gray neared retirement, the Rev. David A. Elliott III, then rector of St. James' Church in Greenville and someone who had known Gray since Elliot was growing up in Meridian at St. Paul's, reflected on the program and Gray's relationship with his clergy. He wrote of Gray, "His compassion, understanding, and spirit of reconciliation have guided this diocese and made us the 'family' we are. It [the annual consultation] has been and still is a needed part of the pastoral care of this diocese. [At] our last annual clergy conference [1990] . . . there was a rapport and one-ness present in our family that other dioceses lack and we are fortunate to have."[45]

During the first several years of Gray's episcopate, issues other than liturgical revision and women's ordination had also filled his plate, and the issue of race had by no means disappeared.

Less than a year after Gray's consecration, he agreed to take part in a lawsuit against the Mississippi History Textbook Rating Committee and the Mississippi State Textbook Purchasing Board. Like several other parents who took part in the suit, he did so on behalf of his child, in Gray's case his daughter Catherine, then a student at St. Andrew's Episcopal School in Jackson. The plaintiffs also included James W. Loewen and Charles Sallis, professors at Tougaloo College and Millsaps College in Jackson (where the Grays' older daughter, Anne, was a student) and authors of the Mississippi history textbook *Mississippi: Conflict and Change*, "the first state history

textbook to take a 'non-traditional' view of race in Mississippi."[46] The Textbook Rating Committee had refused to approve Loewen and Sallis's text as
one which the state would agree to supply to school systems throughout
Mississippi, agreeing instead to approve only another text written in 1964
which presented a more "traditional" view of race relations. Loewen and
Sallis wrote potential plaintiffs, "From various sources, we have been informed that our treatment of such topics as slavery, Reconstruction, lynching, and civil rights met with [the committee's] disapproval."[47] Among other
things, the suit asked for an injunction against the defendants to prevent
them "from engaging in policies or practices which discriminate against
textbooks containing perspectives on history at odds with those traditionally acceptable in Mississippi."[48] The plaintiffs eventually prevailed.

Catherine's enrollment at St. Andrew's was itself controversial, reflecting what was to become, for privileged whites, and later also for privileged
blacks, one of the increasingly vexing moral problems of school integration,
especially the socioeconomic variety in an urban setting. Before what its
opponents called "massive integration," not only was the number of African
Americans who attended predominantly white schools small enough not to
set off "white flight" in all but the most committed segregationists, but, far
more important, those African Americans who did attend predominantly
white schools were almost always the children of middle-class professional
families. Their background and their values were not so different from those
of the white children with whom they went to school. Once desegregation
became general, however, white liberals began to worry about the quality
of their children's education, since now so many of the African American
children who began attending the formerly white public schools were children who showed the scars of generations of poverty and poor education,
going back to the days of slavery. The choice of public or private became a
moral dilemma as it had not been before.

After federal courts had ordered immediate desegregation of Mississippi
public schools in 1969, many so-called seg academies had quickly organized
in order to provide continued segregated education to Mississippi's white
children. These "academies" drew the scorn and condemnation of white
Mississippi liberals. In Jackson, however, another kind of group called Mississippians for Public Education (MPE) also organized with the goal of encouraging white support for public education throughout the state. Ruthie
Gray was a member of the group, but other members came to Gray to complain about St. Andrews. The school had a few black students at the time,
but Gray recalls that the MPE group said to him, "'All they're doing is taking
all the smart black students out of the public schools,' because St. Andrew's

academic standards were high. I told them, 'Well, we'll do what we can to see that they don't limit it to the top academic students, but I can't tell them that they can't do that.' I appreciated what they *were* doing. In terms of the private schools in this area, they were way ahead of what the others were doing. St. Andrew's wasn't a 'seg academy.' It had been established long before *Brown v. Board of Education.* My sister Isabel went to St. Andrew's.[49]

But those facts didn't cut ice with everyone as some Mississippians strove to support public education and desegregation by keeping their children in public schools that were undergoing the turmoil that resulted from two groups of children, black and white, being thrown together for the first time in large numbers, many distrustful of or even despising members of the other group, and with teachers and other school staff often setting a similar example.

"People from Mississippians for Public Education gave me trouble about Catherine being at St. Andrew's. Of course our children, including Catherine, had gone through integration of the public schools in Meridian, and there were a lot of private schools that opened up there at that point. But they hadn't done nearly as good a job of integration in Jackson as they had in Meridian, and they were paying the price.

"A couple of Episcopalians came to me, and we went into great detail about Catherine at St. Andrew's. She had African Americans in her class at St. Andrew's—not many, but it was at least open. But these Episcopalians were saying that Catherine shouldn't be at St. Andrew's. And I said that I was real sorry, but this was something that she's been very much interested in, and she's got friends there that she knew before we ever moved to Jackson. And it *was* desegregated. It might not be fully integrated, but it's not like it's a segregation academy."

Slowly, quietly, Gray continued, "And we decided we'd let Catherine go to St. Andrew's. And I don't regret it, although we had some guilty feelings about it for a while." With more energy, he concluded, "It was a good experience for her and prepared her well for her future. And it got her an A. B. Duke Scholarship to Duke!"[50]

Although socioeconomic issues were becoming more important in school integration, race was still far from the back burner in Mississippi in other areas. In 1979, Gray gave an address entitled "Race Relations and Religion in Mississippi" at Millisaps College. He began the talk by quoting writer Marshall Frady, who had observed that during the Civil Rights Movement, white churches in the South "had rather the air of God in James Joyce's *Portrait of the Artist as a Young Man:* 'invisible, refined out of existence, indifferent, paring his fingernails,'" and added, "Considering that he was talking about the predominantly *white* churches in the South, it was one of the kinder things that was said about these institutions during those critical years." Gray pointed to a number of reasons why Frady's observation was correct, including a too-close connection between Southern religion and culture and the "fiercely democratic polity" of most Protestant denominations, which in turn made clergy who attempted to challenge cultural assumptions highly vulnerable. While acknowledging the truth of Frady's observation, Gray went on to argue that it was also true that Southern churches and church properties, both black and white, had been practically the sole place during Jim Crow that whites and black could meet together in something approaching greater equality. He also reminded his audience of the leadership of individual whites in the fight for racial justice and said, "Most of the prophetic voices that were heard in those days came from church-oriented persons. . . . The Church as an institution may have done little, but many of her sons and daughters, clergy and lay alike, provided what leadership there was in the white community in Mississippi. Such things are not to be overlooked or underestimated." He concluded by saying, "The churches in Mississippi may have seemed 'invisible, refined out of existence, indifferent, paring [their] fingernails' during those years of struggle for racial justice, but at least some of the seeds they have planted over the years have borne considerable fruit among both blacks and whites. More important still, they may yet have within them the potential for the *redemption* of our society to go along with the *reformation* of that society which is already so well underway."[51]

Life was not all seriousness that year, however. Gray observed the fifth anniversary of his consecration, and as the second business session of the 1979 Diocesan Council drew to a close, Gray's Canon to the Ordinary [a bishop's assistant for parish ministry] Fred Bush read the meeting a take-off on Clement Moore's "T'was the Night Before Christmas," entitled "T'was the Night Before Council," a composition that portrayed an uncharacteristically impatient and self-centered Gray anxious about the upcoming council meeting and fretting because apparently no one had remembered his anniversary. The poem concluded:

> *He paced and he fretted and then cried in a blurt,*
> *"Nobody remembered! My feelings are hurt.*
> *This is the fifth Annual Council at which I've presided.*
> *You'd think someone would have decided*
> *To throw a shindig today*
> *And celebrate this year in some sort of way."*

> *Then he dismissed us and turned his back.*
> *We smiled as we left and disregarded his flack.*
> *'Cause, Bishop, we DID remember and do present herewith,*
> *With love and appreciation, a fifth for YOUR fifth.*

As Bush handed Gray a fifth of scotch, "with love and laughter, Council joined in the commemoration."[52]

While there is no record of Gray's hearers' response to his Millsaps talk on race and religion, Gray had a clear recollection of a response he got to a 1982 talk at historically black Tougaloo College. Gray began by telling his audience, which included Charles Evers, Medgar Evers' brother,

> In early June of this year I received a telephone call from a reporter for one of the Jackson newspapers who was writing a story about the late Medgar Evers. She was trying to get a feel for what he was like and what Mississippi was like in the days preceding his assassination. In due time, the inevitable question was raised: Have there been any *real* changes since 1963? As one who feels like there is quite a bit of difference between 1963 and 1982, I was trying to make a list of some of the changes when it occurred to me how I might make the point. "Go back to your 'morgue,'" I said, "and read the copies of your own newspaper of that period, particularly the editorials and local columnists, and compare those with your newspaper today. That may provide as clear an indication of the difference than anything I could say.[53]

Gray went on to describe his daughter Catherine's reaction when she read 1962 (the year she was born) and 1963 clippings from the Jackson papers: she "simply cannot believe the things she reads in the Jackson newspapers of that day. The attitudes, the comments, the whole world which those molders of opinion communicate is something strange and foreign to one who was born at the very time that those words were written, and in the very place where those words bore such bitter fruit." Reminding his hearers of the events surrounding Meredith's enrollment at Ole Miss, Gray raised the question of responsibility for the violence and hatred, and concluded, as was his practice, "In short, we were *all* involved; and I think we came to see this as a kind of turning point" in the struggle for racial justice. When Gray used the words "turning point" with reference to a sense of corporate responsibility, he had in mind the fact that white businessmen in Jackson had spoken out against the violence surrounding Meredith's enrollment, but

Charles Evers had something very different on his mind, and in response to the phrase, he burst out, "My brother was killed the very next year!" By the early 1980s, blacks' and whites' perception of the same events and times had clearly and publicly diverged.[54]

In 1983, Gray and his wife traveled to England again, this time to spend a three-month sabbatical in directed study with MacQuarrie, following up on the contact the two had made five years earlier during Lambeth. "He had taken us everywhere through Christ Church College and told us to call him 'Ian.' That all sort of established a relationship that made me feel comfortable asking to come do my sabbatical with him." The time was an experience that Gray described as "wonderful! It was one of the high points of my life! Ruthie and I were there in Oxford—we stayed on the third floor of the MacQuarries' flat—and under no great pressure. I could go to lectures and be part of a class without having to take final exams or anything! I could read what I wanted to read and then go talk to someone like Dr. Mac-Quarrie about it. As for its theological impact, I think it reinforced what I already felt. That's one of the reasons I had enjoyed reading his books so much before I even met him. It was a very, very happy time."[55] The following year when the national House of Bishops met in Jackson for the first time in its history, Gray brought MacQuarrie there, first as chaplain to the earlier annual diocesan clergy conference and then as speaker to the House of Bishops.[56]

Although by his twelfth year in office, Gray was generally well-loved throughout the diocese, a number of Mississippi congregants found reason to complain about the episcopal vestments he chose to wear—or not wear—when he visited their churches. These complaints were numerous enough that in 1986 he produced what was, in effect, a form letter addressing the concerns of those who noticed his failure to wear a miter (the tall, pointed hat worn by some bishops). After a beginning which read, "I can understand how that [the miter] might be your preference in Episcopal vestments, but I trust you can understand if my preference is different," Gray gave a history of the use of the miter in the Christian church and in the Anglican tradition which noted that in the latter, the miter had been dispensed with at the time of the English Reformation and had only recently made a comeback. "Indeed," he wrote, "I think you will find that Bishop Allin was the first Presiding Bishop of the Episcopal Church ever to wear a miter." In addition to Gray's "low church" preferences, the use or not of the miter was also clearly linked to his personal approach to authority, which was always, if possible, collaborative rather than coercive. Later in the letter he noted, "The miter, with its association with 'prelacy,' suggested an authoritarian exercise of the Episcopal office, and this has never been a very comfortable 'tradition' in the Episcopal Church. We are accustomed to a much more democratically oriented type of Church polity." His conclusion typified not only traditional Anglican flexibility, but also his own non-authoritarianism: "I treasure one part of our tradition in a special way while you treasure another. Still, I believe we can respect each of these traditions and appreciate what each has to offer to the whole of Anglicanism. I trust you will understand, and I thank you for giving me this opportunity to respond."[57]

Four years later, after almost fifteen years of service as Mississippi's bishop, Gray asked the delegates to the annual Diocesan Council to approve election of a bishop coadjutor to assist him. He told the council, "Geographically speaking, Mississippi is a large diocese, and I find it more difficult now than I did fifteen years ago to get around the diocese to carry out the duties of my office and ministry as I would like and as you would like." Gray, who was sixty-three at the time, also told the delegates that he wasn't "eager or anxious to be put on the shelf just yet!" He noted that the Episcopal Church allows bishops to retire as early as sixty-five and requires that they retire by age seventy-two and told his hearers that his retirement would "come somewhere between those two limits."[58]

The council unanimously approved Gray's request, and with a process much more methodical than the one that had selected him as bishop in 1974, five candidates were nominated for the post. At a reconvened 1991 Diocesan Council, the assembled representatives selected Alfred Clark (Chip) Marble Jr. as Gray's coadjutor. Marble was a native Mississippian who had served parishes in Mississippi before leaving to become suffragan bishop of the Diocese of Eastern North Carolina. He was ordained as coadjutor on June 15, 1991.

In the spring of 1991, Gray was elected to the position of chancellor of the University of the South. Nearly forty years earlier he had opposed Bishop R. Bland Mitchell of Arkansas, who had held that same position then, because of Mitchell's efforts to prevent the admission of African American students to the seminary. In 1991, after his selection was announced in the media, Gray, of course, received a number of letters congratulating him on his new position, but none was more apropos, yet also poignant than the one from a Nashville man, who wrote,

When I saw the headline of the enclosed article, I immediately thought of your name and was pleased to find when I read the article that, indeed, it did refer to you. Since you are the only Mississippi Episcopal priest I ever met, I didn't have many names to choose from!

I met you 35 years ago and the circumstances had a real impact on my life. Do you remember the Religious Emphasis Week at Mississippi State in February 1956? I was a senior at State and you were talking to a group of us at Rev. Bob Walkup's Presbyterian church in Starkville when a newspaper reporter in the audience asked you about the Bible and segregation. Your reply, that the Bible and segregation were incompatible, was on the front page of the Jackson newspapers the next day, and the state-wide furor that followed forced the cancellation of RE week. The only organized meeting permitted was listening to Dr. Fred Neal (our total "Philosophy Dept.") play the organ in the auditorium. Of course that didn't stop the small "bull-sessions" where many for the first time seriously questioned the segregation of those days. . . .

What you and the others did the day or two you were actually on campus gave me the courage to express my true feelings and I thank you for it, although belatedly. The fact that I took a stand for what I knew to be right led to a great deal of tension between me and my parents and between me and some of the men of my hometown of Winona [MS]. As a result, I wanted to look elsewhere for employment and in 1957 came to Nashville. The intervening years have made me come to appreciate the people of Mississippi and for how far they have come in race relations. I am sure that is due in no small part to people like you who stayed and worked for change. Thank you for that and for being the catalyst in my own evolution.[59]

"I'M NOT A CRUSADER"

Retirement

"I'M NOT A CRUSADER," Gray said often, by which he meant that he never saw himself as someone whose primary vocation is to call God's people to account for their failure to live up to God's demands for justice and righteousness.

The vocation of a Christian minister is sometimes spoken of as combining three biblical roles: priest, prophet, and pastor.

The priest is the one who serves God and God's people by administering God's rites and rituals, and in the Episcopal Church it is those ordained as priests who officiate at the sacraments.

The prophet *is* something of the "crusader," to use Gray's term. The prophet reminds God's people, often forcefully, that by claiming to *be* God's people they have agreed to abide by the terms of a covenant they have made with God; they have agreed to attempt to *imitate* God's compassion and loving kindness as well as God's justice and righteousness. Although sometimes biblical prophets offer words of comfort, their message always contains accusations of failure and, therefore, is very seldom a welcome one to those who need to hear it.

Finally, the pastor, the term most familiar to many Christians, is the one "who cares for his sheep," the shepherd. But as any number of preachers and writers have noted, in real life sheep are dirty, timid, stupid, and stubborn, with any number of bad habits. So although our image of the shepherd is often, in the poetic sense, *pastoral*, romanticized, the *good* shepherd not only comforts the sheep, but, out of caring for them, *herds* the sheep in the interest of their well-being.

It was as pastor that Gray excelled, whether as rector in a parish or bishop in a diocese. It was as pastor that many people loved him, even when he was speaking in a prophetic voice to them. He loved them and they knew it, even as he chastised them. After all, he always genuinely included himself among those who need to be chastised, the sinners. Imitating God is extremely difficult work.

The Christian theological term that encompasses Gray's ministry is *chairos*, the Greek word meaning "time," but specifically "the time chosen by God in which God *acts*" in a particular place and person. When the New Testament says that God sent his Son "in the fullness of time," it is speaking of *chairos*.

Gray would have been an excellent pastor in any time or place, but from a Christian theological perspective, he was an excellent pastor in racist Mississippi in the latter part of the twentieth century as a result of God's *chairos*. Because he was primarily a loving pastor and because he was "one of them," he could speak prophetic words to his congregations, to his communities, and even to elected officials such as the racist governor. The fact that he had Christian love for all these people didn't mean that they would like the words he spoke or even that they would heed them, but it did mean that he could say them in a way that many others could not. Because he was a loving pastor, he could also be elected bishop by the clergy and laity of the Diocese of Mississippi only a few years after many had reviled him for his stands on racial justice and reconciliation.

Gray's election as bishop in 1974 was also evidence of how much white Mississippi had changed in twenty years, and Gray himself was a significant part of that change. As his Nashville correspondent suggested to Gray when he wrote him in 1991 after Gray was elected chancellor of Sewanee, no small part of his everyday sainthood was that he *stayed* in Mississippi and he *worked for change*.

* * *

Gray retired as bishop of Mississippi on September 30, 1993, shortly after his sixty-fifth birthday. Like many active retirees, he immediately took up new responsibilities, in his case as interim chaplain at Sewanee for the 1993–94 academic year. The former Anwyn Hawkins, now Anwyn Myers, the first woman Gray had ordained to the priesthood in Mississippi, was already on the chapel staff and served as his assistant. Gray fulfilled his term as chancellor in 1997, and during the following years served in a variety of part-time posts, including giving his services as what he referred to as the position of "rent-a-bishop" for the Diocese of Central Florida during the busy Lenten season. By 2008, Gray complained that his memory was not what it once was, but he continued an active life as a clergyman, husband, father, grandfather, and, by then, great-grandfather. In the words of the hymn with which I began, he remained a man who "followed the right for Jesus' sake the whole of [his] good life long."[1]

NOTES

PREFACE

1. *The Hymnal According to the Use of the Episcopal Church* (1940) (New York: The Church Hymnal Corporation, 1961), 243.
2. Bob Dylan, http://www.bobdylan.com (accessed May 20, 2009).
3. Hannah Arendt, *The Human Condition* (Chicago: University of Chicago Press, 1958), 74.
4. *The Hymnal*, 243.

CHAPTER 1

1. Walter Lord, *The Past That Would Not Die* (New York: Pocket Books, 1967), 182; Taylor Branch, *Parting the Waters: America in the King Years, 1954–1963* (New York: Simon and Schuster, 1988), 656.
2. Quoted in Ellen Douglas, *A Long Night* (Jackson, MS: Nouveau Press, 1986), 12.
3. Quoted in Douglas, 3.
4. Duncan M. Gray Jr., interview with author, Sewanee, TN, October 31, 1995. Duncan M. Gray Jr. is hereafter cited as simply Gray; first names are used with other Gray family members.
5. Ibid.
6. Branch, *Parting the Waters*, 46. See Constance Baker Motley, *Equal Justice under Law: An Autobiography of Constance Baker Motley* (New York: Farrar, Strauss and Giroux, 1998), 162–192, for a fuller, "insider" account of Meredith as a person.
7. Nadine Cohodas, *The Band Played Dixie* (New York: The Free Press, 1997), 58.
8. Motley, 162.
9. Quoted in Russell H. Barrett, *Integration at Ole Miss* (Chicago: Quadrangle Books, 1965), 39.
10. Quoted in Barrett, 40.
11. Barrett, 40.
12. Ibid., 33.
13. James Silver, *Mississippi: The Closed Society* (New York: Harcourt Brace & World, 1964), 93–94; Cohodas, 62–63. See also Motley, 165.
14. Barrett, 41–42.
15. Quoted in Barrett, 43.
16. Barrett, 44–45.
17. Quoted in Barrett, 69–70.
18. Duncan M. Gray Jr., interview by Gordon G. Henderson, June 1965, Civil Rights

Documentation Project: Oral History Transcripts. http://www.usm.edu/crdp/html/
millsaps.shtml (accessed October 29, 2009). Courtesy of Millsaps College Oral
History Project, Millsaps College, Jackson, MS.
19. Ibid.
20. Duncan M. Gray Jr., personal files, Jackson, MS; hereafter cited as Gray's files.
21. Quoted in Cohodas, 71.
22. Motley, 174.
23. Quoted in Barrett, 78–79.
24. Barrett, 79.
25. Ibid., 78.
26. Motley, 175–178.
27. Barrett, 88.
28. Quoted in Barrett, 89.
29. *Book of Common Prayer* (New York: The Seabury Press, 1953), 206.
30. Gray's files.
31. Quoted in Barrett, 88–91.
32. Barrett, 91–92.
33. Ibid., 94.
34. Quoted in Barrett, 93.
35. Barrett, 94.
36. Gray, Civil Rights Documentation Project.
37. Gray's files.
38. Quoted in Barrett, 97.
39. Gray, Civil Rights Documentation Project.

CHAPTER 2

1. Barrett, 103.
2. Quoted in Barrett, 103.
3. Barrett, 98–99.
4. Quoted in Barrett, 100.
5. Barrett, 103.
6. Ibid.
7. Ibid.
8. Ibid., 104.
9. Gray, Civil Rights Documentation Project.
10. Quoted in Barrett, 105.
11. Quoted in Barrett, 107.
12. Barrett, 107.
13. Gray, Civil Rights Documentation Project.
14. Quoted in Barrett, 109.
15. Gray's files.
16. Quoted in Barrett, 111.
17. Barrett, 111–113.
18. Ibid., 114.
19. Branch, *Parting the Waters*, 649. Branch is the best source for the state-federal po-
    litical dimension of the crisis, especially the negotiations between Barnett and the
    Kennedy administration, which involved both the attorney general and the president.

20. Quoted in Barrett, 115.
21. Gray, Civil Rights Documentation Project.
22. Quoted in Barrett, 118.
23. Gray, Civil Rights Documentation Project.
24. Quoted in Barrett, 118.
25. Quoted in Barrett, 119.
26. Ibid.
27. Quoted in Barrett, 119.
28. Lord, 191; Barrett, 121.
29. Gray's files.
30. Branch, *Parting the Waters*, 661–662.
31. Gray, interview by author, Jackson, MS, June 6, 1997; Gray, Civil Rights Documentation Project.
32. Ibid.
33. Ibid.
34. Ibid.
35. Ibid.
36. Ibid.

CHAPTER 3

1. Edward McCrady, "The deBernieres of Normandy," unpublished manuscript, Gray's files.
2. Ibid.
3. Ibid.
4. Ibid.
5. Gray's files.
6. Ibid.
7. Ibid.
8. Letter from Joseph Elsbury, "who has spent his life investigating the Fuquas," Lafayette, LA, December 15, 1987, Gray's files.
9. Ibid.
10. Ibid.
11. Ibid.
12. Ibid.
13. Associated Press obituary published in the (Cleveland, MS) *Bolivar Commercial*, April 18, 1929.
14. William F. Holmes, *The White Chief: James K. Vardaman* (Baton Rouge: Louisiana State University Press, 1970), 34. Neither Bilbo's nor his constituents' prejudices were confined to African Americans. According to Mississippi lore, Bilbo, a skilled campaigner and not an ignorant man, famously accused his opponents of being "thespians," a term his ill-educated supporters supposedly confused with "lesbians." According to the story, this was another term about whose meaning the supporters were somewhat unclear beyond the certainly that it wasn't something they favored.
15. *The Episcopal Church in Mississippi: 1763–1992* (Jackson, MS: The Episcopal Diocese of Mississippi, 1992), 93.
16. Clipping of "Shavin's," by Carl Walters, from unidentified newspaper, no date, Gray's files.

17. Gray's files.
18. Gray, interview with author, Jackson, MS, June 14, 1999.
19. Ibid.
20. Ibid.
21. Clipping from (Greenwood) *Commonwealth*, October 27, 1942, Gray's files.
22. Gray, interview with author, Atlanta, GA, October 23, 1996.
23. Gray, interview with author, Jackson, MS, June 14, 1999.
24. Cecil Jones Jr., interview with author, Tupelo, MS, June 20, 1997.
25. Ibid.
26. Ibid.
27. Gray's files.
28. Ibid.
29. Ibid.
30. Ibid.
31. Ibid.
32. Clipping, *The Tiger Talks*, March 23, 1944, Gray's files.
33. Clipping, *The Tiger Talks*, n.d., Gray's files.
34. Gray's files.
35. Unidentified clipping, n.d., Gray's files.
36. Gray, interview with author, Atlanta, GA, October 23, 1996.
37. Ibid.

CHAPTER 4

1. James G. Schneider, *The Navy V-12 Program: Leadership for a Lifetime* (Champaign, IL: Marlow Books, 1987), 102.
2. Schneider, 44.
3. Schneider, 1.
4. Quoted in Schneider, 5–6.
5. Quoted in Schneider, 6.
6. Quoted in Schneider, 150.
7. Ibid.
8. Schneider, 150–151.
9. Ibid., 150–154.
10. Gray, interview with author, Jackson, July 15, 2002.
11. Ibid.
12. Schneider, 105–109.
13. Ibid., 109.
14. Gray, interview with author, July 15, 2002.
15. Schneider, 112–113.
16. Gray, interview with author, July 15, 2002.
17. Schneider, 106.
18. Ibid., 272.
19. Newspaper clipping, n.d., Gray's files.
20. Gray, interview with author, July 15, 2002.
21. Schneider, 102.
22. Ibid.
23. Gray, interview with author, July 15, 2002.

24. Ibid.
25. Ibid.
26. Ibid.
27. Ibid.
28. Ibid.
29. Ibid.
30. Ibid.
31. Ibid.
32. Ruth Gray, interviews with author, Jackson, MS, July 17, 2002, and September 15, 2009.
33. Gray, interview with author, July 15, 2002.
34. Ibid.
35. Ibid.
36. Ibid.
37. Ruth Gray, interview with author, Jackson, MS, July 16, 2002.
38. Ibid.
39. Gray, interview, July 15, 2002.
40. Ibid.
41. Ibid.
42. Ibid.
43. Ruth Gray, interview, July 16, 2002.
44. Gray, interview, July 16, 2002.
45. Ibid.
46. Ibid.
47. Ibid.
48. Ibid.
49. Ibid.
50. Ruth Gray, interview, July 16, 2002.
51. Gray, interview, July 16, 2002.
52. Ruth Gray, interview, July 17, 2002.
53. Gray, interview, July 16, 2002.
54. Ibid.

CHAPTER 5

1. David Vance Guthrie, "Bury My Heart in Arcady," 1986, Gray's files, 1.
2. Personal communication, Gerald T. Smith, Professor of Religion, University of the South, October 7, 2010.
3. Guthrie, 1.
4. Ibid., 2–3.
5. Gray, interview, Jackson, July 16, 2002.
6. Ibid.
7. Ruth Gray, interview with author, Jackson, July 16, 2002.
8. Ibid.
9. Ibid.
10. Ibid.
11. Ibid.
12. Ibid.

13. Transcript, the University of the South, Gray's files.
14. *Sewanee Theological Review* 46, no. 2 (Easter 2003): 177, 179–180, 213.
15. *Sewanee Theological Review* 46, no. 2 (Easter 2003): 219.
16. Gray, interview with author, Jackson, MS, July 16, 2002.
17. Ibid.
18. Ibid.
19. Gray's files.
20. Ibid.
21. Ibid.
22. Ibid.
23. Ibid.
24. Ibid.
25. Ibid.
26. Ibid.
27. Davis Carter, interview with author, Aberdeen, MS, July 27, 2001.
28. Gray, interview with author, Kanuga Conference Center, Hendersonville, NC, August 8, 2003.
29. Ibid.
30. Ibid.
31. Ibid.
32. Ibid.
33. Ibid.
34. "Appraisal," October 29, 1952, Gray's files.
35. Ibid.
36. Ibid.
37. Gray, interview, August 8, 2003.

CHAPTER 6

1. Donald S. Armentrout, "A Documentary History of the Integration Crisis at the School of Theology at The University of the South," *Sewanee Theological Review* 46, no. 2 (Easter 2003): 173. See also Donald S. Armentrout, *The Quest for an Informed Priesthood* (Sewanee, TN: The University of the South, 1979), for an earlier account of this period.
2. *Journal of the Diocese of Florida* (1951): 78–79. Quoted in Armentrout, "Documentary," 173–174.
3. Frank S. Mead and Samuel S. Hill, *Handbook of Denominations in the United States*, 11th ed. (Nashville: Abingdon Press, 2001), 132–133.
4. The seminary had been founded by the trustees of Virginia Theological Seminary in 1878. Armentrout, "Documentary," 174.
5. Armentrout, "Documentary," 174.
6. Quoted in ibid.
7. Ibid.
8. Armentrout, "Documentary," 174–175.
9. Quoted in ibid., 176.
10. Quoted in Armentrout, "Documentary," 176–177.
11. Armentrout, "Documentary," 180.

12. Ibid.

13. Gray, "Sewanee: There and Back Again," *Sewanee Theological Review* 46, no. 2 (Easter 2003): 218.

14. Armentrout, "Documentary," 181–182.

15. Quoted in ibid., 182–183.

16. Quoted in Armentrout, "Documentary," 183.

17. For example, Mitchell sent a letter to the Very Reverend James Pike, dean of the Cathedral of St. John the Divine, taking issue with Pike's stand on the integration of the seminary. In that letter, Mitchell wrote Pike about his actions, "I think the day has not come—at least in this part of the world—when bad manners constitute good religion" (May 29, 1953, copy, Gray's files).

18. Guthrie, 6.

19. Armentrout, "Documentary," 182.

20. Quoted in ibid.

21. Gray, "Sewanee: There and Back Again," 217.

22. Quoted in Armentrout, "Documentary," 184.

23. Armentrout, "Documentary," 184–185.

24. Quoted in ibid., 185–186.

25. Quoted in Armentrout, "Documentary," 190.

26. Quoted in Armentrout, "Documentary," 195.

27. Ibid.

28. Quoted in Armentrout, "Documentary," 195.

29. Gray, "Sewanee: There and Back Again," 217.

30. Ibid.

31. Armentrout, "Documentary," 196.

32. Gray's files, no page numbers.

33. Guthrie, 8.

34. Quoted in Armentrout, "Documentary," 196.

35. Armentrout, "Documentary," 196.

36. Quoted in ibid., 196–197.

37. Quoted in Armentrout, "Documentary," 196.

38. Armentrout, "Documentary," 196.

39. Quoted in ibid., 197.

40. Armentrout, "Documentary," 197–198; Gray's files; Gray, interview with author, July 15, 2002.

41. Gray's files.

42. Letter from Pugh to Gray, n.d., Gray's files.

43. Quoted in Armentrout, "Documentary," 199.

44. Quoted in Armentrout, "Documentary," 200.

45. Ibid.

46. Armentrout, "Documentary," 201.

47. Quoted in ibid., 201–202.

48. Armentrout, "Documentary," 203.

49. Quoted in ibid., 203.

50. Quoted in Armentrout, "Documentary," 206.

51. Armentrout, "Documentary," 207.

52. Quoted in ibid.

53. Guthrie, 11.

54. Guthrie, 11–12.

55. Guthrie, 12.

56. Copy of letter from Pike to McCrady, July 14, 1952, Gray's files.

57. Copy of letter from McCrady to Pike, July 19, 1952, Gray's files.

58. Pike letter, July 14, 1952, Gray's files.

59. McCrady to Pike, July 19, 1952.

60. Copy of letter from Pike to McCrady, February 10, 1953, Gray's files.

61. Ibid.

62. Armentrout, "Documentary," 209.

63. Unidentified newspaper clipping dated February 13, 1953, Gray's files.

64. Letter from Mrs. Raymond Clark Pierce to Gray, March 4, 1953, Gray's files.

65. Penick Report, 12, Gray's files.

66. Ibid., 13.

67. Ibid., 15.

68. Ibid., 17.

69. Ibid., 19–20, 23–25.

70. Armentrout, "Documentary," 209–210.

71. Ibid., 210–211.

72. Quoted in Ibid., 212.

73. *Episcopal Churchnews*, June 21, 1953, Gray's files.

CHAPTER 7

1. Linton Weeks, *Cleveland: A Centennial History* (Cleveland, MS: City of Cleveland, 1985), 68.

2. Will Campbell, *And Also with You* (Franklin, TN: Providence House Publishers, 1997), 120.

3. Ruth Gray, interview with author, Jackson, MS, July 24, 2004.

4. Campbell, 120.

5. Quoted in James C. Cobb, *The Most Southern Place on Earth: The Mississippi Delta and the Roots of Southern Identity* (Oxford: Oxford University Press, 1992), 6.

6. Cobb, 7.

7. Ibid.

8. Weeks, 175.

9. Ibid., 118.

10. Quoted in Cobb, 201.

11. Ibid.

12. Quoted in Weeks, 185.

13. Cobb, 211.

14. Weeks, 185.

15. Howell Raines, *My Soul Is Rested: The Story of the Civil Rights Movement in the Deep South* (New York: Putnam, 1985), 233. Quoted in Cobb, 211.

16. Quoted in Cobb, 211.

17. Gray, interview with author, Jackson, MS, July 15, 2002.

18. Gray, interview with author, Atlanta, GA, October 16, 1996.

19. Ibid.

20. Ruth Gray, interview with author, Jackson, MS, July 23, 2004.

21. Gray, interview with author, Jackson, MS, July 23, 2004.

22. Ruth Gray, interview with author, Jackson, MS, July 24, 2004.

23. Ruth Gray, interview with author, Jackson, MS, June 21, 1999.

24. Ibid.

25. Gray, interview with author, Atlanta, GA, October 23, 1996.

26. Gray, interviews with author, Sewanee, TN, October 12, 1995, and Jackson, MS, July 23, 2004.

27. Quoted in John Dittmer, *Local People: The Struggle for Civil Rights in Mississippi* (Urbana: University of Illinois Press, 1995), 32.

28. Gray, interview, July 23, 2004.

29. Quoted in Dittmer, 33.

30. Quoted in Weeks, 32.

31. Gray, interview with author, Sewanee, TN, October 13, 1995.

32. Gray's files.

33. Ibid.

34. Dittmer, 33.

35. Numan Bartley, *The Rise of Massive Resistance: Race and Politics in the South during the 1950s* (Baton Rouge: Louisiana State University Press, 1999), 55.

36. Gray, interview, October 13, 1995.

37. Ibid.

38. Quoted in Bartley, *Rise of Massive Resistance*, 57.

39. Gray, interview, October 13, 1995.

40. Gray, interview, October 23, 1996.

41. Bartley, *Rise of Massive Resistance*, 85.

42. Neil McMillen, *The Citizens' Council: Organized Resistance to the Second Reconstruction* (Urbana: University of Illinois Press, 1971), 161.

43. McMillen, 6.

44. Bartley, *Rise of Massive Resistance*, 85.

45. Gray, interview with author, Atlanta, GA, October 23,1996.

46. Bartley, *Rise of Massive Resistance*, 248.

CHAPTER 8

1. Gray, interview with author, Jackson, MS, July 23, 2006.

2. "The Church Considers the Supreme Court Decision," Gray's files, 1.

3. Ibid., 2.

4. Ibid., 5.

5. Ibid., 6–7.

6. Ibid., 7.

7. Ibid., 8–9.

8. Ibid., 11.

9. Gray, interview with author, Jackson, MS, July 23, 2004.

10. Letter from Carter to Gray, September 13, 1954, Gray's files.

11. Letter from Brown to Gray, October 2, 1954, Gray's files.

12. Letter from Trinity Church, November 13, 1954, copy in Gray's files.

13. Ibid.

14. Copy of letter from Gray to Charles Jacobs, Walter Sillers, and W. D. Alexander, September 1, 1954, Gray's files.

15. Letter from Jacobs to Gray, September 4, 1954, Gray's files.

16. Letter from Alexander to Gray, September 6, 1954, Gray's files.

17. Letter from Munger to Gray, n.d., Gray's files.

18. Gray's files.

19. Gray, interview with author, Atlanta, GA, October 23, 1996.

20. Ruth Gray, interview with author, Jackson, MS, July 24, 2004.

21. Gray, interview, October 23, 1996.

22. Press release, Public Relations Division, Protestant Episcopal Church, n.d., Gray's files.

23. Gardner H. Shattuck, *Episcopalians and Race: Civil War to Civil Rights* (Lexington: University of Kentucky Press, 2005), 68.

24. Province Four document, n.d., Gray's files.

25. Draft document, May 1955, Gray's files, 7–8.

26. Ibid., 8–9.

27. Bartley, *Rise of Massive Resistance*, 82.

28. Charles Eagles, "The Closing of Mississippi Society: Will Campbell, *The Sixty-Four Thousand Dollar Question*, and Religious Emphasis Week at the University of Mississippi," *Journal of Southern History* 67, no. 2 (May 2001): 333.

29. Dittmer, 53.

30. Ibid., 56–57.

31. Gray, interview, July 23, 2004.

32. Cobb, 220–221.

33. Gray, interview, July 23, 2004.

34. Dittmer, 54.

35. Cobb, 221–222.

36. Quoted in ibid., 222.

37. Quoted in Dittmer, 58.

38. Gray, interview, October 13, 1995.

39. Eagles, 337.

40. Ibid., 341–364, passim.

41. Gray, interview, October 13, 1995.

42. Gray, interview, October 23, 1996.

43. Ibid.

44. Ibid.

45. Gray's files.

46. Gray, interview, October 23, 1996.

47. Ibid.

48. Gray's files.

49. Numan Bartley, *The New South, 1945–1980* (Baton Rouge: Louisiana State University Press, 1995), 29–30.

50. David Chappell, *Inside Agitators: White Southerners and Civil Rights* (Baltimore: The Johns Hopkins University Press, 1994), 46.

51. Ibid.

52. Bartley, *New South*, 30.

53. Gray, interview, October 13, 1995.

54. Dittmer, 59.
55. Dittmer, 59–60.
56. Eagles, 365.

CHAPTER 9

1. Ruth Gray, interview with author, Jackson, MS, July 26, 2005.
2. Duncan M. Gray III, interview with author, Oxford, MS, June 18, 1997.
3. Lloyd Gray, interview with author, Tupelo, MS, June 23, 1997.
4. Duncan M. Gray III, interview with author, Oxford, MS, June 18, 1997.
5. Parochial report to diocese, St. Peter's Episcopal Church files, Oxford, MS.
6. St. Peter's files.
7. Gray, interview with author, Atlanta, GA, October 3, 1996.
8. Ibid.
9. Gray's files.
10. Joseph Blotner, *Faulkner: A Biography*, vol. 2 (New York: Random House, 1974), 1842.
11. Gray's files.
12. Ibid.
13. Sally Wolff King, "He Liked to Call Me Padre: Bishop Duncan Gray Remembers William Faulkner," draft of an article later published in the *Southern Quarterly*, 6.
14. King, 5.
15. Gray, "Some Random Observations of the Life and Writings of William Faulkner," an address delivered at St. Philip's Cathedral, Atlanta, GA, October 2, 1996, Gray's files.
16. Gray's files.
17. Gray, "Some Random Observations."
18. Gray, interview with author, Atlanta, GA, October 2, 1996.
19. Gray, "Some Random Observations."
20. Gray, interview, October 2, 1996.
21. Gray, interview with author, Atlanta, GA, October 3, 1996.
22. William Doyle, *An American Insurrection: The Battle of Oxford, Mississippi, 1962* (New York: Doubleday, 2001), 174–175.
23. Ibid., 347.
24. Ibid., 175.
25. Ibid., 179–181, 183–185.
26. Ibid., 181.
27. Ibid., 186–189
28. Ibid., 198–205.
29. Ibid., 177, 211–215 passim.
30. Quoted in Doyle, 217–218.
31. Doyle, 234–238.
32. Ibid., 239.
33. Ibid., 239–254.
34. Ibid., 254.
35. Ibid., 256; Barrett, 165.
36. Gray, interview, October 13, 1995.
37. Ibid.
38. Ibid.

39. Doyle, 280–281.
40. Gray's files.
41. Patricia Brown Young, interview with author, Oxford, MS, July 9, 1997.
42. Doyle, 289–292.
43. Gray, interview, October 3, 1996.
44. Ibid.
45. Duncan M. Gray III, interview, June 18, 1997.
46. Ibid.
47. Ibid.

CHAPTER 10

1. Gray, interview with author, Sewanee, TN, October 14, 1995.
2. Letter from Henry to Gray, Gray's files.
3. Letter from Beittel to Gray, Gray's files.
4. Letters from Wheatley's, Brown, and Carr to Gray, Gray's files.
5. Gray's files.
6. Ibid.
7. Ibid.
8. Ibid.
9. Ibid.
10. Ibid.
11. Ibid.
12. Ibid.
13. Ibid.
14. Ibid.
15. Ibid.
16. Ibid.
17. Ibid.
18. Ibid.
19. Ibid.
20. Ibid.
21. Ibid.
22. Ibid.
23. Ibid.
24. Ibid.
25. Ibid.
26. Copy sent to Gray, Gray's files.
27. Gray's files.
28. Ibid.
29. Ibid.
30. Ibid.
31. Copy of letter in Gray's files, November 19, 1962, Gray's files.
32. Gray, interview with author, Atlanta, GA, October 3, 1996.
33. Lloyd Gray, interview with author, Tupelo, MS, June 23, 1997.
34. Duncan M. Gray III, interview with author, Oxford, MS, June 18, 1997.
35. Lloyd Gray, interview with author, June 23, 1997.

36. Anne Gray Finley, interview with author, Adams, TN, June 5, 2006.

37. Gray, interview with author, Atlanta, GA, October 23, 1996.

38. Ibid.

39. Gray, interview, October 14, 1995.

40. Ibid.

41. Frank Peddle, interview with author, Oxford, MS, June 7, 1997.

42. Italics are Gray's, Gray's files.

43. "The Church and Race," an address delivered at St. Mark's Episcopal Church, Houston, TX, December 11, 1962, Gray's files.

44. Minutes of special meeting, February 10, 1963, St. Peter's files.

45. Duncan M. Gray III, interview with author, Oxford, MS, June 18, 1997.

46. Letter from Hicks to Duncan Gray Sr., May 26, 1963, Gray's files.

47. Gray, interview, October 14, 1995.

48. Ibid.

49. Ibid.

50. "Chooky" Falkner, interview with author, Oxford, MS, June 23, 1997.

51. Ibid.

52. Gray, interviews, October 14, 1995, and October 23, 1996.

53. Jimmy Falkner, telephone conversation with author, Oxford, MS, July 7, 1997.

54. The *Oxford Eagle*, September 14, 1962.

55. Gray, interview, October 14, 1995.

56. Parochial reports to diocese, St. Peter's files.

57. Gray, interview, October 14, 1995.

58. Gray, interview, October 23, 1996.

59. Ibid.

60. Gray, interview, October 14, 1995.

61. Duncan M. Gray III, interview, June 18, 1997.

62. Gray, interview, October 14, 1995.

CHAPTER 11

1. Julian Bond, "1964 Freedom Summer," in *Freedom Is a Constant Struggle: An Anthology of the Mississippi Civil Rights Movement*, ed. Susie Erenrich (Montgomery, AL: Black Belt Press, 1999), 78–79.

2. Ibid., 79.

3. Ibid.

4. Copy of letter in Gray's files.

5. Gray's files.

6. Gray, interview with author, Jackson, MS, July 15, 2002.

7. Bond, 81–82.

8. William Bradford Huie, *Three Lives for Mississippi* (New York: WCC Books, 1965), 88–89.

9. Quoted in Jack Nelson, *Terror in the Night: The Klan's Campaign Against the Jews* (New York, Simon and Schuster, 1993) 105.

10. Quoted in Huie, 117.

11. Nelson, 107–108.

12. Obie Clark, interview with Donald Williams, March 13, 1999, Civil Rights Documentation Project: Oral History Transcripts, http://www.usm.edu/crdp/html/

transcripts/clark_obie.shtml, courtesy of Tougaloo College Oral History Collection, Tougaloo, MS.

13. Charles Lemuel Young Sr., interview with Donald Paul Williams, November 14, 1998, Civil Rights Documentation Project: Oral History Transcripts, http://www.usm.edu/crdp/html/transcripts/young_charles-i.shtml, courtesy of Tougaloo College Oral History Collection, Tougaloo, MS.

14. Nelson, 108.

15. Ibid., 12, 124.

16. Clark, Civil Rights Documentation Project.

17. Young, Civil Rights Documentation Project.

18. Gray, interview with author, Jackson, MS, June 6, 1997.

19. Quoted in Huie, 141.

20. Quoted in Howard Ball, *Murder in Mississippi*, United States v. Price *and the Struggle for Civil Rights* (Lawrence: University Press of Kansas, 2004), 35–36. See Charles Marsh, *God's Long Summer: Stories of Faith and Civil Rights* (Princeton: Princeton University Press, 1997), for an extended account and analysis of Bowers' theology.

21. Marsh, 49.

22. Huie, 103.

23. Ibid., 124.

24. Ibid., 140.

25. Ball, 58.

26. Ibid., 59.

27. Ibid., 60.

28. Huie, 146–147.

29. Ibid., 153.

30. Ibid., 155.

31. Ibid., 159.

32. Ball, 60.

33. Huie, 173.

34. Ibid., 186–189, passim.

35. Dittmer, 247–248.

36. Ibid., 257–261; Charles Payne, *I've Got the Light of Freedom: The Organizing Tradition and the Mississippi Freedom Struggle* (Berkeley: University of California Press, 1995), 302–303.

37. Report on Freedom Summer from Gray to Dunbar, Gray's files.

38. Ibid.

39. Ibid.

CHAPTER 12

1. Ball, 32.

2. Ibid., 32–33.

3. Gray, interview with author, Sewanee, TN, October 14, 1995.

4. James LeLaurin, *St. Paul's Church: The First Hundred Years* (n.p., n.d.), 6–8.

5. Ibid., 31.

6. Ibid.

7. Tile Howard, interview with author, Meridian, MS, June 18, 2007.

8. LeLaurin, 36.

9. Gil Carmichael, interview with author, Meridian, MS, June 18, 2007.

10. Tile Howard, interview, June 18, 2007.

11. Deanie Carmichael, interview with author, Meridian, MS, June 18, 2007.

12. Ibid.

13. Gil Carmichael, interview, June 18, 2007.

14. Tile Howard, interview, June 18, 2007.

15. Deanie and Gil Carmichael, interview, June 18, 2007.

16. Ibid.

17. Anne Gray Finley, interview with author, Adams, TN, June 5, 2006.

18. Ibid.

19. Ibid.

20. Ball, 152.

21. Ibid., 95–96.

22. Quoted in ibid., 97.

23. Ball, 98–100.

24. Ibid., 153.

25. Ibid.

26. Deanie and Gil Carmichael, interview, June 18, 2007.

27. Gray, interview, October 14, 1995.

28. Ball, 141.

29. Ibid., 132. Killen was finally brought to trial in Mississippi state court in 2005, and
a Neshoba County jury of nine whites and three blacks found him guilty on three
counts of manslaughter, not murder as the prosecutors had asked. He was sentenced
to sixty years in jail.

30. Quoted in Ball, 134.

31. Gray's files.

32. Nelson, 65.

33. Ibid., 28.

34. Ibid., 28–29. In 1998, a Mississippi jury of six whites, five blacks, and one Asian
found Bowers guilty of the murder. He could have been eligible for parole in 2008,
but died in November 2006.

35. Nelson, 25.

36. Ibid., 29.

37. Ibid., 29–30.

38. Ibid., 30–31.

39. Ibid., 31–52 passim.

40. Gray, interview with author, Kanuga Conference Center, Hendersonville, NC, August
10, 2006.

41. Obie Clark, interview with Donald Paul Williams, Civil Rights Documentation
Project, courtesy of Tougaloo College Archives, Tougaloo, MS.

42. Nelson, 56.

43. Ibid., 61–66 passim.

44. Ibid., 66–67.

45. Ibid., 68.

46. Ibid., 70.

47. Ibid., 109–110.

48. Gil Carmichael, interview, June 18, 2007.

49. Ibid.
50. Ibid.
51. Anne Gray Finley, interview, June 5, 2006.
52. Ibid.
53. Nelson, 111–113, passim.
54. Ibid., 119.
55. Gray's files.

CHAPTER 13

1. Bill Johnson, interview with author, Meridian, MS, June 19, 2007.
2. Flyer, Gray's files.
3. Gray's files.
4. Nelson, 120.
5. Ibid., 121.
6. Campbell, 181–182.
7. Nelson, 121.
8. Gray's files, quotation from Psalm 127.
9. Flyer, Gray files
10. Nelson, 79.
11. Ibid., 147.
12. Ibid., 151–153.
13. Quoted in Nelson, 157–158.
14. COINTELPRO activity became public in 1971 and stirred public outrage after it became clear that its unorthodox methods had also been used by F.B.I. agents against such organizations as Martin Luther King's Southern Christian Leadership Conference. These revelations brought an official end to the program. The scope of COINTELPRO activities was more fully revealed in 1976 when Senator Frank Church of Idaho led a Senate investigation into its activities. The committee's final report concluded, "Many of the techniques used would be intolerable in a democratic society even if all the targets had been involved in violent activity, but COINTELPRO went far beyond that." The Church Committee, *Book III: The Final Report of the Select Committee to Study Governmental Operations with Respect to Governmental Activities: Summary Detailed Reports of Intelligence Activities and the Rights of Americans* (Washington, DC, U.S. Government Printing Office, 1976).
15. Nelson, 198.
16. Gray, interview, October 13, 1995.
17. Nelson, 158–175, passim.
18. Ibid., 176.
19. Ibid., 179–180.
20. Ibid., 180–183. Although Kathy Ainsworth had been killed, somehow Tarrants survived his multiple wounds. In another bizarre twist to a bizarre story, he later had what turned out to be a genuine religious conversion while an inmate in Mississippi's infamous Parchman Penitentiary and became as zealous for the Gospel as he had earlier been for right-wing causes. After he was released, he spent years as a Christian minister, establishing an inner-city ministry in Washington, D.C., and preaching racial reconciliation. Some would say, "Only in Mississippi!"
21. Gray's files.

22. Anne Gray Finley, interview, June 5, 2006.

23. Johnnie Faye Inge, interview with Donald Paul Williams, Civil Rights Documentation Project: Oral History Transcripts, http://www.usm.edu/crdp/html/transcripts/inge_faye.shtml (accessed November 28, 1998), courtesy of Tougaloo College Archives, Tougaloo, MS.

24. Copy of speech, Gray's files.

CHAPTER 14

1. Unlike the Roman Catholic Church and some Anglican provinces, the Episcopal Church does not have archbishops. Presiding bishops are elected to nine-year terms by the House of Bishops, and that election must be confirmed by the House of Deputies, whose members are priests and laypeople. Often referred to as "the PB," his or her role is to serve as spiritual leader to the 2.4 million Episcopalians in the United States and to oversee the planning, development, implementation, and assessment of the church's programs.

2. *The Episcopal Church in Mississippi, 1763–1992* (Jackson, MS: Episcopal Diocese of Mississippi, 1992), 133.

3. Ibid.

4. Gray, interview with author, Jackson, MS, June 2, 2008.

5. Gray's files.

6. Ibid.

7. Gray, interview, June 2, 2008.

8. Vote tally, Gray's files.

9. Gray's files; *Episcopal Church in Mississippi*, 135.

10. Gray, interview, June 2, 2008.

11. Ibid.

12. Copy in Gray's files.

13. Robert Prichard, *A History of the Episcopal Church* (Harrisburg, PA: Morehouse Publishing, 1991), 249.

14. Ibid., 249–250.

15. Ibid., 262.

16. Gray, interview, June 2, 2008.

17. Gray, interview, June 2, 2008.

18. Apostolic succession is the claim that one can trace an unbroken line of episcopal consecration back through the church's history to the time of the apostles. This claim, which the Anglican communion shares with the Roman Catholic, requires that for ordination of a priest or a deacon to be effective, that person must be ordained by a bishop in apostolic succession who, in turn, has been ordained and consecrated by a bishop in apostolic succession, and so on back to the time of the apostles.

19. Prichard, 255–256.

20. Gray, interview, June 2, 2008.

21. Ibid.

22. Jean Caffey Lyles, "Episcopal Agony Over Ecclesiastical Disobedience," *Christian Century* 91, no. 30 (September 4–11, 1974): 813.

23. Gray, interview, June 2, 2008.

24. Ibid.

25. Ibid.

26. *Episcopal Church in Mississippi*, 140.

27. Copy in Gray's files.

28. Gray's files.

29. *The Journal of the 150th Annual Council* (Jackson: The Diocese of Mississippi, 1977), 51.

30. Ibid., 52.

31. Ibid., 52.

32. Ibid., 164–167 passim.

33. Copy in Gray's files.

34. Gray's files.

35. *Journal of the 151st Annual Council* (Jackson: The Diocese of Mississippi, 1978), 59.

36. *Episcopal Church in Mississippi*, 141.

37. Ibid.; *Journal of the 153rd Annual Council* (Jackson: Episcopal Diocese of Mississippi, 1980), 53–59.

38. *The Church News* (Jackson: The Episcopal Diocese of Mississippi, September 1978), 9.

39. Ibid.

40. Ibid., 9–10.

41. Ibid., 10; Gray, interview, June 2, 2008.

42. *The Church News*, 9; Gray, interview, June 2, 2006.

43. *The Church News*, 10.

44. Gray, interviews with author, Atlanta, GA, October 14, 1996, and Jackson, MS, June 3, 2008.

45. Quoted in *Episcopal Church in Mississippi*, 143.

46. "Fact sheet for prospective plaintiffs in a suit against the Mississippi State Textbook Purchasing Board and its Rating Committee regarding the rejection of *Mississippi: Conflict and Change*," Gray's files.

47. Ibid.

48. Copy of "Complaint" filed in the United States in the Northern District of Mississippi, Civil Action GC75–147–S, filed November 5, 1975, Gray's files.

49. Gray, interview, June 2, 2008.

50. Ibid.

51. Gray's files.

52. *The Journal of the One Hundred and Fifty-Second Annual Council* (Jackson: The Episcopal Diocese of Mississippi, 1979), 39.

53. Gray's files.

54. Gray, interview, June 2, 2008.

55. Gray, interviews, Atlanta, GA, October 23, 1996, and Jackson, MS, June 2, 2008.

56. Gray, interview, June 2, 2008.

57. Copy, Gray's files.

58. Quoted in *Episcopal Church in Mississippi*, 162.

59. Gray's files.

AFTERWORD

1. *The Hymnal According to the Use of the Episcopal Church* (1940) (New York: Church Hymnal Corporation, 1961), 243.

BIBLIOGRAPHY

BOOKS AND ARTICLES

Arendt, Hannah. *The Human Condition*. Chicago: University of Chicago Press, 1958.

Armentrout, Donald. "A Documentary History of the Integration Crisis at the School of Theology at The University of the South." *Sewanee Theological Review* 46, no. 2 (Spring 2003): 173–212.

———. *The Quest for an Informed Priesthood*. Sewanee, TN: University of the South, 1979.

Ball, Howard. *Murder in Mississippi: United States v. Price and the Struggle for Civil Rights*. Lawrence: University Press of Kansas, 2004.

Barnard, Hollinger F., ed. *Outside the Magic Circle*. University: University of Alabama Press, 1986.

Barrett, Russell H. *Integration at Ole Miss*. Chicago: Quadrangle Books, 1965.

Bartley, Numan V. *The New South, 1945–1980*. Baton Rouge: Louisiana State University Press, 1995.

———. *The Rise of Massive Resistance: Race and Politics in the South during the 1950s*. Baton Rouge: Louisiana State University Press, 1999.

Belfrage, Sally. *Freedom Summer*. Greenwich, CT: Fawcett, 1990.

Blotner, Joseph. *Faulkner: A Biography*. Vol. 2. New York: Random House, 1974.

The Book of Common Prayer (1928). N.p.: n.d.

Branch, Taylor. *Freedom Summer*. New York: Simon and Schuster, 1998.

———. *Parting the Waters: America in the King Years, 1954–1963*. New York: Simon and Schuster, 1988.

———. *Pillar of Fire: America in the King Years, 1963–1965*. New York: Simon and Schuster, 1998.

Campbell, Will. *And Also with You*. Franklin, TN: Providence House Publishers, 1997.

Carson, Thomas H. "The Way We Were: Life at Sewanee in 1953." *Sewanee Theological Review* 46, no. 2 (Spring 2003): 213–216.

Carter, Hodding, III. *The South Strikes Back*. Garden City, NY: Doubleday, 1959.

Chappell, David. *Inside Agitators: White Southerners and Civil Rights*. Baltimore: The Johns Hopkins University Press, 1994.

Cobb, James C. *The Most Southern Place on Earth: The Mississippi Delta and the Roots of Regional Identity*. Oxford: Oxford University Press, 1992.

Cohodas, Nadine. *The Band Played Dixie*. New York: Free Press, 1997.

Daniel, Pete. *Lost Revolutions: The South in the 1950s*. Chapel Hill: University of North Carolina Press, 2000.

Dittmer, John. *Local People: The Struggle for Civil Rights in Mississippi*. Urbana: University of Illinois Press, 1995.

Douglas, Ellen. *A Long Night*. Jackson, MS: Nouveau Press, 1986.

Doyle, William. *An American Insurrection: The Battle of Oxford, Mississippi, 1962.* New York: Doubleday, 2001.

Eagles, Charles, ed. *The Civil Rights Movement in America.* Jackson, MS: University Press of Mississippi, 1986.

———. "The Closing of Mississippi Society: Will Campbell, 'The Sixty-Four Thousand Dollar Question' and Religious Emphasis Week at the University of Mississippi." *Journal of Southern History* 67, no. 2 (May 2001): 331–372.

Egerton, John. *Speak Now against the Day: The Generation before the Civil Rights Movement.* Chapel Hill: University of North Carolina Press, 1994.

The Episcopal Church in Mississippi: 1763–1992. Jackson, MS: Episcopal Diocese of Mississippi, 1992.

Episcopal Diocese of Mississippi. *Diocesan Convention Proceedings.* Jackson: Episcopal Diocese of Mississippi, 1977, 1978, 1979.

Erenrich, Susie. *Freedom Is a Constant Struggle: An Anthology of the Mississippi Civil Rights Movement.* Montgomery, AL: Black Belt Press, 1999.

Gray, Duncan M., Jr. "Sewanee: There and Back Again." *Sewanee Theological Review* 46, no. 2 (Spring 2003): 217–221.

Green, A. Wigfall. *The Man Bilbo.* Greenwood, MS: Greenwood Press, 1976.

Hendrickson, Paul. *Sons of Mississippi: A Story of Race and Its Legacy.* New York: Alfred A. Knopf, 2003.

Henry, Aaron. *Aaron Henry: The Fire Ever Burning.* Jackson, MS: University Press of Mississippi, 2000.

Holmes, William F. *The White Chief: James K. Vardaman.* Baton Rouge: Louisiana State University Press, 1970.

Huie, William Bradford. *Three Lives for Mississippi.* New York: WCC Books, 1965.

The Hymnal According to the Use of the Episcopal Church (1940). New York: The Church Hymnal Corporation, 1961.

Lord, Walter. *The Past That Would Not Die.* New York: Pocket Books, 1967.

Mars, Florence. *Witness in Philadelphia.* Baton Rouge: Louisiana State University Press, 1977.

Marsh, Charles. *God's Long Summer: Stories of Faith and Civil Rights.* Princeton: Princeton University Press, 1997.

Massengill, Reed. *Portrait of a Racist: The Real Life of Byron de la Beckwith.* New York: St. Martin's Griffin, 1996.

McAdam, Doug. *Freedom Summer.* New York: Oxford University Press, 1988.

McMillan, Neil. *The Citizens' Council: Organized Resistance to the Second Reconstruction, 1954–1964.* Urbana: University of Illinois Press, 1971.

Motley, Constance Baker. *Equal Justice under Law: An Autobiography of Constance Baker Motley.* New York: Farrar, Strauss and Giroux, 1998.

Nelson, Jack. *Terror in the Night: The Klan's Campaign against the Jews.* New York: Simon and Schuster, 1993.

Niebuhr, Reinhold, and Hodding Carter III. *Mississippi Black Paper.* New York: Random House, 1965.

Payne, Charles. *I've Got the Light of Freedom: The Organizing Tradition and the Mississippi Freedom Struggle.* Berkeley: University of California Press, 1995.

Perkins, John, Thomas Tarrants Jr., and David Wimbish. *He's My Brother: Former Racial Foes Offer Strategy for Reconciliation.* Grand Rapids: Chosen Books, 1994.

Schneider, James G. *The Navy V-12 Program: Leadership for a Lifetime.* Champaign, IL: Marlow Books, 1987.

Shattuck, Gardiner H. *Episcopalians and Race: Civil War to Civil Rights.* Lexington: University Press of Kentucky, 2005.

Silver, James. *Mississippi: The Closed Society.* New York: Harcourt Brace & World, 1964.

Sims, Patsy. *The Klan.* New York: Stein and Day, 1978.

Tarrants, Thomas. *The Conversion of a Klansman: The Story of a Former Ku Klux Klan Terrorist.* Garden City, NY: Doubleday & Co., 1979.

Weeks, Lincoln. *Cleveland: A Centennial History.* Cleveland, MS: City of Cleveland, 1985.

Whitehead, Don. *Attack on Terror: The F.B.I. Against the Ku Klux Klan in Mississippi.* New York: Funk & Wagnalls, 1970.

UNPUBLISHED SOURCES

Guthrie, David Vance. "Bury My Heart in Arcady." 1986. Personal files, Duncan M. Gray Jr., Jackson, MS.

McCrady, Edward. "The deBernieres of Normandy." Personal files, Duncan M. Gray Jr., Jackson, MS.

Parish files, St. Peter's Episcopal Church, Oxford, MS.

Personal files, the Right Reverend Duncan M. Gray Jr., Jackson MS.

Woolf-King, Sally. "He Liked to Call Me Padre: Bishop Duncan Gray Remembers William Faulkner," draft of article later published in *Southern Quarterly.*

INTERVIEWS

The Reverend Canon Fred Bush, Jackson, MS, July 1, 2002.

Ms. Ormond Gray Caldwell and David Caldwell, Atlanta, GA, August 14, 2002.

The Reverend Davis Carter, Aberdeen, MS, July 26, 2001.

Ms. Catherine Gray Clark, Hendersonville, NC, August 1, 2006.

Dr. John Crews, Oxford, MS, July 3, 1997.

Mr. Murray C. ("Chooky") Falkner, Oxford, MS., July 2, 1997.

Ms. Anne Gray Finley, Adams, TN, June 5, 2006.

The Right Reverend Duncan Gray Jr., Sewanee, TN, October 13, 1995; April 10, 1996; Atlanta, GA, October 23–24, 1996; Jackson, MS, June 12, 1997; June 21, 1999; July 14, 2000; July 15–16, 2002; July 23, 2004; July 25, 2005; Hendersonville, NC, August 1, 2006; Jackson, MS, June 16–17, 2007; Jackson, MS, June 3, 2008.

The Right Reverend Duncan M. Gray III, Oxford, MS, June 18, 1997.

Mr. Lloyd Spivey Gray, Tupelo, MS, June 23, 1997.

Mrs. Ruth Spivey Gray, Sewanee, TN, April 1997; Jackson, MS, July 24, 2004; July 26, 2005; Hendersonville, NC, August 1, 2006.

Dr. Evans Harrington, Oxford, MS, June 25, 1997.

The Reverend Cecil Jones Jr., Tupelo, MS, June 20, 1997.

Ms. Isabel Gray Kelly, Jackson, MS, June 22, 1997.

The Right Reverend Alfred ("Chip") Marble, Jackson, MS, July 10, 2002.

The Reverend Anwyn Meyers, Sewanee, TN, March 11, 1997.

The Reverend Tom Ward, Sewanee, TN, April 10, 1996.

INDEX

African Americans: changes in self-understanding following World War II, 121; experiences as applicants to Mississippi universities, 8–9; life in Mississippi in 1960s, 195

Barnett, Ross: address at Ole Miss–University of Kentucky football game, 31; negotiations with R. Kennedy over Meredith admission, 30, 33; resistance to Meredith admission, 22, 28–29
Beckwith, Byron de la: Gray's relationship to, 153–54; suspected of shooting into Greenwood home, 153–54
Beittel, A. D., letter to Gray after riot, 176
Bowers, Sam: background and philosophy, 201; work with Tarrants, 217

Cameron, Ben, 47; grants stay of Fifth Circuit Court of Appeals' rulings in Meredith's favor, 15–16; home in middle of Tarrants's attempted bombing, 233
Campbell, Will: advice to Gray before riot, 163; on American flags in Oxford after riot, 184; organizes 1956 Religious Emphasis week at Ole Miss, 149
Carmichael, Deanie: background, 220; on Klan blacklist in Meridian, 220–21; on St. Paul's clergy, 210
Carmichael, Gil: aid to Michael Schwerner, 220; background, 220; on Klan blacklist, 220–21; on St. Paul's clergy, 210
Carter, Hodding: advice to Gray about Religious Emphasis Week appearance, 149–50; editorial in *Living Church* on

Sewanee "crisis," 137; reaction to "The Church Considers the Supreme Court Decision," 137
"Church Considers the Supreme Court Decision, The": Gray as author, 136–38; Gray sends copies to Mississippi legislators, 139; reaction to pamphlet, 139–41
Citizens Council: formation, 132; ideology, 133; issue of class, 133–34; pressure tactics, 134; spread of, 133
Clark, Catherine Gray, 253
Clark, Obie: on FBI response to Klan bombing of African American churches, 218; on Meridian, 200
Cleveland, Mississippi, twentieth century growth, 120
Clingman, Charles, response to Sewanee faculty statement, 104
Columbus, Mississippi, character of town, 48–49
Committee of Conscience (Committee of Concern): Day of Conscience, 228–29; Day of Restoration, 226; Gray as public relations chair, 226; origin, 225–26

DeBernieres family, 43–44
Dennis, Delmar, relationship with Gray, 213

Episcopal Church in the United States of America (ECUSA): apostolic succession and, 278; General Convention Special Programs (GCSP), 242; prayer book revision, 243–44; "theological reorientation," 241–42; turmoil over prayer book revision and women's ordination, 241; women's ordination, 244